Connected Mathematics 2

Prime Time
Bits and Pieces I
Shapes and Designs
Bits and Pieces II
Covering and Surrounding
Bits and Pieces III
How Likely Is It?
Data About Us

Glenda Lappan
James T. Fey
William M. Fitzgerald
Susan N. Friel
Elizabeth Difanis Phillips

Boston, Massachusetts · Glenview, Illinois · Shoreview, Minnesota · Upper Saddle River, New Jersey

Connected Mathematics™ was developed at Michigan State University with financial support from the Michigan State University Office of the Provost, Computing and Technology, and the College of Natural Science.

This material is based upon work supported by the National Science Foundation under Grant No. MDR 9150217 and Grant No. ESI 9986372. Opinions expressed are those of the authors and not necessarily those of the Foundation.

The Michigan State University authors and administration have agreed that all MSU royalties arising from this publication will be devoted to purposes supported by the MSU Mathematics Education Enrichment Fund.

13-digit ISBN 978-0-13-366107-1
10-digit ISBN 0-13-366107-5
9 10 V063 12

Authors of Connected Mathematics

(from left to right) Glenda Lappan, Betty Phillips, Susan Friel, Bill Fitzgerald, Jim Fey

Glenda Lappan is a University Distinguished Professor in the Department of Mathematics at Michigan State University. Her research and development interests are in the connected areas of students' learning of mathematics and mathematics teachers' professional growth and change related to the development and enactment of K–12 curriculum materials.

James T. Fey is a Professor of Curriculum and Instruction and Mathematics at the University of Maryland. His consistent professional interest has been development and research focused on curriculum materials that engage middle and high school students in problem-based collaborative investigations of mathematical ideas and their applications.

William M. Fitzgerald *(Deceased)* was a Professor in the Department of Mathematics at Michigan State University. His early research was on the use of concrete materials in supporting student learning and led to the development of teaching materials for laboratory environments. Later he helped develop a teaching model to support student experimentation with mathematics.

Susan N. Friel is a Professor of Mathematics Education in the School of Education at the University of North Carolina at Chapel Hill. Her research interests focus on statistics education for middle-grade students and, more broadly, on teachers' professional development and growth in teaching mathematics K–8.

Elizabeth Difanis Phillips is a Senior Academic Specialist in the Mathematics Department of Michigan State University. She is interested in teaching and learning mathematics for both teachers and students. These interests have led to curriculum and professional development projects at the middle school and high school levels, as well as projects related to the teaching and learning of algebra across the grades.

CMP2 Development Staff

Teacher Collaborator in Residence

Yvonne Grant
Michigan State University

Administrative Assistant

Judith Martus Miller
Michigan State University

Production and Field Site Manager

Lisa Keller
Michigan State University

Technical and Editorial Support

**Brin Keller, Peter Lappan, Jim Laser,
Michael Masterson, Stacey Miceli**

Assessment Team

June Bailey and **Debra Sobko** (Apollo Middle School, Rochester, New York), **George Bright** (University of North Carolina, Greensboro), **Gwen Ranzau Campbell** (Sunrise Park Middle School, White Bear Lake, Minnesota), **Holly DeRosia, Kathy Dole,** and **Teri Keusch** (Portland Middle School, Portland, Michigan), **Mary Beth Schmitt** (Traverse City East Junior High School, Traverse City, Michigan), **Genni Steele** (Central Middle School, White Bear Lake, Minnesota), **Jacqueline Stewart** (Okemos, Michigan), **Elizabeth Tye** (Magnolia Junior High School, Magnolia, Arkansas)

Development Assistants

At Lansing Community College *Undergraduate Assistant:* **James Brinegar**

At Michigan State University *Graduate Assistants:* **Dawn Berk, Emily Bouck, Bulent Buyukbozkirli, Kuo-Liang Chang, Christopher Danielson, Srinivasa Dharmavaram, Deb Johanning, Kelly Rivette, Sarah Sword, Tat Ming Sze, Marie Turini, Jeffrey Wanko;** *Undergraduate Assistants:* **Daniel Briggs, Jeffrey Chapin, Jade Corsé, Elisha Hardy, Alisha Harold, Elizabeth Keusch, Julia Letoutchaia, Karen Loeffler, Brian Oliver, Carl Oliver, Evonne Pedawi, Lauren Rebrovich**

At the University of Maryland *Graduate Assistants:* **Kim Harris Bethea, Kara Karch**

At the University of North Carolina (Chapel Hill) *Graduate Assistants:* **Mark Ellis, Trista Stearns;** *Undergraduate Assistant:* **Daniel Smith**

Advisory Board for CMP2

Thomas Banchoff
Professor of Mathematics
Brown University
Providence, Rhode Island

Anne Bartel
Mathematics Coordinator
Minneapolis Public Schools
Minneapolis, Minnesota

Hyman Bass
Professor of Mathematics
University of Michigan
Ann Arbor, Michigan

Joan Ferrini-Mundy
Associate Dean of the College of
Natural Science; Professor
Michigan State University
East Lansing, Michigan

James Hiebert
Professor
University of Delaware
Newark, Delaware

Susan Hudson Hull
Charles A. Dana Center
University of Texas
Austin, Texas

Michele Luke
Mathematics Curriculum
Coordinator
West Junior High
Minnetonka, Minnesota

Kay McClain
Professor of Mathematics
Education
Vanderbilt University
Nashville, Tennessee

Edward Silver
Professor; Chair of Educational
Studies
University of Michigan
Ann Arbor, Michigan

Judith Sowder
Professor Emerita
San Diego State University
San Diego, California

Lisa Usher
Mathematics Resource Teacher
California Academy of
Mathematics and Science
San Pedro, California

Field Test Sites for CMP2

During the development of the revised edition of *Connected Mathematics* (CMP2), more than 100 classroom teachers have field-tested materials at 49 school sites in 12 states and the District of Columbia. This classroom testing occurred over three academic years (2001 through 2004), allowing careful study of the effectiveness of each of the 24 units that comprise the program. A special thanks to the students and teachers at these pilot schools.

Arkansas
Magnolia Public Schools
Kittena Bell*, Judith Trowell*; *Central Elementary School:* Maxine Broom, Betty Eddy, Tiffany Fallin, Bonnie Flurry, Carolyn Monk, Elizabeth Tye; *Magnolia Junior High School:* Monique Bryan, Ginger Cook, David Graham, Shelby Lamkin

Colorado
Boulder Public Schools
Nevin Platt Middle School: Judith Koenig
St. Vrain Valley School District, Longmont
Westview Middle School: Colleen Beyer, Kitty Canupp, Ellie Decker*, Peggy McCarthy, Tanya deNobrega, Cindy Payne, Ericka Pilon, Andrew Roberts

District of Columbia
Capitol Hill Day School: Ann Lawrence

Georgia
University of Georgia, Athens
Brad Findell
Madison Public Schools
Morgan County Middle School: Renee Burgdorf, Lynn Harris, Nancy Kurtz, Carolyn Stewart

Maine
Falmouth Public Schools
Falmouth Middle School: Donna Erikson, Joyce Hebert, Paula Hodgkins, Rick Hogan, David Legere, Cynthia Martin, Barbara Stiles, Shawn Towle*

Michigan
Portland Public Schools
Portland Middle School: Mark Braun, Holly DeRosia, Kathy Dole*, Angie Foote, Teri Keusch, Tammi Wardwell
Traverse City Area Public Schools
Bertha Vos Elementary: Kristin Sak; *Central Grade School:* Michelle Clark; Jody Meyers; *Eastern Elementary:* Karrie Tufts; *Interlochen Elementary:* Mary McGee-Cullen; *Long Lake Elementary:* Julie Faulkner*, Charlie Maxbauer, Katherine Sleder; *Norris Elementary:* Hope Slanaker; *Oak Park Elementary:* Jessica Steed; *Traverse Heights Elementary:* Jennifer Wolfert; *Westwoods Elementary:* Nancy Conn; *Old Mission Peninsula School:* Deb Larimer; *Traverse City East Junior High:* Ivanka Berkshire, Ruthanne Kladder, Jan Palkowski, Jane Peterson, Mary Beth Schmitt; *Traverse City West Junior High:* Dan Fouch*, Ray Fouch
Sturgis Public Schools
Sturgis Middle School: Ellen Eisele

Minnesota
Burnsville School District 191
Hidden Valley Elementary: Stephanie Cin, Jane McDevitt
Hopkins School District 270
Alice Smith Elementary: Sandra Cowing, Kathleen Gustafson, Martha Mason, Scott Stillman; *Eisenhower Elementary:* Chad Bellig, Patrick Berger, Nancy Glades, Kye Johnson, Shane Wasserman, Victoria Wilson; *Gatewood Elementary:* Sarah Ham, Julie Kloos, Janine Pung, Larry Wade; *Glen Lake Elementary:* Jacqueline Cramer, Kathy Hering, Cecelia Morris,

Robb Trenda; *Katherine Curren Elementary:* Diane Bancroft, Sue DeWit, John Wilson; *L. H. Tanglen Elementary:* Kevin Athmann, Lisa Becker, Mary LaBelle, Kathy Rezac, Roberta Severson; *Meadowbrook Elementary:* Jan Gauger, Hildy Shank, Jessica Zimmerman; *North Junior High:* Laurel Hahn, Kristin Lee, Jodi Markuson, Bruce Mestemacher, Laurel Miller, Bonnie Rinker, Jeannine Salzer, Sarah Shafer, Cam Stottler; *West Junior High:* Alicia Beebe, Kristie Earl, Nobu Fujii, Pam Georgetti, Susan Gilbert, Regina Nelson Johnson, Debra Lindstrom, Michele Luke*, Jon Sorenson
Minneapolis School District 1
Ann Sullivan K-8 School: Bronwyn Collins; Anne Bartel* (Curriculum and Instruction Office)
Wayzata School District 284
Central Middle School: Sarajane Myers, Dan Nielsen, Tanya Ravnholdt
White Bear Lake School District 624
Central Middle School: Amy Jorgenson, Michelle Reich, Brenda Sammon

New York
New York City Public Schools
IS 89: Yelena Aynbinder, Chi-Man Ng, Nina Rapaport, Joel Spengler, Phyllis Tam*, Brent Wyso; *Wagner Middle School:* Jason Appel, Intissar Fernandez, Yee Gee Get, Richard Goldstein, Irving Marcus, Sue Norton, Bernadita Owens, Jennifer Rehn*, Kevin Yuhas

---

* indicates a Field Test Site Coordinator

Ohio

Talawanda School District, Oxford
Talawanda Middle School: Teresa Abrams, Larry Brock, Heather Brosey, Julie Churchman, Monna Even, Karen Fitch, Bob George, Amanda Klee, Pat Meade, Sandy Montgomery, Barbara Sherman, Lauren Steidl

Miami University
Jeffrey Wanko*

Springfield Public Schools
Rockway School: Jim Mamer

Pennsylvania

Pittsburgh Public Schools
Kenneth Labuskes, Marianne O'Connor, Mary Lynn Raith*; *Arthur J. Rooney Middle School:* David Hairston, Stamatina Mousetis, Alfredo Zangaro; *Frick International Studies Academy:* Suzanne Berry, Janet Falkowski, Constance Finseth, Romika Hodge, Frank Machi; *Reizenstein Middle School:* Jeff Baldwin, James Brautigam, Lorena Burnett, Glen Cobbett, Michael Jordan, Margaret Lazur, Melissa Munnell, Holly Neely, Ingrid Reed, Dennis Reft

Texas

Austin Independent School District
Bedichek Middle School: Lisa Brown, Jennifer Glasscock, Vicki Massey

El Paso Independent School District
Cordova Middle School: Armando Aguirre, Anneliesa Durkes, Sylvia Guzman, Pat Holguin*, William Holguin, Nancy Nava, Laura Orozco, Michelle Peña, Roberta Rosen, Patsy Smith, Jeremy Wolf

Plano Independent School District
Patt Henry, James Wohlgehagen*; *Frankford Middle School:* Mandy Baker, Cheryl Butsch, Amy Dudley, Betsy Eshelman, Janet Greene, Cort Haynes, Kathy Letchworth, Kay Marshall, Kelly McCants, Amy Reck, Judy Scott, Syndy Snyder, Lisa Wang; *Wilson Middle School:* Darcie Bane, Amanda Bedenko, Whitney Evans, Tonelli Hatley, Sarah (Becky) Higgs, Kelly Johnston, Rebecca McElligott, Kay Neuse, Cheri Slocum, Kelli Straight

Washington

Evergreen School District
Shahala Middle School: Nicole Abrahamsen, Terry Coon*, Carey Doyle, Sheryl Drechsler, George Gemma, Gina Helland, Amy Hilario, Darla Lidyard, Sean McCarthy, Tilly Meyer, Willow Neuwelt, Todd Parsons, Brian Pederson, Stan Posey, Shawn Scott, Craig Sjoberg, Lynette Sundstrom, Charles Switzer, Luke Youngblood

Wisconsin

Beaver Dam Unified School District
Beaver Dam Middle School: Jim Braemer, Jeanne Frick, Jessica Greatens, Barbara Link, Dennis McCormick, Karen Michels, Nancy Nichols*, Nancy Palm, Shelly Stelsel, Susan Wiggins

Milwaukee Public Schools
Fritsche Middle School: Peggy Brokaw, Rosann Hollinger*, Dan Homontowski, David Larson, LaRon Ramsey, Judy Roschke*, Lora Ruedt, Dorothy Schuller, Sandra Wiesen, Aaron Womack, Jr.

---

* indicates a Field Test Site Coordinator

Reviews of CMP to Guide Development of CMP2

Before writing for CMP2 began or field tests were conducted, the first edition of *Connected Mathematics* was submitted to the mathematics faculties of school districts from many parts of the country and to 80 individual reviewers for extensive comments.

School District Survey Reviews of CMP

Arizona
Madison School District #38 (Phoenix)

Arkansas
Cabot School District, Little Rock School District, Magnolia School District

California
Los Angeles Unified School District

Colorado
St. Vrain Valley School District (Longmont)

Florida
Leon County Schools (Tallahassee)

Illinois
School District #21 (Wheeling)

Indiana
Joseph L. Block Junior High (East Chicago)

Kentucky
Fayette County Public Schools (Lexington)

Maine
Selection of Schools

Massachusetts
Selection of Schools

Michigan
Sparta Area Schools

Minnesota
Hopkins School District

Texas
Austin Independent School District, The El Paso Collaborative for Academic Excellence, Plano Independent School District

Wisconsin
Platteville Middle School

Individual Reviewers of CMP

Arkansas
Deborah Cramer; Robby Frizzell *(Taylor)*; Lowell Lynde *(University of Arkansas, Monticello)*; Leigh Manzer *(Norfork)*; Lynne Roberts *(Emerson High School, Emerson)*; Tony Timms *(Cabot Public Schools)*; Judith Trowell *(Arkansas Department of Higher Education)*

California
José Alcantar *(Gilroy)*; Eugenie Belcher *(Gilroy)*; Marian Pasternack *(Lowman M. S. T. Center, North Hollywood)*; Susana Pezoa *(San Jose)*; Todd Rabusin *(Hollister)*; Margaret Siegfried *(Ocala Middle School, San Jose)*; Polly Underwood *(Ocala Middle School, San Jose)*

Colorado
Janeane Golliher *(St. Vrain Valley School District, Longmont)*; Judith Koenig *(Nevin Platt Middle School, Boulder)*

Florida
Paige Loggins *(Swift Creek Middle School, Tallahassee)*

Illinois
Jan Robinson *(School District #21, Wheeling)*

Indiana
Frances Jackson *(Joseph L. Block Junior High, East Chicago)*

Kentucky
Natalee Feese *(Fayette County Public Schools, Lexington)*

Maine
Betsy Berry *(Maine Math & Science Alliance, Augusta)*

Maryland
Joseph Gagnon *(University of Maryland, College Park)*; Paula Maccini *(University of Maryland, College Park)*

Massachusetts
George Cobb *(Mt. Holyoke College, South Hadley)*; Cliff Kanold *(University of Massachusetts, Amherst)*

Michigan
Mary Bouck *(Farwell Area Schools)*; Carol Dorer *(Slauson Middle School, Ann Arbor)*; Carrie Heaney *(Forsythe Middle School, Ann Arbor)*; Ellen Hopkins *(Clague Middle School, Ann Arbor)*; Teri Keusch *(Portland Middle School, Portland)*; Valerie Mills *(Oakland Schools, Waterford)*; Mary Beth Schmitt *(Traverse City East Junior High, Traverse City)*; Jack Smith *(Michigan State University, East Lansing)*; Rebecca Spencer *(Sparta Middle School, Sparta)*; Ann Marie Nicoll Turner *(Tappan Middle School, Ann Arbor)*; Scott Turner *(Scarlett Middle School, Ann Arbor)*

Minnesota
Margarita Alvarez *(Olson Middle School, Minneapolis)*; Jane Amundson *(Nicollet Junior High, Burnsville)*; Anne Bartel *(Minneapolis Public Schools)*; Gwen Ranzau Campbell *(Sunrise Park Middle School, White Bear Lake)*; Stephanie Cin *(Hidden Valley Elementary, Burnsville)*; Joan Garfield *(University of Minnesota, Minneapolis)*; Gretchen Hall *(Richfield Middle School, Richfield)*; Jennifer Larson *(Olson Middle School, Minneapolis)*; Michele Luke *(West Junior High, Minnetonka)*; Jeni Meyer *(Richfield Junior High, Richfield)*; Judy Pfingsten *(Inver Grove Heights Middle School, Inver Grove Heights)*; Sarah Shafer *(North Junior High, Minnetonka)*; Genni Steele *(Central Middle School, White Bear Lake)*; Victoria Wilson *(Eisenhower Elementary, Hopkins)*; Paul Zorn *(St. Olaf College, Northfield)*

New York
Debra Altenau-Bartolino *(Greenwich Village Middle School, New York)*; Doug Clements *(University of Buffalo)*; Francis Curcio *(New York University, New York)*; Christine Dorosh *(Clinton School for Writers, Brooklyn)*; Jennifer Rehn *(East Side Middle School, New York)*; Phyllis Tam *(IS 89 Lab School, New York)*;

Marie Turini *(Louis Armstrong Middle School, New York)*; Lucy West *(Community School District 2, New York)*; Monica Witt *(Simon Baruch Intermediate School 104, New York)*

Pennsylvania
Robert Aglietti *(Pittsburgh)*; Sharon Mihalich *(Pittsburgh)*; Jennifer Plumb *(South Hills Middle School, Pittsburgh)*; Mary Lynn Raith *(Pittsburgh Public Schools)*

Texas
Michelle Bittick *(Austin Independent School District)*; Margaret Cregg *(Plano Independent School District)*; Sheila Cunningham *(Klein Independent School District)*; Judy Hill *(Austin Independent School District)*; Patricia Holguin *(El Paso Independent School District)*; Bonnie McNemar *(Arlington)*; Kay Neuse *(Plano Independent School District)*; Joyce Polanco *(Austin Independent School District)*; Marge Ramirez *(University of Texas at El Paso)*; Pat Rossman *(Baker Campus, Austin)*; Cindy Schimek *(Houston)*; Cynthia Schneider *(Charles A. Dana Center, University of Texas at Austin)*; Uri Treisman *(Charles A. Dana Center, University of Texas at Austin)*; Jacqueline Weilmuenster *(Grapevine-Colleyville Independent School District)*; LuAnn Weynand *(San Antonio)*; Carmen Whitman *(Austin Independent School District)*; James Wohlgehagen *(Plano Independent School District)*

Washington
Ramesh Gangolli *(University of Washington, Seattle)*

Wisconsin
Susan Lamon *(Marquette University, Hales Corner)*; Steve Reinhart *(retired, Chippewa Falls Middle School, Eau Claire)*

Table of Contents

Prime Time
Factors and Multiples

Table of Contents

Bits and Pieces I
Understanding Fractions, Decimals, and Percents

Bits and Pieces I

Table of Contents

Shapes and Designs

Shapes and Designs

Table of Contents

Bits and Pieces II
Understanding Fraction Operations

Bits and Pieces II

Table of Contents

Covering and Surrounding
Two-Dimensional Measurement

Covering and Surrounding

Table of Contents

Bits and Pieces III
Computing With Decimals and Percents

Table of Contents

How Likely Is It?
Understanding Probability

Table of Contents

Data About Us
Statistics

Prime Time

Factors and Multiples

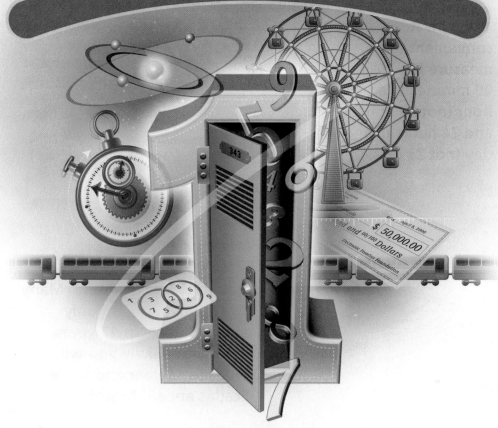

Glenda Lappan
James T. Fey
William M. Fitzgerald
Susan N. Friel
Elizabeth Difanis Phillips

PEARSON

Boston, Massachusetts · Glenview, Illinois · Shoreview, Minnesota · Upper Saddle River, New Jersey

Prime Time

Why is it convenient to measure time using 60 minutes in an hour (not 59 or 61) and 24 hours in a day (not 23 or 25)?

Insects called cicadas (si KAY dahs) spend most of their lives underground. Many come above ground only every 13 years or 17 years. Why is it unlikely you will ever see 13-year and 17-year cicadas appear together?

Why does your birthday fall on a different day of the week from one year to the next? Why is the same also true for New Year's Day and the Fourth of July?

Think for a minute about some of the ways in which you use numbers. You use numbers to count, to measure, to make comparisons, and to describe where places are located. Numbers help you communicate, find information, use technology, and make purchases. Numbers can also help you think about situations such as those on the previous page.

Whole numbers have interesting properties and structures you may not have thought about. For example, some numbers can be divided evenly by many numbers, while others can be divided evenly by only a few numbers. Some pairs of numbers have lots of factors in common, while others share only one factor. The investigations in *Prime Time* will help you learn to use ideas about the structure of numbers to explain some curious patterns, to solve problems, and to think about some interesting questions, such as those on the previous page.

Mathematical Highlights

Factors and Multiples

In *Prime Time,* you will explore important properties of whole numbers, especially properties related to multiplication and division.

You will learn how to

- Understand relationships among factors, multiples, divisors, and products

- Recognize and use properties of prime and composite numbers, even and odd numbers, and square numbers

- Use rectangles to represent the factor pairs of numbers

- Develop strategies for finding factors and multiples, least common multiples, and greatest common factors

- Recognize and use the fact that every whole number can be written in exactly one way as a product of prime numbers

- Use factors and multiples to solve problems and to explain some numerical facts of everyday life

- Develop a variety of strategies for solving problems—building models, making lists and tables, drawing diagrams, and solving simpler problems

When you encounter a new math problem, ask yourself questions about the numbers and relationships involved in the problem. In this unit, you might ask questions such as these:

Will breaking a number into factors help me solve the problem?

What relationships will doing that help me see?

What do the factors and multiples of the numbers tell me about the situation?

How can I find the factors of the numbers?

How can I find the multiples?

What common factors and common multiples do the numbers have?

Unit Project

My Special Number

Many people have a number that they think is interesting. Choose a whole number between 10 and 100 that you especially like.

In your notebook:

• record your number

• explain why you chose that number

• list three or four mathematical facts about your number

• list three or four connections you can make between your number and your world

As you work through the investigations in *Prime Time*, you will learn a lot about numbers. Think about how these new ideas apply to your special number. Add any new information about your number to your notebook. You may want to designate one or two "special-number" pages in your notebook, to record this information. At the end of the unit, your teacher will ask you to find an interesting way to report to the class about your special number.

Factors and Products

Jamie is 12 years old. Her cousin, Emilio, is 2 years old. Her brother, Cam, is 3. Her neighbor, Esther, is 8. The following number sentences say that Jamie is

6 times as old as Emilio,   4 times as old as Cam,   and $1\frac{1}{2}$ times as old as Esther.

$$12 = 6 \times 2$$ $$12 = 4 \times 3$$ $$12 = 1\frac{1}{2} \times 8$$

Notice that each of the whole numbers 2, 3, 4, and 6 can be multiplied by another whole number to get 12. For this reason, 2, 3, 4, and 6 are called *whole-number factors*, or *whole-number divisors*, of 12.

Although 8 *is* a whole number, it *is not* a whole-number factor of 12 because you cannot multiply 8 by another whole number to get 12.

To save time, we will simply use the words **factor** and **divisor** to refer to whole-number factors and whole-number divisors of a number.

1.1 Playing the Factor Game

Playing the Factor Game is a fun way to practice finding factors of whole numbers. If you pay close attention, you may learn some interesting things about numbers that you didn't know before! To play the game, you need a Factor Game Board and colored pens, pencils, or markers.

For: Factor Game Activity
Visit: PHSchool.com
Web Code: amd-1101

The Factor Game

1	2	3	4	5
6	7	8	9	10
11	12	13	14	15
16	17	18	19	20
21	22	23	24	25
26	27	28	29	30

Factor Game Rules

1. Player A chooses a number on the game board and circles it.

2. Using a different color, Player B circles all the proper factors of Player A's number. The **proper factors** of a number are all the factors of that number, except the number itself. For example, the proper factors of 12 are 1, 2, 3, 4, and 6. Although 12 is a factor of itself, it is not a proper factor.

3. Player B circles a new number, and Player A circles all the factors of the number that are not already circled.

4. The players take turns choosing numbers and circling factors.

5. If a player circles a number that has no factors left that have not been circled, then that player does not get the points for the number circled and loses the next turn.

6. The game ends when there are no numbers left with uncircled factors.

7. Each player adds the numbers that are circled with his or her color. The player with the greater total is the winner.

The First Five Moves of a Sample Game

This table shows the first five moves of a game between Cathy and Keiko. The first column describes the moves the players made. The other columns show the game board and the score after each move.

Action	Game Board	Score

Cathy circles 24. Keiko circles 1, 2, 3, 4, 6, 8, and 12 (the proper factors of 24).

Game Board:

1	2	3	4	5
6	7	8	9	10
11	12	13	14	15
16	17	18	19	20
21	22	23	24	25
26	27	28	29	30

Cathy	Keiko
24	36

Keiko circles 28. Cathy circles 7 and 14 (the factors of 28 that are not already circled).

Game Board:

1	2	3	4	5
6	7	8	9	10
11	12	13	14	15
16	17	18	19	20
21	22	23	24	25
26	27	28	29	30

Cathy	Keiko
24	36
21	28

Cathy circles 27. Keiko circles 9 (the only factor of 27 that is not already circled).

Game Board:

1	2	3	4	5
6	7	8	9	10
11	12	13	14	15
16	17	18	19	20
21	22	23	24	25
26	27	28	29	30

Cathy	Keiko
24	36
21	28
27	9

Keiko circles 30. Cathy circles 5, 10 and 15 (the factors of 30 that are not already circled).

Game Board:

1	2	3	4	5
6	7	8	9	10
11	12	13	14	15
16	17	18	19	20
21	22	23	24	25
26	27	28	29	30

Cathy	Keiko
24	36
21	28
27	9
30	30

Cathy circles 25. All the factors of 25 are circled. Cathy does not receive any points for this turn and loses her next turn.

Game Board:

1	2	3	4	5
6	7	8	9	10
11	12	13	14	15
16	17	18	19	20
21	22	23	24	25
26	27	28	29	30

Cathy	Keiko
24	36
21	28
27	9
30	30
0	0

Problem 1.1 Finding Proper Factors

A. Play the Factor Game several times with a partner. Take turns making the first move. Look for moves that will give you more points than your opponent. As you play, write down any strategies or patterns you find.

B. How can you test to determine whether a number is a factor of another number?

C. If you know a factor of a number, can you find another factor? Explain your thinking.

D. Give an example of a number that has many factors and an example of a number that has few factors.

E. Make a list of the factors of 18. Make a list of the divisors of 18. Are the factors of a number also divisors of the number? Explain your thinking.

F. How do you know when you have found all the factors of a number?

ACE Homework starts on page 14.

1.2 Playing to Win the Factor Game

Did you notice that some numbers are better than others to choose for the first move in the Factor Game? For example, if you choose 22, you get 22 points and your opponent gets only $1 + 2 + 11 = 14$ points. However, if you choose 18, you get 18 points, and your opponent gets $1 + 2 + 3 + 6 + 9 = 21$ points!

Now you will make a table to analyze the Factor Game and look for patterns. Your table might start like this:

First Move	Proper Factors	My Score	Opponent's Score
1	None	Lose a Turn	0
2	1	2	1
3	1	3	1
4	1, 2	4	3

Problem 1.2 Prime and Composite Numbers

A. 1. Make a table of all the possible first moves (numbers from 1 to 30) in the Factor Game.

   2. For each move, list the proper factors of the number, and record the scores you and your opponent would receive.

   3. Describe an interesting pattern you see in your table.

B. What is the best first move? Why?

C. Which first move would make you lose your next turn? Why?

D. Other than your answer to Question C, what is the worst first move? Why?

E. List all the first moves that allow your opponent to score only one point. These numbers are called *prime numbers*.

F. Are all prime numbers good first moves? Explain. (Remember, a number is a *good first move* if the player choosing the number scores more points than his or her opponent.)

G. List all the first moves that allow your opponent to score more than one point. These numbers also have a special name. They are called *composite numbers*.

H. Are composite numbers good first moves? Explain.

ACE Homework starts on page 14.

Did You Know?

Large prime numbers are used to encode top-secret information. In 1999, Nayan Hajratwala found a prime number with more than 2 million digits. In type this size, that number would be more than 2 miles long! The Electronic Frontier Foundation awarded Mr. Hajratwala $50,000 for discovering the first prime number with more than 1,000,000 digits. The EFF now offers a prize of $250,000 to the first person to find a prime number with over 1,000,000,000 digits!

Mathematicians have always been puzzled about fast ways of determining whether really big numbers are prime. In August, 2002, Dr. Manindra Agrawal and two college students, Neeraj Kayal and Nitin Saxena, made a breakthrough. They surprised and delighted mathematicians with an elegant way of determining whether really huge numbers are prime. You can find more information about this in the August 8, 2002, issue of *The New York Times*.

Go Online
PHSchool.com **For:** Information about prime numbers
Web Code: ame-9031

1.3 The Product Game

You learned about factors of a number in Problems 1.1 and 1.2. In the next game you will learn about multiples of numbers. A **multiple** of a number is the product of that number and another whole number. For example, 24 is a multiple of 6 because $4 \times 6 = 24$. Multiples and factors have an interesting back-and-forth relationship.

If a number is a multiple of 5, then 5 is a factor of that number. These five sentences describe how the numbers 3, 5, and 15 are related.

$$5 \times 3 = 15$$

5 is a factor of 15.

3 is a factor of 15.

15 is a multiple of 5.

15 is a multiple of 3.

You can probably think of other ways to show the relationship. For example, you could add these to the list:

15 is divisible by 5.

15 is divisible by 3.

In the Factor Game, you start with a number and find its factors. In the Product Game, you start with factors and find their product. The Product Game board consists of a list of factors and a grid of products. The object is to mark four products in a row—up and down, across, or diagonally—before your opponent does.

active math online

For: Product Game Activity
Visit: PHSchool.com
Web Code: amd-1103

The Product Game

1	2	3	4	5	6
7	8	9	10	12	14
15	16	18	20	21	24
25	27	28	30	32	35
36	40	42	45	48	49
54	56	63	64	72	81

Factors:

1 2 3 4 5 6 7 8 9

To play the game, you need a Product Game Board, two paper clips, and colored markers or chips—one color for each player.

Product Game Rules

1. Player A puts a paper clip on a number in the factor list. Player A does not mark a square on the product grid because only one factor has been marked. It takes two factors to make a product.

2. Player B puts the other paper clip on any number in the factor list (including the same number marked by Player A). Player B then shades or covers the product of the two factors on the product grid. An example is shown on the next page.

3. Player A moves *either* paper clip to another number, leaving one in its original place, and then shades or covers the new product.

4. Each player, in turn, moves a paper clip and marks a product. If a product is already marked, the player does not get a mark for that turn. The winner is the first player to mark four squares in a row—up and down, across, or diagonally.

A. Play the Product Game several times with a partner. Look for interesting patterns and strategies that might help you win. Make notes on your observations.

B. Examine the Product Game Board. Is it possible to get every number on the product grid by multiplying two of the numbers in the factor list? Justify your answer.

C. Can you find two numbers in the list of factors for the game whose product is *not* on the product grid?

D. Suppose that a game is in progress and you want to cover the number 12 on the grid. Describe one way this can happen. Can you get 12 in more than one way?

E. 1. Suppose that a game is in progress and one of the paper clips is on 5. What products can you make by moving the other paper clip?

    2. List five multiples of 5 that are not on the game board.

ACE Homework starts on page 14.

The Product Game

1	2	3	4	5	6
7	8	9	10	12	14
15	16	18	20	21	24
25	27	28	30	32	35
36	40	42	45	48	49
54	56	63	64	72	81

Factors:
1   2   3   4   5   6   7   8   9

How can I get 12?

Applications

1. Ben claims that 12 is a factor of 24. How can you check to determine whether he is correct?

2. What factor is paired with 6 to give 24?

3. What factor is paired with 5 to give 45?

4. What factor is paired with 3 to give 24?

5. What factor is paired with 6 to give 54?

6. How would you test to see whether 7 is a factor of 291?

7. **Multiple Choice** Which of these numbers has the most factors?

   A. 6   **B.** 17   **C.** 25   **D.** 36

8. Lareina understands factors, but sometimes she has trouble finding all the factors of a number. What advice would you give to help her find all the factors of a number? Demonstrate by finding all the factors of 110.

9. Find two numbers that have 2, 3, and 5 as factors. What other factors do the two numbers have in common?

10. **a.** What do you get when you use your calculator to divide 84 by 14? What does this tell you about 14 and 84?

    b. What do you get when you use your calculator to divide 84 by 15? What does this tell you about 15 and 84?

11. Ramona says the Factor Game might also be called the Divisor Game. Do you agree? Why or why not?

12. a. Is 6 a divisor of 18? Why or why not?

   b. Is 18 a divisor of 6? Why or why not?

13. Which of these numbers are divisors of 64?

    2   6   8   12   16

14. In Exercise 13, Evan noticed that some of the proper factors of 64 can be multiplied to get another proper factor of 64. For example, 2 and 8 are factors of 64, and 16 is also a factor of 64. Does every number have some factors for which this is true?

For: Help with Exercise 14
Web Code: ame-1114

15. a. A **prime number** has exactly two factors, 1 and itself. If you circle a prime number in the Factor Game, your opponent will receive at most one point. Explain why. Give some examples.

   b. A **composite number** has more than two factors. If you circle a composite number in the Factor Game, your opponent might receive more points than you. Explain why. Give some examples.

16. Why is the set of factors of a number not the same as the set of proper factors of that number?

17. Using the terms *factor*, *divisor*, *multiple*, *product*, and *divisible by*, write as many statements as you can about the number sentence 4 × 7 = 28.

18. Dewayne and Todd are playing the Product Game. Dewayne's markers are on 16, 18, and 28, and Todd's markers are on 14, 21, and 30. The paper clips are on 5 and 6. It is Dewayne's turn to move a paper clip.

   a. List the moves Dewayne can make.

   b. Which move(s) would give Dewayne three markers in a row?

   c. Which move(s) would allow him to block Todd?

   d. Which move do you think Dewayne should make? Explain.

The Product Game

1	2	3	4	5	6
7	8	9	10	12	**14**
15	**16**	**18**	20	**21**	24
25	27	**28**	**30**	32	35
36	40	42	45	48	49
54	56	63	64	72	81

Factors:

1 2 3 4 5 6 7 8 9

Investigation 1 Factors and Products   **15**

19. a. Suppose that one paper clip on the Product Game board is on 3. What products can you make by moving the other paper clip?

b. List five multiples of 3 that are not on the game board.

c. How many multiples of 3 are there?

20. Davis just marked 18 on the Product Game board. On which factors might the paper clips be placed? List all the possibilities.

21. Find two products on the Product Game board, other than 18, that can be made in more than one way. List all the pairs of factors that give each product.

22. Multiple Choice Which set represents all the factors of 12?

F. {1, 2, 3, 4, 6, 12}   **G.** {12, 24, 36, 48, . . . }

H. {0, 1, 2, 3, 4, 6, 12}   **J.** {1, 2, 3, 4, 6}

23. Use the ideas from this investigation to list at least five facts about the number 30.

24. Determine whether each of the following numbers can be made in more than one way in the Product Game. State whether the number is prime or composite.

a. 36   **b.** 5   **c.** 7   **d.** 9

25. Salvador said that the Product Game might also be called the Multiple Game. Do you agree? Why or why not?

26. On the Product Game board, which number is both a prime number and an even number?

27. Jose says the Factor Game and the Product Game are similar because both involve multiplication. Marcus says they are not similar. With whom do you agree and why?

Connections

28. Twenty-five classes from Martin Luther King Elementary School will play the Factor Game at their math carnival. Each class has 32 students. How many game boards are needed if each pair of students is to play the game once?

29. As part of the carnival, the school will hold a Factor Game marathon. It takes Archie and Kel an average of 12 minutes to finish one game. About how many games will they finish if they play nonstop from 9:00 A.M. to 2:30 P.M.?

30. Multiple Choice This week Carlos read a book for language arts class. He finished the book on Friday. On Monday he read 27 pages; on Tuesday he read 31 pages; and on Wednesday he read 28 pages. On Thursday and Friday he read the same number of pages each day. The book had 144 pages. How many pages did he read on Thursday?

A. 28   **B.** 29   **C.** 31   **D.** 58

31. Write a problem like Exercise 30 about a book you have read recently.

32. Long ago, people observed the sun's rising and setting over and over at about equal intervals. They decided to use the amount of time between two sunrises as the length of a day. They divided the day into 24 hours. Use what you know about factors to answer these questions:

a. Why is 24 a more convenient choice for the number of hours in a day than 23 or 25?

b. If you could select a number different from 24 to represent the number of hours in a day, what number would you choose? Why?

33. a. In developing the ways in which we calculate time, astronomers divided an hour into 60 minutes. Why is 60 a good choice (better than 59 or 61)?

b. If you could select another number to represent the number of minutes in an hour, what would be a good choice? Why?

34. a. Is 132 divisible by 12? By 3? By 4?

b. Is 160 divisible by 10? By 2? By 5?

c. Is 42 divisible by 6? By 3? By 2?

d. What patterns do you see in parts (a), (b), and (c)?

Go Online
PHSchool.com
For: Multiple-Choice Skills Practice
Web Code: ama-1154

For Exercises 35–37, find two numbers that can be multiplied to give each product. Do not use 1 as one of the numbers.

35. 84   **36.** 145   **37.** 300

38. a. Ms. Diaz wants to divide her class of 30 students into 10 groups, not necessarily of equal size. What are some of her choices?

b. Ms. Diaz wants to divide her class of 30 students into equal-sized groups. What are her choices?

c. How is the thinking you did in part (a) different from the thinking you did in part (b)?

Extensions

39. Jocelyn and Moesha decide to play the Factor Game on a 100-board, which includes the whole numbers from 1 to 100.

a. What will Jocelyn's score be if Moesha chooses 100 as her first move?

b. What will Jocelyn's score be if Moesha chooses 99 as her first move?

c. What is the best first move on a 100-board?

40. What is my number?

Clue 1 When you divide my number by 5, the remainder is 4.

Clue 2 My number has two digits, and both digits are even.

Clue 3 The sum of the digits is 10.

41. The Factor Game can be played on a 49-board, which includes the whole numbers from 1 to 49.

   a. Use your table for analyzing first moves on a 30-board from Problem 1.2. Extend it to include all the numbers on a 49-board.

   b. What new primes do you find?

The Factor Game

1	2	3	4	5	6	7
8	9	10	11	12	13	14
15	16	17	18	19	20	21
22	23	24	25	26	27	28
29	30	31	32	33	34	35
36	37	38	39	40	41	42
43	44	45	46	47	48	49

42. Lana and Luis are playing the Factor Game on a 49-board. Lana has the first move and chooses 49.

   a. How many points does Luis score for this round?

   b. How many points does Lana score for this round?

43. What is the best first move on a 49-board? Why?

44. What is the worst first move on a 49-board? Why?

45. What three factors were used to make this Product Game board? What product is missing from the grid?

4	6	9
14	?	49

Factors: ___ ___ ___

46. What four factors were used to make this Product Game board? What product is missing from the grid?

9	15	18	
21	?	30	35
	36	42	49

Factors: ___ ___ ___ ___

47. The sum of the proper factors of a number may be greater than, less than, or equal to the number. Ancient mathematicians used this idea to classify numbers as *abundant*, *deficient*, and *perfect*. Each whole number greater than 1 falls into one of these three categories.

    a. Draw and label three circles as shown below. The numbers 12, 15, and 6 have been placed in the appropriate circles. Use your factor table to determine what each label means. Then, write each whole number from 2 to 30 in the correct circle.

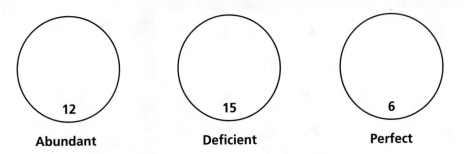

           12   **15**   **6**

        Abundant   **Deficient**   **Perfect**

    b. Do the labels seem appropriate? Why or why not?

    c. In which circle would 36 belong?

    d. In which circle would 55 belong?

48. Look at the Product Game board you used in Problem 1.3. Which of the numbers on that board can be formed by placing both paper clips on the same number? These numbers are called *square numbers*. Why do you think they have this name?

49. a. Suppose you choose 16 as a first move in the Factor Game. How many points does your opponent get? How does your opponent's score for this turn compare to yours?

    b. Suppose you choose 4 as a first move. How many points does your opponent get? How does your opponent's score for this turn compare to yours?

    c. Find some other numbers that have the same pattern of scoring as 4 and 16. These numbers could be called *near-perfect numbers*. Why do you think this name fits?

Did You Know?

Is there a largest perfect number? Mathematicians have been trying for hundreds of years to find the answer to this question. You might like to know that the next largest perfect number after 6 and 28 is 496.

Go Online
PHSchool.com

For: Information about perfect numbers
Web Code: ame-9031

Mathematical Reflections 1

In this investigation, you played and analyzed the Factor Game and the Product Game. These questions will help you summarize what you have learned.

Think about your answers to these questions. Discuss your ideas with other students and your teacher. Then write a summary of your findings in your notebook.

1. What are the factors of a number and how do you find them?

2. What did you learn about prime numbers and composite numbers while you were playing the Factor Game? Is the number 1 prime or composite? Explain.

3. What are the multiples of a number and how do you find them?

Unit Project What's Next?

Write something new that you have learned about your special number now that you have played the Factor Game and the Product Game.

Would your special number be a good first move in either game? Why or why not?

Investigation 2

Whole-Number Patterns and Relationships

Because you have been using whole numbers since you were young, you may think there is not much more to learn about them. However, there are many interesting relationships involving whole numbers that you may never have considered. To notice these relationships, it is sometimes helpful to break whole numbers into factors or to multiply them by other numbers.

2.1 Finding Patterns

In the Factor Game and the Product Game, you found that factors occur in pairs. Once you know one factor of a number, you can find another factor. For example, 3 is a factor of 12, and because $3 \times 4 = 12$, 4 is also a factor of 12. We call the pair 3, 4 a **factor pair.**

Every year, Meridian Shopping Mall has an exhibit of arts and crafts. People who want to display their work rent a space for $20 per square yard. Exhibitors are given carpet squares to lay out their spaces. Each carpet square measures 1 square yard. All exhibit spaces must have a rectangular shape.

Terrapin Crafts wants to rent a space of 12 square yards. Use 12 square tiles to represent the carpet squares.

- What are all the possible ways the Terrapin Crafts owner can arrange the squares to make a rectangle?

- How are the rectangles you found and the factors of 12 related?

You just found all the possible rectangles that can be made from 12 tiles. These rectangles are *models* for the number 12. The models are useful because they allow you to "see" the factors of 12. You can make rectangle models such as these for any whole number.

In Problem 2.1, you and your classmates will use grid paper to create all the possible rectangle models for all the whole numbers from 1 to 30. When the rectangles are displayed, you can look for interesting patterns.

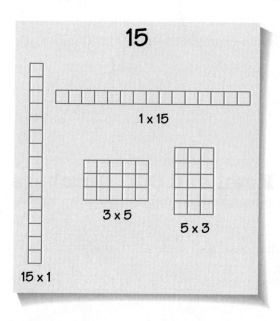

Your teacher will assign your group a few of the numbers from 1 to 30. Work with your group to decide how to distribute the numbers you have been assigned.

A. From grid paper, cut out all the possible rectangle models you can make for each of your numbers. You may want to use tiles to help you find the rectangles.

Write each number at the top of a sheet of paper, and tape all the rectangles for that number to the sheet. List the factors of the number from least to greatest at the bottom of the paper.

Display the sheets of rectangles in order from 1 to 30 around the room. When all the numbers are displayed, look for patterns.

B. 1. Which numbers have the most rectangles? What kind of numbers are these?

  2. Which numbers have the fewest rectangles? What kind of numbers are these?

  3. Which numbers are **square numbers** (numbers whose tiles can be arranged to form a square)?

  4. How can you use the rectangle models for a number to list the factors of the number? Use an example to show your thinking.

ACE Homework starts on page 30.

2.2 Reasoning With Even and Odd Numbers

An **even number** is a number that has 2 as a factor. An **odd number** is a number that does not have 2 as a factor.

Tilo makes models for whole numbers by arranging square tiles in a special pattern. Here are Lilo's tile models for the numbers from 1 to 7.

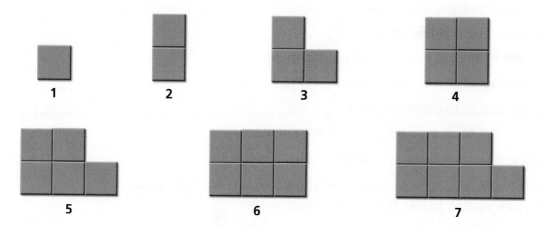

- How are the models of even numbers different from the models of odd numbers?

- Describe the models for 50 and 99.

When you tell what you think will happen in a mathematical situation, you are making a conjecture. A **conjecture** is your best guess about a pattern or a relationship that you observe. You can use models, drawings, or other kinds of evidence to support your conjectures.

Make a conjecture about what happens when you add two even numbers. Do you get an even number or an odd number? Why?

Problem 2.2 asks you to think of other conjectures to make about even and odd numbers.

When I add two even numbers, the sum is...

Problem 2.2 Reasoning with Even and Odd Numbers

A. Make conjectures about whether the results below will be even or odd. Then use tile models or some other method to support your conjectures.

  1. the sum of two even numbers

  2. the sum of two odd numbers

  3. the sum of an even number and an odd number

  4. the product of two even numbers

  5. the product of two odd numbers

  6. the product of an even number and an odd number

B. Is 0 an even number or an odd number? How do you know?

C. Without building a tile model, how can you determine whether a sum of numbers, such as $127 + 38$, is even or odd?

D. A problem occurs when we compute $6 + 3 \times 9$. You can get 81 or 33 as the answer! How can you get 81? How can you get 33? The *order of operations* rule says that you do all multiplications and divisions before you add or subtract. This makes 33 the correct answer.

Compute each number and tell whether it is even or odd.

  1. $3 + 5 \times 7$ **2.** $25 - 3 \times 2$ **3.** $11 \times 5 + 3 \times 9$

  4. $43 - 25 \div 5 + 2$ **5.** $43 - 7 + 5 \times 2$ **6.** $6 + 18 - 24 \div 6$

ACE Homework starts on page 30.

2.3 Classifying Numbers

A **Venn diagram** uses circles to group things that belong together. You can use Venn diagrams to explore relationships among whole numbers. For example, suppose that you want to group the whole numbers from 1 to 9 according to whether they are prime or multiples of 2. First, list the numbers that fall into each category:

    Prime Numbers: 2, 3, 5, 7   Multiples of 2: 2, 4, 6, 8

Next, draw and label two overlapping circles, one that represents the prime numbers and one that represents the multiples of 2. Put each number from 1 to 9 in the appropriate region. The numbers that don't fall into either category belong outside of the circles. The numbers that are in both categories belong in the overlap of the circles.

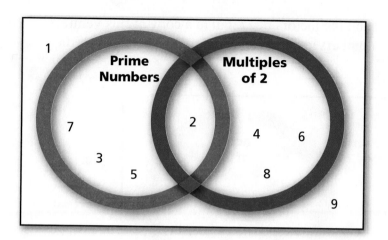

Problem 2.3 Classifying Numbers

The Venn diagrams in Questions A–D are related to the ideas you studied in Investigation 1.

A. List the factors of 30 and 36. Fill in a copy of this Venn diagram with all whole numbers less than or equal to 40. Then answer the questions below.

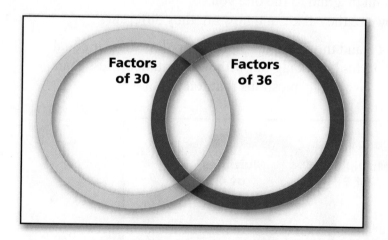

1. What do the numbers in the intersection (the "overlap") of the circular regions have in common?

2. List five numbers that fall in the region outside the circles and explain why they belong outside the circles.

3. Explain how you can use your completed diagram to find the greatest factor that 30 and 36 have in common. What is this *greatest common factor*?

4. What is the least number that falls in the intersection?

B. List the factors of 20 and the factors of 27. Fill in a copy of this Venn diagram with whole numbers less than or equal to 30. Then answer the questions below.

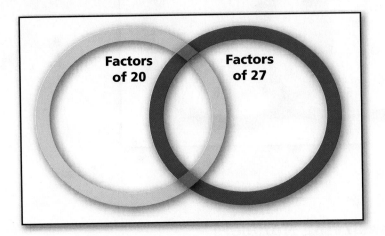

1. What do the numbers in the intersection of the circular regions have in common?

2. Explain how you can use your completed diagram to find the greatest factor that 20 and 27 have in common. What is this greatest common factor?

3. Compare this Venn diagram to the one you completed in Question A. How are they alike, and how are they different?

C. List the multiples of 5 and the multiples of 4 that are less than or equal to 40. Fill in a copy of this Venn diagram with whole numbers less than or equal to 40. Then answer the questions that follow.

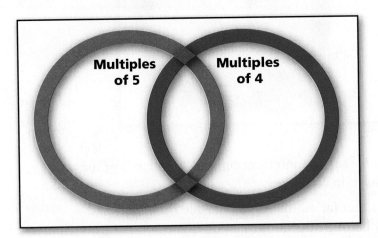

1. What do the numbers in the intersection of the circular regions have in common?

2. Explain how you can use your completed diagram to find the least multiple that 5 and 4 have in common. What is this *least common multiple*?

3. List five more numbers that would be in the intersection if numbers greater than 40 were allowed. What would be the greatest possible number in the intersection if you could use any number?

D. List the multiples of 6 and the multiples of 8 that are less than or equal to 48. Fill in a copy of this Venn diagram with whole numbers less than or equal to 48. Then answer the questions below.

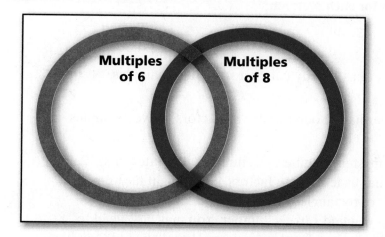

1. What do the numbers in the intersection have in common?

2. Explain how you can use your completed diagram to find the least multiple that 6 and 8 have in common. What is this least common multiple?

3. Compare this Venn diagram to the one you completed in Question C. How are they alike? How are they different?

ACE Homework starts on page 30.

Applications

For Exercises 1–6, give the dimensions of each rectangle that can be made from the given number of tiles. Then use the dimensions of the rectangles to list all the factor pairs for each number.

1. 24   **2.** 32   **3.** 48   **4.** 45   **5.** 60   **6.** 72

7. What type of number has exactly two factors? Give examples.

8. What type of number has an odd number of factors? Give examples.

9. Luke has chosen a mystery number. His number is greater than 12 and less than 40, and it has exactly three factors. What might his number be? Use the display of rectangles for the numbers 1 to 30 from Problem 2.1 to help you find Luke's number. You may also need to think about what the displays for the numbers 31 to 40 would look like.

For Exercises 10–13, make a conjecture about whether each result will be odd or even. Use models, pictures, or other reasoning to support your conjectures.

10. An even number minus an even number

11. An odd number minus an odd number

12. An even number minus an odd number

13. An odd number minus an even number

14. How can you tell whether a number is even or odd? Explain or illustrate your answer in at least two ways.

15. How can you determine whether a sum of several numbers, such as $13 + 45 + 24 + 17$, is even or odd?

For: Help with Exercise 15
Web Code: ame-1215

16. Insert operation signs to make the answer correct.

   a. 2 ■ 5 ■ 3 = 17   **b.** 2 ■ 5 ■ 3 = 13

   c. 2 ■ 5 ■ 3 = 30   **d.** 2 ■ 5 ■ 3 = 7

17. Copy this Venn diagram and place whole numbers from 1 to 36 in the appropriate regions. Do you notice anything unusual about the diagram?

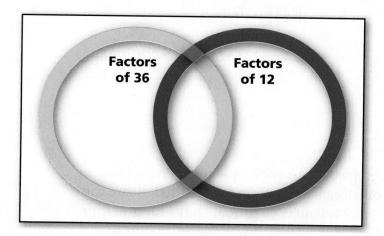

18. Copy this Venn diagram and find at least five numbers that belong in each region.

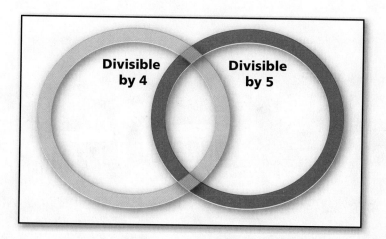

19. **a.** Draw and label a Venn diagram in which one circle represents the multiples of 3 and another circle represents the multiples of 5. Place whole numbers from 1 to 45 in the regions of the diagram.

   b. List four numbers between 1 and 45 that fall in the region outside the circles.

   c. The *common multiples* of 3 and 5 (the numbers that are multiples of both 3 and 5) should be in the intersection of the circles. What is the least common multiple of 3 and 5?

20. **a.** Draw and label a Venn diagram in which one circle contains the divisors of 42 and another circle contains the divisors of 60.

   b. The *common factors* of 42 and 60 (the numbers that are divisors of both 42 and 60) should be in the intersection of the circles. What is the greatest common factor of 42 and 60?

21. Find all the common multiples of 4 and 11 that are less than 100.

Connections

22. The Olympic photograph below inspired a school pep club to design card displays for football games. Each display uses 100 square cards, At a game, groups of 100 volunteers will hold up the cards to form complete pictures. They are most effective if the volunteers sit in a rectangular arrangements. What rectangular seating arrangements are possible? Which arrangements would you choose? Why?

23. A school band has 64 members. The band marches in the form of a rectangle. What rectangles can the band director make by arranging the members of the band? Which of these arrangements is most appealing to you? Why?

24. How many rectangles can you build with a prime number of square tiles?

25. Multiple Choice What is my number?

Clue 1 My number has two digits, and both digits are even.

Clue 2 The sum of my number's digits is 10.

Clue 3 My number has 4 as a factor.

Clue 4 The difference between the two digits of my number is 6.

A. 28   **B.** 46   **C.** 64   **D.** 72

26. a. List all the numbers less than or equal to 50 that are divisible by 5.

   b. Describe a pattern you see in your list that you can use to determine whether a large number—such as 1,276,549—is divisible by 5.

   c. Which numbers in your list are divisible by 2?

   d. Which numbers in your list are divisible by 10?

   e. How do the lists in parts (c) and (d) compare? Why does this result make sense?

27. Allie wants to earn some money for a new bike. She tells her dad she will wash the dishes for 2 cents on Monday, for 4 cents on Tuesday, and for 8 cents on Wednesday. If this pattern continued, how much would Allie earn on Thursday? How much would she earn altogether in 14 days?

28. Allie's eccentric aunt, May Belle, hides $10,000 in $20 bills under her mattress. If she spends one $20 bill every day, how many days will it take her to run out of bills?

29. a. What factor is paired with 6 to give 48?

   b. What factor is paired with 11 to give 121?

30. Using the terms *factor*, *divisor*, *multiple*, *product*, and *divisible by*, write as many statements as you can about the number sentence $6 \times 8 = 48$.

31. Multiple Choice Which number is a prime number?

   F. 91   **G.** 51   **H.** 31   **J.** 21

32. Multiple Choice Which number is a composite number?

A. 2   **B.** 79   **C.** 107   **D.** 237

Go Online
PHSchool.com

For: Multiple-Choice Skills Practice
Web Code: ama-1254

Extensions

33. Multiple Choice Which number is a square number?

F. 128   **G.** 225   **H.** 360   **J.** 399

34. Find three numbers you can multiply to get 300.

35. a. Below is the complete list of the proper factors of a certain number. What is the number?

1, 2, 3, 4, 6, 7, 12, 14, 21, 28, 42, 49, 84, 98, 147, 196, 294

b. List each of the factor pairs for the number.

c. How is the list of factor pairs related to the rectangles that could be made to show the number?

36. a. Find at least five numbers that belong in each region of the Venn diagram below.

b. What do the numbers in the intersection have in common?

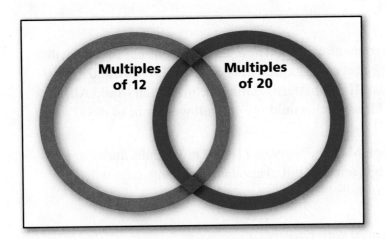

Consecutive numbers are whole numbers in a row, such as 31, 32, 33, or 52, 53, 54. Think of different series of consecutive numbers when you work on Exercises 37–40.

37. For any three consecutive numbers, what can you say about odd numbers and even numbers? Explain.

38. Mirari conjectures that, in every three consecutive whole numbers, one number would be divisible by 3. Do you think Mirari is correct? Explain.

39. How many consecutive numbers do you need to guarantee that one of the numbers is divisible by 5?

40. How many consecutive numbers do you need to guarantee that one of the numbers is divisible by 6?

41. Jeff is trying to determine when to quit looking for more whole number factors of a number. He has collected data about several numbers. For example, 30 has 1×30, 2×15, 3×10, 5×6, and then he can stop looking, because the factor pairs repeat. For 36, he can stop looking when he gets to 6×6. For 66, there are no new factor pairs after 6×11. Copy and complete the table below. Is there any pattern that would help him know when to stop looking?

Number	16	30	36	40	50	64	66
Last Factor Pair	■	5×6	6×6	■	■	■	6×11

Did You Know?

Many conjectures involving whole numbers seem simple, but are actually very difficult to justify. For example, in 1742, a mathematician named Christian Goldbach conjectured that any even number, except 2, could be written as the sum of two prime numbers. For example:

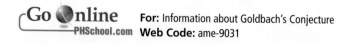

$$4 = 2 + 2 \qquad 12 = 7 + 5$$
$$36 = 17 + 19 \qquad 162 = 59 + 103$$

This seems like a pretty simple idea, doesn't it? However, in over 260 years, no one has been able to prove that it is true or find an even number that is not the sum of two prime numbers!

Go Online
PHSchool.com   **For:** Information about Goldbach's Conjecture
Web Code: ame-9031

Mathematical Reflections 2

In this investigation, you classified numbers, analyzed factor pairs, and made conjectures about sums and products of odd and even numbers. These questions will help you summarize what you have learned.

Think about your answers to these questions. Discuss your ideas with other students and your teacher. Then write a summary of your findings in your notebook.

1. Think about the grid paper models in Problem 2.1. For any number, how can you use grid paper models to find the factor pairs for that number?

2. What are Venn diagrams? How are they useful for showing relationships among numbers?

3. What strategy do you use to find a complete list of factors for a given number? How do you know when you have found all the possible factors?

4. What do you know about the sums and products of odd and even numbers? Justify your statements.

Unit Project What's Next?

Write about your special number. What can you say about your number now?

Is your number even? Is it odd?

How many factor pairs does your number have?

Investigation 3

Common Multiples and Common Factors

Many things happen over and over again in fixed cycles. For example, a morning news program may have a traffic report every 7 minutes. A train may arrive at a particular station every 12 minutes. A cuckoo clock may sound every 15 minutes.

How can you figure out when two events with different cycles can occur at the same time? Thinking about common factors and common multiples can help you solve such problems.

Let's start by comparing the multiples of 20 and 30.

- The multiples of 20 are 20, 40, 60, 80, 100, 120, 140, 160, 180, . . .
- The multiples of 30 are 30, 60, 90, 120, 150, 180, . . .

The numbers 60, 120, 180, 240, . . . , are multiples of both 20 and 30. We call these numbers **common multiples** of 20 and 30. Of these multiples, 60 is the *least common multiple*.

Now let's compare the factors of 12 and 30.

- The factors of 12 are 1, 2, 3, 4, 6, and 12.
- The factors of 30 are 1, 2, 3, 5, 6, 10, 15, and 30.

The numbers 1, 2, 3, and 6, are factors of both 12 and 30. We call these numbers **common factors** of 12 and 30. Of these factors, 6 is the *greatest common factor*.

3.1 Riding Ferris Wheels

One of the more popular rides at a carnival or amusement park is the Ferris wheel.

Problem 3.1 Choosing Common Multiples or Common Factors

Jeremy and his little sister, Deborah, are at a carnival. There are both a large and a small Ferris wheel. Jeremy gets on the large Ferris wheel at the same time his sister gets on the small Ferris wheel. The rides begin at the same time. For each situation below, decide how many seconds will pass before Jeremy and Deborah are both at the bottom again.

A. The large wheel makes one revolution in 60 seconds and the small wheel makes one revolution in 20 seconds.

B. The large wheel makes one revolution in 50 seconds and the small wheel makes one revolution in 30 seconds.

C. The large wheel makes one revolution in 10 seconds and the small wheel makes one revolution in 7 seconds.

D. For Questions A–C, determine the number of times each Ferris wheel goes around before Jeremy and his sister are both on the ground again.

ACE Homework starts on page 42.

Cicadas (si KAY dahs) spend most of their lives underground. Some populations of cicadas come above ground every 13 years, while others come up every 17 years. Although cicadas do not cause damage directly to fruits and vegetables, they can damage orchards because the female makes slits in trees to lay her eggs.

Did You Know?

Cicadas are sometimes mistakenly called locusts. A locust is actually a type of grasshopper that looks nothing like a cicada. The error originated when early European settlers in North America encountered large outbreaks of cicadas. The swarms of insects reminded the settlers of stories they knew about swarms of locusts in Egypt.

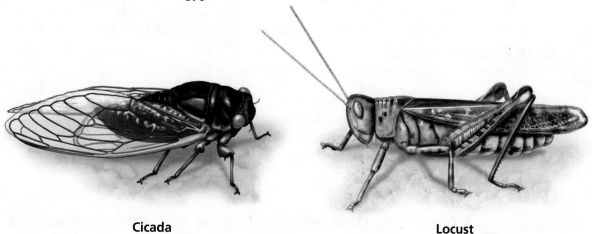

Cicada   Locust

Female cicadas lay their eggs in tree branches. When the young cicadas hatch, they drop to the ground and burrow into the soil. They remain underground for 13 or 17 years, feeding off juices from tree roots. Several months before they emerge, cicadas tunnel to the surface and wait to come out.

The mass emergence of cicadas is the key to their survival. There may be up to 1.5 million cicadas per acre! Many will be eaten by predators. However, enough will survive to lay eggs, so a new generation can emerge in 13 or 17 years.

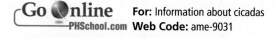

Go Online
PHSchool.com   **For:** Information about cicadas
Web Code: ame-9031

Problem 3.2 Choosing Common Multiples or Common Factors

Stephan's grandfather told him about a terrible year when the cicadas were so numerous that they wrecked the buds on all the young trees in his orchard. Stephan conjectured that both 13-year and 17-year cicadas came up that year. Assume that Stephan's conjecture is correct.

A. How many years after an appearance of 13-year and 17-year cicadas together will both types of cicadas appear together again? Explain.

B. Suppose there were 12-year, 14-year, and 16-year cicadas, and they all came up this year. How many years will elapse before they all come up together again? Explain.

C. For Questions A and B, tell whether the answer is less than, greater than, or equal to the product of the cicada cycles.

ACE Homework starts on page 42.

3.3 Bagging Snacks

You have used common multiples to analyze events that repeat in cycles. Now you will explore problems about sharing items equally. Common factors can help you solve "sharing" problems.

Problem 3.3 Choosing Common Multiples or Common Factors

Jane and her friends are going on a hiking trip. Jane wants to make snack packs of apples and trail mix to take on the trip. She has 24 apples and 36 small bags of trail mix.

A. 1. What is the greatest number of snack packs Jane can make if each pack must have exactly the same number of apples and exactly the same number of bags of trail mix? She doesn't want any apples or trail mix left over. Explain.

2. Could Jane make a different number of snack packs so that the treats are shared equally? If so, describe each possibility.

3. Which possibility seems most reasonable to you? Why?

B. Suppose that Jane's pet canary has bitten into six of the packages of trail mix and ruined them. Now what is the greatest number of snack packs Jane can make so that the apples and the remaining trail mix are shared equally?

ACE Homework starts on page 42.

3.4 Planning a Picnic

Miriam's uncle runs a small convenience store. He often donates treats for Miriam's school parties.

Problem 3.4 Choosing Common Multiples or Common Factors

Miriam's uncle donated 120 cans of juice and 90 packs of cheese crackers for the school field trip. Each student is to receive the same number of cans of juice and the same number of packs of crackers.

A. What is the greatest number of students that can go on the field trip and share the food equally with no food left over? How many cans of juice and how many packs of crackers will each student receive? Explain.

B. Suppose Miriam's uncle eats two packs of crackers before he sends the supplies to school. What is the greatest number of students that can go on the field trip and share the food equally? How many cans of juice and how many packs of crackers will each student receive?

ACE Homework starts on page 42.

Applications

For Exercises 1–8, list the common multiples from 1 to 100 for each pair of numbers. Then find the least common multiple for each pair.

1. 8 and 12

2. 3 and 15

3. 7 and 11

4. 9 and 10

5. 24 and 36

6. 20 and 25

7. 42 and 14

8. 30 and 12

9. a. Find three pairs of numbers for which the least common multiple equals the product of the two numbers.

   b. Look at the pairs of numbers you found in part (a). What is true about all three pairs of numbers?

For Exercises 10–13, find two pairs of numbers with the given number as their least common multiple.

10. 10

11. 36

12. 60

13. 105

14. a. A restaurant is open 24 hours a day. The manager wants to divide the day into work shifts of equal length. The shifts should not overlap, and all shift durations should be a whole number of hours. Describe the different ways this can be done.

   b. The restaurant's two neon signs are turned on at the same time. Both signs blink as they are turned on. One sign blinks every 9 seconds. The other sign blinks every 15 seconds. In how many seconds will they blink together again?

15. The school cafeteria serves pizza every sixth day and applesauce every eighth day. If pizza and applesauce are both on today's menu, in how many days will they be together on the menu again?

For Exercises 16–23, list the common factors for each pair of numbers. Then find the greatest common factor for each pair.

16. 18 and 30

17. 9 and 25

18. 60 and 45

19. 23 and 29

20. 49 and 14

21. 140 and 25

22. 142 and 148

23. 84 and 105

Go Online
PHSchool.com
For: Multiple-Choice Skills Practice
Web Code: ama-1354

24. Multiple Choice For which pair is the greatest common factor 8?

A. 2 and 4

B. 7 and 15

C. 32 and 64

D. 56 and 72

25. Multiple Choice For which pair is the greatest common factor 15?

F. 60 and 75

G. 30 and 60

H. 10 and 25

J. 3 and 5

26. Multiple Choice For which pair is the greatest common factor 1?

A. 5 and 10

B. 8 and 4

C. 8 and 10

D. 8 and 15

27. Mr. Mendoza and his 23 students are planning to have hot dogs at their class picnic. Mr. Mendoza can buy hot dogs in packages of 12 and hot dog buns in packages of 8.

Homework Help Online
PHSchool.com
For: Help with Exercise 27
Web Code: ame-1327

a. Mr. Mendoza plans that everyone will get the same number of hot dogs and buns and there will be no leftovers. What are the least number of hot dog packages and the least number of bun packages Mr. Mendoza can buy? How many hot dogs and buns will each person get?

b. Suppose that the class invites the principal, the secretary, the bus driver, and three parents to help supervise. How many packages of hot dogs and buns will Mr. Mendoza need to buy so that everyone will get the same number of hot dogs and buns with no leftovers? How many hot dogs and buns will each person get?

Investigation 3 Common Multiples and Common Factors   **43**

28. The cast of a play had a party at the drama teacher's house. There were 20 cookies and 40 carrot sticks served as refreshments. Each cast member had the same number of whole cookies and the same number of whole carrot sticks. Nothing was left over. The drama teacher did not eat. How many cast members might have been at the party? Explain.

29. Make up a word problem that you can solve by finding common factors. Then make up a different word problem that you can solve by finding common multiples. Solve your problems, and explain how you know that your answers are correct.

30. Multiple Choice Neena has 54 smiley-face stickers, 36 glittery stickers, and 81 heart stickers. She wants to divide the stickers evenly among her friends. Find the greatest number that Neena can use to divide the stickers evenly.

F. 3   **G.** 9   **H.** 18   **J.** 27

Connections

31. Use the terms *factor, divisor, multiple, product,* and *divisible by* to write as many statements as you can about the number sentence below.

$$7 \times 9 = 63$$

32. a. What factor is paired with 12 to give 48?

b. What factor is paired with 11 to give 110?

33. Use the fact that $135 \times 37 = 4,995$ to find the value of $1,350 \times 3,700$.

34. a. Suppose a jet travels 60 kilometers in 5 minutes. How many kilometers will it travel in 2 hours? In 6 hours?

b. How many more kilometers will the jet travel in 6 hours than in 2 hours?

c. Suppose that Nodin flew on this jet to the Dominican Republic. If his trip took 4 hours, how many kilometers did he travel?

35. Mario's watch runs fast. In 1 day, it gains an hour; so in 12 days, it gains 12 hours and is correct again. Julio's watch also runs fast. In 1 day, it gains 20 minutes. If they both set their 12-hour watches correctly at 9:00 A.M. on Monday, when will their watches both be correct again at the same time?

36. $3 \times 5 \times 7 = 105$. Use this fact to find each product.

    a. $9 \times 5 \times 7$ **b.** $3 \times 5 \times 14$

    c. $3 \times 50 \times 7$ **d.** $3 \times 25 \times 7$

Extensions

37. Ms. Santiago has many pens in her desk drawer. She says that if you divide the total number of pens by 2, 3, 4, 5, or 6, you get a remainder of 1. What is the smallest number of pens that could be in Ms. Santiago's drawer?

38. What is the mystery number pair?

    Clue 1 The greatest common factor of the mystery pair is 7.

    Clue 2 The least common multiple of the mystery pair is 70.

    Clue 3 Both of the numbers in the mystery pair have two digits.

    Clue 4 One of the numbers in the mystery pair is odd and the other is even.

39. Suppose that, in some distant part of the universe, there is a star with four orbiting planets. One planet makes a trip around the star in 6 Earth years, the second planet takes 9 Earth years, the third takes 15 Earth years, and the fourth takes 18 Earth years. Suppose that at some time the planets are lined up as pictured below. This phenomenon is called *conjunction*. How many years will it take before the planets return to this position?

40. Eric and his friends practice multiplying by using dominoes such as those above. Each half of a domino has dots on it to show a number from 0 to 6. The students use the two numbers on a domino as factors. So when Eric sees a domino like the one below, he answers 12.

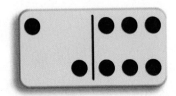

a. What is the greatest product you can make from numbers on dominoes?

b. What is the least product you can make from numbers on dominoes?

c. Eric reasons that he has to know the answers for $0 \times 0, 0 \times 1,$ $0 \times 2, 0 \times 3, 0 \times 4, 0 \times 5, 0 \times 6, 1 \times 0, 1 \times 1,$ and so on. Because there are seven different numbers, $0, 1, 2, 3, 4, 5,$ and $6,$ that can occur on each half of the domino, he reasons that he needs to know 49 different answers. This is too many. What did he forget?

41. Examine the number pattern below. You can use the tiles to help you see a pattern.

Row 1:	1	= 1
Row 2:	1 + 3	= 4
Row 3:	1 + 3 + 5	= 9
Row 4:	1 + 3 + 5 + 7	= 16

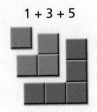

a. Complete the next four rows in the number pattern.

b. What is the sum in row 20?

c. In what row will the sum be 576? What is the last number (addend) in the sum in this row? Explain.

42. Examine the pattern below. Using tiles or making a diagram may help you see a pattern.

Row 1: 2   = 2

Row 2: 2 + 4   = 6

Row 3: 2 + 4 + 6   = 12

Row 4: 2 + 4 + 6 + 8 = 20

  a. Complete the next four rows in the pattern.

  b. What is the sum in row 20?

  c. In what row will the sum be 110? What is the last number (addend) in the sum in this row? Explain.

43. a. Suppose that cicadas have predators with 2-year cycles. How often would 12-year cicadas face their predators? Would life be better for 13-year cicadas? Explain.

  b. Suppose that 12-year and 13-year cicadas have predators with both 2-year and 3-year cycles. Suppose that both kinds of cicadas and both kinds of predators came up this year. When would the 12-year cicadas again have to face both kinds of predators at the same time? When would the 13-year cicadas face both? Which type of cicada do you think is better off?

"BELIEVE ME, THEY'RE NOT EXPECTING US. WE'RE 387-YEAR LOCUSTS."

44. While Nina was reading through her old journals, she noticed that on November 9, 1999, she had written the date 11-9-99. It looked like a multiplication problem, $11 \times 9 = 99$. Nina wondered if there were any other such dates from 1900 to 1999. Are there? Explain.

Mathematical Reflections 3

In this investigation, you used common factors and common multiples to help you solve problems. These questions will help you summarize what you have learned.

Think about your answers to these questions. Discuss your ideas with other students and your teacher. Then write a summary of your findings in your notebook.

1. Look at the four problems in this investigation. Explain how you can decide if finding common multiples or common factors is helpful in solving a problem.

2. Describe how you can find the common factors and the greatest common factor of two numbers.

3. Describe how you can find the common multiples and the least common multiple of two numbers.

Unit Project What's Next?

Don't forget to write about your special number!

Investigation 4

Factorizations: Searching for Factor Strings

Some numbers can be written as the product of several different pairs of factors. For example, 100 can be written as 1×100, 2×50, 4×25, 5×20, and 10×10. It is also possible to write 100 as the product of three factors, such as $2 \times 2 \times 25$ and $2 \times 5 \times 10$.

Getting Ready for Problem 4.1

Can you find a longer string of factors with a product of 100?

4.1 The Product Puzzle

The Product Puzzle is a number-search puzzle in which you look for strings of factors with a product of 840. Two factor strings have been marked in the puzzle at the right.

How many factor strings can you find?

The Product Puzzle

5	42	14	15	56	3
20	3	4	420	28	5
70	12	35	210	2	168
120	24	14	2	28	84
7	280	3	4	6	10
3	2	105	140	4	5
20	40	8	21	2	7

Problem 4.1 Finding Factor Strings

In the Product Puzzle, find as many factor strings for 840 as you can. When you find a string, draw a line through it. Keep a list of the strings you find.

A. What is the longest factor string you found?

B. If possible, name a factor string with a product of 840 that is longer than any string you found in the puzzle. Do not consider strings that contain 1.

C. Choose a factor string with two factors. How can you use this string to find a factor string with three factors?

D. How do you know when you have found the longest possible string of factors for a number?

E. How many distinct longest strings of factors are there for 840? Strings are *distinct* if they are different in some way other than the order in which the factors are listed.

ACE **Homework starts on page 56.**

The Product Puzzle

5	42	14	15	56	3
20	3	4	420	28	5
70	12	35	210	2	168
120	24	14	2	28	84
7	280	3	4	6	10
3	2	105	140	4	5
20	40	8	21	2	7

4.2 Finding the Longest Factor String

The strings of factors of a number are called **factorizations** of that number. In Problem 4.1, you saw that the longest possible factor string for 840 is made up of prime numbers. We call this string the **prime factorization** of 840. In fact, the longest factor string for any whole number is the prime factorization. Can you explain why?

Getting Ready for Problem 4.2

When you look for the prime factorization of a number, it helps to have a list of prime numbers handy. Look back at the table of first moves you made for the Factor Game. Make a list of all prime numbers less than 30.

One method for finding the prime factorization of a number is described below. In this example, you'll find the prime factorization of 100.

- First, find one prime factor of 100. You can start with 2. Divide 100 by 2, showing the work as an upside-down division problem.

$$2\,\overline{)\,100\,} \\ \quad\ \ 50$$

- Next, find a prime factor of 50. You can use 2 again. Add another step to the division problem.

$$2\,\overline{)\,100\,} \\ \ \ 2\,\overline{)\,50\,} \\ \qquad 25$$

- Now, find a prime factor of 25. The only possibility is 5.

$$2\,\overline{)\,100\,} \\ \ \ 2\,\overline{)\,50\,} \\ \ \ 5\,\overline{)\,25\,} \\ \qquad 5$$

You are left with a prime number, 5. From the final diagram, you can read the prime factorization of 100: $100 = 2 \times 2 \times 5 \times 5$.

You could also use a *factor tree* to find the prime factorization of a number. Here are the steps to make a factor tree for 100.

- First, find a factor pair of 100. You might use 10 and 10. Write 100 and then draw branches from 100 to each factor.

- If possible, break each factor you chose into the product of two factors. Draw branches to show how the factors are related to the numbers in the row above.

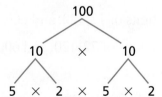

- Because all the numbers in the bottom row are prime, the tree is complete. The prime factorization of 100 is $5 \times 2 \times 5 \times 2$.

Here are two more factor trees for 100:

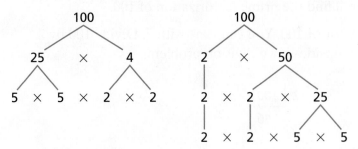

- In the tree at the right, notice that the 2 in the second row does not break down further. Draw a single branch, and repeat the 2 in the next rows.

You can see that the bottom row of each tree contains the same factors, although the order of the factors is different. You can also see that factor trees give you the same prime factorization for 100 as the previous method.

You can use a shorthand notation to write prime factorizations. For example, you can write $5 \times 5 \times 2 \times 2$ as $5^2 \times 2^2$. The small raised number is an exponent. An **exponent** tells you how many times a factor is used. For example, $2^2 \times 5^4$ means a 2 is used twice as a factor and a 5 is used four times. So, $2^2 \times 5^4$ is the same as $2 \times 2 \times 5 \times 5 \times 5 \times 5$.

You can read some exponents in more than one way.

Example	Ways to read
3^2	3 to the second power OR 3 squared
5^3	5 to the third power OR 5 cubed
2^4	2 to the fourth power

Problem 4.2 Finding the Longest Factor String

A. Why do we say *the* prime factorization of 100 instead of *a* prime factorization of 100?

B. Find the prime factorizations of 72, 120, and 600.

C. Write the prime factorizations of 72, 120, and 600 using exponents.

D. Choose a composite factor of 72.

   1. Show how this composite factor can be found in the prime factorization of 72.

   2. This composite factor is part of a factor pair for 72. How can you use the prime factorization to find the other factor in the pair?

E. Find a multiple of 72. What will the prime factorization of this multiple have in common with the prime factorization of 72?

ACE Homework starts on page 56.

Derrick wanted to find the common factors and common multiples of 24 and 60. He made Venn diagrams similar to the ones you made in Problem 2.3. He conjectured that he could use prime factorization to find common factors.

First, he found the prime factorizations of 24 and 60.

$$24 = 2 \times 2 \times 2 \times 3$$
$$60 = 2 \times 2 \times 3 \times 5$$

Both prime factorizations contain 2×2, which shows that 4 is a common factor.

$$24 = \boxed{2 \times 2} \times 2 \times 3$$
$$60 = \boxed{2 \times 2} \times 3 \times 5$$

Both prime factorizations contain 2×3, which shows that 6 is a common factor.

$$24 = 2 \times 2 \times \boxed{2 \times 3}$$
$$60 = 2 \times \boxed{2 \times 3} \times 5$$

Derrick noticed that the longest string common to both factorizations is $2 \times 2 \times 3$, so 12 must be the greatest common factor. He then checked a Venn Diagram and found that he was right.

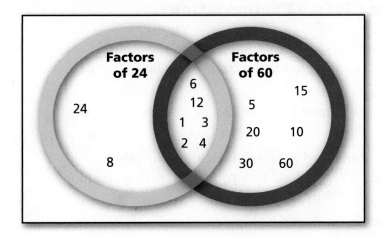

Derrick wondered if he could use a similar method to find the least common multiple. He realized that the prime factorization of any multiple of 24 will include its prime factorization, $2 \times 2 \times 2 \times 3$. The prime factorization of any multiple of 60 will contain its prime factorization, $2 \times 2 \times 3 \times 5$.

So, Derrick thought the prime factorization of any common multiple should include $2 \times 2 \times 2 \times 3 \times 5$. Is he right? Check this on the Venn diagram below:

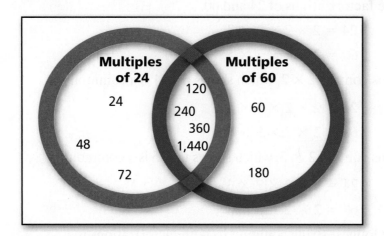

Problem 4.3 Using Prime Factorizations

A. 1. Write the prime factorizations of 72 and 120 that you found in Problem 4.2. What is the longest string common to both factorizations?

2. What is the greatest common factor of 72 and 120? How do you know?

B. 1. What is the shortest string of factors that includes the prime factorizations of both 72 and 120? Can you find a smaller common multiple of 72 and 120? Why or why not?

2. Can you find a greatest common multiple of 72 and 120? Why or why not?

C. Numbers whose greatest common factor is 1, such as 25 and 12, are **relatively prime.** How can you determine that 25 and 12 are relatively prime by looking at their prime factorizations? Find another pair of relatively prime numbers.

D. 1. Find two pairs of numbers whose least common multiple is the product of the numbers. For example, $5 \times 6 = 30$, and the least common multiple of 5 and 6 is 30.

    2. Find two pairs of numbers whose least common multiple is less than the product of the numbers. For example, $6 \times 8 = 48$, but the least common multiple of 6 and 8 is 24.

    3. How can you determine from the prime factorizations whether the least common multiple of two numbers is the product of the numbers or is less than the product of the two numbers? Explain your thinking.

E. If you multiply the greatest common factor of 12 and 16 by the least common multiple of 12 and 16, you get 192, which is equal to 12×16. Does this work for any two numbers? Why or why not?

ACE Homework starts on page 56.

Did You Know?

In all mathematics, there are a few relationships that are so basic that they are called *fundamental theorems*. There is the Fundamental Theorem of Calculus, the Fundamental Theorem of Algebra, and you have found the Fundamental Theorem of Arithmetic. The Fundamental Theorem of Arithmetic states that every whole number greater than one has exactly *one* prime factorization (except for the order in which the factors are written).

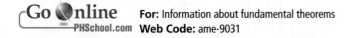

Go Online
PHSchool.com   **For:** Information about fundamental theorems
                       Web Code: ame-9031

Applications

Connections

Extensions

Applications

To solve a multiplication maze, you must find a path of numbers from the entrance to the exit so that the product of the numbers in the path equals the puzzle number. No diagonal moves are allowed. Below is the solution of a multiplication maze for 840.

Multiplication Maze 840

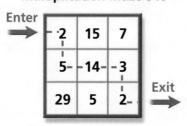

Solve each multiplication maze. Hint: It may help to find the longest factor string of the puzzle number.

1. **Multiplication Maze 840**

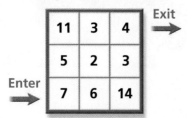

2. **Multiplication Maze 360**

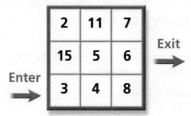

3. Make a multiplication maze for 720. Be sure to record your solution.

For Exercises 4–11, find the prime factorization of each number.

4. 36	**5.** 180	**6.** 525	**7.** 165
8. 293	**9.** 760	**10.** 216	**11.** 231

12. Use exponents to rewrite the prime factorizations you found in Exercises 4–11.

13. To indicate multiplication, you can use a raised dot symbol. For example, $3 \times 5 = 3 \cdot 5$. Find the prime factorization of 312 using raised dot symbols.

14. Multiple Choice What is the prime factorization of 240?

    A. $10 \cdot 24$ **B.** $2 \cdot 3 \cdot 5$

    C. $2^3 \cdot 3 \cdot 5$ **D.** $2^4 \cdot 3 \cdot 5$

15. Jill and Jamahl are comparing their special numbers. Jill's number has a prime factorization with six prime numbers. Jamahl's number has a prime factorization with only three numbers. Jill says this means her number is greater than Jamahl's. Jamahl says that is not necessarily true. Who is right?

16. Find all the numbers less than 100 that have at least one 2 and at least one 5 in their prime factorization. What do you notice about these numbers?

17. Multiple Choice Choose the number that is the product of exactly three different prime numbers.

    F. 15   **G.** 20   **H.** 30   **J.** 57

Homework Help Online
PHSchool.com

For: Help with Exercise 18
Web Code: ame-1418

18. Find all the numbers less than 100 that are the product of exactly three different prime numbers.

For Exercises 19–24, find the greatest common factor and the least common multiple for each pair of numbers.

19. 36 and 45   **20.** 30 and 75   **21.** 78 and 104

22. 15 and 60   **23.** 32 and 45   **24.** 37 and 12

Connections

25. Mr. Rawlings has 60 cookies. He wants to give each of his 16 grandchildren the same number of cookies for a snack. What is the greatest number of cookies he can give each child? After he gives his grandchildren their cookies, how many cookies will he have left for himself?

26. Mr. and Mrs. Fisk have 8 children. Each of those children has 8 children. How many grandchildren do Mr. and Mrs. Fisk have? If each grandchild has 8 children, how many great-grandchildren do Mr. and Mrs. Fisk have?

27. Rosa claims the longest string of prime factors for 30 is $2 \times 3 \times 5$. Tyee claims there is a longer string, $1 \times 2 \times 1 \times 3 \times 1 \times 5$. Who is correct? Why?

28. The number 1 is not prime. Why do you think mathematicians decided not to call 1 a prime number?

29. a. Find the multiples of 9 that are less than 100.

    b. Find the multiples of 21 that are less than 100.

    c. Find the common multiples of 9 and 21 that are less than 100.

    d. What is the next common multiple of 9 and 21?

For: Multiple-Choice Skills
Practice
Web Code: ama-1454

30. For each part below, use your birth year or the birth year of one of your family members as your number.

    a. Find the prime factorization of your number.

    b. Describe your number to a friend, giving your friend as much information as you can about the number. Here are some ideas to include: Is the number square, prime, even, or odd? How many factors does it have? Is it a multiple of some other number?

31. Tomas and Sharlina work on weekends and holidays doing odd jobs around the neighborhood. They are paid by the day, not the hour. They each earn the same whole number of dollars per day. Last month Tomas earned $184 and Sharlina earned $207. How many days did each person work? What is their daily pay?

32. What is my number?

    Clue 1 My number is a multiple of 2 and 7.

    Clue 2 My number is less than 100 but greater than 50.

    Clue 3 My number is the product of three different prime numbers.

33. What is my number?

    Clue 1 My number is a perfect square.

    Clue 2 The only prime number in its prime factorization is 2.

    Clue 3 My number is a factor of 32.

    Clue 4 The sum of its digits is odd.

Extensions

Connections Extensions

34. Most years contain 365 days, but certain years, called *leap years*, contain 366 days. Leap years occur in years divisible by four, with some exceptions. Years divisible by 100 are *not* leap years—unless they are divisible by 400. So 1896 was a leap year, but 1900 wasn't. Both 1996 and 2000 were leap years. A week has 7 days.

a. How many weeks are in each type of year?

b. January 1, 2004, fell on a Thursday. On what dates did the next three Thursdays of 2004 occur?

c. The year 2004 was a leap year. It had 366 days. What day of the week was January 1, 2005?

d. What is the pattern, over several years, for the days on which your birthday will fall?

35. The Fundamental Theorem of Arithmetic was first stated by the Greek mathematician Euclid. He wrote: "If a number is the least that is measured by prime numbers, it will not be measured by any prime except those originally measuring it." After studying prime factorizations in this Investigation, what do you suppose Euclid meant?

36. Mr. Barkley has a box of books. He says the number of books in the box is divisible by 2, 3, 4, 5, and 6. How many books could be in the box? Add another factor so that there is only one possible solution.

Did You Know?

If you were born on any day other than February 29, leap day, it takes at least 5 years for your birthday to come around to the same day of the week. It follows a pattern of 5 years, then 6 years, then 11 years, and then 6 years (or some variation of that pattern), to fall on the same day of the week. If you were born on February 29, it takes 28 years for your birthday to fall on the same day of the week!

Mathematical Reflections 4

In this investigation, you found factor strings for numbers, and you saw how the prime factorizations of numbers could be used to find common factors and multiples. These questions will help you summarize what you have learned.

Think about your answers to these questions. Discuss your ideas with other students and your teacher. Then write a summary of your findings in your notebook.

1. **a.** Does every number have a prime factorization?

   b. How many prime factorizations does a number have?

   c. Why is it important that 1 is not a prime number?

2. **a.** How can you use the prime factorization of two numbers to find their least common multiple? Give examples.

   b. How can you use the prime factorization of two numbers to find their greatest common factor? Give examples.

   c. How can you use the prime factorization of two numbers to determine whether they are relatively prime? Give examples.

3. If you know the greatest common factor of two numbers is 1, can you predict what the least common multiple will be?

Unit Project | What's Next?

Don't forget your special number! What is its prime factorization?

Investigation 5

Putting It All Together

You have learned many things about factors and multiples of whole numbers. Now you'll have a chance to use what you know to solve an interesting problem.

5.1 Unraveling the Locker Problem

There are 1,000 lockers in a long hall of Westfalls High. In preparation for the beginning of school, the janitor cleans the lockers and paints fresh numbers on the locker doors. The lockers are numbered from 1 to 1,000. When the 1,000 Westfalls High students return from summer vacation, they decide to celebrate the beginning of the school year by working off some energy.

The first student, Student 1, runs down the row of lockers and opens every door.

Student 2 closes the doors of Lockers 2, 4, 6, 8, and so on to the end of the line.

Student 3 *changes the state of* the doors of Lockers 3, 6, 9, 12, and so on to the end of the line. (This means the student opens the door if it is closed and closes the door if it is open.)

Student 4 changes the state of the doors of Lockers 4, 8, 12, 16, and so on.

Student 5 changes the state of every fifth door, Student 6 changes the state of every sixth door, and so on, until all 1,000 students have had a turn.

active math
online
For: Locker Problem Activity
Visit: PHSchool.com
Web Code: amd-1501

Getting Ready for Problem 5.1

Consider this question:

When all the students have finished, which locker doors are open?

Make a conjecture about the answer to this question. Then, describe a strategy you might use to try to find the answer.

Did You Know?

A famous mathematician, George Polya, wrote a book titled *How to Solve It* about problem-solving strategies. He suggests that if you can't solve a problem right away, you might first try to solve a related problem or a simplified version of the problem so that you can look for patterns and strategies to help you. He also suggests drawing pictures. Professor Polya solved some very complicated math problems that way!

Go Online
PHSchool.com
For: Information about prime numbers
Web Code: ame-9031

Problem **5.1** Using Multiples and Factors

A. Model the problem for the first 30 students and the first 30 lockers. What patterns do you see as the students put their plan into action?

B. When the 1,000 students are finished, which locker doors are open? Explain why your answer makes sense. What kind of numbers are these?

C. Give the numbers of several lockers that were touched by exactly

    1. two students. What kind of numbers are these?

    2. three students.

    3. four students.

D. How can you determine exactly how many students have touched a given locker?

E. Which was the first locker touched by

    1. both Student 6 and Student 8?

    2. both Student 12 and Student 30?

    3. both Student 7 and Student 13?

    4. both Student 100 and Student 120?

F. Given two student numbers, how can you determine which locker will be the first touched by both students? How can you determine which locker will be the last touched by both students?

G. Which students touched

    1. both Locker 24 and Locker 36?

    2. both Locker 100 and Locker 120?

    3. both Locker 42 and Locker 273?

H. Given two lockers, how can you determine which students touched both?

ACE Homework starts on page 65.

Applications

For Exercises 1–3, refer to Problem 5.1.

1. Give the numbers of several lockers that were touched by exactly five students.

2. Which was the first locker touched by both

   a. Students 3 and 5?

   b. Students 12 and 20?

   c. Students 72 and 84?

   d. Students 210 and 315?

3. Which students touched both

   a. Lockers 13 and 81?

   b. Lockers 140 and 210?

   c. Lockers 165 and 330?

   d. Lockers 196 and 294?

Connections

4. There are 50 lockers, numbered 1 through 50, in a short hall at Phillips Middle School. Mr. Giannetti hid treats for his class in one of the lockers. He gave the class the following clues about the number of the locker where the treats are located.

   Clue 1 The number is even.

   Clue 2 The number is divisible by 3.

   Clue 3 The number is a multiple of Mr. Giannetti's lucky number, 7.

   In which locker are the treats located?

5. How many factors does each of the following numbers have?

    a. 100   **b.** 101   **c.** 102   **d.** 103

6. Write a mathematical story about the number 648. For example, you might describe its factors and its multiples. You might also give some examples of its relationship to other numbers. Use at least five vocabulary words from this unit in your story.

7. What is the least prime number greater than 50?

8. Ivan said that if a number ends in 0, both 2 and 5 are factors of the number. Is he correct? Why or why not?

Homework Help **Online**
PHSchool.com
For: Help with Exercise 8
Web Code: ame-1508

9. What is my number?

    Clue 1 My number is a multiple of 5 and is less than 50.
    Clue 2 My number is a multiple of 3.
    Clue 3 My number has exactly 8 factors.

10. What is my number?

    Clue 1 My number is a multiple of 5, but it does not end in 5.

    Clue 2 The prime factorization of my number is a string of three numbers.

    Clue 3 Two of the numbers in the prime factorization are the same.

    Clue 4 My number is greater than the seventh square number.

11. Now it's your turn! Make up a set of clues for a mystery number. You might want to use your special number as the mystery number. Include as many ideas from this unit as you can. Try out your clues on a classmate.

For Exercises 12 and 13, describe the numbers that have both of the given numbers as factors.

12. 2 and 3   **13.** 3 and 5

Go **Online**
PHSchool.com
For: Multiple-Choice Skills Practice
Web Code: ama-1554

14. a. Find all the numbers between 1 and 1,000 that have 2 as their only prime factor.

    b. What is the next number after 1,000 that has 2 as its only prime factor?

15. The numbers 2 and 3 are prime, consecutive numbers. Are there other such pairs of *adjacent primes*? Why or why not?

16. Which group of numbers—evens or odds—contains more prime numbers? Why?

Extensions

17. Goldbach's Conjecture is a famous conjecture that has never been proved true or false. The conjecture states that every even number, except 2, can be written as the sum of two prime numbers. For example, 16 can be written as 5 + 11, which are both prime numbers.

  a. Write the first six even numbers greater than 2 as the sum of two prime numbers.

  b. Write 100 as the sum of two primes.

  c. The number 2 is a prime number. Can an even number greater than 4 be written as the sum of two prime numbers if you use 2 as one of the primes? Why or why not?

18. Multiple Choice Choose the number that is divisible by four different prime numbers.

  A. 77   **B.** 105   **C.** 225   **D.** 1,155

19. Find the least number that is divisible by four different prime numbers.

20. Prime numbers that differ by 2, such as 3 and 5, are called *twin primes*. Starting with the twin primes 5 and 7, look carefully at the numbers between twin primes. What do they have in common? Why?

21. Try to discover a method for finding all the factors of a number using its prime factorization. Use your method to find all the factors of 36. Then use your method to find all the factors of 480.

22. Suppose a number has 2 and 6 as factors. What other numbers must be factors of the number? Explain.

23. Suppose a number is a multiple of 12. Of what other numbers is it a multiple? Explain.

24. Suppose 10 and 6 are common factors of two numbers. What other factors must the numbers have in common? Explain.

25. The chart below shows the factor counts for the numbers from 975 to 1,000. Each star stands for one factor. For example, the four stars after 989 indicate that 989 has four factors.

975	★★★★★★★★★★★★
976	★★★★★★★★★★
977	★★
978	★★★★★★★★
979	★★★★
980	★★★★★★★★★★★★★★★★★★
981	★★★★★★
982	★★★★
983	★★
984	★★★★★★★★★★★★★★★★
985	★★★★
986	★★★★★★★★
987	★★★★★★★★
988	★★★★★★★★★★★★
989	★★★★
990	★★★★★★★★★★★★★★★★★★★★★★★★
991	★★
992	★★★★★★★★★★★★
993	★★★★
994	★★★★★★★★
995	★★★★
996	★★★★★★★★★★★★
997	★★
998	★★★★
999	★★★★★★★★
1,000	★★★★★★★★★★★★★★★★

Boris thinks that numbers that have many factors, such as 975 and 996, must be abundant numbers. (Recall that an *abundant number* is a number whose proper factors have a sum greater than the number.) Is Boris correct? Explain.

Mathematical Reflections 5

Working on the locker problem gave you an opportunity to use what you know about whole numbers, factors, and multiples. These questions will help you summarize what you have learned.

Think about your answers to these questions. Discuss your ideas with other students and your teacher. Then write a summary of your findings in your notebook.

1. What can you say about a number if all you know is that it has an odd number of factors? Justify your answer.

2. Describe how the following ideas were used in solving parts of the Locker Problem:

   a. prime numbers

   b. divisors

   c. multiples

   d. square numbers

   e. least common multiple

   f. greatest common factor

Unit Project | What's Next?

Don't forget your special number. What new things can you say about your number?

Unit Project

My Special Number

At the beginning of this unit, you chose a special number and wrote several things about it in your journal. As you worked through the investigations, you used the concepts you learned to write new things about your number.

Now it is time for you to show off your special number. Write a story, compose a poem, make a poster, or find some other way to highlight your number.

Your teacher will use your project to determine how well you understand the concepts in this unit, so be sure to include all the things you have learned while working through the investigations. You may want to start by looking back through your journal to find the things you wrote after each investigation. In your project, be sure you use all the vocabulary your teacher has asked you to record in your journals for *Prime Time*.

Looking Back and Looking Ahead

Go Online
PHSchool.com

For: Vocabulary Review
Puzzle
Web Code: amj-1051

While working on the problems in this unit, you investigated some important properties of whole numbers. Finding factors and multiples of numbers and identifying prime numbers helps in answering questions about clocks and calendars, puzzles and games, and rectangular patterns of tiles. Factoring also focuses attention on the properties of even and odd numbers, square numbers, greatest common factors, and least common multiples.

Use Your Understanding: Number Patterns

Test your understanding of multiples, factors, and prime numbers, by solving the following problems.

1. The Red Top Taxi company wants to keep its cars in good operating condition. It has a schedule for regular maintenance checks on each car. Oil is to be changed once every 6 weeks. Brakes are to be inspected and repaired every 10 weeks.

   a. After a new cab is put in service, is there ever a week when that cab is scheduled for both an oil change and a brake inspection? If so, what is the first such time?

   b. Suppose the oil change time is extended to 8 weeks and the brake inspection to 12 weeks. Is there ever a week when the cab is due for both an oil change and brake inspection? If so, when will such a coincidence first occur?

2. The Mystate University marching band consists of 60 members. The band director wants to arrange the band into a rectangular array for the halftime activities.

   a. In how many ways can she arrange the band? Make a sketch of each arrangement.

   b. How many rectangular arrangements are possible if the band adds one member and becomes a 61-member band?

3. The prime factorization of Tamika's special number is $2 \times 2 \times 3 \times 11$ and the prime factorization of Cyrah's special number is $3 \times 3 \times 5 \times 5$.

   a. What is the least common multiple of the two special numbers?

   b. What is the greatest common factor of the two special numbers?

   c. List all the factors of Tamika's number.

   d. Is Tamika's number even or odd? Is Cyrah's number even or odd?

   e. Is Tamika's number a square number? Is Cyrah's number a square number?

4. Shani gave three clues for her secret number.

   Clue 1 *My number is a factor of 90.*

   Can you determine what Shani's secret number is?

   a. What is the smallest Shani's number can be? What is the largest Shani's number can be?

   b. Brandon says the secret number must also be a factor of 180. Is he correct?

   Clue 2 *My number is prime.*

   c. Now can you determine what the secret number is?

   Clue 3 *Twenty-one is a multiple of my secret number.*

   d. Now can you determine what the secret number is?

Explain Your Reasoning

To answer Questions 1–4 you had to use knowledge of factors and multiples of a number.

5. What strategies can be used to find

   a. all the factors of a number?

   b. the least common multiple of two numbers?

   c. the greatest common factor of two numbers?

6. How you can you decide whether a number is a(n)

   a. prime number?

   b. square number?

   c. even number?

   d. odd number?

7. Decide whether each statement is *true* or *false*. Explain your reasoning. (A statement is true if it is correct for *every* pair of numbers. If you can find a pair of numbers that makes the statement incorrect, then the statement is false.)

   a. If a number is greater than a second number, then the first number has more factors than the second number.

   b. The sum of two odd numbers is even.

   c. The product of an even number and an odd number is odd.

   d. The least common multiple of two different prime numbers is the product of those numbers.

   e. The greatest common factor of two numbers is less than either of those numbers.

Look Ahead

You will use ideas about factors, multiples, and primes in many future units of *Connected Mathematics*, especially those that deal with properties of other numbers like fractions and decimals.

English / Spanish Glossary

A

abundant number A number for which the sum of all its proper factors is greater than the number itself. For example, 24 is an abundant number because its proper factors, 1, 2, 3, 4, 6, 8, and 12, add to 36.

número abundante Un número con factores propios que sumados resultan en un número mayor que el número mismo. Por ejemplo, 24 es un número abundante porque la suma de sus factores propios, 1, 2, 3, 4, 6, 8 y 12, es 36.

C

common factor A factor that two or more numbers share. For example, 7 is a common factor of 14 and 35 because 7 is a factor of 14 $(14 = 7 \times 2)$ and 7 is a factor of 35 $(35 = 7 \times 5)$.

factor común Un factor que es compartido por dos o más números. Por ejemplo, 7 es factor común de 14 y 35 porque 7 es factor de 14 $(14 = 7 \times 2)$ y 7 es factor de 35 $(35 = 7 \times 5)$.

common multiple A multiple that two or more numbers share. For example, the first few multiples of 5 are 5, 10, 15, 20, 25, 30, 35, 40, 45, 50, 55, 60, 65, and 70. The first few multiples of 7 are 7, 14, 21, 28, 35, 42, 49, 56, 63, 70, 77, 84, 91, and 98. From these lists, we can see that two common multiples of 5 and 7 are 35 and 70.

múltiplo común Un múltiplo compartido por dos o más números. Por ejemplo, los primeros múltiplos de 5 son 5, 10, 15, 20, 25, 30, 35, 40, 45, 50, 55, 60, 65 y 70. Los primeros múltiplos de 7 son 7, 14, 21, 28, 35, 42, 49, 56, 63, 70, 77, 84, 91 y 98. Estas listas nos indican que dos múltiplos comunes de 5 y 7 son el 35 y el 70.

composite number A whole number with factors other than itself and 1 (that is, a whole number that is not prime). Some composite numbers are 6, 12, 20, and 1,001.

número compuesto Un número entero con otros factores además del número mismo y el 1 (es decir, un número entero que no es primo). Algunos números compuestos son 6, 12, 20 y 1,001.

conjecture A guess about a pattern or relationship based on observations.

conjetura Suposición acerca de un patrón o relación, basada en observaciones.

deficient number A number for which the sum of all its proper factors is less than the number itself. For example, 14 is a deficient number because its proper factors, 1, 2, and 7, add to 10. All prime numbers are deficient.

número deficiente Un número con factores propios que sumados resultan en un número menor que el número mismo. Por ejemplo, 14 es un número deficiente porque la suma de sus factores 1, 2 y 7 equivale a 10. Todos los números primos son deficientes.

dimensions The dimensions of a rectangle are the lengths of its sides. For example, the rectangle below has side lengths of 5 and 3. We can refer to this rectangle as a 5 × 3 rectangle.

dimensiones Las dimensiones de un rectángulo son las longitudes de sus lados. Por ejemplo, el rectángulo de abajo tiene longitudes de lados de 3 y 5. Podemos referirnos a este rectángulo como un rectángulo de 5 × 3.

divisor A number that divides a given number leaving a zero remainder. For example, 5 is a divisor of 20 since 20 ÷ 5 = 4 has a remainder of 0. A divisor of a given number is also known as a factor of that number. Another way to determine if 5 is a divisor of 20 is to ask whether there is a whole number that, when multiplied by 5, gives 20. The number is 4. 5 × 4 = 20.

divisor Número que divide a otro número sin dejar ningún resto. Por ejemplo, 5 es un divisor de 20 porque 20 ÷ 5 = 4 tiene resto cero. El divisor de un número determinado también se conoce como un factor de ese número. Otra manera de determinar si 5 es divisor de 20 es preguntando si hay un número entero que, al ser multiplicado por 5, dé 20. El número es 4. 5 × 4 = 20.

even number A multiple of 2. When you divide an even number by 2, the remainder is 0. Examples of even numbers are 0, 2, 4, 6, 8, and 10.

número par Un múltiplo de 2. Cuando divides un número par por 2, el resto es 0. Los siguientes son ejemplos de números pares: 0, 2, 4, 6, 8 y 10.

exponent The small raised number that tells how many times a factor is used. For example, 5^3 means 5 × 5 × 5. 3 is the exponent.

exponente El pequeño número elevado que dice cuántas veces se usa un factor. Por ejemplo, 5^3 significa 5 × 5 × 5. 3 es el exponente.

factor One of two or more whole numbers that are multiplied to get a product. For example, 13 and 4 are both factors of 52 because $13 \times 4 = 52$.

factor Uno de dos o más números enteros que se multiplican para obtener un producto. Por ejemplo, tanto 13 como 4 son factores de 52 porque $13 \times 4 = 52$.

factor pair Two whole numbers that are multiplied to get a product. For example, in the pair 13, 4 is a factor pair of 52 because $13 \times 4 = 52$.

par de factores Dos números enteros que se multiplican para obtener un producto. Por ejemplo, el par 13, 4 es un par factor de 52 porque $13 \times 4 = 52$.

factorization A product of numbers, perhaps with some repetitions, resulting in the desired number. A number can have many factorizations. For example, two factorizations of 60 are 3×20 and $2 \times 2 \times 15$.

factorización Producto de números, con posibles repeticiones, que resultan en el número deseado. Un número puede tener muchas factorizaciones. Por ejemplo, dos factorizaciones de 60 son 3×20 y $2 \times 2 \times 15$.

Fundamental Theorem of Arithmetic The theorem stating that, except for the order of the factors, every whole number greater than 1 can be factored into prime factors in only one way.

Teorema fundamental de la aritmética Teorema que enuncia que, salvo por el orden de los factores, todos los números enteros mayores de 1 pueden descomponerse en factores primos de una sola manera.

greatest common factor The greatest factor that two or more numbers share. For example, 1, 2, 3, and 6 are common factors of 12 and 30, but 6 is the greatest common factor.

máximo común factor El factor mayor que comparten dos o más números. Por ejemplo, 1, 2, 3 y 6 son factores comunes de 12 y 30, pero 6 es el máximo común factor.

least common multiple The least multiple that two or more numbers share. Common multiples of 6 and 8 include 24, 48, and 72, but 24 is the least common multiple.

mínimo común múltiplo El múltiplo menor que comparten dos o más números. Los múltiplos comunes de 6 y 8 incluyen 24, 48 y 72, pero 24 es el mínimo común múltiplo.

multiple The product of a given whole number and another whole number. For example, some multiples of 3 are 3, 6, 9, and 12. Note that if a number is a multiple of 3, then 3 is a factor of the number. For example, 12 is a multiple of 3, and 3 is a factor of 12.

múltiplo El producto de un número entero dado y otro número entero. Por ejemplo, algunos múltiplos de 3 son 3, 6, 9 y 12. Observa que si un número es múltiplo de 3, entonces 3 es factor de ese número. Por ejemplo, 12 es múltiplo de 3, y 3 es factor de 12.

near-perfect number A number for which the sum of all its proper factors is one less than the number. All powers of 2 are near-perfect numbers. For example, 32 is a near-perfect number because its proper factors, 1, 2, 4, 8, and 16, add to 31.

número casi perfecto Un número con factores propios que sumados resultan en 1 menos que ese número. Todas las potencias de 2 son números casi perfectos. Por ejemplo, 32 es un número casi perfecto porque sus factores propios 1, 2, 4, 8 y 16 suman 31.

odd number A whole number that is not a multiple of 2. When an odd number is divided by 2, the remainder is 1. Examples of odd numbers are 1, 3, 5, 7, and 9.

número impar Un número entero que no es múltiplo de 2. Cuando un número impar se divide por 2, el resto es 1. Los siguientes son ejemplos de números impares: 1, 3, 5, 7 y 9.

perfect number A number for which the sum of all its proper factors is the number itself. For example, 6 is a perfect number because its proper factors, 1, 2, and 3, add to 6.

número perfecto Un número con factores propios que, cuando se suman, el resultado es ese número exacto. Por ejemplo, 6 es un número perfecto porque la suma de sus factores propios, 1, 2 y 3, es 6.

prime factorization A product of prime numbers, perhaps with some repetitions, resulting in the desired number. For example, the prime factorization of 7,007 is $7 \times 7 \times 11 \times 13$. The prime factorization of a number is unique except for the order of the factors.

descomposición en factores primos Un producto de números primos, con posibles repeticiones, que resulta en el número deseado. Por ejemplo, la descomposición en factores primos de 7,007 es $7 \times 7 \times 11 \times 13$. La descomposición en factores primos de un número es única salvo por el orden de los factores.

English/Spanish Glossary

prime number A number with exactly two factors, 1 and the number itself. Examples of primes are 11, 17, 53, and 101. The number 1 is not a prime number because it has only one factor.

número primo Un número que tiene exactamente dos factores: 1 y él mismo. Los siguientes son ejemplos de números primos: 11, 17, 53 y 101. El número 1 no es un número primo porque tiene sólo un factor.

proper factors All the factors of a number, except the number itself. For example, the proper factors of 16 are 1, 2, 4, and 8.

factores propios Todos los factores de un número salvo el número mismo. Por ejemplo, los factores propios de 16 son 1, 2, 4 y 8.

relatively prime numbers A pair of numbers with no common factors except for 1. For example, 20 and 33 are relatively prime because the factors of 20 are 1, 2, 4, 5, 10, and 20, while the factors of 33 are 1, 3, 11, and 33. Notice that neither 20 nor 33 is itself a prime number.

números relativamente primos Par de números que no tienen factores comunes salvo 1. Por ejemplo, 20 y 33 son números relativamente primos porque los factores de 20 son 1, 2, 4, 5, 10 y 20 mientras que los factores de 33 son 1, 3, 11 y 33. Observa que ni el 20 ni el 33 son en sí mismos números primos.

square number A number that is a result of the product of a number multiplied by itself. For example, 9 and 64 are square numbers because $9 = 3 \times 3$ and $64 = 8 \times 8$. A square number represents a number of square tiles that can be arranged to form a square.

número al cuadrado Número que es el resultado del producto de un número multiplicado por sí mismo. Por ejemplo, 9 y 64 son números al cuadrado porque $9 = 3 \times 3$ y $64 = 8 \times 8$. Un número al cuadrado representa un número de mosaicos cuadrados que se pueden colocar para formar un cuadrado.

Venn diagram A diagram in which overlapping circles are used to show relationships among sets of objects that have certain attributes. Two examples are shown below.

diagrama de Venn Un diagrama en el que se usan círculos superpuestos para representar relaciones entre conjuntos de objetos que tienen ciertos atributos. A continuación se muestran dos ejemplos. En uno se muestran factores de 24 y factores de 60, y en el otro se muestran múltiplos de 24 y múltiplos de 60.

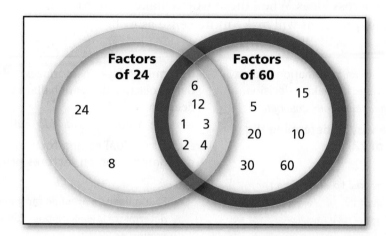

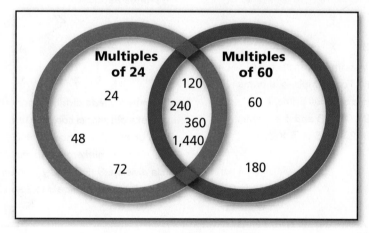

Academic Vocabulary

The following terms are important to your understanding of the mathematics in this unit. Knowing and using these words will help you in thinking, reasoning, representing, communicating your ideas, and making connections across ideas. When these words make sense to you, the investigations and problems will make more sense as well.

D

determine To use the given information and any related facts to find a value or make a decision.
related terms: decide, find, calculate, conclude

Sample: What is one way to determine the prime factorization of 27?

I could use a factor tree to determine the prime factorization of 27.

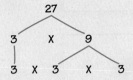

I can also divide 27 by prime numbers until I have a prime quotient. For example, 3 is prime and 27 ÷ 3 = 9. Since 9 is not prime, I continue to divide. 9 ÷ 3 = 3 and 3 is prime. The prime factors for 27 are 3 × 3 × 3.

determinar Usar la información dada y cualesquiera datos relacionados para hallar un valor o tomar una decisión.
términos relacionados: decidir, hallar, calcular, concluir

Ejemplo: ¿Cuál es una forma de determinar la descomposición en factores primos de 27?

Podría usar un árbol de factores para determinar la descomposición en factores primos de 27.

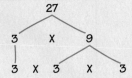

También puedo dividir 27 por números primos hasta obtener el cociente primo. Por ejemplo, 3 es un número primo y 27 ÷ 3 = 9. Puesto que 9 no es un número primo, puedo continuar con la división. 9 ÷ 3 = 3 y 3 es un número primo. Los factores primos de 27 son 3 × 3 × 3.

E

explain To give facts and details that make an idea easier to understand. Explaining can involve a written summary supported by a diagram, chart, table, or a combination of these.
related terms: analyze, clarify, describe, justify, tell

Sample: Amara is thinking of a number that is the least common multiple of 5 and 6. What is the number? Explain your reasoning.

Multiples of 5: 5, 10, 15, 20, 25, 30, 35...
Multiples of 6: 6, 12, 18, 24, 30, 36, 42...
The first common multiple is 30. So, Amara's number is 30.

explicar Dar hechos y detalles que hacen que una idea sea más fácil de comprender. Explicar puede implicar un resumen escrito apoyado por hechos, un diagrama, una gráfica, una tabla o una combinación de éstos.
términos relacionados: analizar, aclarar, describir, justificar, decir

Ejemplo: Amara está pensando en un número que es el mínimo común múltiplo de 5 y 6. ¿Cuál es el número? Explica tu razonamiento.

Múltiplos de 5: 5, 10, 15, 20, 25, 30, 35...
Múltiplos de 6: 6, 12, 18, 24, 30, 36, 42...
El primer común múltiplo es 30. Así que el número de Amara es 30.

justify To support your answers with reasons or examples

related terms: validate, explain, defend

Sample: Jeffrey claims that 12 and 14 are relatively prime numbers. Is Jeffrey correct? Justify your answer.

Jeffrey is not correct. The Venn diagram shows that 12 and 14 have both 1 and 2 as common factors. Since 12 and 14 share two factors they cannot be relatively prime.

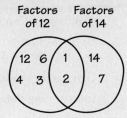

justificar Apoyar tus respuestas con razones o ejemplos.

términos relacionados: validar, explicar, defender

Ejemplo: Jeffrey afirma que 12 y 14 son números primos entre sí. ¿Es correcta la afirmación de Jeffrey? Justifica tu respuesta.

La afirmación de Jeffrey no es correcta. El diagrama de Venn muestra que 12 y 14 tienen 1 y 2 como factores comunes. Puesto que 12 y 14 comparten dos factores no pueden ser números primos entre sí.

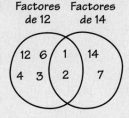

represent To stand for or take the place of something else. Symbols, equations, charts, and tables are often used to represent particular situations.

related terms: symbolize, stand for

Sample: Which of the following sets of numbers represents the factors of 16? Explain.

A. {1, 2, 3, 4, 9, 16}   C. {1, 2, 4, 8, 16}

B. {2, 4, 8}   D. {16, 32, 48, 64}

Set C represents the factors of 16. Set A does not represent the factors of 16 since 3 and 9 are not factors of 16. Set B does not include 1 and 16, which are factors of 16. Set D contains multiples of 16 instead of factors of 16.

representar Significar o tomar el lugar de algo más. Con frecuencia se usan símbolos, ecuaciones, gráficas y tablas para representar situaciones particulares.

términos relacionados: simbolizar, significar

Ejemplo: ¿Cuál de los siguientes conjuntos de números representa los factores de 16? Explica tu respuesta.

A. {1, 2, 3, 4, 9, 16}   C. {1, 2, 4, 8, 16}

B. {2, 4, 8}   D. {16, 32, 48, 64}

El conjunto C representa los factores de 16. El conjunto A no representa los factores de 16 puesto que 3 y 9 no son factores de 16. El conjunto B no incluye 1 y 16, los cuales son factores de 16. El conjunto D contiene múltiplos de 16 en lugar de factores de 16.

Academic Vocabulary

Index

Looking for a pattern, 9–10, 13, 25, 37–40, 64, 71
ACE, 18–19, 33, 35, 42–47, 57, 59, 67

Making an organized list, 9–10, 13, 36
ACE, 16, 19, 33–34

Manipulatives
game pieces, 7–13
tiles, 23–24, 26, 30, 32, 36, 46–47

Mathematical Highlights, 4

Mathematical Reflections, 21, 36, 48, 60, 69

Model
area model (*see also* tile), 23–26, 46, 75, 78
grid paper, *see* tile
picture, 8, 20, 30, 63, 72
rectangle (*see also* tile), 4, 23–25, 32, 34, 75
tile, 23–26, 30, 32, 36, 46–47, 78

Multiple, 11, 13, 77
ACE, 14–20, 30–35, 42–47, 56–59, 65–68
common, 4, 28–29, 31–32, 34, 37–40, 42–76
least common, 28–29, 31, 37, 40, 42–76

Multiplication maze, 56

Near-perfect number, 20, 77

Notebook, 5, 21, 36, 48, 60, 69–70

Number
abundant, 20, 68, 74
classifying, 26–29
composite, 4, 10, 15–16, 21, 33, 74
consecutive, 34–35, 67
deficient, 20, 75
even, 4, 24–26, 30–31, 34–35, 36, 67, 72–73, 75
near-perfect, 20, 77
odd, 4, 24–26, 30–31, 34, 36, 67, 72–73, 77
perfect, 20, 77
prime, *see* Prime number
rectangular, 23–25, 32, 34

relatively prime, 54, 60, 78
square, 4, 20, 24, 34, 69, 72–73, 78
whole, 4, 22–36

Odd number, 4, 24–26, 36, 72–73, 77
ACE, 30–31, 34, 67

Order of Operations, 26
ACE, 31

Patterns, factor, 22–24

Perfect number, 20, 77

Pictorial model, *see* Model

Prime factorization, 4, 50–55, 60, 72, 77
ACE, 56–59, 66–67

Prime number, 4, 10–11, 21, 26–73, 77–78
ACE, 15–16, 19, 32–33, 57–59, 66–67
adjacent primes, 67
factor tree, 51–52
large, 10–11
relatively prime, 54, 60, 78
twin primes, 67

Problem-solving strategies
acting it out, 7–13, 23–24, 26, 30, 32, 36, 46–47
drawing a picture, 20, 30, 63, 72
drawing a Venn diagram, 26–29, 31–32
looking for a pattern, 9–10, 13, 18–19, 25, 33, 35, 37–40, 42–47, 57, 59, 64, 67, 71
making a factor tree, 51–52
making an organized list, 9–10, 13, 16, 19, 33–34, 36
making a table, 7, 9–10, 35, 56
solving a simpler problem, 63
using tiles, 23–24, 26, 30, 32, 36, 46–47

Product Game, 11–13, 21, 22
ACE, 15–16, 19–20
designing, 12–13
playing, 11–13
rules, 12–13

Product Puzzle, 49–50

Proper factor, 7–8, 74–75, 78
ACE, 15, 34

Reasonableness, *see* **Check for reasonableness**

Rectangle model (*see also* **Model, tile**), 4, 23–25, 32, 34, 75

Rectangular numbers, 23–25, 32, 34

Relatively prime numbers, 54, 60, 78

Solve 40, 44

Solving a simpler problem, 63

Square number, 4, 20, 24, 34, 69, 72–73, 78

Table, 7–9, 12–13, 49–50
ACE, 15–16, 19–20, 35, 56
making a table, 7, 9–10, 35, 56

Tile model, 23–26, 36, 78
ACE, 30, 32, 46–47
using, 23–24, 26, 30, 32, 36, 46–47

Time
day, 17, 44, 59
hour, 17, 42, 44
leap year, 59
year, 39, 40, 45, 47, 59

Tree diagram, *see* **Factor tree**

Twin primes, 67

Unit project
My Special Number, 5, 21, 57, 60, 69, 70

Venn diagram, 26–29, 36, 53–54, 79
ACE, 31–32, 34
drawing, 26–29, 31–32

Whole number, 4, 22–36

Whole-number divisor, 6

Whole-number factor, 6

Index

Acknowledgments

Team Credits

The people who made up the **Connected Mathematics2** team—representing editorial, editorial services, design services, and production services—are listed below. Bold type denotes core team members.

Leora Adler, Judith Buice, Kerry Cashman, Patrick Culleton, Sheila DeFazio, Richard Heater, **Barbara Hollingdale, Jayne Holman,** Karen Holtzman, **Etta Jacobs,** Christine Lee, Carolyn Lock, Catherine Maglio, **Dotti Marshall,** Rich McMahon, Eve Melnechuk, Kristin Mingrone, Terri Mitchell, **Marsha Novak,** Irene Rubin, Donna Russo, Robin Samper, Siri Schwartzman, **Nancy Smith,** Emily Soltanoff, **Mark Tricca,** Paula Vergith, Roberta Warshaw, Helen Young

Additional Credits

Diana Bonfilio, Mairead Reddin, Michael Torocsik, nSight, Inc.

Technical Illustration

WestWords, Inc.

Cover Design

tom white.images

Photos

2, Frank Cezus/Getty Images, Inc.; **3 t,** Adrian Peacock/ImageState; **3 b,** Peter Hvizdak/ The Image Works; **5,** Richard Haynes; **6 t,** Michael Newman/PhotoEdit; **6 bl,** BananaStock/SuperStock; **6 bm,** Michael Newman/PhotoEdit; **6 br,** Ryan McVay/Getty Images, Inc.; **10,** Declan McCullagh Photography; **13,** Richard Haynes; **17,** Frank Cezus/Getty Images, Inc.; **22,** Rex Butcher/Getty Images, Inc.; **25,** Richard Haynes; **32,** Bettmann/Corbis; **37,** Lester Lefkowitz/Corbis; **38,** Ron Chapple/Thinkstock/Alamy Images; **41,** Ariel Skelley/Corbis; **42,** joSon/SuperStock; **47,** ©1991 by Sydney Harris, From "You Want Proof, I'll Give You Proof!", WH. Freeman, New York; **57,** Peter Usbeck/Alamy Images; **58,** David Young-Wolff/PhotoEdit; **65,** Digital Vision/Getty Images, Inc.; **66,** Richard Haynes

Data Sources

Information on Prime Numbers on pages 10-11 from THE NEW YORK TIMES, August 8, 2002. Copyright © 2002 The New York Times Company.

Connected Mathematics 2

Bits and Pieces I

Understanding Fractions, Decimals, and Percents

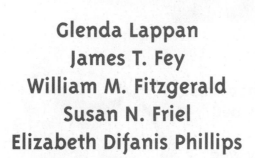

Glenda Lappan

James T. Fey

William M. Fitzgerald

Susan N. Friel

Elizabeth Difanis Phillips

PEARSON

Boston, Massachusetts · Glenview, Illinois · Shoreview, Minnesota · Upper Saddle River, New Jersey

Bits and Pieces I

Understanding Fractions, Decimals, and Percents

Bryce and Rachel are collecting food for the local food bank. Bryce's goal is to collect 32 items. Rachel's goal is to collect 24 items. Suppose Rachel and Bryce each meet their goal. What fraction of Bryce's goal does Rachel collect?

Sarah and her uncle, Takota, go fishing in the Grand River. Each person catches one fish. Sarah's fish is $\frac{5}{8}$ of a foot long. Takota's fish is $\frac{2}{3}$ of a foot long. Which fish is longer?

A survey asked cat owners, "Does your cat have bad breath?" Out of the 200 cat owners surveyed, 80 answered yes to this question. What percent of the cat owners answered yes?

You often encounter situations in which a whole number cannot communicate information precisely. Sometimes you need to talk about parts of wholes: "What fraction of the students going on this trip are eighth-graders?" "Water occupies more than 71% of the Earth's surface." You also need a way to discuss how to share, divide, or measure things: "What part of the pizza will we each get?" or "How tall are you?" Fractions, decimals, and percents are all ways of expressing quantities or measures that are not whole numbers.

People have been working on ways to talk about fractions and to do operations with them for almost 4,000 years. A document written in Egypt around 1850 B.C. (now called the Moscow Papyrus) may contain the first record of people working with fractions. The word *fraction* comes from the Latin word *fractio,* which means "a breaking."

In *Bits and Pieces I,* you will develop skill with fractions, decimals, and percents. Your new skill can help you make sense of situations like the ones on the facing page.

Mathematical Highlights

Understanding Fractions, Decimals, and Percents

In *Bits and Pieces I*, you will explore relationships among fractions, decimals, and percents. You will learn that fractions and decimals are also part of a larger set of numbers called *rational numbers*.

You will learn how to

- Model situations involving fractions, decimals, and percents

- Understand and use equivalent fractions to reason about situations

- Compare and order fractions and decimals

- Move flexibly among fraction, decimal, and percent representations

- Use benchmarks, such as $0, \frac{1}{2}, 1, 1\frac{1}{2}$, and 2, to help estimate the size of a number or sum

- Develop and use benchmarks that relate different forms of rational numbers (for example, 50% is the same as $\frac{1}{2}$ or 0.5)

- Use context, physical models, drawings, patterns, or estimation to help reason about situations involving rational numbers

As you work on problems in this unit, ask yourself questions about situations that involve rational numbers and relationships:

What models or diagrams might be helpful in understanding the situation and the relationships among quantities?

Do I want to express the quantities in the situation as fractions, decimals, or percents?

What strategies can I use to find equivalent forms of fractions, decimals, or percents?

What strategies can I use to compare or order a set of fractions, decimals, and percents?

Investigation 1

Fundraising Fractions

Students at Thurgood Marshall Middle School are organizing three fundraising projects to raise money. The eighth-grade class will sell calendars, the seventh-grade class will sell popcorn, and the sixth-grade class will sell art, music, and sports posters. The three grades are competing to see which will reach its fundraising goal first.

1.1 Reporting Progress

The school's principal has a chart that looks like a thermometer in front of her office. The chart shows progress on the fundraising. She analyzes the progress shown on the thermometer using fractions and whole numbers. Then she announces the progress of the classes over the loudspeaker.

Problem 1.1 Whole Numbers and Fractions

A. Based on the thermometer at the right for Day 2, which of the following statements could the principal use to describe the sixth-graders' progress?

- The sixth-graders have raised $100.

- The sixth-graders have reached $\frac{1}{4}$ of their goal.

- The sixth-graders have reached $\frac{2}{8}$ of their goal.

- The sixth-graders only have $225 left to meet their goal.

- The sixth-graders have completed 50% of their goal.

- At this pace, the sixth-graders should reach their goal in six more days.

B. Make up two more statements the principal could use in the announcement.

C. 1. What are two claims the sixth-graders can make if they collect $15 on the third day?

　　2. Draw and shade the thermometer for Day 3.

ACE Homework starts on page 12.

Fractions like the ones the principal uses can be written using two whole numbers separated by a bar. For example, one half is written $\frac{1}{2}$ and two eighths is written $\frac{2}{8}$. The number above the bar is the **numerator,** and the number below the bar is the **denominator.**

As you work on the problems in this unit, think about what the numerators and denominators of your fractions are telling you about each situation.

Goal
$300

Day 2

1.2 Folding Fraction Strips

One way to think about fractions is to make fraction strips by folding strips of paper into fractional parts of equal size. In this problem you will fold fraction strips that can help you with other problems in the unit. As you are folding your strips, think about the strategies you use to make the different fraction strips.

Problem 1.2 Folding Fraction Strips

A. 1. Use strips of paper that are $8\frac{1}{2}$ inches long. Fold the strips to show halves, thirds, fourths, fifths, sixths, eighths, ninths, tenths, and twelfths. Mark the folds so you can see them better.

2. What strategies did you use to fold your strips?

B. 1. How could you use the halves strip to fold eighths?

2. How could you use the halves strip to fold twelfths?

C. What fraction strips can you make if you start with a thirds strip?

D. Which of the fraction strips you folded have at least one mark that lines up with the marks on the twelfths strip?

E. 1. Sketch a picture of a fifths strip and mark $\frac{1}{5}, \frac{2}{5}, \frac{3}{5}, \frac{4}{5}$, and $\frac{5}{5}$ on the strip.

2. Show $\frac{1}{10}, \frac{2}{10}, \frac{3}{10}, \frac{4}{10}, \frac{5}{10}, \frac{6}{10}, \frac{7}{10}, \frac{8}{10}, \frac{9}{10}$, and $\frac{10}{10}$ on the fifths strip that you sketched.

F. What do the numerator and denominator of a fraction tell you?

ACE Homework starts on page 12.

The thermometers on the next page show the progress of the sixth-grade poster sales after 2, 4, 6, 8, and 10 days. The principal needs to know what fraction of the goal the sixth-grade class has achieved after each day.

Problem 1.3 Finding Fractional Parts

A. Use the thermometers on the facing page. What fraction of their goal did the sixth-graders reach after each day?

B. What do the numerator and denominator of each fraction tell you about each thermometer?

C. What strategies did you use to estimate the fraction of the goal achieved for each day?

D. How much money had the sixth-graders raised at the end of each day?

E. At the end of Day 9, the sixth-graders had raised $240.

    1. What fraction of their goal had they reached?

    2. Show how you would shade a thermometer for Day 9 on a blank thermometer.

ACE **Homework starts on page 12.**

Sixth-Grade Fundraiser

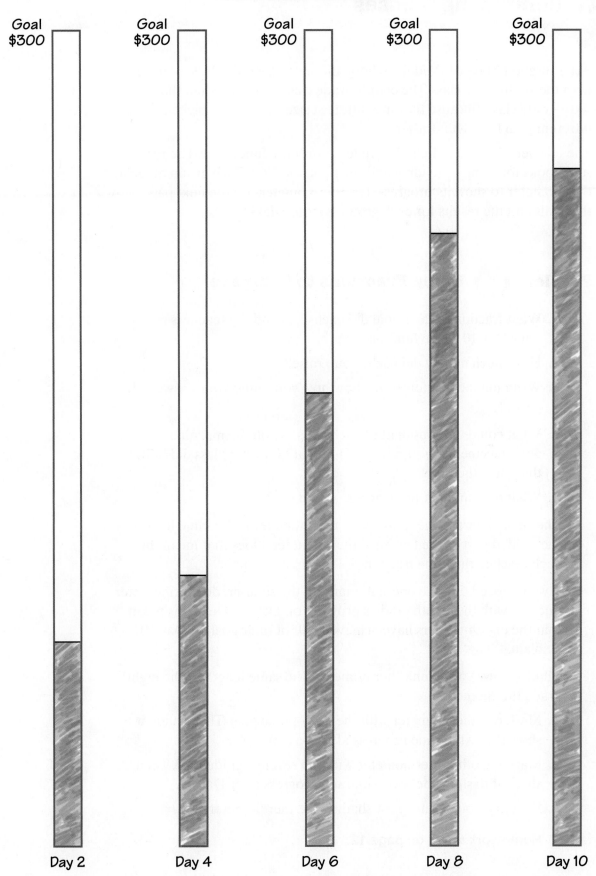

Goal $300 Goal $300 Goal $300 Goal $300 Goal $300

Day 2   Day 4   Day 6   Day 8   Day 10

Comparing Classes

At Thurgood Marshall Middle School, the seventh-grade class is larger than the sixth-grade class. The eighth-grade class is smaller than the sixth-grade class. Because they are different sizes, each class picked a different goal for its fundraiser.

The teachers decided to help the students with the fundraiser. The teachers sold books for summer reading and set a goal of $360. Each group made a thermometer to show its progress. The thermometers on the next page show the goals and the results for each group after ten days.

Problem 1.4 Using Fractions to Compare

A. 1. What fraction of their goal did each class and the teachers reach after Day 10 of the fundraiser?

2. How much money did each group raise?

3. Write number sentences to show how you found your answers in part (2).

B. 1. What could the president of each class say on the morning announcements to support a claim that his or her class did better than the other two?

2. What do you think the teachers would say?

C. The shaded part of the sixth-grade thermometer is the same length as the shaded part of the teachers' thermometer. Does that mean they each reached the same fraction of their goal? Explain.

D. Gwen noticed that the one-half mark on the sixth-grade thermometer lines up with the eighth grade's progress on Day 10. Does this mean that the eighth-graders have achieved half of their goal on Day 10? Explain.

E. Make (or use) two blank thermometers the same length as the eighth-grade thermometer.

1. Mark one thermometer with the sixth-grade goal. Then shade it to show the sixth-grade progress after Day 10.

2. Mark the other thermometer with the seventh-grade goal. Then shade it to show the seventh-grade progress after Day 10.

3. Describe your strategy for shading the thermometers.

ACE Homework starts on page 12.

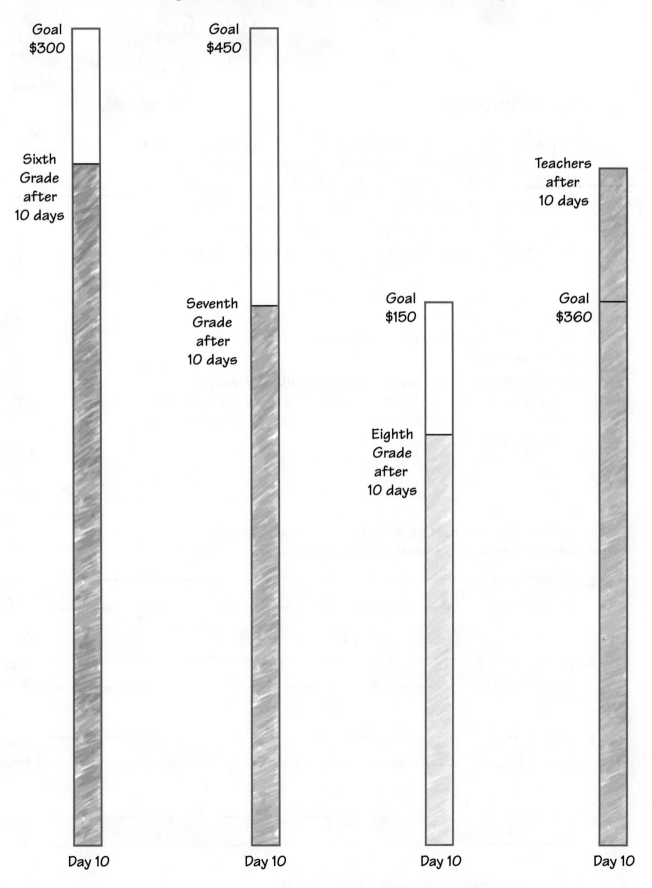

Goal
$300

Sixth
Grade
after
10 days

Day 10

Goal
$450

Seventh
Grade
after
10 days

Day 10

Goal
$150

Eighth
Grade
after
10 days

Day 10

Teachers
after
10 days

Goal
$360

Day 10

Applications Connections Extensions

ACE

Applications

1. Mountview Middle School conducted the same type of fundraiser as Thurgood Marshall Middle School. The Mountview sixth-grade thermometer for Day 2 is shown at the right.

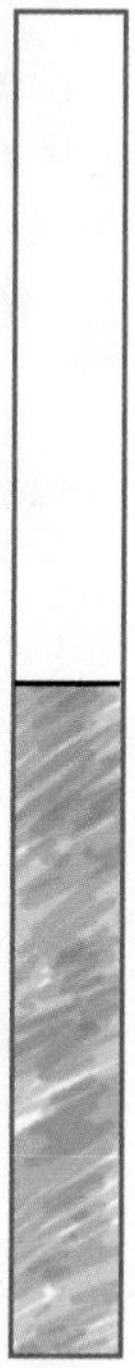
Goal
$300
Day 2

   a. Write three statements that the principal could make when reporting the results of the progress made by the sixth-graders.

   b. What are two claims that the sixth-graders could make if they collected $50 on the third day?

   c. Draw and shade a thermometer for Day 3.

2. a. What fraction strips could you make if you started with a fourths strip?

   b. If your teacher gave you an eighths strip like the one you made in Problem 1.2, which of the fraction strips you folded for Problem 1.2 would have more than one mark that lines up with the marks on the eighths strip?

For Exercises 3–6, fold fraction strips or use some other method to estimate the fraction of the fundraising thermometer that is shaded.

3.

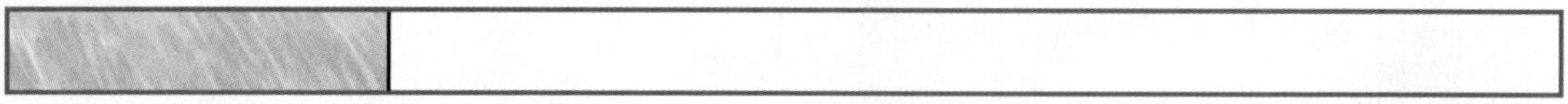
Goal
$400

4.

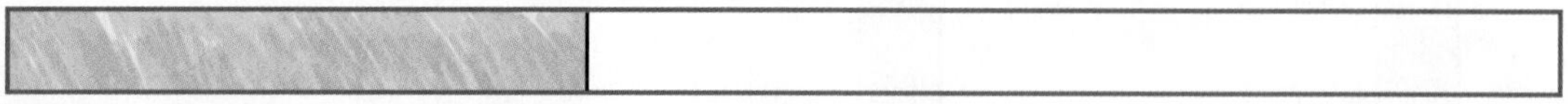
Goal
$400

5.

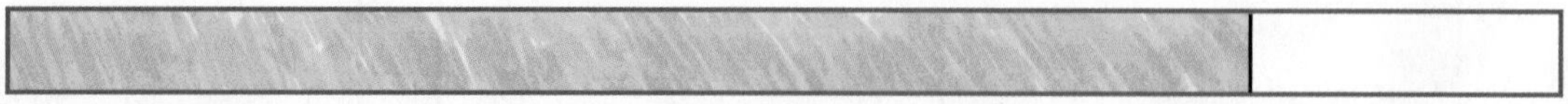
Goal
$400

6.

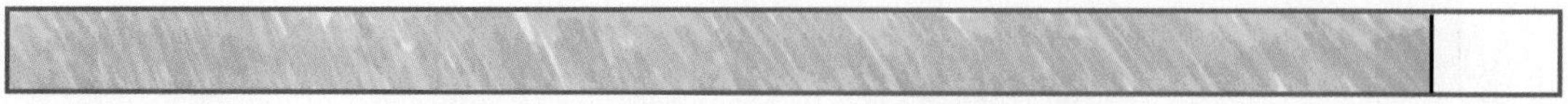
Goal
$400

For Exercises 7–11, use this illustration of a drink dispenser. The gauge on the side of the dispenser shows how much of the liquid remains in the dispenser. The dispenser holds 120 cups.

7. **a.** About what fraction of the dispenser is filled with liquid?

   b. About how many cups of liquid are in the dispenser?

   c. About what fraction of the dispenser is empty?

   d. About how many more cups of liquid would it take to fill the dispenser?

8. For parts (a)–(c), sketch the gauge and tell whether each dispenser is *almost empty, about half full,* or *almost full.*

   a. five sixths $\left(\frac{5}{6}\right)$ of a full dispenser

   b. three twelfths $\left(\frac{3}{12}\right)$ of a full dispenser

   c. five eighths $\left(\frac{5}{8}\right)$ of a full dispenser

9. **Multiple Choice** Which gauge shows about 37 out of 120 cups remaining?

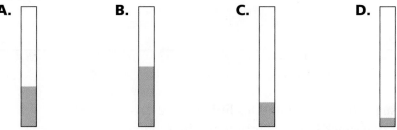

10. **Multiple Choice** Which gauge shows about 10 out of 120 cups remaining?

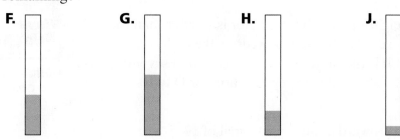

11. In Exercises 9 and 10, about what fraction is shaded in each gauge you chose?

12. Suppose you were trying to measure progress on a fundraising thermometer with your fifths strip, but the progress was between $\frac{3}{5}$ and $\frac{4}{5}$. What could you do to find a more exact answer?

For Exercises 13–15, use the information below.

You can also use fraction strips to name points on a number line. The point on this number line is at $\frac{1}{2}$.

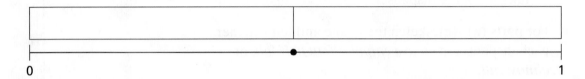

Copy each number line. Use fraction strips or some other method to name the point with a fraction.

13.

14.

15.

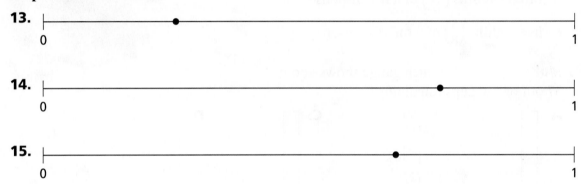

16. Samuel is getting a snack for himself and his little brother, Adam. Samuel takes half of one snack bar for himself and half of another snack bar for Adam. Adam complains that Samuel got more. Samuel says that he got half and Adam got half. What might be the problem?

17. In Problem 1.4, the eighth-grade thermometer is smaller than the sixth- and seventh-grade thermometers. Redraw the eighth-grade thermometer so that it is the same size as the sixth- and seventh-grade thermometers, but still shows the correct fraction for Day 10.

For: Help with Exercise 17
Web Code: ame-2117

18. If a class collects $155 toward a fundraising goal of $775, what fraction represents the class's progress toward its goal?

19. Bryce and Rachel are collecting food for the local food bank. Bryce's goal is to collect 32 items. Rachel's goal is to collect 24 items. If Rachel and Bryce each meet their goal, what fraction of Bryce's goal does Rachel collect?

Connections

20. Is 450 divisible by 5, 9, and 10? Explain.

21. Explain your answer to each question.
   a. Is 12 a divisor of 48?
   b. Is 4 a divisor of 150?
   c. Is 3 a divisor of 51?

22. Multiple Choice Choose the number that is not a factor of 300.
   A. 5   **B.** 6   **C.** 8   **D.** 20

23. Multiple Choice Choose the answer that shows all of the factors of 48.
   F. 2, 4, 8, 24, and 48   **G.** 1, 2, 3, 4, 5, and 6
   H. 48, 96, 144   **J.** 1, 2, 3, 4, 6, 8, 12, 16, 24, and 48

24. a. Miguel says that numbers that are divisible by 2 can easily be separated into halves of the number. Do you agree? Why or why not?
   b. Manny says that if Miguel is correct, then any numbers that are divisible by 3 can easily be separated into thirds. Do you agree? Why or why not?
   c. Lupe says that if any number is divisible by n, it can be easily separated into $n$ths. Do you agree with her? Explain.

25. a. If you had a fraction strip folded into twelfths, what fractional lengths could you measure with the strip?
   b. How is your answer in part (a) related to the factors of 12?

26. a. If you had a fraction strip folded into tenths, what fractional lengths could you measure with the strip?
   b. How is your answer in part (a) related to the factors of 10?

27. Ricky found a beetle that has a body one fourth $\left(\frac{1}{4}\right)$ the length of the fraction strips used in Problem 1.2.

a. How many beetle bodies, placed end to end, would have a total length equal to the length of a fraction strip?

b. How many beetle bodies, placed end to end, would have a total length equal to three fraction strips?

c. Ricky drew 13 paper beetle bodies, end to end, each the same length as the one he found. How many fraction strips long is Ricky's line of beetle bodies?

For Exercises 28–30, use the bar graph below, which shows the number of cans of juice three sixth-grade classes drank.

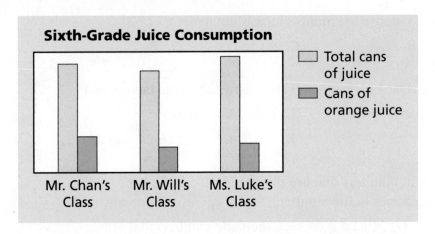

28. In each class, what fraction of the cans were orange juice?

29. In which class would you say orange juice was most popular?

30. a. Students in Mr. Chan's class drank a total of ten cans of orange juice. About how many cans of orange juice did the students in each of the other two classes drink?

b. About how many total cans of juice did each of the three classes drink?

Extensions

31. Dario made three pizzas, which he sliced into quarters. After considering how many people he would be sharing with, he thought to himself, "Each person can have half."

    a. Is it possible that there was only one other person to share with? Explain.

    b. Is it possible that there were 5 other people to share with? Explain.

    c. Is it possible that there were 11 other people to share with?

For Exercises 32–35, copy the number line. Use fraction strips or some other method to name the point with a fraction.

32.

33.

34.

35.

36. Write a numerator for each fraction to make the fraction close to, but not equal to, $\frac{1}{2}$. Then write a numerator to make each fraction close to, but greater than, 1.

    a. $\frac{\blacksquare}{22}$ **b.** $\frac{\blacksquare}{43}$ **c.** $\frac{\blacksquare}{17}$

37. Write a denominator to make each fraction close to, but not equal to, $\frac{1}{2}$. Then write a denominator to make each fraction close to, but greater than, 1.

    a. $\frac{22}{\blacksquare}$ **b.** $\frac{43}{\blacksquare}$ **c.** $\frac{17}{\blacksquare}$

Mathematical Reflections 1

In this investigation, you made fraction strips to help you identify fractional parts of a whole. These questions will help you summarize what you have learned.

Think about your answers to these questions. Discuss your ideas with other students and your teacher. Then write a summary of your findings in your notebook.

1. Two different classes reached $\frac{3}{5}$ of their fundraising goals. Did the two classes raise the same amount of money? Explain.

2. What do the numerator and the denominator of a fraction tell you?

3. If a class goes over its goal, what can you say about the fraction of their goal they have reached?

Investigation 2

Sharing and Comparing With Fractions

In Investigation 1, you used fraction strips to help determine what fraction of a fundraising goal students had reached. You interpreted fractions as parts of a whole. In this investigation, you will explore situations in which fractions are used to make comparisons.

2.1 Equivalent Fractions and Equal Shares

Sid and Susan are going hiking on the Appalachian Trail in Virginia with a group of friends. They are packing snack foods that are easy to carry and to eat. Their favorite is licorice (LIK uh rish) lace, a rope candy that looks like a long, round shoelace. Sid packs a licorice lace to share on the hike.

The licorice lace is 48 inches long and difficult to break into pieces. Sid can mark the licorice lace by cutting partway through. Then it will be easy to break and share later.

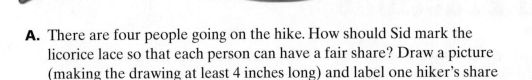

A. There are four people going on the hike. How should Sid mark the licorice lace so that each person can have a fair share? Draw a picture (making the drawing at least 4 inches long) and label one hiker's share of the lace.

B. Two more friends join the hike! Each wants a fair share of the licorice lace. Sid has to add more marks to the lace. He is stuck with the marks he has already made. Sid makes new marks so that the new marks together with the old marks make equal-size pieces.

   1. Draw a picture to show how Sid can add more marks to the licorice lace so it has equal-size pieces and can be broken to serve six people. Label one hiker's share.

   2. What fraction of the licorice lace will each of the six hikers get?

C. Well, you've probably guessed what happens next! Two more join the hike. Poor Sid has to re-mark the licorice lace he made for six people with additional marks. The new marks along with the old marks must form equal-size pieces to break off and share equally among eight friends. How should he re-mark the lace?

   1. Draw a picture and label one hiker's share of the licorice lace.

   2. How many inches of the lace will each of the eight hikers get?

How can I re-mark the licorice so all eight people get the same amount?

D. Use your drawing for Question C. Are there any marks that could be labeled with more than one fraction? If so, give some examples.

E. Carlotta bought a 48-inch blueberry lace. She cut off a part for her friend Brianna.

Blueberry Lace

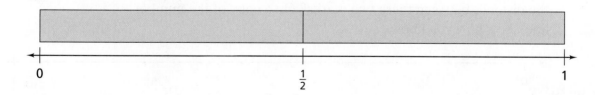

Brianna's part

1. What fraction of the blueberry lace did she give to Brianna?

2. How many inches of the blueberry lace did Brianna get?

ACE Homework starts on page 28.

2.2 Finding Equivalent Fractions

When you compare your fraction strips to each other, you find marks that match even though the total number of parts on each fraction strip is different. The places where marks match show **equivalent fractions.** Fractions that are equivalent represent the same amount even though their names are different.

Getting Ready for Problem 2.2

• Below is a fraction strip that shows a mark for $\frac{1}{2}$. What are five other fractions that are equivalent to $\frac{1}{2}$?

Problem 2.2 Finding Equivalent Fractions

A. **1.** On a number line like the one below, carefully label marks that show where $\frac{1}{3}$ and $\frac{2}{3}$ are located.

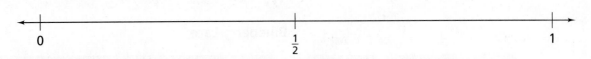

2. Use the same number line. Mark the point that is halfway between 0 and $\frac{1}{3}$ and the point that is halfway between $\frac{2}{3}$ and 1.

3. Label these new marks with appropriate fraction names.

4. What are additional ways to label $\frac{1}{3}, \frac{1}{2}$, and $\frac{2}{3}$? Explain.

5. Use the same number line. Mark halfway between each of the marks that were already made.

6. Label the new marks on your number line. Add additional names to the marks that were already named.

7. Write three number sentences that show equivalent fractions on your number line. $\left(\text{Here is an example: } \frac{1}{2} = \frac{3}{6}.\right)$

8. Write two number sentences to show fractions that are equivalent to $\frac{9}{12}$.

B. **1.** On your number line, the distance between the $\frac{1}{2}$ mark and the 1 mark is $\frac{1}{2}$ of a unit. The distance between the 0 mark and the $\frac{1}{3}$ mark on your number line is $\frac{1}{3}$ of a unit. Name two other fractions that are $\frac{1}{3}$ of a unit apart on your number line.

2. What is the distance between the $\frac{1}{3}$ and $\frac{1}{2}$ marks on your number line? How do you know?

3. Name at least two other fraction pairs that are the same distance apart as $\frac{1}{3}$ and $\frac{1}{2}$.

4. Describe the distance between $\frac{2}{3}$ and $\frac{5}{6}$ in two ways.

C. **1.** Here is another number line with a mark for $\frac{7}{10}$ and for $\frac{3}{5}$. What is the distance between these two marks? On a copy of the number line, show how you know.

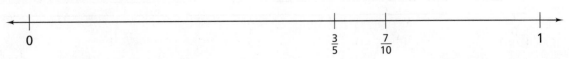

2. Suppose a number line is marked with tenths. Which marks can also be labeled with fifths?

D. 1. Find three fractions that are equivalent to $\frac{2}{7}$.

2. Find every fraction with a whole-number denominator less than 50 that is equivalent to $\frac{10}{15}$.

3. Describe a strategy for finding equivalent fractions.

4. How does renaming fractions help you find distances between fractions?

ACE Homework starts on page 28.

Did You Know?

Hieroglyphic inscriptions show that, with the exception of $\frac{2}{3}$, Egyptian mathematicians only used fractions with 1 in the numerator. These fractions, such as $\frac{1}{2}$ and $\frac{1}{16}$, are known as *unit fractions*. Other fractions were expressed as sums of unit fractions. For example, the fraction $\frac{5}{12}$ was expressed as $\frac{1}{4} + \frac{1}{6}$ (as shown in the second and third pieces of the hieroglyphics below). Check with fraction strips to see if $\frac{1}{4} + \frac{1}{6} = \frac{5}{12}$.

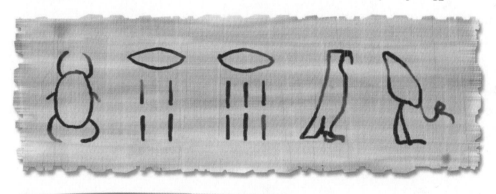

2.3 Comparing Fractions to Benchmarks

When you solve problems involving fractions, you may find it useful to estimate the size of fractions quickly. One way is to compare each fraction to $0, \frac{1}{2}$, and 1. These values serve as **benchmarks** —or reference points. First, you can decide whether a fraction is between 0 and $\frac{1}{2}$, between $\frac{1}{2}$ and 1, or greater than 1. Then decide whether the fraction is closest to $0, \frac{1}{2}$, or 1.

Problem 2.3 Comparing Fractions to Benchmarks

A. Decide whether each fraction below is in the interval between 0 and $\frac{1}{2}$, the interval between $\frac{1}{2}$ and 1, or between 1 and $1\frac{1}{2}$. Record your information in a table that shows which fractions are in each interval.

$$\frac{1}{5} \qquad \frac{4}{5} \qquad \frac{1}{3} \qquad \frac{2}{3} \qquad \frac{1}{10} \qquad \frac{6}{10} \qquad \frac{7}{10} \qquad \frac{8}{10} \qquad \frac{3}{8}$$

$$\frac{17}{12} \qquad \frac{7}{8} \qquad \frac{9}{8} \qquad \frac{7}{9} \qquad \frac{3}{4} \qquad \frac{3}{12} \qquad \frac{5}{6} \qquad \frac{3}{7} \qquad \frac{4}{7}$$

B. Decide whether each fraction above is closest to $0, \frac{1}{2}, 1$, or $1\frac{1}{2}$. Record your information in a table that also includes the categories "Halfway Between 0 and $\frac{1}{2}$" and "Halfway Between $\frac{1}{2}$ and 1."

C. Compare each pair of fractions using benchmarks and other strategies. Then copy the fractions and insert the *less than* ($<$), *greater than* ($>$), or *equals* ($=$) symbol. Describe your strategies.

1. $\frac{5}{8} \ \blacksquare \ \frac{6}{8}$ **2.** $\frac{5}{6} \ \blacksquare \ \frac{5}{8}$ **3.** $\frac{2}{3} \ \blacksquare \ \frac{3}{9}$

4. $\frac{13}{12} \ \blacksquare \ \frac{6}{5}$ **5.** $\frac{6}{12} \ \blacksquare \ \frac{5}{9}$ **6.** $\frac{3}{4} \ \blacksquare \ \frac{12}{16}$

D. Use benchmarks and other strategies to help you write each set of fractions in order from least to greatest.

1. $\frac{2}{3}, \frac{7}{9}, \frac{3}{7}$ **2.** $\frac{4}{5}, \frac{4}{12}, \frac{7}{10}, \frac{5}{6}$

ACE Homework starts on page 28.

2.4 Fractions Between Fractions

Fractions seem to behave differently than whole numbers. For example, there is no whole number between 1 and 2. You already know that between $\frac{1}{4}$ and $\frac{1}{2}$ there are other fractions—for example, $\frac{1}{3}$.

As you do Problem 2.4, consider this question:
Can you always find another fraction between any two fractions?

Problem 2.4 Fractions Between Fractions

A. Find a fraction between each pair of fractions.

    1. $\frac{3}{10}$ and $\frac{7}{10}$ **2.** $\frac{1}{5}$ and $\frac{2}{5}$

    3. $\frac{1}{8}$ and $\frac{1}{4}$ **4.** $\frac{1}{10}$ and $\frac{1}{9}$

B. Find two fractions between each pair of fractions.

    1. $\frac{4}{7}$ and $\frac{5}{7}$ **2.** $\frac{5}{11}$ and $\frac{6}{11}$

C. Describe the strategies you used in answering Questions A and B.

ACE Homework starts on page 28.

2.5 Naming Fractions Greater Than 1

The whole numbers on a number line follow one another in a simple, regular pattern. Between every pair of whole numbers are many other points that may be labeled with fractions.

A number such as $2\frac{1}{2}$ is called a **mixed number** because it has a whole number part and a fraction part.

Getting Ready for Problem 2.5

- How would you label the marks halfway between the whole numbers on this number line?

- Betty says that the mark between 2 and 3 should be labeled $\frac{1}{2}$. Do you agree? Why?

- If you made a new mark halfway between 2 and $2\frac{1}{2}$, how would you label it?

Alyssa asked whether a mixed number can be written as a fraction with no whole number part. For example,

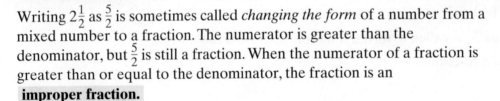

Alyssa: Can you write $2\frac{1}{2}$ as a fraction?

Sammy: Yeah, that's a good question.

Alyssa: Let's see. How many halves does the number 2 represent?

Sammy: Since there are two halves for each of the two wholes, 2 represents four halves.

Alyssa: Does knowing this help us write $2\frac{1}{2}$ as a fraction?

Sammy: Yes, now that we know that $2\frac{1}{2}$ represents five halves (4 + 1), we can write $2\frac{1}{2}$ as $\frac{5}{2}$.

Writing $2\frac{1}{2}$ as $\frac{5}{2}$ is sometimes called *changing the form* of a number from a mixed number to a fraction. The numerator is greater than the denominator, but $\frac{5}{2}$ is still a fraction. When the numerator of a fraction is greater than or equal to the denominator, the fraction is an **improper fraction.**

There is really nothing improper about such fractions! This is just a name used to distinguish between fractions less than 1 and those greater than 1.

Problem 2.5 Naming Fractions Greater Than 1

Each student activity group at Johnson School agreed to pick up litter along a 10-mile stretch of highway.

For each problem, use a number line to show what the problem describes and how you solved it. Show your answers as both a mixed number and an improper fraction.

 A. Kate and Julianna are in the Marching Band. They work together to clean a section of highway that is $\frac{9}{4}$ miles long. Write this length as a mixed number.

B. The Math Club divided their 10-mile section into 2-mile segments that were assigned to the group members. Adrian and Ellie's section starts at the 2-mile point.

 1. If they start at the 2-mile point and clean for $\frac{5}{3}$ miles, how far are they from the start of the Math Club section? Explain.

 2. How many more miles of their 2-mile segment are left to clean?

C. The Drama Club's stretch of highway is very hilly and filled with litter. Working their hardest, club members can clean $1\frac{2}{3}$ miles each day.

 1. How far will they be at the end of the second day?

 2. At this rate, how many days will it take them to clean their 10-mile section?

 3. Jacqueline says that in four days they can clean $\frac{19}{3}$ miles. Thomas says they can clean $6\frac{2}{3}$ miles in four days. Who is right? Why?

D. The 10 miles assigned to the Chess Club start at the 10-mile point and go to the 20-mile point. When the Chess Club members have cleaned $\frac{5}{8}$ of their 10-mile section, between which miles will they be?

E. The Gardening Club has a section of highway between the 20- and 30-mile points. The club members set their goal for the first day to reach the 24-mile point. What fraction of the Gardening Club's total distance do they plan to cover on the first day?

 **ACE** Homework starts on page 28.

Did You Know?

Whole numbers, mixed numbers, and fractions all belong to the set of **rational numbers.** If you can write a number in fraction form using a whole number for each numerator and denominator $\left(\text{as in } \frac{3}{4}, \frac{5}{1}, \text{ or } \frac{7}{2}\right)$, it is a rational number.

The word *rational* comes from the Latin word *ratio*, which means "relation." You will learn more about ratios and see other examples of rational numbers later in this unit.

Applications

1. Cheryl, Rita, and four of their friends go to a movie and share equally a 48-ounce bag of popcorn and three 48-inch licorice laces. Find the fraction of popcorn each gets and the fraction of licorice each gets.

2. The Lappans buy three large sandwich wraps to serve at a picnic. Nine people in all will be at the picnic. Show three different ways to cut the sandwiches so that each person gets an equal share.

3. Three neighbors are sharing a rectangular strip of land for a garden. They divide the land into 24 equal-sized pieces. What fraction of the land does each person get if they share it equally? Write the answer in more than one way.

For Exercises 4–7, decide whether the statement is *correct* or *incorrect*. Explain your reasoning in words or by drawing pictures.

4. $\frac{1}{3} = \frac{4}{12}$
5. $\frac{4}{6} = \frac{2}{3}$
6. $\frac{2}{5} = \frac{1}{3}$
7. $\frac{2}{5} = \frac{5}{10}$

For Exercises 8 and 9, draw fraction strips to show that the two fractions are equivalent.

8. $\frac{2}{5}$ and $\frac{6}{15}$
9. $\frac{1}{9}$ and $\frac{2}{18}$

Homework Help Online
PHSchool.com
For: Help with Exercise 8
Web Code: ame-2208

10. Write an explanation to a friend telling how to find a fraction that is equivalent to $\frac{3}{5}$. You can use words and pictures to help explain.

11. When you save or download a file, load a program, or open a page on the Internet, a status bar is displayed on the computer screen to let you watch the progress. Use the fraction strips shown to find three fractions that describe the status of the work in progress.

Downloading file ...

Compare each pair of fractions in Exercises 12–23 using benchmarks and other strategies. Then copy the fractions, and insert the *less than* (<), *greater than* (>), or *equals* (=) symbol.

12. $\frac{8}{10}$ ■ $\frac{3}{8}$ 13. $\frac{2}{3}$ ■ $\frac{4}{9}$ 14. $\frac{3}{5}$ ■ $\frac{5}{12}$ 15. $\frac{1}{3}$ ■ $\frac{2}{3}$

16. $\frac{3}{4}$ ■ $\frac{3}{5}$ 17. $\frac{3}{2}$ ■ $\frac{7}{6}$ 18. $\frac{8}{12}$ ■ $\frac{6}{9}$ 19. $\frac{9}{10}$ ■ $\frac{10}{11}$

20. $\frac{3}{12}$ ■ $\frac{7}{12}$ 21. $\frac{5}{6}$ ■ $\frac{5}{8}$ 22. $\frac{3}{7}$ ■ $\frac{6}{14}$ 23. $\frac{4}{5}$ ■ $\frac{7}{8}$

For: Multiple-Choice Skills Practice
Web Code: ama-2254

24. Find a fraction between each pair of fractions.

   a. $\frac{1}{8}$ and $\frac{1}{4}$ **b.** $\frac{1}{6}$ and $\frac{1}{12}$ **c.** $\frac{1}{6}$ and $\frac{2}{6}$ **d.** $\frac{1}{4}$ and $\frac{2}{5}$

Between which two benchmarks ($0, \frac{1}{2}, 1, 1\frac{1}{2}$, and 2) does each fraction in Exercises 25–33 fall? Tell which is the nearer benchmark.

25. $\frac{3}{5}$ 26. $1\frac{2}{6}$ 27. $\frac{12}{10}$

28. $\frac{2}{18}$ 29. $1\frac{8}{10}$ 30. $1\frac{1}{10}$

31. $\frac{12}{24}$ 32. $\frac{9}{6}$ 33. $1\frac{12}{15}$

34. Describe, in writing or with pictures, how $\frac{7}{3}$ compares to $2\frac{1}{3}$.

35. **Multiple Choice** Which fraction is the greatest?

   A. $\frac{7}{6}$ **B.** $\frac{9}{8}$ **C.** $\frac{13}{12}$ **D.** $\frac{14}{15}$

36. **Multiple Choice** On a number line from 0 to 10, where is $\frac{13}{3}$ located?

    F. between 0 and 1   **G.** between 4 and 5

    H. between 5 and 6   **J.** between 6 and 7

37. Copy the number line below. Locate and label marks representing $\frac{9}{10}$, $\frac{11}{10}$, $2\frac{3}{10}$, and $2\frac{5}{10}$. For each point you mark, give two other fractions that are equivalent to the fraction given.

38. Copy the number line below. Locate and label marks representing $2\frac{1}{4}$, $1\frac{9}{10}$, and $\frac{15}{4}$.

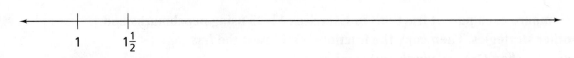

39. Copy the number line below. Locate and label a fraction represented by each point described.

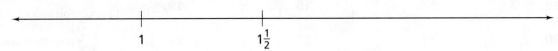

    a. a point close to but greater than 1

    b. a point close to but less than $1\frac{1}{2}$

    c. a point close to but greater than $1\frac{1}{2}$

    d. a point close to but less than 2

40. Copy the number line below. Locate and label marks representing 16, $15\frac{1}{2}$, $19\frac{1}{2}$, and $20\frac{1}{4}$.

41. Copy and complete the table.

Fraction	$\frac{5}{3}$	▪	▪	$\frac{19}{6}$	$\frac{37}{4}$	▪
Mixed Number	▪	$2\frac{4}{5}$	$9\frac{3}{7}$	▪	▪	$6\frac{2}{3}$

42. Kelly and Sean work together to clean a section of highway that is $\frac{10}{3}$ miles long. Write this distance as a mixed number.

43. The Chess Club is cleaning a very littered section of highway. Each day the members clean $1\frac{3}{4}$ miles of highway. After four days of hard work, Lakeisha says they have cleaned $\frac{28}{4}$ miles of highway. Glenda says they have cleaned 7 miles of roadway. Who is right? Why?

44. Change each mixed number into an improper fraction.

   a. $1\frac{2}{3}$ **b.** $6\frac{3}{4}$ **c.** $9\frac{7}{9}$ **d.** $4\frac{2}{7}$

45. Change each improper fraction into a mixed number.

   a. $\frac{22}{4}$ **b.** $\frac{10}{6}$ **c.** $\frac{17}{5}$ **d.** $\frac{36}{8}$

Connections

For Exercises 46 and 47, write a fraction to describe how much pencil is left, compared to a new pencil. Measure from the left edge of the eraser to the point of the pencil.

46.

47.

48. These bars represent trips that Ms. Axler took in her job this week.

300 km

180 km

200 km

a. Copy each bar and shade in the distance Ms. Axler traveled after going one third of the total distance for each trip.

b. How many kilometers had Ms. Axler traveled when she was at the one-third point in each trip? Explain your reasoning.

49. Multiple Choice Find the least common multiple of the following numbers: 3, 4, 5, 6, 10, and 15.

A. 1 **B.** 15 **C.** 60 **D.** 54,000

50. Use what you found in Exercise 49. Write the fractions in equivalent form, all with the same denominator.

$\frac{1}{3}$ $\frac{1}{4}$ $\frac{1}{5}$ $\frac{1}{6}$ $\frac{1}{10}$ $\frac{1}{15}$

Find the greatest common factor of each pair of numbers.

51. 12 and 48 **52.** 6 and 9

53. 24 and 72 **54.** 18 and 45

Use your answers from Exercises 51–54 to write a fraction equivalent to each fraction given.

55. $\frac{12}{48}$ **56.** $\frac{6}{9}$ **57.** $\frac{24}{72}$ **58.** $\frac{18}{45}$

Extensions

For Exercises 59–64, copy each number line. Estimate and mark where the number 1 would be.

59.

0          $\frac{2}{5}$

60.

0                              $\frac{9}{10}$

61.

```
←——+———————+————————————————————→
    0         1/3
```

62.

```
←——+——————————————————————————+————→
    0                          5/2
```

63.

```
←——+——————————————————————————+————→
    0                          3/4
```

64.

```
←——+——————————————————————+—————————→
    0                      6/4
```

For Exercises 65–67, find every fraction with a denominator less than 50 that is equivalent to the given fraction.

65. $\frac{3}{15}$ **66.** $\frac{8}{3}$ **67.** $1\frac{4}{6}$

68. Use the information in *Did You Know?* after Problem 2.2 to figure out how to name the sums below with a single fraction. (Your strips might be helpful.) Explain your reasoning.

 a. $\frac{1}{2} + \frac{1}{4} = \blacksquare$ **b.** $\frac{1}{12} + \frac{1}{6} = \blacksquare$ **c.** $\frac{1}{4} + \frac{1}{6} + \frac{1}{12} = \blacksquare$

69. A *unit fraction* is a fraction with 1 in the numerator. Find a set of unit fractions whose sum equals each of the following. Try to find more than one answer for each.

 a. $\frac{7}{8}$ **b.** $\frac{7}{12}$

70. Find five fractions between $\frac{8}{10}$ and $\frac{5}{4}$.

71. Does $\frac{4}{5}, \frac{17}{23}$, or $\frac{51}{68}$ represent the greatest part of a whole? Explain your reasoning.

72. Copy the number line below. Locate and label marks representing $0, \frac{3}{4}$, $\frac{1}{8}$, and $2\frac{2}{3}$.

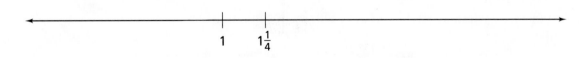

```
←————————————+———————+————————————————→
             1      1 1/4
```

Connections Extensions

Mathematical Reflections 2

In this investigation, you explored equivalent fractions, compared fractions to benchmarks, and considered fractions greater than 1. These questions will help you summarize what you have learned.

Think about your answers to these questions. Discuss your ideas with other students and your teacher. Then write a summary of your findings in your notebook.

1. Describe your strategy for finding a fraction equivalent to a given fraction.

2. Describe strategies you have found for deciding whether a fraction is between 0 and $\frac{1}{2}$ or between $\frac{1}{2}$ and 1.

3. Explain how you can decide which of two fractions is greater.

4. Describe how to write a mixed number as a fraction.

5. Describe how to write a fraction greater than 1 as a mixed number.

Moving Between Fractions and Decimals

You see decimals every day, in lots of different places. Can you tell where each of the decimals below was found?

3.1 Making Smaller Parts

Decimals give us a way to write special fractions that have denominators of 10 or 100 or 1,000 or 10,000 or even 100,000,000,000. In Investigation 1, you folded fraction strips. One of the strips you made was a tenths strip, shown on the next page.

Suppose you need more marks to show a fraction. Look at the tenths strip.

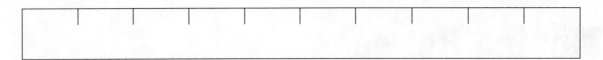

- How could you fold a tenths strip to get a hundredths strip?
- How would you label this new fraction strip?

A *tenths grid* is also divided into ten equal parts. It resembles a tenths fraction strip, but it is square. Below is a tenths grid that shows the fraction and its decimal equivalent represented by each section of the grid.

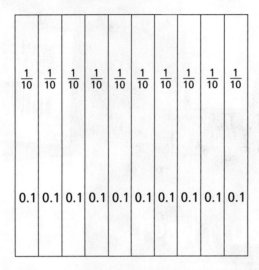

Here are some examples of fractions represented on tenths grids. The fraction name and decimal name for the shaded part are given below each drawing.

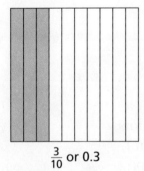

$\frac{3}{10}$ or 0.3

$\frac{5}{10}$ or 0.5

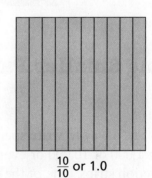

$\frac{10}{10}$ or 1.0

You can further divide a tenths grid by drawing horizontal lines to make ten rows. This makes 100 parts. This is called a *hundredths grid*.

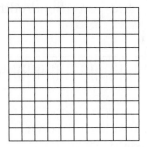

Fractions can also be represented on a hundredths grid. You can write fractional parts of 100 as decimal numbers, as in the following examples:

Fraction	Decimal	Representation on a Hundredths Grid
$\frac{7}{100}$	0.07	
$\frac{27}{100}$	0.27	
$\frac{20}{100}$	0.20	

Problem 3.1 Using Tenths and Hundredths

A. 1. Mark and label the fractions $\frac{1}{4}$, $\frac{2}{4}$, $\frac{3}{4}$, and $\frac{4}{4}$ on a hundredths fraction strip like the one shown.

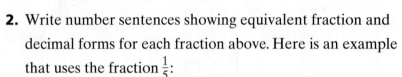

2. After marking each fraction, shade that fraction on a hundredths grid like the one at the right.

3. Write a fraction that shows how many hundredths you shaded.

4. Write a decimal that shows how many hundredths you shaded.

B. 1. Which of the fractions could be easily shown on a tenths grid or a tenths fraction strip?

2. Write number sentences showing equivalent fraction and decimal forms for each fraction above. Here is an example that uses the fraction $\frac{1}{5}$:

$$\frac{1}{5} = \frac{2}{10} = 0.2 \text{ and } \frac{1}{5} = \frac{20}{100} = 0.20$$

C. Rewrite the fractions below using denominators of 10 or 100. Then, write a decimal for each fraction.

1. $\frac{2}{5}$ **2.** $\frac{26}{50}$ **3.** $\frac{4}{20}$ **4.** $\frac{4}{5}$

D. Lin, a sixth-grader at Pleasant Valley School, won a giant fruit bar for selling the most posters in the school fundraiser. The bar is 10 inches by 10 inches and is marked into 100 square-inch sections. Lin decides to share her fruit bar with some friends.

1. Lin gives 0.1 of the bar to Bailey. Describe two ways Lin could cut the bar to share it with Bailey.

2. Lin gives 0.25 of the bar to Lula. Describe two ways that she could cut the bar to share it with Lula.

3. Lin gives $\frac{1}{5}$ of the bar to her little sister, Donna, who helped her sell the posters for the fundraiser. Write two decimals that represent how much of the bar Donna gets.

4. Lin gives $\frac{1}{50}$ of the bar to Patrick. Write a decimal that represents how much of the bar Patrick gets.

5. Shade a hundredths grid to show one way that Lin could cut all of the sections to give to her friends.

Certificate
of Award

Pleasant Valley School

Top Seller

Lin Chang

6. Who got more of the fruit bar—Bailey, Lula, Donna, or Patrick? Explain.

7. How much of the bar was left for Lin?

ACE **Homework starts on page 47.**

3.2 Making Even Smaller Parts

The place value chart below shows a set of special numbers in both fraction and decimal form. Think about these questions as you look at the chart:

What do you notice about the denominators of the fractions as you move to the right from the decimal point?

Why are these denominators useful in writing fractions as decimals?

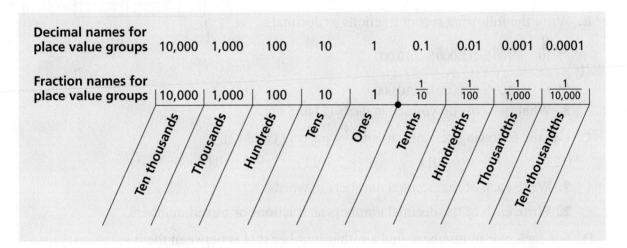

Decimal names for place value groups	10,000	1,000	100	10	1	0.1	0.01	0.001	0.0001
Fraction names for place value groups	10,000	1,000	100	10	1	$\frac{1}{10}$	$\frac{1}{100}$	$\frac{1}{1,000}$	$\frac{1}{10,000}$
	Ten thousands	Thousands	Hundreds	Tens	Ones	Tenths	Hundredths	Thousandths	Ten-thousandths

Some fractions can be written as decimals using only the tenths place.

$$\frac{4}{5} = \frac{8}{10} = 0.8$$

Some fractions, like $\frac{1}{4}$, are difficult to represent with tenths. You can write $\frac{1}{4}$ as an equivalent fraction with a denominator of 100 to find the decimal representation.

$$\frac{1}{4} = \frac{25}{100} = 0.25$$

You can think of $\frac{1}{4}$ as 25 hundredths or as 2 tenths and 5 hundredths. For some fractions, you may need to section a grid into even more parts to represent denominators such as 1,000 or 10,000.

- What might a hundredths grid look like if each square were subdivided into 10 equal parts? How many parts would the new grid have?

- What is a fraction name for the smallest part of this new grid? What is its decimal name?

Problem 3.2 Place Values Greater Than Hundredths

A. 1. What fraction of the grid at the right is shaded?

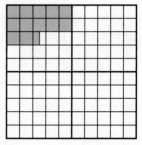

   2. How many hundredths are shaded? Write your answer as a fraction and as a decimal.

   3. If you shaded the same fraction on a *thousandths grid*, how many thousandths would be shaded? Write your answer as a fraction and as a decimal.

B. Write the following sets of fractions as decimals.

   1. $\frac{9}{10}$, $\frac{9}{100}$, $\frac{9}{1,000}$, $\frac{9}{10,000}$

   2. $\frac{43}{10}$, $\frac{43}{100}$, $\frac{43}{1,000}$, $\frac{43}{10,000}$

   3. What patterns do you see in parts (1) and (2)?

C. Use the following decimals to answer parts (1) and (2).

   0.23   0.7011   2.7011   0.00006

   1. Write each of the decimal numbers in words.

   2. Write each of the decimal numbers as fractions or mixed numbers.

D. For each pair of numbers, find another number that is between them.

   1. 0.8 and 0.85   **2.** 0.72 and 0.73

   3. 1.2 and 1.205   **4.** 0.0213 and 0.0214

   5. Describe one strategy that you used to find numbers between decimals in parts (1)–(4).

ACE Homework starts on page 47.

Below are representations of $\frac{3}{4}$ on a hundredths grid and on a number line.

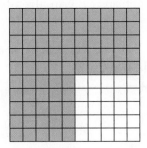

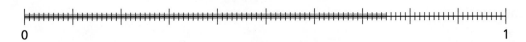

Consider these questions:

Each representation shows that $\frac{3}{4}$ is 75 out of 100 parts. How would you write this as a decimal?

Different representations are usually good for different things. Which representation, the grid or the number line, do you find most useful?

Sometimes knowing a little can go a long way! With decimals and fractions, knowing just a few fractions and their decimal equivalents can help you think about many other fractions and their decimal equivalents. In Problem 3.3 you will make a list of benchmarks that show equivalent fractions and decimals.

Mary wants to make a list of decimal benchmarks for these fraction benchmarks:

$$\frac{1}{2} \qquad \frac{1}{3} \qquad \frac{1}{4} \qquad \frac{1}{5} \qquad \frac{1}{6} \qquad \frac{1}{8} \qquad \frac{1}{10}$$

A. 1. For which of Mary's benchmark fractions do you already know the decimal equivalent? Show how you know.

   2. Use hundredths grids to find decimals that represent or are close approximations for the ones you do not know.

   3. Compare your decimals for $\frac{1}{4}$ and $\frac{1}{8}$.

   4. Compare your decimals for $\frac{1}{3}$ and $\frac{1}{6}$.

B. Use your work with Mary's benchmark list to help you find decimal equivalents for the following groups of fractions:

   1. $\frac{2}{5}$ $\quad$ $\frac{3}{5}$ $\quad$ $\frac{4}{5}$ $\quad$ $\frac{6}{5}$

   2. $\frac{2}{8}$ $\quad$ $\frac{3}{8}$ $\quad$ $\frac{4}{8}$ $\quad$ $\frac{5}{8}$ $\quad$ $\frac{6}{8}$ $\quad$ $\frac{7}{8}$

   3. $\frac{4}{20}$ $\quad$ $\frac{2}{6}$ $\quad$ $\frac{3}{12}$ $\quad$ $\frac{3}{6}$

   4. Describe strategies you used to find decimal equivalents.

C. Which fraction benchmark is each decimal nearest?

   1. 0.18 $\qquad$ **2.** 0.46 $\qquad$ **3.** 0.225 $\qquad$ **4.** 0.099

   5. Describe one strategy that you used to find answers to parts (1)–(4).

`ACE` **Homework starts on page 47.**

Did You Know?

Fractions like $\frac{1}{2}, \frac{1}{4}, \frac{1}{5}$, and $\frac{1}{10}$ all can be represented easily by decimals. However, a fraction such as $\frac{1}{3}$ requires careful thinking. It is easy to see that $\frac{1}{3}$ is between 0.3 and 0.4, and also between 0.33 and 0.34. We could go on and see that $\frac{1}{3}$ is between 0.333 and 0.334.

Where do we stop and get an exact value? It turns out that we do not *ever* get an exact answer if we stop finding additional decimal places! To write something like an exact value, we would need to write $\frac{1}{3}$ as 0.33333 . . . , where the "..." means that we go on and on, without stopping. When we need to stop somewhere, we write approximations for fractions. We often approximate $\frac{1}{3}$ by decimals such as 0.33, 0.333, or even 0.3333. We can use as many 3's as we need for whatever accuracy is appropriate.

3.4 Moving From Fractions to Decimals

In August 2004, Hurricane Charley swept though Cuba, Jamaica, and Florida. It destroyed many homes and caused lots of damage to land and buildings. Many people had no place to live and little clothing and food. In response, people from all over collected clothing, household items, and food to send to the victims of the hurricane.

One group of students decided to collect food to distribute to families whose homes were destroyed. They packed what they collected into boxes to send to the families. The students had to solve some problems while they were packing the boxes.

Problem 3.4 Moving From Fractions to Decimals

The students had 14 boxes for packing the food they collected. They wanted to share the supplies equally among the 14 families who would receive the boxes. They had bags and plastic containers to repack items for the individual boxes. They also had a digital scale that measured in kilograms or grams. (Remember that 1 kilogram = 1,000 grams.)

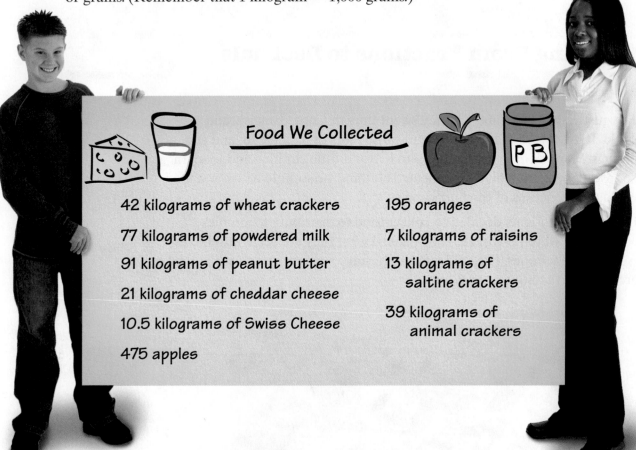

Food We Collected

42 kilograms of wheat crackers

77 kilograms of powdered milk

91 kilograms of peanut butter

21 kilograms of cheddar cheese

10.5 kilograms of Swiss Cheese

475 apples

195 oranges

7 kilograms of raisins

13 kilograms of saltine crackers

39 kilograms of animal crackers

A. How much of each item should the students include in each box? Explain how you found your answer.

B. One student calculated the amount of powdered milk by writing $\frac{77}{14}$, then $\frac{11}{2}$, or 5.5 kilograms per box. Use this method to calculate the amount of the other items per box.

C. Another student calculated the amount of Swiss cheese to include in each box by entering 10.5 into her calculator and dividing by 14. Is this a good method? Why or why not?

D. How does this problem suggest a way to change a fraction to a decimal? Explain.

ACE Homework starts on page 47.

3.5 Ordering Decimals

The decimal number system is based on place value. The value of a digit in a number depends on the place where it is written. So the "2" in "20" has a different meaning from the "2" in "0.02." The chart below shows the place value for each digit of the number 5,620.301.

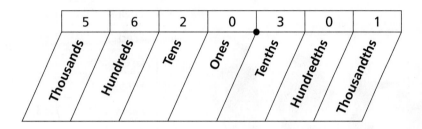

5	6	2	0	3	0	1
Thousands	Hundreds	Tens	Ones	Tenths	Hundredths	Thousandths

When you read decimal numbers that are greater than one, you say "and" to separate the whole number and decimal parts. For 2.5 you say "2 *and* 5 tenths."

Getting Ready for Problem 3.5

Consider these numbers:

$$2 \qquad 0.2 \qquad 20 \qquad 0.00002$$

- How does place value tell you which number is greatest?

Decimals can also help you to answer questions like the following:

> *How tall am I?*
>
> *Who is the tallest person in our class?*
>
> *How many people are injured by doors every year?*

As you work with decimals in this problem, think about place value and how it helps you to sort numbers.

A. The table at the right shows the heights of a class of sixth-graders.

1. Write Beth and Lana's heights as fractions. Who is taller?

2. Order the students according to height from the shortest to the tallest.

Students' Heights

Student	Height (m)
Alan	1.45
Beth	1.52
Juan	1.72
Dave	1.24
Eddie	1.22
Fred	1.66
Greg	1.3
Hiroko	1.26
Abey	1.63
Joan	1.58
Karl	1.23
Lana	1.5
Maria	1.27

B. The federal government keeps track of all kinds of interesting data. The table at the right shows the number of people injured by various household items in a recent year per thousand U.S. residents.

1. Order these items by the number of people injured from the least to the greatest.

2. Which are more dangerous: beds or carpets? How do you know?

3. Which item injured about twice as many people as ladders?

4. Which item injured about 10 times as many people as televisions?

C. What strategies did you use to order and compare the decimals in each situation?

ACE Homework starts on page 47.

Injuries From Household Items

Item	People Injured (per thousand U.S. residents)
Bathtubs and showers	0.674
Beds	1.569
Carpets and rugs	0.404
Ceilings and walls	0.894
Chairs	1.008
Doors	1.143
Ladders	0.563
Tables	1.051
Televisions	0.140
Toilets	0.195
Windows	0.446

SOURCE: U.S. Census Bureau. Go to **www.PHSchool.com** for a data update. Web Code: amg-9041

Applications

For Exercises 1–5, the whole is one hundredths grid. Write fraction and decimal names for the shaded part.

1.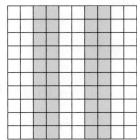

2.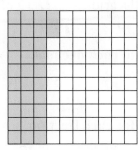

3.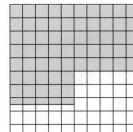

4.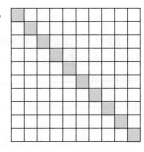

5.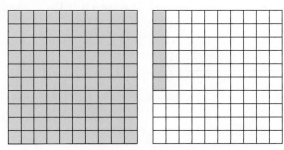

6. Name three fractions whose decimal equivalent is 0.25. Explain how you know each fraction is equivalent to 0.25. Draw a picture if it helps you explain your thinking.

7. Name three fractions whose decimal equivalent is 0.40. Explain how you know each fraction is equivalent to 0.40. Draw a picture if it helps you explain.

8. In parts (a)–(f), use blank hundredths grids to shade the given fractional part. Write the fraction as an equivalent decimal.

   a. $\frac{1}{2}$ of the hundredths grid   **b.** $\frac{3}{4}$ of the hundredths grid

   c. $\frac{99}{100}$ of the hundredths grid   **d.** $1\frac{3}{10}$ of the hundredths grids

   e. $2\frac{7}{10}$ of the hundredths grids   **f.** $1\frac{3}{5}$ of the hundredths grids

Write a fraction equivalent to each decimal.

   9. 0.08   **10.** 0.4   **11.** 0.04   **12.** 0.84

Go Online
PHSchool.com

For: Multiple-Choice Skills
   Practice
Web Code: ama-2354

Write a decimal equivalent for each fraction.

   13. $\frac{3}{4}$ **14.** $\frac{7}{50}$ **15.** $\frac{13}{25}$ **16.** $\frac{17}{25}$ **17.** $\frac{1}{20}$ **18.** $\frac{7}{10}$

For Exercises 19–21, copy the part of the number line given. Then find the "step" by determining the difference from one mark to another. Label the unlabeled marks with decimal numbers.

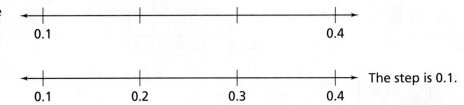

Sample

0.1   0.4

0.1   0.2   0.3   0.4   The step is 0.1.

19.

0.15   0.17

20.

0.028   0.029

21.

1.8   2.1

22. For each pair of numbers, find another number that is between them.

   a. 0.7 and 0.75   **b.** 0.65 and 0.68

   c. 1.4 and 1.410   **d.** 0.0322 and 0.323

23. Write each decimal in words.

    a. 3.620   **b.** 0.14   **c.** 0.00002

24. Name each decimal as a fraction or mixed number.

    a. 3.4   **b.** 0.35   **c.** 7.0003

25. For parts (a)–(c), use number lines to show the given fractional amount. Write the fraction as an equivalent decimal.

    a. $\frac{20}{25}$ **b.** $\frac{5}{8}$ **c.** $\frac{13}{26}$

26. Pilar divided 1 by 9 on her calculator and found that $\frac{1}{9}$ was approximately 0.1111. Find decimal approximations for each of the following fractions.

    a. $\frac{2}{9}$ **b.** $\frac{11}{9}$ **c.** $\frac{6}{9}$ **d.** $\frac{2}{3}$

    e. Describe any patterns that you see.

27. Ella says that she can find the decimal equivalent for lots of fractions because she knows that the decimal equivalent for $\frac{1}{5}$ is 0.2. Name three fractions for which Ella could find the decimal equivalent. Explain how Ella would use $\frac{1}{5}$ to find the decimal for each fraction.

28. Which fraction benchmark below is each decimal nearest?

    $\frac{1}{2}$ $\frac{1}{3}$ $\frac{1}{4}$ $\frac{1}{5}$ $\frac{1}{6}$ $\frac{1}{8}$ $\frac{1}{10}$

    a. 0.30   **b.** 0.50   **c.** 0.12333   **d.** 0.15

29. a. Sarah and her uncle, Takota, went fishing in the Grand River, and each caught one fish. Sarah's fish was $\frac{5}{8}$ of a foot long and Takota's was $\frac{2}{3}$ of a foot long. Which fish is longer? Explain.

    b. If Sarah and Takota measured their fish in decimals, would it be easier for them to tell which fish is longer? Explain.

30. Belinda used her calculator to find the decimal for the fraction $\frac{21}{28}$. When she entered 21 ÷ 28, the calculator gave an answer that looked familiar. Why do you think she recognized it?

31. Multiple Choice The orchestra at Johnson School is responsible for cleaning a 15-mile section of highway. There are 45 students in the orchestra. If each orchestra member cleans an equal section, what decimal represents this section?

A. 0.3　　　　**B.** 0.33　　　　**C.** 0.3333 . . .　　　　**D.** 3.0

32. Suppose a new student starts school today and your teacher asks you to teach her how to find decimal equivalents for fractions. What would you tell her? How would you convince her that your method works?

Copy each pair of numbers in Exercises 33–42. Insert <, >, or = to make a true statement.

33. 0.205 ▦ 0.21　　　　　　　**34.** 0.1 ▦ 0.1000

35. 0.04 ▦ 0.050　　　　　　　**36.** 1.03 ▦ 0.03

37. $\frac{5}{10}$ ▦ 0.6　　　　　　　　**38.** $\frac{3}{5}$ ▦ 0.3

39. 0.4 ▦ $\frac{2}{5}$　　　　　　　　**40.** 0.7 ▦ $\frac{1}{2}$

41. 0.52 ▦ $\frac{2}{4}$　　　　　　　　**42.** 0.41 ▦ 0.405

43. For each pair of numbers in Exercises 33–42, write a number that is between the two given numbers. If this is not possible, explain why.

44. Which is greater, 0.45 or 0.9? Explain your reasoning. Draw a picture if it helps explain your thinking.

45. Which is greater, seventy-five hundredths or six tenths? Explain. Draw a picture if needed.

46. Which is greater, 0.6 or 0.60? Explain. Draw a picture if needed.

For Exercises 47–50, rewrite the numbers in order from least to greatest.

47. 0.33, 0.12, 0.127, 0.2, $\frac{45}{10}$　　　**48.** $\frac{45}{10}$, $\frac{3}{1,000}$, 0.005, 0.34

49. 0.418, $\frac{4}{10}$, $\frac{40}{1,000}$, 0.481　　　**50.** 0.827, 1.23, $\frac{987}{100}$, $\frac{987}{1,000}$

For: Help with Exercise 47
Web Code: ame-2347

Connections

51. Ten students went to a pizza parlor together. They ordered eight small pizzas.

   a. How much will each student receive if they share the pizzas equally? Express your answer as a fraction and as a decimal.

   b. Explain how you thought about the problem. Draw a picture that would convince someone that your answer is correct.

52. If you look through a microscope that makes objects appear ten times larger, 1 centimeter on a metric ruler looks like this:

   a. Copy this microscope's view of 1 cm. Divide the length for 1 cm into ten equal parts. What fraction of the "centimeter" does each of these parts represent?

   b. Now think of dividing one of these smaller parts into ten equal parts. What part of the original "centimeter" does each of the new segments represent?

   c. If you were to divide one of these new small parts into ten parts again, what part of the original "centimeter" would each of the new small parts represent?

53. Copy the number line below. Show 0.4 and 0.5 on your number line.

$$\begin{array}{c} \hspace{0.5cm} \\ 0 \hspace{6cm} 1 \end{array}$$

a. Can you place five numbers between 0.4 and 0.5? If yes, place them on your number line with labels. If no, explain why not.

b. Now, enlarge the line segment from 0.4 to 0.5. Make your new line segment approximately the length of the original number line. Place 0.4, 0.45, and 0.50 on your new number line. Can you find five numbers that belong between 0.45 and 0.50? If yes, place them on your number line with labels. If no, explain why not.

54. Hana says division should be called a "sharing operation." Why might she say this?

Extensions

For Exercises 55–60, find an estimate if you cannot find an exact answer. You may find that drawing a number line, a hundredths grid, or some other diagram is useful in solving the problem. Explain your reasoning.

55. What is $\frac{1}{4}$ of 12?

56. What is $\frac{3}{4}$ of 8?

57. What is $\frac{2}{9}$ of 18?

58. What is $\frac{2}{9}$ of 3?

59. What is $\frac{1}{4}$ of 3?

60. What is $\frac{3}{4}$ of 3?

Mathematical Reflections 3

In this investigation, you studied relationships between fractions and decimals. These questions will help you summarize what you have learned.

Think about your answers to these questions. Discuss your ideas with other students and your teacher. Then write a summary of your findings in your notebook.

1. Describe how to find a decimal equivalent to a given fraction. How can you check your strategy to see that it works?

2. Describe how to find a fraction equivalent to a given decimal. Explain why your strategy works.

3. When comparing two decimals—such as 0.57 and 0.559—how can you decide which decimal represents the greater number?

Working With Percents

In this unit you have represented quantities as fractions and decimals to make sense of questions asking "how much?" or "how good?" or "which is better?" Below is a typical situation where a comparison is needed.

Getting Ready for Problem 4.1

When voters pass a school bond, they agree to a tax increase to pay for school construction. Based on the following data from a survey, which neighborhood—Whitehills or Bailey—is more positive about the proposed school bond to build a new gymnasium?

**People Favorable to
School Bond**

Neighborhood	Yes	No
Whitehills	31	69
Bailey	17	33

To make meaningful comparisons in a situation like this, you need to rewrite the amounts so that you are using a common unit of comparison. One way to compare this data would be to figure out what the numbers in each neighborhood would be if 100 people were polled and the rate of support stayed the same. Think about how this might be done.

Fractions that have 100 as their denominator are very useful because you can easily write such fractions as decimals and then compare them to other decimals.

Another useful way to express a fraction with a denominator of 100 is to use a special symbol called the percent symbol—%. **Percent** means "out of 100." So, 8% means 8 out of 100.

In the fifteenth century, the phrase *per cento* stood for "per 100." Writing "per cento" over and over again probably got tiresome. Manuscripts on arithmetic from about 1650 show that people began to replace "per cento" with "per $\frac{0}{0}$" or "p $\frac{0}{0}$."

Later, the "per" was dropped and the symbol $\frac{0}{0}$ appeared alone.

Over time, $\frac{0}{0}$ became the symbol % which we use today.

Go Online
PHSchool.com
For: Information about early arithmetic manuscripts
Web Code: ame-9031

Who's the Best?

Sports statistics are often given in percents. An important statistic for basketball players is their successful free-throw percent. Two well-known players are Yao Ming and Shaquille O'Neal. Mathematics can help us to compare their basketball statistics.

During a recent year, Yao Ming made 301 out of 371 free-throw attempts and Shaquille O'Neal made 451 out of 725 attempts. It is hard from these raw numbers to tell who was better at free throws. But in sports, the announcers give these raw numbers as percents.

A. Will said that he drew some pictures to help him think about the percent of free throws made by Yao Ming and Shaquille O'Neal, but then he got stuck! Here are Will's pictures.

1. Describe one way that Will could use his pictures to estimate the percentage of free throws made by each player.

2. Where would the mark for 50% be on the bottom scale in each picture?

3. Estimate the number that should sit on the top scale above 50% in each picture.

4. For each player, estimate the position for the mark representing the number of free throws made. Use a benchmark fraction to describe this location.

B. Alisha says that it is easy to tell who has the best free-throw record. She says, "Yao Ming made 301 free throws and Shaquille O'Neal made 451. So, Shaquille O'Neal has the better record!" Do you agree? Why or why not?

ACE **Homework starts on page 61.**

4.2 Choosing the Best

The Portland Tigers are playing the Coldwater Colts in basketball. The game is tied 58 to 58, but in the excitement both coaches step onto the court just as the buzzer sounds. A referee calls a technical foul on each coach.

Each coach has to choose one player to make the free-throw attempt. The winning team may be determined by the free throw.

Problem 4.2 Using Percents to Compare

A. The Portland coach will choose among three players to make the free-throw attempt. In their pre-game warm-ups:

- Angela made 12 out of 15 free throws
- Emily made 15 out of 20 free throws
- Cristina made 13 out of 16 free throws

Which player should the Portland coach select to make the free-throw attempt? Explain your reasoning.

B. The coach of the Coldwater Colts must choose the best player for free throws from the four players listed below. Which player should the coach select? Explain.

- Naomi made 10 out of 13 free throws
- Bobbie made 8 out of 10 free throws
- Kate made 36 out of 50 free throws
- Carmen made 16 out of 20 free throws

C. Find a way to support your conclusions in A and B that uses percents. What is the advantage of using percents when making comparisons?

ACE Homework starts on page 61.

Basketball was invented in 1891 by James Naismith. He was a physical education teacher who wanted to create a team sport that could be played indoors during the winter. The game was originally played with a soccer ball, peach baskets, and a ladder.

Go Online
PHSchool.com
For: Information about the origins of basketball
Web Code: ame-9031

4.3 Finding a General Strategy

One of the powerful things about mathematics is that you can often find ways to solve one problem that can also be used to solve similar problems.

For example, it is easy to find percents when exactly 100 people are surveyed, since percent means "out of 100." However, surveys often involve more than or fewer than 100 people. Here is an example.

A survey asked cat owners, "Does your cat have bad breath?" Out of the 200 cat owners surveyed, 80 answered yes to this question. What percent of the cat owners answered yes?

Problem 4.3 Expressing Data in Percent Form

As you work on these questions, try to find a way to describe strategies you can use for solving these kinds of problems.

A. Suppose 80 out of 400 cat owners surveyed said their cats have bad breath. What percent of the cat owners is this? Is this percent greater than, equal to, or less than the percent represented by 80 out of 200 cat owners? Explain.

B. If 120 out of 300 seventh-graders surveyed said mathematics is their favorite subject, how would you express this as a fraction? Write this fraction as a decimal and as a percent.

C. Suppose 30 out of 50 adults surveyed said they enjoy their jobs. How would you express this as a fraction, as a decimal, and as a percent?

D. Suppose 34 out of 125 sixth-graders surveyed said they would like to try hang gliding. What fraction, decimal, and percent is this?

E. Five out of 73 middle-school students said they look forward to practicing fire drills. What fraction, decimal, and percent is this?

F. **1.** Write an explanation for the different strategies you used to express the survey data in percent form.

2. What general process will cover all of the cases?

ACE Homework starts on page 61.

Did You Know?

Percents, fractions, and decimals are ways to represent ratios. A **ratio** is a comparison of two quantities. If you survey 200 people and report that $\frac{3}{5}$, 0.6, or 60% of the people have driver's licenses, you are comparing the number of people with licenses (120) to the total number of people you asked (200). A phrase such as "120 out of 200" is another way to represent a ratio.

4.4 Changing Forms

There are many different ways to talk about number relationships. When you are telling a story with data, you have choices about how you express the relationships. Fractions or decimals or percents may be more suitable in certain situations.

A survey asked a group of cat owners this question:

During the first year that you owned your cat, how much did it cost?

The table shows how the cat owners responded.

The First-Year Cost of Cat Ownership

Cost	Percent	Decimal	Fraction
$600 and up	▪	0.11	▪
From $500 to $599	25%	▪	▪
From $400 to $499	▪	▪	$\frac{2}{5}$
From $300 to $399	18%	▪	▪
From $200 to $299	▪	▪	$\frac{1}{25}$
Under $200	▪	0.02	▪

Problem 4.4 Moving Between Representations

A. Copy the table above and fill in the missing information.

B. 1. Starting at 0%, shade in different parts of a single percent bar like the one below. Use different colors or shading styles to show the percent corresponding to each of the six choices.

0% _____ 100%

2. Add a key to your percent bar to show what each color or type of shading represents. When you finish, the percent bar should be completely shaded. Explain why.

C. 1. What percent of cat owners had less than $400 in first-year costs?

2. What percent of cat owners had less than $600 in first-year costs?

D. 1. Write each decimal as a percent.

   a. 0.3   **b.** 0.21   **c.** 0.115

   d. 0.2375   **e.** 2.37

2. Write each percent as a decimal.

   a. 17%   **b.** 17.5%

   c. 132%   **d.** 132.5%

E. If you were asked to write a story about the first-year costs of cat ownership, would you use data expressed as percents, as fractions, or as decimals? Explain why you think your choice is best.

ACE Homework starts on page 61.

Applications

1. In a recent year, Karl Malone made 474 out of 621 free-throw attempts and John Stockton made 237 out of 287 free-throw attempts. Copy the percent bars and use them to answer each question.

```
0                                              621
┌──────────────────────────────────────────────┐
│ KARL MALONE                                    │
└──────────────────────────────────────────────┘
0%                                             100%
```

```
0                                         287
┌──────────────────────────────────────────┐
│ JOHN STOCKTON                              │
└──────────────────────────────────────────┘
0%                                          100%
```

a. What fraction benchmark is near the fraction of free throws made by each player?

b. Estimate the percent of free throws made by each player.

2. Use the data at the right. Which neighborhood (Elmhurst or Little Neck) is more in favor of the proposed school bond to build a new sports complex? Explain your reasoning.

People Favorable to School Bond

Neighborhood	Yes	No
Elmhurst	43	57
Little Neck	41	9

3. **Multiple Choice** Choose the best score on a quiz.

   A. 15 points out of 25   **B.** 8 points out of 14

   C. 25 points out of 45   **D.** 27 points out of 50

4. **Multiple Choice** Choose the best score on a quiz.

   F. 150 points out of 250   **G.** 24 points out of 42

   H. 75 points out of 135   **J.** 75 points out of 150

5. **Multiple Choice** What is the percent correct for a quiz score of 14 points out of 20?

   A. 43%   **B.** 53%   **C.** 70%   **D.** 75%

Homework Help Online
PHSchool.com
For: Help with Exercise 5
Web Code: ame-2405

6. Multiple Choice What is the percent correct for a quiz score of 26 points out of 60?

    F. about 43%   **G.** about 57%   **H.** about 68%   **J.** about 76%

For Exercises 7–15, use the cat data in the table.

Distribution of Cat Weights

Weight (lb.)	Males		Females	
	Kitten	Adult	Kitten	Adult
0–5.9	8	1	7	4
6–10.9	0	16	0	31
11–15.9	2	15	0	10
16–20	0	4	0	2
Total	10	36	7	47

7. a. What fraction of the cats are female?

   b. What fraction of the cats are male?

   c. Write each fraction as a decimal and as a percent.

8. a. What fraction of the cats are kittens?

   b. What fraction of the cats are adults?

   c. Write each fraction as a decimal and a percent.

9. a. What fraction of the kittens are male?

   b. Write the fraction as a decimal and as a percent.

10. What percent of the cats weigh from 11 to 15.9 pounds?

11. What percent of the cats weigh from 0 to 5.9 pounds?

12. What percent of the cats are male kittens and weigh from 11 to 15.9 pounds?

13. What percent of the cats are female and weigh from 6 to 15.9 pounds?

14. What percent of the cats are kittens and weigh from 16 to 20 pounds?

15. What percent of the females weigh from 0 to 5.9 pounds?

For Exercises 16–19 use the following information:

In a recent survey, 150 dog owners and 200 cat owners were asked what type of food their pets liked. Here are the results of the survey.

Pet Food Preferences

Preference	Out of 150 Dog Owners	Out of 200 Cat Owners
Human Food Only	75	36
Pet Food Only	45	116
Human and Pet Food	30	48

16. Find the food category that the greatest number of dog owners say is favored by their pets. Write the number in this category as a fraction, as a decimal, and as a percent of the total dog owners surveyed.

17. Find the food category that the greatest number of cat owners say is favored by their pets. Write the number in this category as a fraction, as a decimal, and as a percent of the total cat owners surveyed.

18. Suppose only 100 dog owners were surveyed, with similar results. Estimate how many would have answered in each of the three categories.

19. Suppose 50 cat owners were surveyed, with similar results. Estimate how many would have answered in each of the three categories.

20. Elisa's math test score, with extra credit included, was $\frac{26}{25}$. What percent is this?

21. Suppose 12% of students surveyed said they have tried rock climbing. Estimate how many would say they have tried rock climbing if

   a. 100 students were surveyed

   b. 200 students were surveyed

   c. 150 students were surveyed

22. When surveyed, 78% of pet owners said they live in a town where there is a pooper-scooper law in effect.

   a. How would you express this percent as a decimal?

   b. How would you express this percent as a fraction?

   c. What percent of people surveyed said they do not live in a town with a pooper-scooper law? Explain your reasoning. Express this percent as a decimal and as a fraction.

   d. Can you determine how many people were surveyed? Why or why not?

23. When surveyed, 66% of dog owners who took their dog to obedience school said their dog passed.

   a. What percent of the dog owners said their dogs did not pass?

   b. Write an explanation for a friend about how to solve part (a) and why your solution works.

24. Copy the table below and fill in the missing parts.

Percent	Decimal	Fraction
62%	■	■
■	■	$\frac{4}{9}$
■	1.23	■
■	■	$\frac{12}{15}$
■	2.65	■
■	0.55	■
48%	■	■
■	■	$\frac{12}{10}$

For: Multiple-Choice Skills Practice
Web Code: ama-2454

25. When Diane and Marla got their partner quiz back, their grade was 105% because they got some of the extra credit problems correct.

   a. Write this percent as a decimal and as a fraction.

   b. If each problem on the test had the same point value, how many problems could have been on the test?

Connections

Compare each pair of fractions in Exercises 26–31 using benchmarks or another strategy that makes sense to you. Copy the fractions and insert $<$, $>$, or $=$ to make a true statement.

26. $\frac{7}{10}$ ▪ $\frac{5}{8}$

27. $\frac{11}{12}$ ▪ $\frac{12}{13}$

28. $\frac{12}{15}$ ▪ $\frac{12}{14}$

29. $\frac{3}{8}$ ▪ $\frac{4}{8}$

30. $\frac{3}{5}$ ▪ $\frac{4}{6}$

31. $\frac{4}{3}$ ▪ $\frac{15}{12}$

32. Copy the table below and fill in the missing parts.

Fraction	Mixed Number
$\frac{13}{5}$	▪
▪	$5\frac{2}{7}$
▪	$9\frac{3}{4}$
$\frac{23}{3}$	▪

33. The following percents are a good set of benchmarks to know because they have nice fraction equivalents and some nice decimal equivalents. Copy the table and fill in the missing parts. Use your table until you have learned these relationships.

Percent	10%	$12\frac{1}{2}$%	20%	25%	30%	$33\frac{1}{3}$%	50%	$66\frac{2}{3}$%	75%
Fraction	▪	▪	▪	▪	▪	▪	▪	▪	▪
Decimal	▪	▪	▪	▪	▪	▪	▪	▪	▪

Extensions

In Exercises 34–36, determine what fraction is the correct label for the mark halfway between the two marked values on the number line. Then write the fraction as a percent and as a decimal.

34.

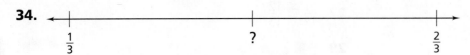

$\frac{1}{3}$? $\frac{2}{3}$

35.

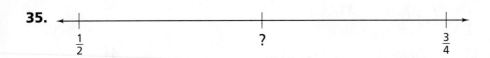

$\frac{1}{2}$? $\frac{3}{4}$

36.

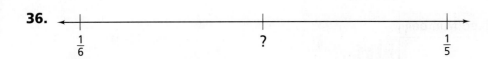

$\frac{1}{6}$? $\frac{1}{5}$

37. What fraction of the square below is shaded? Explain your reasoning.

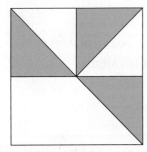

38. In decimal form, what part of the square below is shaded? Explain.

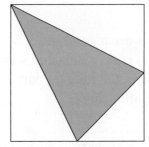

39. What percent of the square below is shaded? Explain.

40. A pet store sells digestible mouthwash for cats. To promote the new product, the store is offering $0.50 off the regular price of $2.00 for an 8-ounce bottle. What is the percent discount on the mouthwash?

In Exercises 41–43, determine what number is the correct label for the place halfway between the two percents marked on the percent bar. Then determine what percent the number represents.

41.

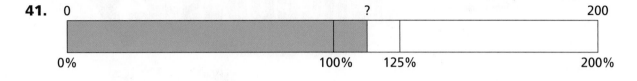

0   ?   200

0%   100% 125%   200%

42.

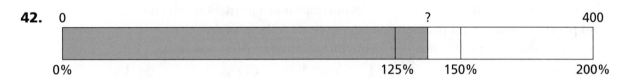

0   ?   400

0%   125% 150%   200%

43.

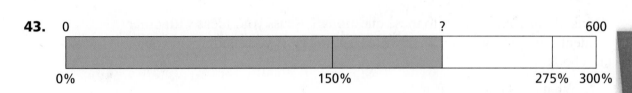

0   ?   600

0%   150%   275% 300%

Extensions

44. A store offers a discount of 30% on all reference books.

    a. If a dictionary costs $12.00 before the discount, what is the amount of the discount?

    b. If a book on insect identification originally costs $15.00, how much will you have to pay for it?

Mathematical Reflections 4

In this investigation, you explored relationships among fractions, decimals, and percents and solved problems using percents to help make comparisons. These questions will help you summarize what you have learned.

Think about your answers to these questions. Discuss your ideas with other students and your teacher. Then write a summary of your findings in your notebook.

1. What does percent mean?

2. a. Describe how you can change a percent to a decimal and to a fraction.

   b. Describe how you can change a fraction to a percent.

   c. Describe how you can change a decimal to a percent.

3. Why are percents useful in making comparisons?

4. Explain how to find what percent one number is of another number. For example, what percent of 200 is 75? Draw a percent bar to help explain your thinking.

Looking Back and Looking Ahead

Working on the problems of this unit extended your knowledge of fractions, decimals, and percents. You learned how

- to relate fractions and decimals to their locations on a number line
- fractions, decimals, and percents are related to each other
- to compare and order fractions and decimals
- to identify equivalent fractions, decimals, and percents

Go Online
PHSchool.com

For: Vocabulary Review Puzzle
Web code: amj-2051

Use Your Understanding: Number Sense

Demonstrate your understanding and skill working with fractions, decimals, and percents by solving the following problems.

1. The diagram shows a puzzle made up of familiar shapes. Find a fraction name and a decimal name for the size of each piece.

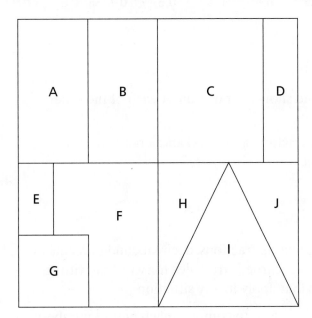

a. What fraction of the puzzle is covered by each piece? Use your measurement estimation skills and reasoning to find each fraction.

b. What decimal represents each part of the puzzle?

2. Jose drew eight cards from a deck of number cards. He was asked to show the position of each number on a number line as a fraction, as a decimal, and as a percent of the distance from zero to one.

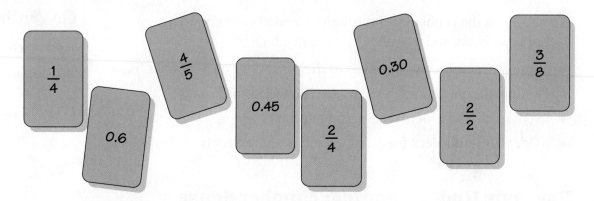

The fraction $\frac{1}{4}$ has already been located on the number line below, along with its corresponding decimal and percent.

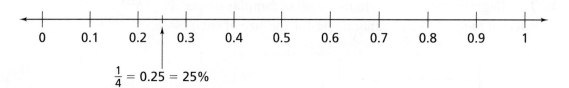

$$\frac{1}{4} = 0.25 = 25\%$$

a. Copy the number line and show the position of each of the other number cards.

b. Label each position as a fraction, a decimal and a percent of the distance from zero to one.

Explain Your Reasoning

You have explored relationships among fractions, decimals, and percents in many different problems. You have learned strategies for working with fractions, decimals, and percents that apply in any situation.

3. Describe a strategy that can be used to compare each pair of numbers.

a. $\frac{5}{8}$ and $\frac{7}{8}$ **b.** $\frac{3}{4}$ and $\frac{3}{5}$ **c.** $\frac{3}{4}$ and $\frac{5}{8}$

d. $\frac{3}{8}$ and $\frac{2}{3}$ **e.** $\frac{3}{4}$ and $\frac{4}{5}$ **f.** $\frac{2}{3}$ and $\frac{5}{8}$

Describe a strategy that can be used to find

4. a fraction equivalent to $\frac{16}{20}$

5. a decimal equivalent to $\frac{16}{20}$

6. a percent for $\frac{16}{20}$

7. a decimal equivalent to 0.18

8. a fraction equivalent to 0.18

9. a percent for 0.18

10. a fraction for 35%

11. a decimal for 3%

Look Ahead

Fractions, decimals, and percents will be used in almost every future unit of *Connected Mathematics.* They are also used in applications of mathematics to problems in science, business, and personal life. You will use them in work on probability, geometry, measurement, and algebra.

In the unit *Bits and Pieces II,* you will learn the operations of addition, subtraction, multiplication, and division of fractions. In *Bits and Pieces III,* you will learn the operations for addition, subtraction, multiplication, and division of decimals and look at additional ways percents are used in the world around us.

English/Spanish Glossary

B

base ten number system The common number system we use. Our number system is based on the number 10 because we have ten fingers with which to group. Each group represents ten of the previous group, so we can write numbers efficiently. By extending the place value system to include places that represent fractions with 10 or powers of 10 in the denominator, we can easily represent very large and very small quantities. Below is a graphic representation of counting in the base ten number system.

sistema numérico de base diez El sistema numérico que usamos habitualmente. Nuestro sistema numérico está basado en el número 10 porque tenemos diez dedos con los cuales agrupar. Cada grupo representa diez del grupo anterior, así podemos escribir números eficazmente. Si extendemos el sistema de valor posicional para incluir lugares que representen fracciones con 10 o con potencias de 10 en el denominador, podemos representar fácilmente cantidades muy grandes o muy pequeñas. Arriba tienes una representación gráfica de cómo contar con el sistema numérico de base diez.

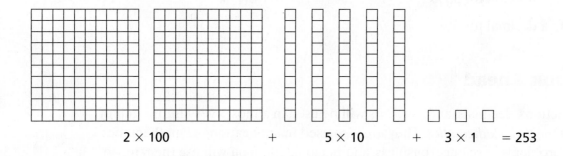

2×100 + 5×10 + 3×1 = 253

benchmark A reference number that can be used to estimate the size of other numbers. For work with fractions, $0, \frac{1}{2}$, and 1 are good benchmarks. We often estimate fractions or decimals with benchmarks because it is easier to do arithmetic with them, and estimates often give enough accuracy for the situation. For example, many fractions and decimals—such as $\frac{37}{50}, \frac{5}{8}$, 0.43, and 0.55—can be thought of as being close to $\frac{1}{2}$. You might say $\frac{5}{8}$ is between $\frac{1}{2}$ and 1 but closer to $\frac{1}{2}$, so you can estimate $\frac{5}{8}$ to be about $\frac{1}{2}$. We also use benchmarks to help compare fractions and decimals. For example, we could say that $\frac{5}{8}$ is greater than 0.43 because $\frac{5}{8}$ is greater than $\frac{1}{2}$ and 0.43 is less than $\frac{1}{2}$.

punto de referencia Un número de comparación que se puede usar para estimar el tamaño de otros números. Para trabajar con fracciones, $0, \frac{1}{2}$ y 1 son buenos puntos de referencia. Por lo general, estimamos fracciones o decimales con puntos de referencia porque nos resulta más fácil hacer cálculos aritméticos con ellos, y las estimaciones suelen ser bastante exactas para la situación. Por ejemplo, muchas fracciones y decimales, como por ejemplo $\frac{37}{50}, \frac{5}{8}$, 0.43 y 0.55, se pueden considerar como cercanas a $\frac{1}{2}$. Se podría decir que $\frac{5}{8}$ está entre $\frac{1}{2}$ y 1, pero más cerca de $\frac{1}{2}$, por lo que se puede estimar que $\frac{5}{8}$ es alrededor de $\frac{1}{2}$ También usamos puntos de referencia para ayudarnos a comparar fracciones y decimales. Por ejemplo, podríamos decir que $\frac{5}{8}$ es mayor que 0.43, porque $\frac{5}{8}$ es mayor que $\frac{1}{2}$ y 0.43 es menor que $\frac{1}{2}$.

decimal A special form of a fraction. Decimals, or decimal fractions, are based on the base ten place-value system. To write numbers as decimals, we use only 10 and powers of 10 as denominators. Writing fractions in this way saves us from writing the denominators because they are understood. When we write $\frac{375}{1,000}$ as a decimal (0.375) the denominator of 1,000 is understood. The digits to the left of the decimal point show whole units. The digits to the right of the decimal point show a portion of a whole unit. The diagram shows the place value for each digit of the number 5,620.301.

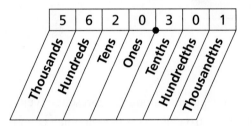

decimal Una forma especial de fracción. Los decimales, o fracciones decimales, se basan en el sistema de valor relativo de base 10. Para escribir números como decimales, usamos solamente 10 y potencias de 10 como denominadores. Escribir fracciones de esta manera nos evita tener que escribir los denominadores, porque están implícitos. Cuando escribimos $\frac{375}{1,000}$ como un decimal, 0.375, se entiende que el denominador es 1,000. Los dígitos que se encuentran a la izquierda del punto decimal muestran unidades enteras, y los dígitos a la derecha del punto decimal muestran una porción de una unidad entera. El diagrama muestra el valor relativo para cada dígito del número 5,620.301.

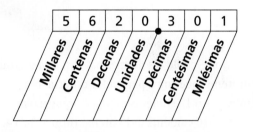

denominator The number written below the line in a fraction. In the fraction $\frac{3}{4}$, 4 is the denominator. In the part-whole interpretation of fractions, the denominator shows the number of equal-size parts into which the whole has been split.

denominador El número escrito debajo de la línea en una fracción. En la fracción $\frac{3}{4}$, 4 es el denominador. En la interpretación de partes y enteros de fracciones, el denominador muestra el número de partes iguales en que fue dividido el entero.

equivalent fractions Fractions that are equal in value, but may have different numerators and denominators. For example, $\frac{2}{3}$ and $\frac{14}{21}$ are equivalent fractions. The shaded part of this rectangle represents both $\frac{2}{3}$ and $\frac{14}{21}$.

fracciones equivalentes Fracciones de igual valor, pero que pueden tener diferentes numeradores y denominadores. Por ejemplo, $\frac{2}{3}$ y $\frac{14}{21}$ son fracciones equivalentes. La parte sombreada de este rectángulo representa tanto $\frac{2}{3}$ como $\frac{14}{21}$.

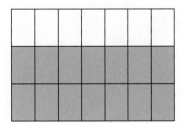

English/Spanish Glossary

(vertical tab, right margin) English/Spanish Glossary

fraction A number (quantity) of the form $\frac{a}{b}$ where *a* and *b* are whole numbers. A fraction can indicate a part of a whole object, set, or measurement unit; a ratio of two quantities; or a division. For the picture below, the fraction $\frac{3}{4}$ shows the part of the rectangle that is shaded. The denominator 4 indicates the number of equal-sized pieces. The numerator 3 indicates the number of pieces that are shaded.

fracción Un número (una cantidad) en forma de $\frac{a}{b}$, donde *a* y *b* son números enteros. Una fracción puede indicar una parte de un objeto, conjunto de objetos enteros, o unidad de la medida; una razón entre dos cantidades; o una división. Para el dibujo de abajo, la fracción $\frac{3}{4}$ muestra la parte del rectángulo que está sombreada. El denominador 4 indica la cantidad de piezas de igual tamaño. El numerador 3 indica la cantidad de piezas que están sombreadas.

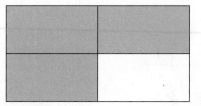

The fraction $\frac{3}{4}$ could also represent three of a group of four items meeting a particular criteria. For example, when 12 students enjoyed a particular activity and 16 students did not, the ratio is 3 to 4. Another example is the amount of pizza each person receives when three pizzas are shared equally among four people ($3 \div 4$ or $\frac{3}{4}$ of a pizza per person).

La fracción $\frac{3}{4}$ también podría representar 3 en un grupo de cuatro elementos que cumplan con un mismo criterio. Por ejemplo, cuando 12 estudiantes participaron en una determinada actividad y 16 estudiantes no lo hicieron, la razón es 3 a 4. Otro ejemplo es la cantidad de pizza que le toca a cada persona cuando se reparten tres pizzas en partes iguales entre cuatro personas ($3 \div 4$ ó $\frac{3}{4}$ de pizza por persona).

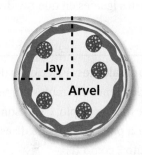

improper fraction A fraction in which the numerator is larger than the denominator. An improper fraction is a fraction that is greater than 1. The fraction $\frac{5}{2}$ is an improper fraction. The fraction $\frac{5}{2}$ means 5 halves and is equivalent to $2\frac{1}{2}$, which is greater than 1.

fracción impropia Una fracción cuyo numerador es mayor que el denominador. Una fracción impropia es una fracción mayor que 1. La fracción $\frac{5}{2}$ es una fracción impropia. La fracción $\frac{5}{2}$ representa 5 mitades y es equivalente a $2\frac{1}{2}$, lo cual es mayor que 1.

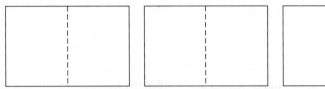

M

mixed number A number that is written with both a whole number and a fraction. A mixed number is the sum of the whole number and the fraction. The number $2\frac{1}{2}$ represents two wholes and one half and can be thought of as $2 + \frac{1}{2}$.

número mixto Un número que se escribe con un número entero y una fracción. Un número mixto es la suma del número entero y la fracción. El número $2\frac{1}{2}$ representa dos enteros y un medio, y se puede considerar como $2 + \frac{1}{2}$.

N

numerator The number written above the line in a fraction. In the fraction $\frac{5}{8}$, 5 is the numerator. When you interpret the fraction $\frac{5}{8}$ as a part of a whole, the numerator represents 5 of 8 equal parts.

numerador El número escrito sobre la línea en una fracción. En la fracción $\frac{5}{8}$, 5 es el numerador. Cuando interpretas la fracción $\frac{5}{8}$ como parte de un entero, el numerador representa 5 de 8 partes iguales.

P

percent "Out of 100." A percent is a special decimal fraction in which the denominator is 100. When we write 68%, we mean 68 out of 100, $\frac{68}{100}$, or 0.68. We write the percent sign (%) after a number to indicate percent. The shaded part of this square is 68%.

porcentaje "La parte de 100". Un porcentaje es una fracción decimal especial en la que el denominador es 100. Cuando escribimos 68%, queremos decir 68 de 100, $\frac{68}{100}$ ó 0.68. Para indicar porcentaje escribimos el signo correspondiente (%) después del número. La parte sombreada de este cuadrado es 68%.

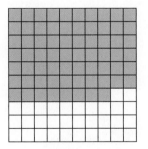

English/Spanish Glossary

R

ratio A number, often expressed as a fraction, used to make comparisons between two quantities. Ratios may also be expressed as equivalent decimals or percents. $\frac{3}{5}$, 0.6, and 60% are all ratios. A phrase such as "120 out of 200" is another way to represent a ratio. Here are three ways to show the same ratio:

$$\frac{3}{5} \qquad 3 \text{ to } 5 \qquad 3 : 5$$

razón Un número, a menudo expresado como fracción, que se usa para hacer comparaciones entre dos cantidades. Las razones también se pueden expresar como decimales equivalentes o porcentajes. $\frac{3}{5}$, 0.6, y 60% también son razones. Una frase como "120 de 200" es otra forma de representar una razón. Aquí están tres maneras de demostrar la misma razón:

$$\frac{3}{5} \qquad 3 \text{ a } 5 \qquad 3 : 5$$

rational number A number that can be written as a quotient of two positive or negative numbers. You are familiar with positive rational numbers like $\frac{3}{4}$, $\frac{107}{5}$, and $3\left(\frac{3}{1}\right)$. Some examples of the negative rational numbers you will see in the future are $^-3$, $\frac{^-2}{5}$, and $^-20$. Both positive and negative rational numbers can be used to represent real-life situations. For example, temperatures or yardage during a football game can be positive, negative, or 0. There are other numbers, such as pi, that are *not* rational numbers.

número racional Número que se puede expresar como cociente de dos números enteros positivos o negativos. Tú ya conoces los números racionales positivos, como $\frac{3}{4}$, $\frac{107}{5}$, y $3\left(\frac{3}{1}\right)$. Algunos ejemplos de números racionales negativos que verás en el futuro son $^-3$, $\frac{^-2}{5}$, y $^-20$. Tanto los números racionales positivos como negativos se pueden usar para representar situaciones de la vida real. Por ejemplo, las temperaturas o las medidas en yardas en un partido de fútbol americano pueden ser positivas, negativas o 0. Hay otros números, como pi, que no son números racionales.

U

unit fraction A fraction with a numerator of 1. In the unit fraction $\frac{1}{13}$, the denominator 13 indicates the number of equal-size parts into which the whole has been split. The fraction represents the quantity of one of those parts.

fracción de unidad Una fracción con numerador 1. En la fracción de unidad $\frac{1}{13}$, el denominador 13 indica la cantidad de partes iguales en las que se ha dividido el entero, y que la fracción representa uno de esas partes.

Academic Vocabulary

The following terms are important to your understanding of the mathematics in this unit. Knowing and using these words will help you in thinking, reasoning, representing, communicating your ideas, and making connections across ideas. When these words make sense to you, the investigations and problems will make more sense as well.

C

compare To tell or show how two things are alike and different.

related terms: analyze, relate

Sample: Compare the fractions $\frac{2}{3}$ and $\frac{3}{8}$.

I set the fractions strips representing $\frac{2}{3}$ and $\frac{3}{8}$ next to each other to see which fraction was greater. $\frac{2}{3} > \frac{3}{8}$

comparar Decir o mostrar en qué se parecen y en qué son diferentes dos cosas.

términos relacionados: analizar, relacionar

Ejemplo: Compara las fracciones $\frac{2}{3}$ y $\frac{3}{8}$.

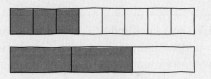

Coloco las tiras de fracciones que representan $\frac{2}{3}$ y $\frac{3}{8}$ una junto a la otra para ver cuál fracción es mayor. $\frac{2}{3} > \frac{3}{8}$

D

describe To explain or tell in detail. A written description can contain facts and other information needed to communicate your answer. A diagram or a graph may also be included.

related terms: express, explain, illustrate

Sample: Describe in writing or with pictures how $\frac{5}{4}$ compares to $1\frac{1}{4}$.

I can use fraction strips divided into fourths to show that $1\frac{1}{4}$ is equal to $\frac{5}{4}$.

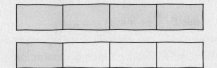

I can also compare using division. 5 divided by 4 is 1 remainder 1. So $\frac{5}{4}$ is the same as $1\frac{1}{4}$.

describir Explicar o decir con detalle. Una descripción escrita puede contener hechos y otra información necesaria para comunicar tu respuesta. También se puede incluir un diagrama o una gráfica.

términos relacionados: expresar, explicar, ilustrar

Ejemplo: Describe por escrito o con imágenes cómo $\frac{5}{4}$ se compara con $1\frac{1}{4}$.

Puedo usar tiras de fracciones divididas en cuartos para mostrar que $1\frac{1}{4}$ es igual a $\frac{5}{4}$.

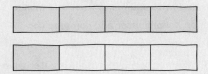

También puedo comparar usando la división. 5 dividido entre 4 es 1 con un residuo de 1. Así, $\frac{5}{4}$ es lo mismo que $1\frac{1}{4}$.

estimate To find an approximate answer that is relatively close to an exact amount.

related terms: approximate, guess

Sample: Estimate and mark where the number 2 should be on the number line below. Explain.

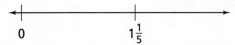

0                    $1\frac{1}{5}$

Since $1\frac{1}{5}$ is the same as $\frac{6}{5}$, I divided the space between 0 and $1\frac{1}{5}$ into six parts. This gives me an idea of the length of $\frac{1}{5}$.

0                $1\frac{1}{5}$ 2

Then I added 4 marks after $1\frac{1}{5}$ to estimate where $1\frac{5}{5}$, or 2, should be on the number line.

estimar Hallar una respuesta aproximada que esté relativamente cerca de una cantidad exacta.

términos relacionados: aproximar, conjeturar

Ejemplo: Estima y marca dónde debería estar el número 2 en la recta numérica que sigue. Explica tu respuesta.

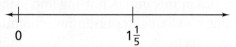

0                    $1\frac{1}{5}$

Puesto que $1\frac{1}{5}$ es lo mismo que $\frac{6}{5}$, divido el espacio entre 0 y $1\frac{1}{5}$ en cinco partes. Esto me da una idea de la longitud de $\frac{1}{5}$.

0                $1\frac{1}{5}$ 2

Luego agrego 4 marcas después de $1\frac{1}{5}$ para estimar donde debería estar $1\frac{5}{5}$, ó 2, en la recta numérica.

---

explain To give facts and details that make an idea easier to understand. Explaining can involve a written summary supported by a diagram, chart, table, or a combination of these.

related terms: analyze, clarify, describe, justify, tell

Sample: Explain why $\frac{9}{10}$ is greater than $\frac{7}{8}$.

I can write the fractions in decimal form and compare digits.

$\frac{9}{10}$	0.900
$\frac{7}{8}$	0.875

Because 9 in the tenths place is greater than 8, $\frac{9}{10}$ is greater than $\frac{7}{8}$.

I can also write equivalent fractions with a common denominator and compare the numerators. Since $\frac{9}{10}$ is equivalent to $\frac{36}{40}$ and $\frac{7}{8}$ is equivalent to $\frac{35}{40}$, and 36 is greater than 35, $\frac{9}{10}$ is greater than $\frac{7}{8}$.

explicar Dar hechos y detalles que hacen que una idea sea más fácil de comprender. Explicar puede implicar un resumen escrito apoyado por hechos, un diagrama, una gráfica, una tabla o una combinación de éstos.

términos relacionados: analizar, aclarar, describir, justificar, decir

Ejemplo: Explica por qué $\frac{9}{10}$ es mayor que $\frac{7}{8}$.

Puedo escribir las fracciones en forma decimal y comparar los dígitos.

$\frac{9}{10}$	0.900
$\frac{7}{8}$	0.875

Puesto que 9 en el lugar de los décimos es mayor que 8, $\frac{9}{10}$ es mayor que $\frac{7}{8}$.

También puedo escribir fracciones equivalentes con un común denominador y comparar los numeradores. Puesto que $\frac{9}{10}$ es equivalente a $\frac{36}{40}$ y $\frac{7}{8}$ es equivalente a $\frac{35}{40}$ y 36 es mayor que 35, $\frac{9}{10}$ es mayor que $\frac{7}{8}$.

Index

Acting it out, 7, 21, 35–36, 38
  ACE, 12–17, 28–29, 33

Algebra
  analyze 5
  denominator 6, 7, 17, 18,
    23, 38, 39
  divisor 15
  equivalent 21
  factor 15
  greatest common factor 32

Analyze 5

Area model
  ACE, 47–48, 66
  for decimals, 36–38, 40–41, 69
  for fractions, 36–38, 40–41, 69,
    73–76
  for percents, 76

Bar graph 16

Benchmarks
  ACE, 29, 49, 61, 65
  decimal, 4, 41–43, 72
  fractional, 4, 23–24, 41–43, 56,
    72
  percents, 4, 65

Check for reasonableness, 8, 24,
  42
  ACE, 12–13, 53

Comparing decimals, 38–40, 42,
  45–46, 57, 59–60
  ACE, 48, 50, 63

Comparing fractions, 7, 10–11, 21,
  24–25, 38–40, 42, 57, 59–60,
  70
  ACE, 12–13, 17, 28–30, 33, 50,
    63, 65–66
  to benchmarks, 4, 23–24, 29,
    41–43, 49, 56, 61, 65

Comparing percents, 57–60
  ACE, 63, 67

Concrete model, *see* **Model**

Data 61

Decimals
  ACE, 47–52, 61–67
  approximating, 42–43
  area model and, 36–38, 40–41,
    69

  as benchmarks, 4, 41–43, 49, 72
  comparing, 38–40, 42, 45–46,
    57, 59–60
  equivalent, 4, 38–42, 44, 58–60
  estimation with, 49
  and fraction strip model, 35–36
  fractions and, 4, 35–46, 53,
    59–60, 71
  on a hundredths grid, 37–39,
    40–41
  ordering, 40, 42, 45–46
  percents and, 4, 54, 58–60, 71
  place value and, 39–40, 45–46,
    73
  on a tenths grid, 36, 38

Denominator, 6, 8, 17, 18, 39, 73

Discounts, 66–67

Divisibility, 15

Divisor 15

Drawing a diagram, 20, 28, 52

Drawing a picture, 47–48, 50–51

Equivalent fractions 21

Equivalent representations
  decimals, 4, 38–42, 44, 47–51,
    58–60, 62–66
  fractions, 4, 6–7, 10–11, 12, 15,
    17, 19–23, 27, 28–29, 31,
    38–42, 44, 47–51, 58–60,
    62–66, 73
  percents, 4, 58–66
  whole numbers, 6

Estimation
  ACE, 12-13, 16, 32, 49, 61, 63
  with decimals, 49
  with fractions, 8–9, 12–13, 16,
    24, 32
  with percents, 61, 63

Factor 15

Fraction, word origin, 3

Fractions
  ACE, 12–17, 28–33, 47–52,
    61–67
  approximations, 42–43
  area model for, 36–38, 40–41,
    69, 73–76
  as benchmarks, 4, 23–24, 41–43,

    56, 73
  comparing, 7, 10–11, 21, 24–25,
    38–40, 42, 57, 59–60, 70
  decimals and, 4, 35–46, 53,
    59–60, 71
  denominator and, 6, 8, 17, 18,
    39, 72–73, 75
  divisibility and, 15
  early use of, 3, 23
  equivalent, 4, 6–7, 10–11,
    19–23, 27, 38–42, 44, 58–60,
    73
  estimation with, 8–9, 12–13, 16,
    24, 32
  and fraction strip model, 7, 18,
    21, 35–36, 38
  fundraising and, 5–11, 18
  greater than one, 10–11, 25–27
  on a hundredths grid, 37–39,
    40–41, 47–48
  improper, 26, 28–33, 75
  mixed numbers and, 25–27,
    28–33, 65, 75
  numerator and, 6, 8, 17, 18, 33,
    73–75
  on a number line, 22–23, 25–26,
    41, 69–70
  ordering, 10, 22, 24–25, 40, 42
  percent and, 4, 54, 59–60, 71
  and place value, 39–40
  of regions, 4, 5–11, 36–38,
    40–41, 73–76
  symbolic form, 6
  on a tenths grid, 36, 38
  unit, 23, 33, 76
  of a whole, 4, 5–11, 12–17, 18
  and whole numbers, 6

Fraction strip model
  ACE, 12–17, 28–33
  for decimals, 35–36
  for fractions, 7, 18, 21, 35–36, 38
  using, 7, 12–17, 21, 28–29, 33,
    35–36, 38

Greatest common factor 32

Hundredths grid, 37–39, 40–41,
  72, 76
  ACE, 47–48
  using, 37–39, 40–41, 47–48, 52,
    72, 76

Acknowledgments

Team Credits

The people who made up the **Connected Mathematics2** team—representing editorial, editorial services, design services, and production services—are listed below. Bold type denotes core team members.

Leora Adler, Judith Buice, Kerry Cashman, Patrick Culleton, Sheila DeFazio, Richard Heater, **Barbara Hollingdale, Jayne Holman,** Karen Holtzman, **Etta Jacobs,** Christine Lee, Carolyn Lock, Cathie Maglio, **Dotti Marshall,** Rich McMahon, Eve Melnechuk, Kristin Mingrone, Terri Mitchell, **Marsha Novak,** Irene Rubin, Donna Russo, Robin Samper, Siri Schwartzman, **Nancy Smith,** Emily Soltanoff, **Mark Tricca,** Paula Vergith, Roberta Warshaw, Helen Young

Additional Credits

Diana Bonfilio, Mairead Reddin, Michael Torocsik

Illustration

Michelle Barbera: 8, 14

Technical Illustration

WestWords, Inc.

Cover Design

9 Surf Studios

Photos

2 t, Peter Beck/Corbis; **2 b,** Dave King/Dorling Kindersley; **3 t,** NASA; **3 b,** Eastcott Momatiuk/Getty Images, Inc.; **5,** Richard Haynes; **6,** Richard Haynes; **16,** Colin Keates/Dorling Kindersley; **19,** Tom Stewart/Corbis; **20,** Richard Haynes; **25,** Richard Haynes; **26 both,** Richard Haynes; **28,** Russ Lappa; **35 all,** Russ Lappa; **41,** Richard Haynes; **43,** AP/Wide World Photos/ J. Pat Carter; **44,** Richard Haynes; **49,** Peter Beck/Corbis; **51,** SW Production/Index Stock Imagery, Inc.; **52,** Richard Haynes; **55,** Rocky Widner/NBAE/Getty Images, Inc.; **58,** Dave King/Dorling Kindersley; **61,** Ron Kimball Stock; **63,** Don Mason/Corbis; **64,** Frank Siteman/Getty Images, Inc.; **67,** Russ Lappa

Note: Every effort has been made to locate the copyright owner of the material reprinted in this book. Omissions brought to our attention will be corrected in subsequent editions.

Shapes and Designs

Two-Dimensional Geometry

Glenda Lappan

James T. Fey

William M. Fitzgerald

Susan N. Friel

Elizabeth Difanis Phillips

PEARSON

Boston, Massachusetts · Glenview, Illinois · Shoreview, Minnesota · Upper Saddle River, New Jersey

Shapes and Designs

Two-Dimensional Geometry

What property of a hexagon makes it a good shape for the cells of a honeycomb?

Why do some shapes occur more often than other shapes in art, rug, and quilt designs?

Why are braces on towers, roofs, and bridges in the shape of triangles and not rectangles or pentagons?

The world is filled with shapes and designs. Your clothes, your home, the games you play, and the tools you work with are built on frames of geometric shapes and decorated with an endless variety of designs. If you look closely, you can even find shapes and designs in the animals and plants around you.

Builders and designers can imagine many different shapes and patterns.

Frank O. Gehry used unique shapes in the design of the Massachusetts Institute of Technology's Stata Center shown below. But there are some simple shapes (triangles, rectangles, circles, and squares) that they use again and again. In this unit, you will discover properties of geometric figures that make them attractive for designs and useful for structures.

Mathematical Highlights

Two-Dimensional Geometry

In *Shapes and Designs*, you will explore important properties of polygons.

You will learn how to

- Identify some important properties of polygons
- Recognize polygonal shapes both in and out of the classroom
- Investigate reflection and rotation symmetries of a shape
- Estimate the measures of angles by comparing them to a right angle or other benchmark angles
- Use an angle ruler to measure an angle
- Explore properties of parallel lines
- Find patterns that help you determine the sum of the interior angle measures of any polygon
- Find which polygons fit together to cover a flat surface and understand why they fit together
- Explain which properties of triangles make them a stable building unit
- Find that the sum of two side lengths of a triangle is greater than the third side length
- Find that the sum of three side lengths of a quadrilateral is greater than the fourth side length
- Draw or sketch polygons with certain properties
- Reason about and solve problems involving shapes

As you work on problems in this unit, ask yourself questions about situations that involve shapes.

What kinds of shapes/polygons will cover a flat surface?

What do these shapes have in common?

How do simple polygons work together to make more complex shapes?

What kinds of polygons are used in buildings and art?

How can angle measures be estimated?

How much accuracy is needed in measuring angles?

Unit Project

What I Know About Shapes and Designs

As you work in this unit, you will be asked to think about the characteristics of different shapes. You will determine how unusual a shape can be and still be a triangle, quadrilateral, pentagon, or hexagon. You will also be asked to think about the relationships among these shapes. It is these characteristics of shapes and the relationships among them that affect the designs you see in your world.

One of the ways you will be asked to demonstrate your understanding of the mathematics in this unit is through a final project. At the end of this unit, you will use what you have learned to create a project. Your project could be a book, a poster, a report, a mobile, a movie, or a slide show.

You can start preparing your project now. Make a special "shapes section" in your notebook, where you can collect information about

- The characteristics of triangles, squares, rectangles, parallelograms, quadrilaterals, pentagons, hexagons, and octagons
- The relationships among these shapes
- Examples of places where these shapes can be found in the world

After each investigation, record all the new information you have learned about shapes. Use as many of the new vocabulary words as you can. As you work through this unit, look for examples of the shapes being used in many ways. Cut out examples from magazines and newspapers. Draw pictures of shapes you see around you. You could use an envelope for collecting and storing your examples.

Use the information you have collected, plus what you learned from this unit, to prepare your final project. Your project should include the following:

- All the facts you know about the relations among the sides of polygons. Consider properties of all polygons and properties of special polygons, such as squares, rectangles, and other parallelograms.
- All the facts you know about the relations among angles of polygons. Again, consider properties of all polygons and properties of special polygons.

Bees and Polygons

Honeybees build nests in the wild called *hives*. About 60,000 bees live in a hive. Bees are fairly small insects, but packing a hive with 60,000 bees and their honey is tricky.

Bees store their honey in a honeycomb, which is filled with tubes. An interesting pattern appears on the face of a honeycomb. It is covered with a design of identical six-sided shapes that fit together like tiles on a floor.

You can also find many different shapes in art, architecture, and nature.

What shapes can you identify in Auguste Herbin's painting below?

In this unit, you will investigate properties that make two-dimensional shapes useful. The unit will focus on *polygons.* First, let's review some basic concepts. A line is a familiar object. In mathematics, *line* means a straight line that has no end in either direction. You can use arrows to show that a line has no ends. A **line segment,** or *segment,* consists of two points of a line and all the points between these two points.

Line   **Line Segment**

Getting Ready for **Problem**

A *polygon* is a group of line segments put together in a special way. For example, some of the shapes below are polygons and some are not.

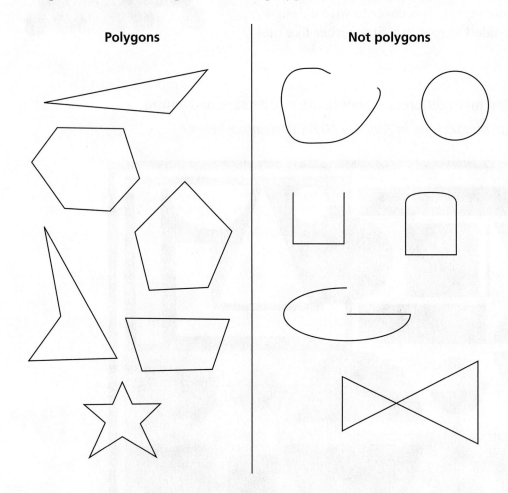

Polygons   **Not polygons**

In order to be a polygon, what properties does a shape need to have?
Draw a polygon that is different from the ones above.
Then draw a shape that is not a polygon.

The line segments in polygons are called **sides.** The points where two sides of a polygon meet are called **vertices.** Polygons have special names based on the number of sides and angles they have. For example, a polygon with six sides and six angles is called a *hexagon*. The table below shows the names of some common polygons.

Common Polygons	
Number of Sides and Angles	**Polygon Name**
3	triangle
4	quadrilateral
5	pentagon
6	hexagon
7	heptagon
8	octagon
9	nonagon
10	decagon
12	dodecagon

You can label a polygon by using a single letter or numeral for the entire shape or by marking each corner, or vertex, with a different letter. To refer to a polygon with lettered vertices, start with any letter and list the letters in order as you move around the polygon in one direction. For the rectangle below, you could say rectangle *CDAB* or rectangle *DCBA* (but not rectangle *ACDB*).

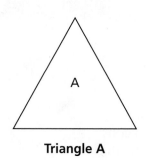

Triangle A

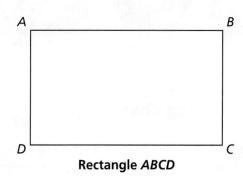

Rectangle *ABCD*

Sorting Shapes

Below are a variety of polygons. Many of these polygons have common properties.

Shapes Set

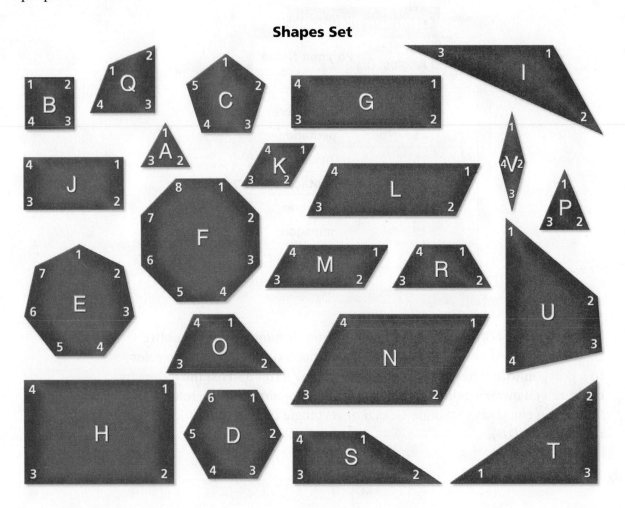

 **Sorting Shapes**

A. Sort the polygons in the Shapes Set into groups so that the polygons in each group have one or more properties in common. Describe the properties the polygons have in common and give the letters of the polygons in each group.

B. Take all the triangles and sort them into two or more groups. Describe the properties you used to form the groups and give the letters of the triangles in each group.

C. Take all the quadrilaterals and sort them into two or more groups. Describe the properties you used to form the groups and give the letters of the quadrilaterals in each group.

D. Rose put Shapes R, O, and S into the same group. What properties do these polygons have in common? Would Shape U belong to this group? Explain.

ACE Homework starts on page 17.

In Problem 1.1, you may have sorted the triangles according to the number of equal-length sides they have. An **equilateral triangle** has three sides the same length. An **isosceles triangle** has two sides the same length. A **scalene triangle** has no sides the same length. (The small marks on the sides of each triangle indicate sides that are the same length.)

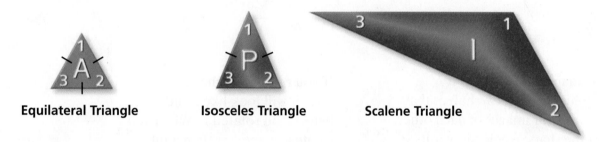

Equilateral Triangle   **Isosceles Triangle**   **Scalene Triangle**

You may have sorted the quadrilaterals according to the number of sides with the same length or the number of angles of the same measure. A **square** is a quadrilateral with four sides the same length and four angles of the same measure. A **rectangle** is a quadrilateral with opposite sides the same length and four angles of the same measure. A **parallelogram** is a quadrilateral with opposite sides the same length and opposite angles of the same measure. (Note: angles 1 and 3 and angles 2 and 4 are opposite angles in the quadrilaterals below.) You will be seeing these shapes throughout this unit.

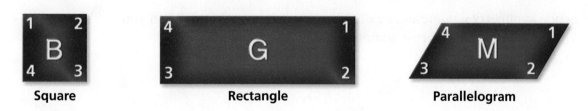

Square   **Rectangle**   **Parallelogram**

1.2 Symmetries of Shapes

As you study the polygons in this unit, look for ways that different combinations of side lengths and angle sizes give different shapes. In particular, look for shapes that have attractive *symmetries*.

Reflection Symmetry

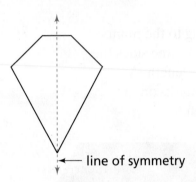

← line of symmetry

Rotation Symmetry

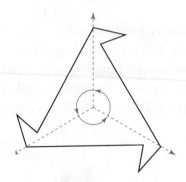

A shape with **reflection symmetry** has two halves that are mirror images of each other. If the shape is folded over its **line of symmetry,** the two halves of the shape match exactly.

If you rotate any shape a full turn, it will look like it did before you rotated it. When you rotate a shape *less* than a full turn about its center point and it looks exactly as it did before it was rotated, it has **rotation symmetry.**

In the polygon shown above, there are three places in the rotation where the polygon will look exactly the same as when you started.

Reflection symmetry is sometimes called *line* or *mirror symmetry*. (Can you see why?) Rotation symmetry is sometimes called *turn symmetry*.

- Which of the following shapes have reflection symmetry?
- Which of the following shapes have rotation symmetry?

Problem Symmetry

Use the Shapes Set from Problem 1.1.

A. Look at the triangles.

   1. Which triangles have reflection symmetry? Trace these triangles and draw all the lines of symmetry.

   2. Which triangles have rotation symmetry?

   3. Which triangles have no symmetries?

B. Look at the quadrilaterals.

   1. Which quadrilaterals have reflection symmetry? Trace these quadrilaterals and draw all the lines of symmetry.

   2. Which quadrilaterals have rotation symmetry?

   3. Which quadrilaterals have no symmetries?

C. Look at the remaining polygons (the polygons that are not triangles or quadrilaterals). What is special about these shapes?

D. Find shapes with symmetry in your classroom. Sketch each shape and describe its symmetries.

ACE Homework starts on page 17.

A regular polygon is a polygon in which all the sides are the same length and all the angles have the same measure. In an **irregular polygon,** all sides are *not* the same length or all the angles are *not* the same measure. The shapes below are regular polygons.

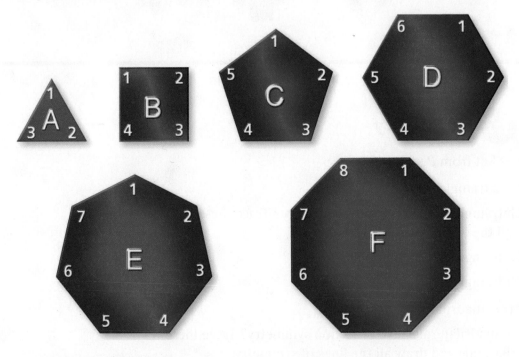

You can find an interesting pattern of regular hexagons on the face of a honeycomb. The hexagons fit together like tiles on a floor.

Tiling means covering a flat surface with shapes that fit together without any gaps or overlaps.

Which regular polygons can be used to tile a surface?

Problem 1.3   Tiling With Regular Polygons

Use Shapes A–F from your Shapes Set or cutouts of those shapes. As you work, try to figure out why some shapes cover a flat surface, while others do not.

A. 1. First, form tile patterns with several copies of the *same* polygon. Try each of the regular polygons. Sketch your tilings.

   2. Which regular polygons fit together, without gaps or overlaps, to cover a flat surface?

B. Next, form tile patterns using combinations of two or more different shapes. Sketch your tilings.

C. The following tiling may be one that you found. Look at a point where the vertices of the polygons meet.

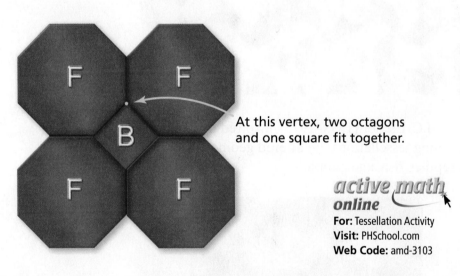

At this vertex, two octagons and one square fit together.

   1. Look back at each tiling you made. Find a point on the tiling where the vertices of the polygons meet.

   2. Describe exactly which polygons fit around this point and the pattern of how they fit together.

   3. Is this pattern the same for all other points where the vertices of the polygons meet in this tiling?

ACE **Homework starts on page 17.**

Investigation 1 Bees and Polygons   **15**

Tilings are also called *tessellations*. Artists, designers, and mathematicians have been interested in tessellations for centuries. The Greek mathematician and inventor Archimedes (c. 287–212 B.C.) studied the properties of regular polygons that tiled the plane. Beginning in the middle of the eighth century, Moorish artists used tessellating patterns extensively in their work.

The Dutch artist M.C. Escher (1898–1972), inspired by Moorish designs, spent his life creating tessellations. He altered geometric tessellating shapes to make birds, reptiles, fish, and people.

Go Online
PHSchool.com

For: Information about tessellations
Web Code: ame-9031

Applications

1. Tell whether each shape is a polygon. If it is, tell how many sides it has.

   a.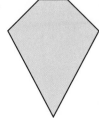

   b.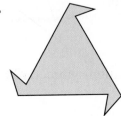

2. Tell whether each figure is a polygon. Explain how you know.

   a.  **b.** 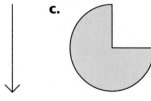 **c.**  **d.**

3. Examine Shapes L, R, and N from the Shapes Set (or look at the drawings from Problem 1.1). How are these polygons alike? How are they different?

4. Examine Shapes A, I, P, and T from the Shapes Set (or look at the drawings from Problem 1.1). How are these polygons alike? How are they different?

5. Tell whether each statement is *true* or *false.* Justify your answers.

   a. All squares are rectangles.

   b. All rectangles are parallelograms.

   c. All rectangles are squares.

   d. All parallelograms are rectangles.

6. a. Copy the shapes below. Draw all the lines of symmetry.

Homework
Help **O**nline
PHSchool.com
For: Help with Exercise 6
Web Code: ame-3106

Shape 1   Shape 2

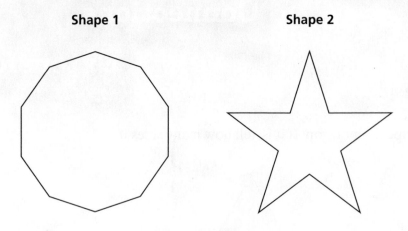

b. Do these shapes have rotation symmetry? Explain.

7. Half of the figure below is hidden. The vertical line is a line of symmetry for the complete figure. Copy the part of the figure shown. Then draw the missing half.

8. Below is a rug design from the Southwest United States.

a. Name some of the polygons in the rug.

b. Describe the symmetries of the design.

9. Here are three state flags.

Arizona

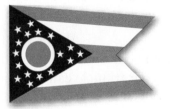

Ohio

New Mexico

  a. Describe the lines of symmetry in each whole flag.

  b. Do any of the shapes or designs within the flags have rotation symmetry? If so, which ones?

  c. Design your own flag. Your flag should have at least one line of symmetry. Your flag should also include three shapes that have rotation symmetry. List the shapes in your flag that have rotation symmetry.

For Exercises 10 and 11, use these quilt patterns.

Pattern A

Pattern B

10. Name some of the polygons in each quilt pattern.

11. Describe the symmetries of each quilt pattern.

12. a. Does a circle have any symmetries? If so, explain and show some examples.

    b. Can you make a tiling pattern with circles? If so, explain and show some examples.

13. Choose a rectangle from your Shapes Set, or draw your own. Find two ways that copies of your rectangle can be used to tile a surface. Sketch your tilings.

Investigation 1 Bees and Polygons   **19**

14. Choose a parallelogram from your Shapes Set, or draw your own. Find two ways that copies of your parallelogram can be used to tile a surface. Sketch your tilings.

15. Choose a scalene triangle from your Shapes Set, or draw your own. Find two ways that copies of your triangle can be used to tile a surface. Sketch your tilings.

16. Find three examples of tilings in your school, home, or community. Describe the patterns and make a sketch of each.

Connections

For each fraction, find two equivalent fractions. One fraction should have a denominator less than the one given. The other fraction should have a denominator greater than the one given.

17. $\frac{4}{12}$ **18.** $\frac{9}{15}$ **19.** $\frac{15}{35}$ **20.** $\frac{20}{12}$

Copy the fractions and insert $<$, $>$, or $=$ to make a true statement.

21. $\frac{5}{12}$ ■ $\frac{9}{12}$ **22.** $\frac{15}{35}$ ■ $\frac{12}{20}$ **23.** $\frac{7}{13}$ ■ $\frac{20}{41}$ **24.** $\frac{45}{36}$ ■ $\frac{35}{28}$

Go Online
PHSchool.com
For: Multiple-Choice Skills Practice
Web Code: ama-3154

25. Multiple Choice Choose the correct statement.

A. $\frac{5}{6} = \frac{11}{360}$ **B.** $\frac{3}{4} = \frac{300}{360}$ **C.** $\frac{1}{4} = \frac{90}{360}$ **D.** $\frac{3}{36} = \frac{33}{360}$

Alberto's little sister Marissa decides to take a ride on a merry-go-round. It is shaped like the one shown. Marissa's starting point is also shown.

26. Multiple Choice Choose the point where Marissa will be after the ride completes $\frac{4}{8}$ of a full turn.

F. point C **G.** point D

H. point E **J.** point G

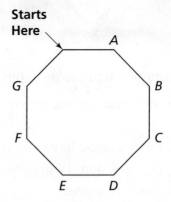

Starts Here

27. Multiple Choice Where will Marissa be after the ride completes $\frac{1}{2}$ of a full turn?

A. point B **B.** point C

C. point D **D.** point F

28. Find all the possible rectangles with whole number side lengths that can be made with the given number of identical square tiles. Give the dimensions of each rectangle.

    a. 30 square tiles   **b.** 24 square tiles

    c. 36 square tiles   **d.** 17 square tiles

    e. How are the dimensions of the rectangles for a given number of square tiles related to factor pairs of the number?

    f. Which of the rectangles you made were squares? Give the dimensions of the squares you made.

Extensions

For Exercises 29–33, one diagonal of each quadrilateral has been drawn. Complete parts (a) and (b) for each quadrilateral.

    a. Is the given diagonal a line of symmetry? Why or why not?

    b. Does the figure have any other lines of symmetry? If so, copy the figure and sketch the symmetry lines.

29. 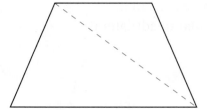   **30.**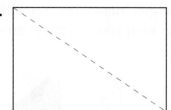

31. 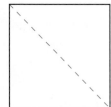   **32.**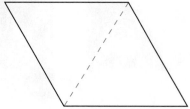

33.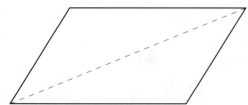

For Exercises 34 and 35, use the two given shapes to form a tiling pattern. Trace and cut out the shapes, or use shapes from your Shapes Set. Sketch your tilings.

34.

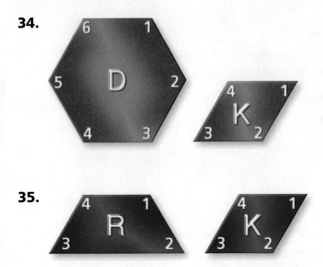

35.

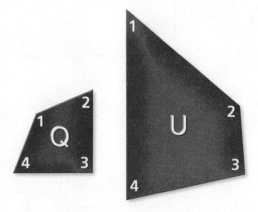

36. Choose an irregular quadrilateral from your Shapes Set, such as Q or U, or draw your own. Cut out several copies of your quadrilateral. See whether you can use the copies to tile a surface. Sketch your findings. Test other irregular quadrilaterals to see if they can be used to tile a surface. Summarize what you find about using irregular quadrilaterals to tile a surface.

Mathematical Reflections 1

In this investigation, you explored some properties of polygons. You saw that some polygons have reflection or rotation symmetry, while others have no symmetries. You also discovered that some polygons fit together like tiles to cover a flat surface, while others do not. These questions will help you summarize what you have learned.

Think about your answers to these questions. Discuss your ideas with other students and your teacher. Then write a summary of your findings in your notebook.

1. a. What does it mean for a figure to have reflection symmetry? Give an example.

   b. What does it mean for a figure to have rotation symmetry? Give an example.

2. a. Using one shape at a time, which regular polygons will fit together to tile a surface? Which regular polygons cannot tile a surface?

   b. Why do you think that some shapes make tilings and some do not?

Unit Project What's Next?

What information about shapes can you add to your *Shapes and Designs* project?

Polygons and Angles

Both the regular decagon and the five-point star below have ten sides of equal length.

What makes these two polygons different?

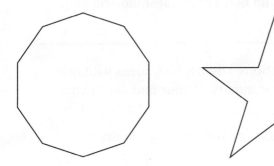

2.1 Understanding Angles

The workers in a honeybee hive fly great distances to find flowers with nectar. They use nectar to make honey. When a bee finds a good patch of flowers, it returns to the hive and communicates the location of the flowers to the other bees.

Did You Know?

Honeybees live in colonies. Each honeybee colony has a single queen and thousands of worker bees. The worker bees find flowers to get nectar. The nectar is used to make honey. Worker bees build the honeycomb and keep the beehive clean. They feed and groom the queen bee and take care of the baby bees. They also guard the hive against intruders.

Scientific observation has shown that honeybees have an amazing method for giving directions to flowers: they perform a lively dance!

For: Information about honeybees
Web Code: ame-9031

During the direction dance, a honeybee moves in a combination of squiggly paths and half circles. The squiggly paths in the dance indicate the direction of the flowers. If the flowers are in the direction of the sun, the middle path of the bee's dance is straight up and down.

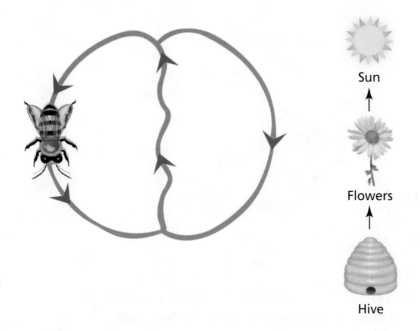

If the flowers are not in the direction of the sun, the direction of the honeybee's dance is tilted. The angle of the tilt is the same as the angle formed by the sun, the hive, and the flowers.

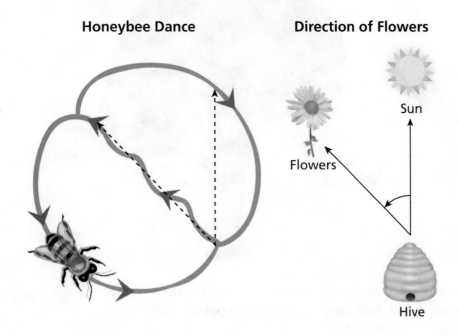

Honeybee Dance   **Direction of Flowers**

The bee dance illustrates one way to think about an angle—as a *turn*. When the honeybee dances in a tilted direction, she is telling the other bees how far to *turn* from the sun to find the flowers.

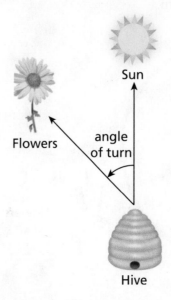

You can also think of an angle as the sides of a *wedge*, like the cut sides of a slice of pizza. Or, you can think of an angle as a point with two sides extending from the point, like branches on a tree.

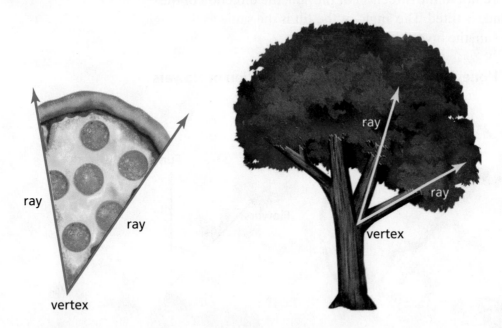

In all of these examples, since each side extends from a point in only one direction, the sides are called **half lines** or **rays.** The point is called the **vertex** of the angle.

In many figures, like in the triangle below, you will see angles without the arrows to indicate the rays.

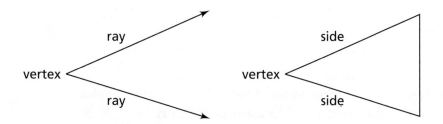

Getting Ready for Problem 2.1

Think of some examples of angles that can be found in your school, your home, in other buildings, or outside. Give at least one example of each type of angle described.

- An angle that occurs as the result of a *turning motion,* such as the opening of a door
- An angle that occurs as a *wedge,* such as a slice of pizza
- An angle that occurs as *two rays with a common vertex,* such as the branches on a tree

How could you compare the size of these angles?

There are several ways to describe the size of an angle. The most common way uses units called **degrees.** An angle with measure 1 degree (also written 1°) is a very small turn, or a very narrow wedge.

The ancient Babylonians measured angles in degrees. They set the measure of an angle that goes all the way around a point to 360°. They may have chosen 360° because their number system was based on the number 60. They may have also considered the fact that 360 has many factors.

Go Online
PHSchool.com

For: Information about Babylonians
Web Code: ame-9031

An angle with a measure of 170° results from a very large turn. You can fit 170 wedges that measure 1° in this angle!

The angles below have sides that meet to form a square corner. Such angles are called right angles. A **right angle** has a measure of 90°. A right angle is sometimes marked with a small square as shown on the angle at the right. When you see an angle marked this way, you can assume it has a measure of 90°.

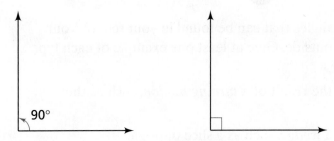

The angle below is one-half the size of a right angle. So, its measure is 45°.

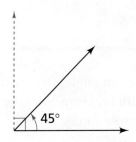

Problem 2.1 Understanding Angles

A. Sketch the angles made by these turns. For each sketch, include a curved arrow indicating the turn and label the angle with its degree measure.

1. One third of a right-angle turn

2. Two thirds of a right-angle turn

3. One quarter of a right-angle turn

4. One and a half right-angle turns

5. Two right-angle turns

6. Three right-angle turns

B. In parts (1)–(6), sketch an angle with *approximately* the given measure. For each sketch, include a curved arrow indicating the turn.

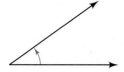

1. 20°   **2.** 70°

3. 150°   **4.** 180°

5. 270°   **6.** 360°

C. Estimate the measure of each angle.

1.
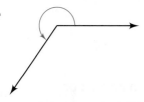

2.

3.
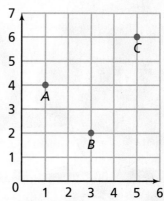

ACE **Homework starts on page 40.**

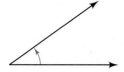 **Developing Angle Benchmarks**

You may know how to locate points on a grid by using ordered pairs of coordinates. Given the ordered pair (1, 4), you first start at (0, 0) and move to the right the number of units given by the first coordinate, 1. From this point, you move up the number of units given by the second coordinate, 4.

On the grid at right, point *A* has coordinates (1, 4). Point *B* has coordinates (3, 2). Point *C* has coordinates (5, 6).

Mathematicians and scientists find it useful to locate points using different kinds of coordinate grids. One way to locate points is to use a circular grid. On this kind of grid, angle measures help describe the location of points.

Two examples of circular grids are shown below. The grid on the left has lines at 45° intervals. The grid on the right has lines at 30° intervals. The circles are numbered, moving out from the center at 0.

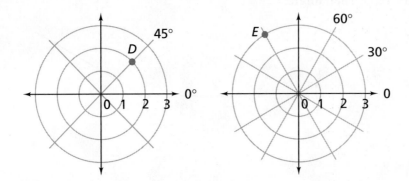

Points on a circular grid are described by giving a distance and an angle. For example, point *D* has coordinates (2, 45°). To locate a point, start at the center of the grid and move to the right the number of units indicated by the first coordinate. Then, move counterclockwise along that circle the number of degrees given by the second coordinate. To locate (2, 45°), move to the right 2 units on the 0° line and then move up (around the circle) to the 45° line.

Can you find the coordinates of point E above?

You can use circular grids to play a game called Four in a Row. Two players or two teams can play the game.

Four in a Row Rules

Choose one of the circular grids, either with 30° intervals or 45° intervals.

- Player A chooses a point where a circle and a grid line meet and says the coordinates of the point aloud.

- Player B checks that the coordinates Player A gave are correct. If they are, Player A marks the point with an X. If they are not, Player A does not get to mark a point.

- Player B chooses a point and says its coordinates. If the coordinates are correct, Player B marks the point with an O.

- Players continue to take turns, saying the coordinates of a point and then marking the point. The first player to get four marks in a row, either along a grid line or around a circle, wins the game.

Problem 2.2 Developing Angle Benchmarks

A. Play Four in a Row several times. Play games with the 30° grid and the 45° grid. Write down any winning strategies you discover.

B. On one of the circular grids, label points *A*, *B*, and *C* that fit the following descriptions:

- The angle measure for point *A* is greater than 120°.
- The angle measure for point *B* is equal to 0°.
- The angle measure for point *C* is less than 90°.

ACE Homework starts on page 40.

Circular grids are examples of *polar coordinate grids*. Sir Isaac Newton introduced polar coordinates. In some real-life settings, such as sea and air navigation, a rectangular coordinate system is not always useful. In these settings, a system similar to a polar coordinate system works better.

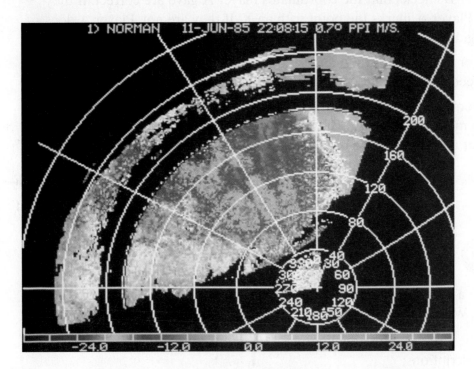

You may have seen grids similar to these polar coordinate grids shown as radar grids in movies or on television. This is because certain types of radar use polar coordinates in order to locate objects. This type of radar is used to find weather patterns, airplanes, and ships at sea.

An object appearing on radar will have an angle measure. It will be based on the direction of the object from the radar site. You measure the angle of the direction by turning clockwise from North.

Go Online
PHSchool.com
For: Information about radar
Web Code: ame-9031

2.3 Using an Angle Ruler

In many situations in which distance and angles are measured, estimates are good enough. But sometimes it is important to measure precisely. If you were navigating an ocean liner, an airplane, or a rocket, you would want precise measurements of the angles needed to plot your course.

There are several tools for measuring angles. One of the easiest to use is the *angle ruler*. An angle ruler has two arms, like the sides of an angle. A rivet joins the arms. This allows them to swing apart to form angles of various sizes. One arm is marked with a circular ruler showing degree measures from 0° to 360°.

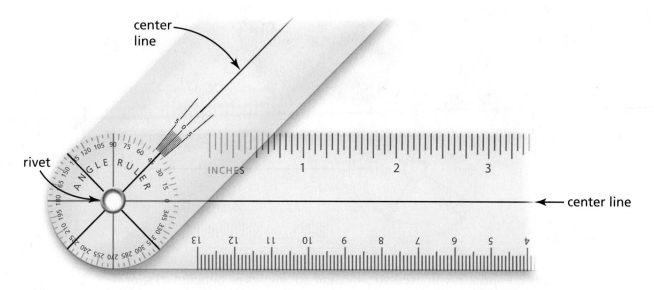

To measure an angle with an angle ruler, first place the rivet over the vertex of the angle. Then set the *center line* of the arm with the ruler markings on one side of the angle. Swing the other arm around counterclockwise until its center line lies on the second side of the angle. The center line on the second arm will pass over a mark on the circular ruler. This tells you the degree measure of the angle.

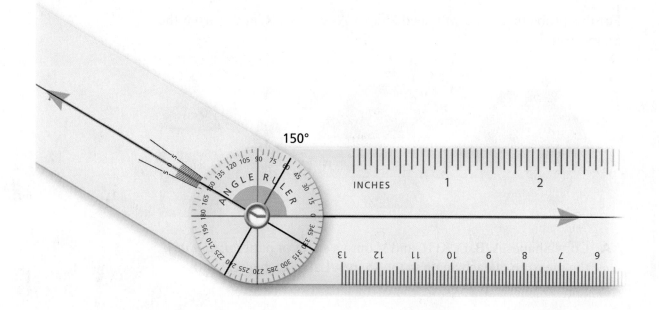

When you are measuring an angle on an actual object, you can place the object between the two arms of the angle ruler as shown here. Then read off the size of the angle. Angle 1 in shape R measures 120°.

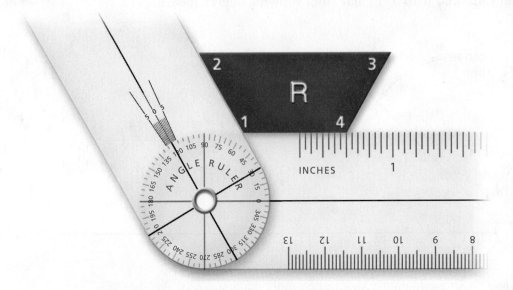

In Problems 2.1 and 2.2, you used 90°, 45°, and 30° angles as benchmarks, or references, to sketch angles and estimate angle measures. In Problem 2.3, you will use these benchmark angles to estimate the angle measures for some of the shapes in the Shapes Set. You can then use an angle ruler to measure the angles.

Problem 2.3 Measuring Angles

For this problem set you will need Shapes A, B, D, K, R, and V from the Shapes Set.

A. Copy Shapes A, B, D, K, R, and V onto a sheet of paper. *Estimate* the measure of each angle in the shapes. Label each angle with your estimate.

B. 1. Use an angle ruler to *measure* each angle of the six shapes. On your drawing of the shapes, label each angle with its measure. Use a different color than you used on Question A.

2. How do your measurements compare with your estimates?

C. Use an angle ruler to find the measure of each angle.

1.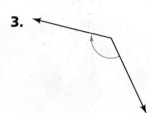

2.

3.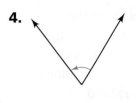

4.

D. 1. Draw an angle whose measure is less than the measure of any of the angles in Question C.

2. Draw an angle whose measure is greater than the measure of any of the angles in Question C.

ACE **Homework starts on page 40.**

The angle ruler's formal name is *goniometer* (goh nee AHM uh tur), which means "angle measurer." Goniometers are used by doctors and physical therapists to measure flexibility (range of motion) in joints such as knees, elbows, and fingers.

A *protractor* is another device used for measuring angles (see Exercise 21 in Investigation 4). Protractors are an alternative to angle rulers.

Go Online
PHSchool.com

For: Information about physical therapists
Web Code: ame-9031

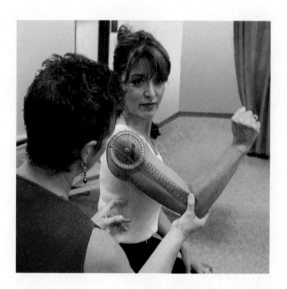

2.4 Analyzing Measurement Errors

In Problem 2.3, you and your classmates may have found slightly different measures for some of the angles. Because no instrument gives absolutely precise measurements, there is some error every time you use a measurement tool. However, in some situations, it is important to make measurements that are as precise as possible. For example, when using angle measures to navigate an airplane, even small errors can lead a flight far astray.

In 1937, the famous aviator Amelia Earhart tried to become the first woman to fly around the world. She began her journey on June 1 from Miami, Florida. She reached Lae, New Guinea, and then headed east toward Howland Island in the Pacific Ocean. She never arrived at Howland Island.

In 1992, 55 years later, investigators found evidence that Earhart had crashed on the deserted island of Nikumaroro, far off her intended course. It appears that an error may have been made in plotting Earhart's course.

The map below shows Lae, New Guinea; Howland Island (Earhart's intended destination); and Nikumaroro Island (the crash site).

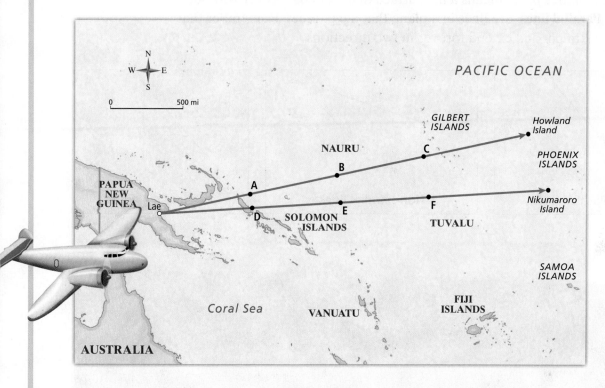

A. How many degrees off course was Earhart's crash site from her intended destination?

B. Suppose two planes fly along the paths formed by the rays of the angle indicated on the map. Both planes leave Lae, New Guinea, at the same time and fly at the same speed. Find the approximate distance in miles between the planes at each pair of points labeled on the map (A and D, B and E, and C and F).

C. Amelia Earhart apparently flew several degrees south of her intended course. Suppose you start at Lae, New Guinea, and are trying to reach Howland, but you fly 20° south. Where might you land?

ACE Homework starts on page 40.

2.5 Angles and Parallel Lines

In mathematics, *plane* means a flat surface that extends forever without edges. **Parallel lines** are lines in a plane that never meet. Remember that lines are straight and extend forever in two directions.

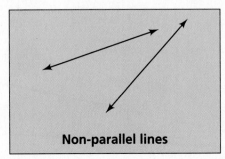

Parallel lines   **Non-parallel lines**   **Non-parallel lines**

The next problem helps you explore some interesting patterns among angles formed when parallel lines are intersected by a third line. A line that intersects two or more lines is called a **transversal.**

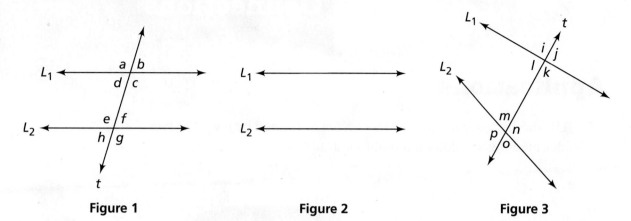

Figure 1   Figure 2   Figure 3

A. In Figure 1, lines L_1 and L_2 are parallel. They are intersected by a transversal t. Measure the angles labeled with small letters. What patterns do you observe among the angle measures?

B. In Figure 2, lines L_1 and L_2 are also parallel.

- Using a copy of Figure 2, draw a transversal t that intersects both lines.

- Measure the angles that are formed.

- What patterns do you observe among the angle measures?

C. In Figure 3, lines L_1 and L_2 are *not* parallel.

- Measure the angles formed by the transversal intersecting lines L_1 and L_2.

- Which patterns you observed in Figures 1 and 2 appear in Figure 3? Explain.

D. Make one or more conjectures about the measures of the angles formed when a transversal intersects two parallel lines.

E. 1. Explain why Shapes B, G, H, J, K, L, M, N, and V in the Shapes Set are called parallelograms.

2. Trace two of the parallelograms. Are any of the lines in the parallelograms transversals? If so, which lines are transversals?

3. Based on the conjectures that you have made in this problem, what do you think is true about the angle measures of a parallelogram? Check your ideas by choosing a parallelogram from the Shapes Set and measuring its angles.

ACE Homework starts on page 40.

Applications

1. Tell whether each diagram shows an angle formed by a wedge, two sides meeting at a common point, or a turn.

   a.

   b.

   c.

2. Give the degree measure of each turn.

   a. One right-angle turn

   b. Four right-angle turns

   c. Five right-angle turns

   d. One half of a right-angle turn

   e. One ninth of a right-angle turn

   f. One fourth of a right-angle turn

3. At the start of each hour, the minute hand of a clock points straight up at the 12. In parts (a)–(f), determine the angle through which the minute hand turns as the given amount of time passes.

Notice that only the minute hand is illustrated on the clock. Make a sketch to illustrate each situation. The curved arrow is pointing clockwise here because that is the direction that the minute hand turns.

a. 15 minutes

b. 30 minutes

c. 20 minutes

d. one hour

e. 5 minutes

f. one and a half hours

4. *Without* using an angle ruler, decide whether the measure of each angle is closest to 30°, 60°, 90°, 120°, 150°, 180°, 270°, or 360°. Be prepared to explain your reasoning.

a.

b.

c.

d.

e.

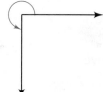

f.

g.

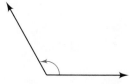

h.

5. You have learned that a 90° angle is called a *right angle*. An angle with measure less than 90° is an **acute angle.** An angle with measure greater than 90° and less than 180° is an **obtuse angle.** An angle with measure exactly 180° is a **straight angle.** Decide whether each angle in Exercise 4 is right, acute, obtuse, straight, or none of these.

For Exercises 6–9, find the measure of the angle labeled *x*, *without* measuring.

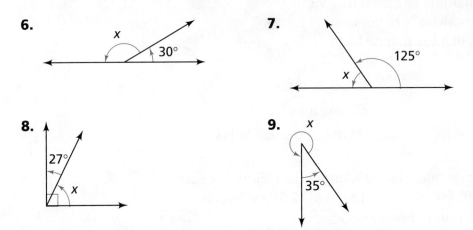

6. x 30°

7. 125° x

8. 27° x

9. x 35°

For Exercises 10–13, a worker bee has located flowers with nectar and is preparing to do her dance. The dots represent the hive, the sun, and flowers. Estimate the measure of each angle. Use an angle ruler to check your estimate.

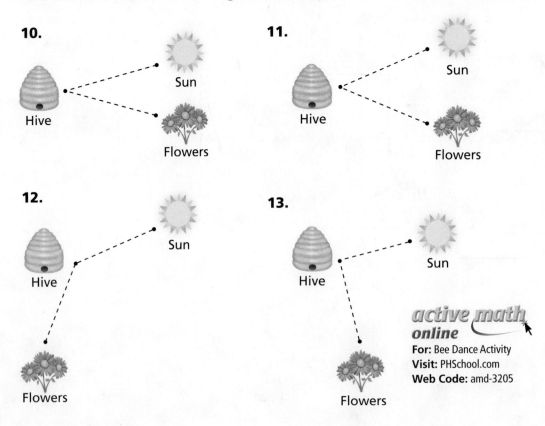

10.

Hive Sun Flowers

11.

Hive Sun Flowers

12.

Hive Sun Flowers

13.

Hive Sun Flowers

14. Draw an angle for each measure. Include a curved arrow indicating the turn.

    a. 45°   **b.** 25°   **c.** 180°   **d.** 200°

15. *Without* measuring, decide whether the angles in each pair have the same measure. If they do not, tell which angle has the greater measure. Then find the measure of the angles with an angle ruler to check your work.

a.

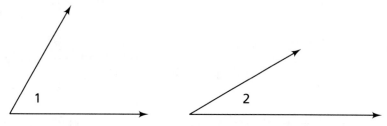

b.

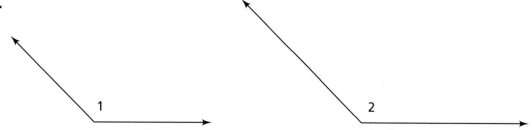

c.

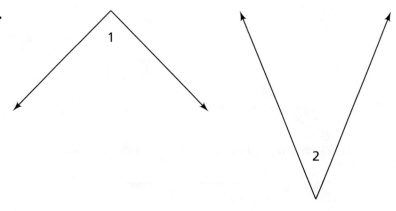

16. Estimate the measure of each angle, then check your answers with an angle ruler.

a.

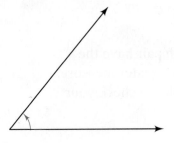

b.

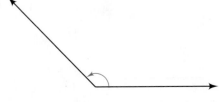

c.

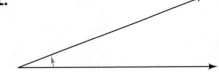

d.

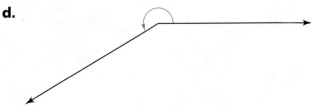

e.

17. For each polygon below, measure the angles with an angle ruler.

a.

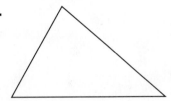

b.

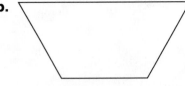

18. You have read about how worker bees communicate the location of flowers. Suppose the angle a worker bee indicates is off by 1°. How will this affect the other bees' ability to locate the flowers? Explain.

19. A bee leaves the hive and wants to fly to a rose but instead ends up at a daisy. How many degrees did the bee travel off course? Estimate your answer. Then check your answer with an angle ruler.

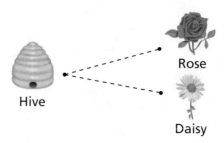

Rose

Hive

Daisy

20. Little Bee left point A for a flower patch. Big Bee left point B for the same flower patch. However, both bees were 15° off course. Little Bee landed on the patch and Big Bee did not. Explain why Big Bee did not hit the patch and Little Bee did, if they were both off course by 15°.

Homework Help Online
PHSchool.com
For: Help with Exercise 20
Web Code: ame-3220

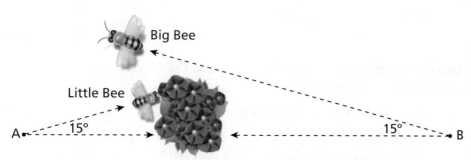

Big Bee

Little Bee

A   15°   15°   B

21. Lines L_1 and L_2 are parallel lines cut by a transversal. The measure of one of the angles is given. Based on what you discovered in Problem 2.5, find the measures of the other angles.

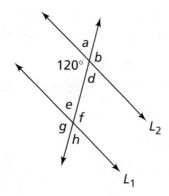

120°

a
b
d
e
f
g
h
L_2
L_1

22. In parts (a)–(c), lines L_1 and L_2 are intersected by a transversal. The measures of some of the angles formed are given. In each part, tell whether you think the lines are parallel. Explain.

a.

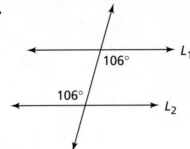

b.

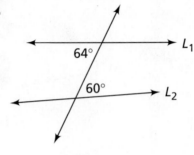

c.

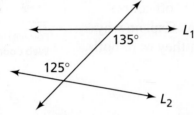

23. a. Draw any two intersecting lines, L_1 and L_2. Measure the four angles formed around the point of intersection.

b. What patterns do you observe among the angle measures?

c. Draw two more pairs of intersecting lines and measure the angles formed. Do you observe the same patterns as in part (b)?

24. Multiple Choice Use the angle measures to determine which of the following shapes is a parallelogram. The shapes may not be drawn to scale.

A.

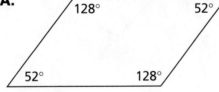

B.

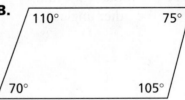

C.

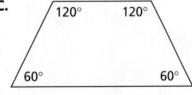

D.

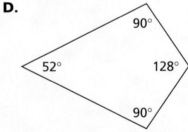

25. How did you know which shape was a parallelogram in Exercise 24?

26. Liang said that an equilateral triangle must have angles totaling 360° because he can cut it into two right triangles, as in the diagram. Is Liang's statement correct? Explain.

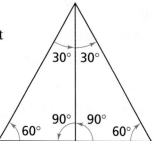

Connections

27. Is the statement below *true* or *false*? Justify your answer.

The region inside a polygon can be tiled by triangles.

28. The number 360 was chosen for the number of degrees in a full turn. The number may have been chosen because it has many factors.

a. List all the factors of 360.

b. What is the prime factorization of 360?

29. A right angle can be thought of as a quarter of a complete rotation.

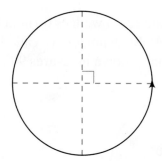

a. How many degrees is $\frac{1}{3}$ of a quarter of a rotation?

b. How many degrees is two times a quarter of a rotation?

c. How many degrees is $2\frac{1}{3}$ times a quarter of a rotation?

Replace the ■ with a number that will make the sentence true.

30. $\frac{1}{2} = \frac{■}{360}$

31. $\frac{1}{10} = \frac{36}{■}$

32. $\frac{1}{■} = \frac{40}{360}$

33. $\frac{■}{3} = \frac{120}{360}$

34. A full turn is 360°. If a bee turns around 180°, like the one at the right, she has made a half turn.

a. What fraction of a turn is 90°?

b. What fraction of a turn is 270°?

c. How many turns is 720°?

d. How many degrees is the fraction $\frac{25}{360}$ of a turn?

35. The minute hand on a watch makes a complete rotation every hour. The hand makes half of a full rotation in 30 minutes.

a. In how many minutes does the hand make $\frac{1}{6}$ of a rotation?

b. In how many minutes does the hand make $\frac{1}{6}$ of half a rotation?

c. What fraction of an hour is $\frac{1}{6}$ of half a rotation?

d. How many degrees has the minute hand moved through in $\frac{1}{6}$ of half a rotation?

36. The circular region is divided into four equal wedges formed by angles with vertices at the center of the circle. Such angles are called **central angles** of the circle. Each central angle shown measures 90°.

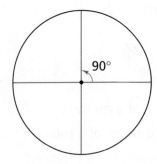

In parts (a)–(c), sketch a circular region divided into the given number of equal wedges. Then find the measure of the central angles.

a. 8 equal edges   b. 6 equal wedges   c. 3 equal wedges

d. Find another way to divide the circular region into equal wedges so that the central angles have whole number degree measures. Give the number of wedges and the measure of the central angles. What strategy did you use?

37. A ruler is used to measure the length of line segments. An angle ruler is used to measure the size of (or turn in) angles.

　a. What is the unit of measurement for each kind of ruler?

　b. Write a few sentences comparing the method for measuring angles to the method for measuring line segments.

38. Skateboarders use angle measures to describe their turns. Explain what a skateboarder would mean by each statement.

　a. I did a 720.　　**b.** I did a 540.　　**c.** I did a 180.

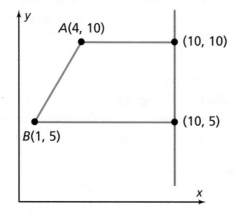

39. In the figure below, the blue segments represent half of a polygon. The red vertical line is the line of symmetry for the complete polygon.

　a. Copy the figure onto a sheet of grid paper. Then draw the missing half of the polygon.

　b. On the "new" half of the figure, what are the coordinates of the point that corresponds to point *A*? What are the coordinates of the point that corresponds to point *B*?

　c. Describe some properties of the polygon.

40. Multiple Choice Which choice is a 180° rotation of the figure below?

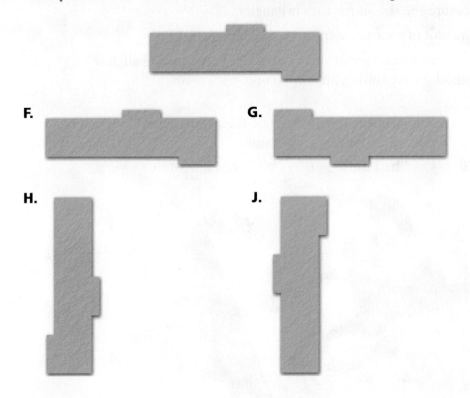

F.

G.

H.

J.

Extensions

41. Design a new polar coordinate grid for playing Four in a Row. Play your game with a friend or a member of your family. Explain the ideas that led to your new design. Compare playing on your new grid to playing on the grids given in Problem 2.2.

42. The **midpoint** of a line segment is the point that divides it into two segments of equal length. Trace the parallelogram below onto a sheet of paper. Connect the midpoints of two opposite sides. Describe the two quadrilaterals that are formed. Are they parallelograms? Explain.

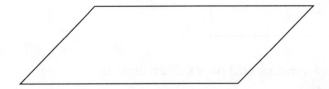

43. a. In the equilateral triangle below, the midpoints of two of the sides have been marked and then connected by a line segment. How does the length of this segment compare to the length of the third side of the triangle? Does the segment appear to be parallel to the third side of the triangle?

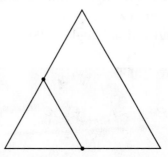

b. Draw an isosceles triangle. Locate the midpoints of two of the sides. Then draw a line segment connecting the midpoints. Compare the segment with the third side of the triangle. Do the observations you made in part (a) also apply in this case? Now connect the midpoints of a different pair of sides. Do the same observations hold?

c. Draw a scalene triangle. Locate the midpoints of two of the sides. Then draw a line segment connecting the midpoints. Compare the segment with the third side of the triangle. Do the observations you made in part (a) also apply in this case? Now connect the midpoints of a different pair of sides. Do the same observations hold?

44. Two lines are **perpendicular** if they intersect to form right angles. Tell whether the statement below is *true* or *false*. Justify your answer.

If a transversal is perpendicular to one line in a pair of parallel lines, then it must also be perpendicular to the other line.

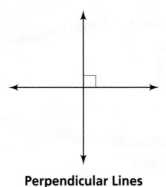

Perpendicular Lines

Astronomers use two types of angles to locate objects in the sky. The *altitudinal* (al tuh too' di nuhl) *angle* is the angle from the horizon to the object. The horizon has an altitudinal angle of 0°. The point directly overhead, called the *zenith*, has an altitudinal angle of 90°.

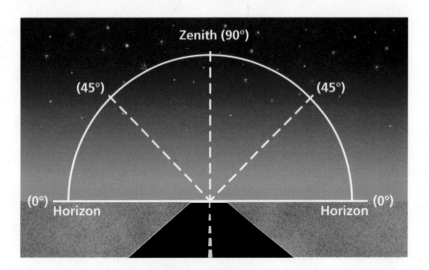

The *azimuthal* (az uh myooth' uhl) *angle* is the angle of rotation from north to the object. To find the azimuthal angle of an object, face north and then rotate clockwise until you are facing the object. The angle through which you turn is the azimuthal angle.

To find the azimuthal angle *between* two objects, face one of the objects and then turn until you are facing the other. The angle through which you turn is the azimuthal angle between the objects.

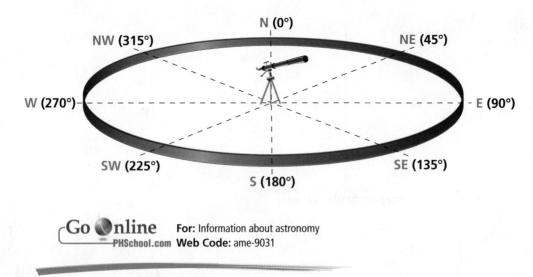

Go Online
PHSchool.com **For:** Information about astronomy
Web Code: ame-9031

Mathematical Reflections 2

In this investigation, you thought about angles that involved turns, sides of wedges, and two sides with a common vertex. You learned to estimate angle measures and to use tools to make more precise measurements. These questions will help you summarize what you have learned.

Think about your answers to these questions. Discuss your ideas with other students and your teacher. Then write a summary of your findings in your notebook.

1. **a.** Explain what the measure of an angle is.

   b. Explain how to measure an angle.

2. Describe some ways to estimate the measure of an angle.

3. **a.** What does it mean for two lines to be parallel?

   b. If two parallel lines are intersected by a transversal, what patterns can you expect to find in the measures of the angles formed?

Unit Project What's Next?

What information about shapes can you add to your *Shapes and Designs* project?

Polygon Properties and Tiling

You learned about angles and angle measure in Investigations 1 and 2. What you learned can help you figure out some useful properties of the angles of a polygon. Let's start with the sum of the measures of all the inside angles at the vertices of a polygon. This sum is called the **angle sum** of a polygon.

3.1 Angle Sums of Regular Polygons

Below are six regular polygons that are already familiar to you.

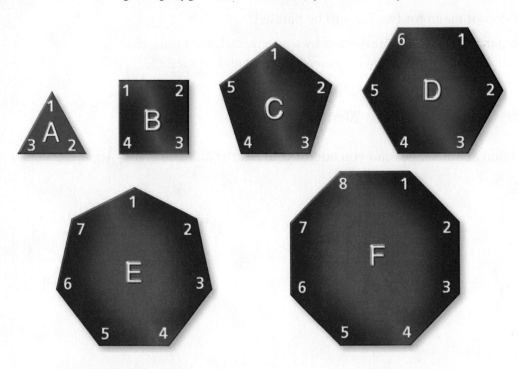

What is the angle sum of each figure?

Do you see a pattern relating the number of sides to the angle sum?

A. 1. In Problem 2.3, you measured the angles of some regular polygons—triangles, squares, and hexagons. Record the number of sides, the angle measures, and the angle sum of a triangle, square, and hexagon in a table like the one below.

Polygon	Number of Sides	Measure of an Angle	Angle Sum
Triangle	■	■	■
Square	■	■	■
Pentagon	■	■	■
Hexagon	■	■	■
Heptagon	■	■	■
Octagon	■	■	■
Nonagon	■	■	■
Decagon	■	■	■

2. Measure an angle of the regular pentagon and regular octagon from your Shapes Set. Record the measures of the angles and the angle sums in your table. What patterns do you see?

3. Use your patterns to fill in the table for a regular polygon with seven, nine, and ten sides.

B. Below are two sets of regular polygons of different sizes. Do the same patterns relating the number of sides, the measures of the angles, and the angle sums apply to these shapes? Explain.

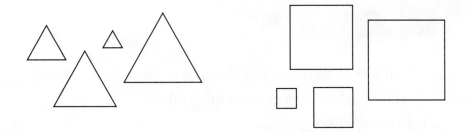

C. Describe how you could find the angle sum of a regular polygon that has *N* sides.

ACE Homework starts on page 62.

Angle Sums of Any Polygon

Do the patterns that you observed for the angle sum of regular polygons apply to all polygons?

Getting Ready for Problem 3.2

Suppose you tear the three corners off of a triangle. You can arrange them this way:

- Based on the picture, what is the sum of angles 1, 2, and 3? How do you know?
- Make a conjecture about the angle sum of any triangle.

You could do the same thing with a quadrilateral.

- Based on the picture, what is the sum of angles 1, 2, 3, and 4? How do you know?
- Make a conjecture about the angle sum of any quadrilateral.
- Do similar patterns hold for other polygons?

Problem 3.2 Angle Sums of Any Polygon

Tia and Cody claim that the angle sum of any polygon is the same as the angle sum of a regular polygon with the same number of sides. They use diagrams to illustrate their reasoning.

A. Tia divides polygons into triangles by drawing all the *diagonals* of the polygons from one vertex, as in the diagrams below:

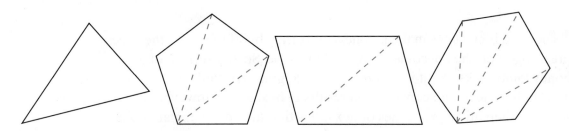

   1. Study Tia's drawings. How can you use Tia's method to find the angle sum of each polygon?

   2. Copy these three polygons. Use Tia's method to find the angle sum of each polygon.

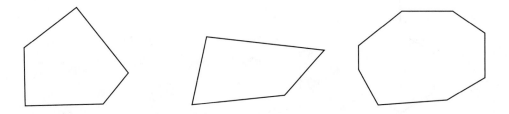

   3. Does Tia's method work for any polygon? Explain.

B. Cody also discovered a method for finding the angle sum of any polygon. He starts by drawing line segments from a point within the polygon to each vertex.

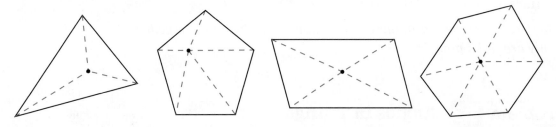

   1. Study Cody's drawings. How can you use Cody's method to find the angle sum of each polygon?

   2. Copy the three polygons from Question A part (2). Use Cody's method to find the angle sum of each polygon.

   3. Does Cody's method work for any polygon? Explain.

C. In Problem 3.1, you found a pattern relating the number of sides of a regular polygon to the angle sum. Does the same pattern hold for any polygon? Explain.

ACE Homework starts on page 62.

3.3 Back to the Bees!

When the honeybees make a honeycomb, they build tubes. As the tubes press together, they become hexagonal in shape. So, the surface of a honeycomb looks like it is covered with hexagons. We can't ask honeybees why their honeycomb construction results in hexagons. However, there are some mathematical properties of hexagons that may offer explanations.

Below is a tiling of regular hexagons. Notice that three angles fit together exactly around any point in the tiling.

Why do these regular hexagons fit together so neatly?

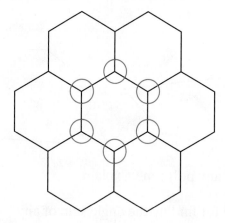

In Problem 1.3, you experimented to find which regular polygons could tile a surface.

What are the properties of these shapes that allow them to fit together so neatly around a point?

Problem 3.3 Angles in Tilings

A. In Problem 1.3, you explored tilings made from a single type of regular polygon. You found that only equilateral triangles, squares, and regular hexagons could be used to tile a surface.

   1. For each of these shapes, make a tiling and sketch the results.

   2. In each case, explain why copies of the shape fit neatly around a point.

B. In Problem 1.3, you also found that regular pentagons, regular heptagons, and regular octagons could not be used to tile a surface. Explain why copies of these polygons do not fit neatly around a point.

C. 1. Find tilings using combinations of two or more shapes from your Shapes Set. Sketch your results.

2. What do you observe about the angles that meet at a point in the tiling?

ACE **Homework starts on page 62.**

Did You Know?

One of the leading golf ball manufacturers developed a pattern using hexagons for golf balls. They claim it is the first design to cover 100% of the surface area of a golf ball. This pattern of mostly hexagons almost eliminates flat spots found on typical golf balls, which interfere with their performance. This new design produces a longer, better flight for the golf ball.

Go Online
PHSchool.com   **For:** Information about golf
Web Code: ame-9031

3.4 Exterior Angles of Polygons

An angle *inside* a polygon, formed by the polygon's sides, is an **interior angle.** By extending a side of a polygon, you can make an **exterior angle,** which is *outside* the polygon. Extending a side of the polygon forms one ray of the exterior angle.

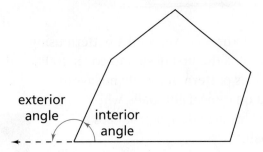

Figure 1 shows the exterior angles made by extending sides as you move counterclockwise around the polygon. Figure 2 shows the exterior angles formed by extending sides as you move clockwise around the polygon.

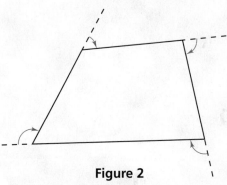

Figure 1
Exterior angles as you
move counterclockwise.

Figure 2
Exterior angles as you
move clockwise.

Problem 3.4 Exterior Angles of Polygons

A skateboarder is skating on a triangular path around a park. In the diagram below, each segment of the path has been extended to show the angle of turn the in-line skater makes as she turns the corner. Each of these angles is an exterior angle of the triangle.

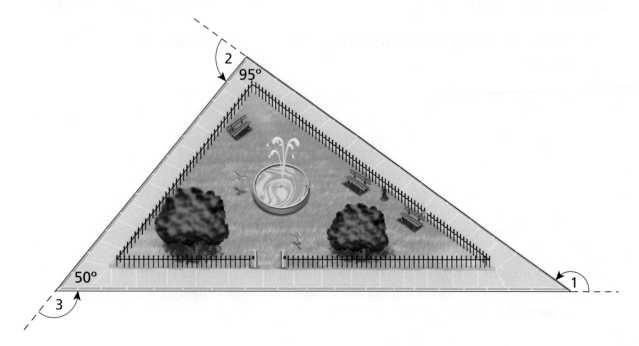

A. 1. What are the measures of the interior angles of the triangle?

2. What is the measure of angle 1?

3. What are the measures of angle 2 and angle 3?

B. Suppose the skateboarder skates once around the park counterclockwise, turning each corner exactly once. What is the sum of the angles through which she turns?

C. 1. Draw another triangle and mark the exterior angles going in one direction around the triangle.

2. Measure the exterior angles and find the sum.

3. Compare the exterior angle sum of your triangle to the sum you found for the triangle in Question B.

4. Can you predict the exterior angle sum for another triangle? Explain.

ACE Homework starts on page 62.

Applications

1. Without measuring, find the measures of the angle labeled *x* in each regular polygon.

   a.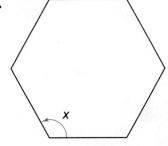

   b.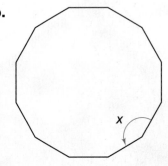

2. Below are sets of regular polygons of different sizes. Does the length of a side of a regular polygon affect the sum of the interior angle measures? Explain.

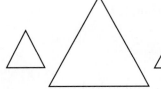

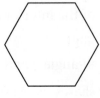

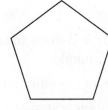

For Exercises 3–9, find the measure of each angle labeled _x_.

3.

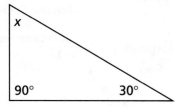

4.

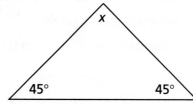

5.

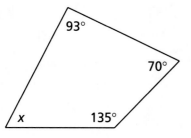

6. This figure is a parallelogram.

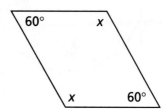

7.

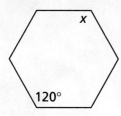

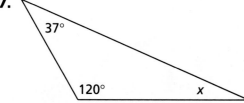

8. This figure is a regular hexagon.

9. This figure is a parallelogram.

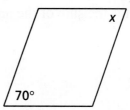

10. A **right triangle** has one right angle and two acute angles. Without measuring, find the sum of the measures of the two acute angles. Explain.

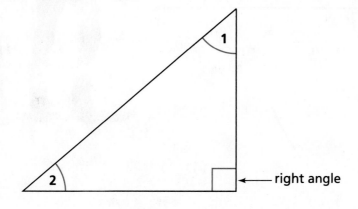

right angle

11. This figure is a regular dodecagon. A dodecagon has 12 sides.

    a. What is the sum of the measures of the angles of this polygon?

    b. What is the measure of each angle?

    c. Can copies of this polygon be used to tile a surface? Explain.

Go Online
PHSchool.com

For: Multiple-Choice Skills Practice

Web Code: ama-3354

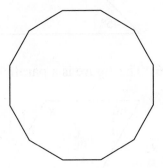

12. Multiple Choice Which of the following will tile a plane?

    A. regular heptagon and equilateral triangle

    B. square and regular octagon

    C. regular pentagon and regular hexagon

    D. regular hexagon and square

13. Suppose an in-line skater skates around a park that has the shape of a quadrilateral. Suppose he skates once around the quadrilateral, turning each corner exactly once. What is the sum of the angles through which he turns?

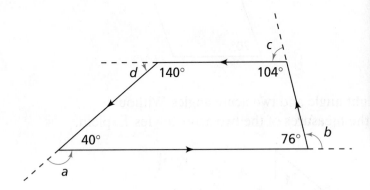

14. a. Suppose an in-line skater skates around a park that has the shape of a regular pentagon. If he skates once around the pentagon, turning each corner exactly once, what is the sum of the angles through which he turns?

b. How many degrees will the skater turn if he skates once around a regular hexagon? A regular octagon? A regular polygon with *N* sides? Explain.

Connections

15. A regular decagon and a star are shown below. Measure the angles inside the star to find the angle sum of the star. Compare your results to the angle sum for a regular decagon.

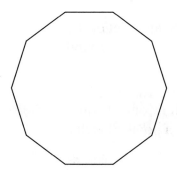

16. In the diagram below, the dashed line is a line of symmetry for the equilateral triangle. Examine the two smaller triangles that are formed by the dashed line. What do you know about the angles and the line segments of triangles *ABD* and *ACD*? Give reasons to support the relationships you find.

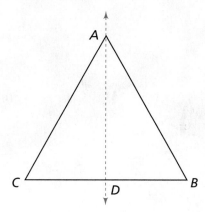

17. Multiple Choice Figure $QSTV$ is a rectangle. The lengths QR and QV are equal. What is the measure of angle x?

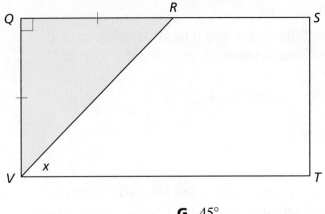

F. 20°

G. 45°

H. 90°

J. 120°

18. Choose a non-rectangular parallelogram from your Shapes Set or draw one of your own. Try to fit copies of the parallelogram exactly around a point. Sketch a picture to help explain what you found.

19. Choose a scalene triangle from your Shapes Set or draw one of your own. Try to fit copies of your triangle exactly around a point. Sketch a picture to help explain what you found.

20. In the diagram below, two parallel lines are cut by a transversal. Use what you learned in Investigation 2 to find the missing angle measures.

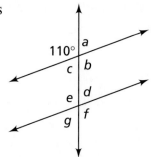

Extensions

21. a. Complete this table about regular polygons and look for a pattern.

Regular Polygons	
Number of Sides	**Measure of Interior Angle**
4	$\frac{1}{2}$ of 180°
6	$\frac{2}{3}$ of 180°
8	$\frac{3}{4}$ of 180°
10	■

b. Does this pattern continue? Explain.

c. Is there a similar pattern for regular polygons with odd numbers of sides?

22. Kele claims that the angle sum of a polygon that he has drawn is 1,660°. Can he be correct? Explain.

23. Look at the polygons below. Does Tia's method of finding the angle sum (Problem 3.2) still work? Does Cody's method also still work? Can you still find the angle sum of the interior angles without measuring? Explain.

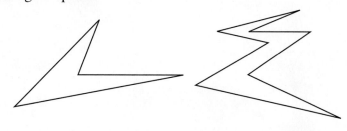

24. Below are a quadrilateral and a pentagon with the diagonals drawn from all the vertices.

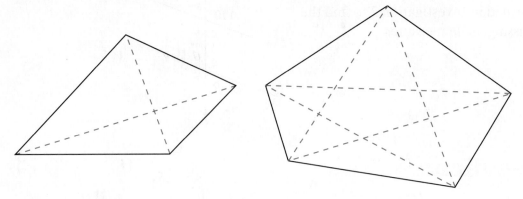

    a. How many diagonals does the quadrilateral have? How many diagonals does the pentagon have?

    b. Find the total number of diagonals for a hexagon and for a heptagon.

    c. Copy the table below and record your results from parts (a) and (b). Look for a pattern relating the number of sides and the number of diagonals to complete the table.

Number of Sides	4	5	6	7	8	9	10	11	12
Number of Diagonals	■	■	■	■	■	■	■	■	■

    d. Write a rule for finding the number of diagonals for a polygon with *N* sides.

25. Would a quadrilateral like the one below tile a plane? Explain.

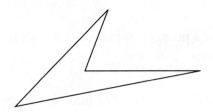

Mathematical Reflections 3

In this investigation, you explored patterns for angle sums of polygons. You also investigated how the interior angle measures of a polygon determine whether copies of the polygon will fit exactly around a point. The questions below will help you summarize what you have learned.

Think about your answers to these questions, and discuss your ideas with other students and your teacher. Then write a summary of your findings in your notebook.

1. **a.** What is the angle sum of a triangle? A quadrilateral? A hexagon? A polygon with N sides?

   b. Describe how you can find the measure of each interior angle of a regular polygon.

   c. As the number of sides in a regular polygon increases, what happens to the measure of an interior angle?

2. Describe how you can find the sum of the measures of the exterior angles of a polygon.

Unit Project What's Next?

What information about shapes can you add to your *Shapes and Designs* project?

Building Polygons

In the last two investigations, you explored the relationship between the number of sides of a polygon and the measure of its interior angles. Now you will turn your attention to the sides of a polygon.

How do the side lengths of a polygon affect its shape?

You can use polystrips and fasteners like these:

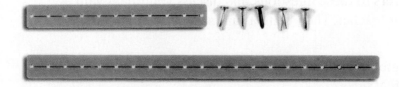

to build polygons with given side lengths and study their properties.

4.1 Building Triangles

Bridges, towers, and other structures contain many triangles in their design.
Why are triangles used so frequently in construction?

Problem 4.1 Building Triangles

Make a triangle using the steps below. Sketch and label your results.

Step 1 Roll three number cubes and record the sum. Do this two more times, so that you have three sums.

Step 2 Using polystrips, try to make a triangle with the three sums as side lengths. If you can build one triangle, try to build a different triangle with the same side lengths.

Repeat Steps 1 and 2 to make several triangles.

A. 1. List each set of side lengths that did make a triangle.

   2. List each set of side lengths that did not make a triangle.

   3. What pattern do you see in each set that explains why some sets of numbers make a triangle and some do not?

   4. Use your pattern to find two new sets of side lengths that will make a triangle. Then find two new sets of side lengths that will not make a triangle.

B. Can you make two different triangles from the same three side lengths?

C. Why do you think triangles are so useful in construction?

ACE Homework starts on page 76.

4.2 Building Quadrilaterals

You need four side lengths to make a quadrilateral.

Will any four side lengths work?

Can you make more than one quadrilateral from four side lengths?

Problem **Building Quadrilaterals**

A. 1. Use polystrips to build quadrilaterals with each of the following sets of numbers as side lengths. Try to build two or more different quadrilaterals using the same set of side lengths.

6, 10, 15, 15   3, 5, 10, 20

8, 8, 10, 10   12, 20, 6, 9

Sketch and label your results to share with your classmates. Record any observations you make.

2. Choose your own sets of four numbers and try to build quadrilaterals with those numbers as side lengths.

B. Use your observations from Question A.

1. Is it possible to make a quadrilateral using any four side lengths? If not, how can you tell whether you can make a quadrilateral from four side lengths?

2. Can you make two or more different quadrilaterals from the same four side lengths?

3. What combinations of side lengths are needed to build rectangles? Squares? Parallelograms?

C. 1. Use four polystrips to build a quadrilateral. Press on the sides or corners of your quadrilateral. What happens?

2. Use another polystrip to add a diagonal connecting a pair of opposite vertices. Now, press on the sides or corners of the quadrilateral. What happens? Explain.

D. 1. Describe the similarities and differences between what you learned about building triangles in Problem 4.1 and building quadrilaterals in this problem.

2. Explain why triangles are used in building structures more often than quadrilaterals.

ACE Homework starts on page 76.

active math **online**

For: Virtual Polystrips Activity
Visit: PHSchool.com
Web Code: amd-3402

Mechanical engineers use the fact that quadrilaterals are not rigid to design *linkages*. Below is an example of a quadrilateral linkage.

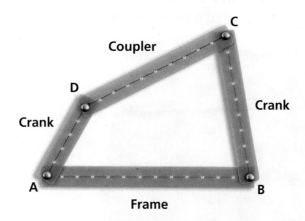

One of the sides is fixed. It is the *frame*. The two sides attached to the frame are the *cranks*. One of the cranks is the driver and the other the follower. The fourth side is called the *coupler*. Quadrilateral linkages are used in windshield wipers, automobile jacks, reclining lawn chairs, and handcars.

In 1883, the German mathematician Franz Grashof suggested an interesting principle for quadrilateral linkages: If the sum of the lengths of the shortest and longest sides is less than or equal to the sum of the lengths of the remaining two sides, then the shortest side can rotate 360°.

The Quadrilateral Game

The Quadrilateral Game will help you explore the properties of quadrilaterals. The game is played by two teams. To play, you need two number cubes, a game grid, a geoboard, and a rubber band.

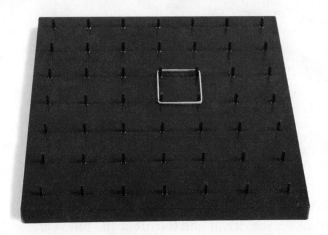

Quadrilateral Game Rules

- Near the center of the geoboard, put the rubber band around a square measuring one unit on each side.

- Team A rolls the number cubes one at a time to locate an entry in the game grid on the next page. The first number locates the row and the second number locates the column. Team A reads the description in this location. Team A then looks at the quadrilateral already on the game board, and forms a new quadrilateral to match the description. They move as few corners of the already existing quadrilateral as possible. Team A receives one point for each corner moved.

- Next, Team B rolls the number cubes and locates the corresponding description on the grid. They make a quadrilateral fitting the new description by moving as few corners of the existing quadrilateral as possible. Team B receives one point for each corner moved.

- Play continues until each team has had five turns. The team with the lowest score at the end is the winner.

Problem 4.3 Properties of Quadrilaterals

A. Play the Quadrilateral Game. Keep a record of interesting strategies and difficult situations. Make notes about when you do not receive a point during a turn. Why did you not need to move any corners on those turns?

B. Write two new descriptions of quadrilaterals that you could include in the game grid.

active math online
For: Quadrilateral Game Activity
Visit: PHSchool.com
Web Code: amd-3403

ACE Homework starts on page 76.

Quadrilateral Game Grid

	Column 1	Column 2	Column 3	Column 4	Column 5	Column 6
Row 6	A quadrilateral that is a square	**Add 1 point to your score and skip your turn**	A rectangle that is not a square	A quadrilateral with two obtuse angles	A quadrilateral with exactly one pair of parallel sides	A quadrilateral with one pair of opposite side lengths equal
Row 5	**Subtract 2 points from your score and skip your turn**	A quadrilateral that is not a rectangle	A quadrilateral with two pairs of consecutive angles that are equal	A quadrilateral with all four angles the same size	A quadrilateral with four lines of symmetry	A quadrilateral that is a rectangle
Row 4	A quadrilateral with no reflection or rotation symmetry	A quadrilateral with four right angles	**Skip a turn**	A quadrilateral with exactly one pair of consecutive side lengths that are equal	A quadrilateral with exactly one right angle	A quadrilateral with two 45° angles
Row 3	A quadrilateral with no angles equal	A quadrilateral with one pair of equal opposite angles	A quadrilateral with exactly one pair of opposite angles that are equal	**Add 2 points to your score and skip your turn**	A quadrilateral with no sides parallel	A quadrilateral with exactly two right angles
Row 2	A quadrilateral with both pairs of adjacent side lengths equal	A quadrilateral with two pairs of equal opposite angles	A quadrilateral with a diagonal that divides it into two identical shapes	A quadrilateral that is a rhombus	A quadrilateral with 180° rotation symmetry	**Subtract 1 point from your score and skip your turn**
Row 1	A quadrilateral with one diagonal that is a line of symmetry	A quadrilateral with no side lengths equal	A quadrilateral with exactly one angle greater than 180°	A parallelogram that is not a rectangle	**Add 3 points to your score and skip your turn**	A quadrilateral with two pairs of opposite side lengths equal

Applications

Follow these directions for Exercises 1–4.

- If possible, build a triangle with the given set of side lengths. Sketch your triangle.
- Tell whether your triangle is the only one that is possible. Explain.
- If a triangle is not possible, explain why.

1. Side lengths of 5, 5, and 3

2. Side lengths of 8, 8, and 8

3. Side lengths of 7, 8, and 15

4. Side lengths of 5, 6, and 10

5. Which set(s) of side lengths from Exercises 1–4 can make each of the following shapes?

    a. an equilateral triangle

    b. an isosceles triangle

    c. a scalene triangle

    d. a triangle with at least two angles of the same measure

For Exercises 6 and 7, draw the polygons described to help you answer the questions.

6. What must be true of the side lengths in order to build a triangle with three angles measuring 60°? What kind of triangle is this?

7. What must be true of the side lengths in order to build a triangle with only two angles the same size? What kind of triangle is this?

8. Giraldo and Maria are building a tent. They have two 3-foot poles. In addition, they have a 5-foot pole, a 6-foot pole, and a 7-foot pole. They want to make a triangular-shaped doorframe for the tent using both 3-foot poles and one of the other poles. Which of the other poles could be used to form the base of the door?

Follow these directions for Exercises 9–12.

- If possible, build a quadrilateral with the given set of side lengths. Sketch your quadrilateral.
- Tell whether your quadrilateral is the only one that is possible. Explain.
- If a quadrilateral is not possible, explain why.

 9. Side lengths of 5, 5, 8, and 8

10. Side lengths of 5, 5, 6, and 14

11. Side lengths of 8, 8, 8, and 8

12. Side lengths of 4, 3, 5, and 14

13. Which set(s) of side lengths from Exercises 9–12 can make each of the following shapes?

   a. a square

   b. a quadrilateral with all angles the same size

   c. a parallelogram

   d. a quadrilateral that is not a parallelogram

14. A quadrilateral with four equal sides is called a **rhombus.** Which set(s) of side lengths from Exercises 9–12 can make a rhombus?

15. A quadrilateral with at least one pair of parallel sides is called a **trapezoid.** Which set(s) of side lengths from Exercises 9–12 can make a trapezoid?

For Exercises 16 and 17, draw the polygons described to help you answer the questions.

16. What must be true of the side lengths of a polygon to build a square?

17. What must be true of the side lengths of a polygon to build a rectangle that is not a square?

18. Li Mei builds a quadrilateral with sides that are each five inches long. To help stabilize the quadrilateral, she wants to insert a ten-inch diagonal. Is this possible? Explain.

For: Help with Exercise 18
Web Code: ame-3418

19. You are playing the Quadrilateral Game. The shape currently on the geoboard is a square. Your team rolls the number cubes and gets the description "A parallelogram that is not a rectangle." What is the minimum number of vertices your team needs to move to form a shape meeting this description?

20. You are playing the Quadrilateral Game. The shape currently on the geoboard is a non-rectangular parallelogram. Your team rolls the number cubes and gets the description "A quadrilateral with two obtuse angles." What is the minimum number of vertices your team needs to move to create a shape meeting this description?

Connections

21. Multiple Choice Which one of the following shaded regions is *not* a representation of $\frac{4}{12}$?

A.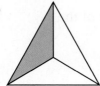

B.

C.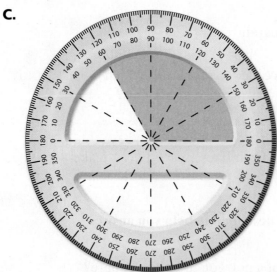

D.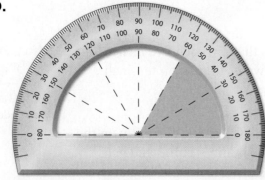

22. a. How are all three quadrilaterals below alike?

b. How does each quadrilateral differ from the other two?

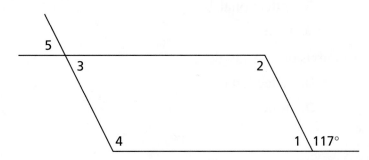

23. In this parallelogram, find the measure of each numbered angle.

Go Online
PHSchool.com

For: Multiple-Choice Skills Practice
Web Code: ame-3454

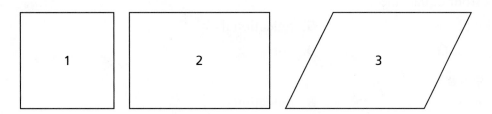

24. Think about your polystrip experiments with triangles and quadrilaterals. What explanations can you now give for the common use of triangular shapes in structures like bridges and antenna towers for radio and television?

25. rhombus (four equal sides)

    F. rotational   **G.** reflectional

    H. both F and G   **J.** none

26. regular pentagon

    A. rotational   **B.** reflectional

    C. both A and B   **D.** none

27. square

    F. rotational   **G.** reflectional

    H. both F and G   **J.** none

28. a parallelogram that is not a rhombus or a rectangle

    A. rotational   **B.** reflectional

    C. both A and B   **D.** none

Extensions

29. In the triangle, a line has been drawn through vertex *A*, parallel to line segment *BC* of the triangle.

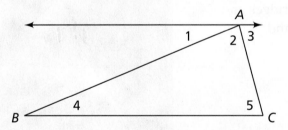

    a. What is the sum of the measures of angles 1, 2, and 3?

    b. Explain why angle 1 has the same measure as angle 4 and why angle 3 has the same measure as angle 5.

    c. How can you use the results of parts (a) and (b) to show that the angle sum of a triangle is 180°?

30. In parts (a)–(b), explore pentagons by using polystrips or by making sketches.

   a. If you choose five numbers as side lengths, can you always build a pentagon? Explain.

   b. Can you make two or more different pentagons from the same side lengths?

31. Refer to the *Did You Know?* after Problem 4.2.

   a. Make a model that illustrates Grashof's principle using polystrips or paper fasteners and cardboard strips. Describe the motion of your model.

   b. How can your model be used to make a stirring mechanism? A windshield wiper?

32. Build the figure below from polystrips. Note that the vertical sides are all the same length, the distance from *B* to *C* equals the distance from *E* to *D*, and the distance from *B* to *C* is twice the distance from *A* to *B*.

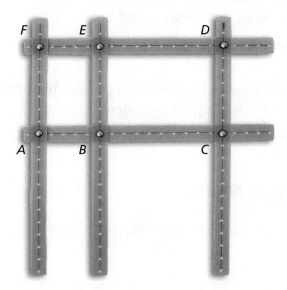

   a. Experiment with holding various strips fixed and moving the other strips. In each case, tell which strips you held fixed, and describe the motion of the other strips.

   b. Fix a strip between points *F* and *B* and then try to move strip *CD*. What happens? Explain why this occurs.

Mathematical Reflections 4

In this investigation, you experimented with building polygons by choosing lengths for the sides and then connecting those sides to make a polygon. These questions will help you summarize what you have learned.

Think about your answers to these questions. Discuss your ideas with other students and your teacher. Then write a summary of your findings in your notebook.

1. a. How can you tell whether three line segments will form a triangle?

   b. If it is possible to build one triangle, is it also possible to build a different triangle with the same three segments? Explain.

2. a. How can you tell whether four line segments will form a quadrilateral?

   b. If it is possible to build one quadrilateral, is it also possible to build a different quadrilateral with the same four segments? Explain.

3. Explain why triangles are useful in building structures.

Unit Project   What's Next?

What information about shapes can you add to your *Shapes and Designs* project?

Looking Back and Looking Ahead

Unit Review

As you worked on the problems of this unit, you have extended your knowledge of two-dimensional geometry—the study of shapes that fit on a flat surface. You have

Go Online
PHSchool.com

For: Vocabulary Review Puzzle
Web Code: amj-3051

- Explored properties of geometric shapes
- Learned how *side lengths* and *angle measures* determine the shapes of *triangles*, *rectangles*, *parallelograms*, and other *polygons*
- Looked at *regular polygons* and discovered why some can fit together to cover a flat surface, while others cannot
- Learned that polygons and angles have important practical uses in the design of buildings, beehives, road signs, and flight paths

Use Your Understanding: Shapes

Test your understanding of shapes by solving the following exercises.

1. This drawing of a building contains many angles.

   a. Which labeled angles appear to measure 90°?

   b. Which labeled angles appear to have measures greater than 90° and less than 180°?

   c. List the labeled angles from smallest to largest, and estimate the degree measure of each. Then use an angle ruler or protractor to measure each as accurately as possible.

2. A designer is experimenting with new shapes for floor tiles. She is considering regular pentagons and regular hexagons.

   a. What is the measure of each interior angle in a regular pentagon?

   b. Is it possible to tile a floor with copies of a regular pentagon? Explain.

   c. What is the measure of each interior angle in a regular hexagon?

   d. What is the measure of each exterior angle in a regular hexagon?

   e. Is it possible to tile a floor with copies of a regular hexagon? Explain.

   f. Describe the symmetries of these two polygons.

   g. Do either of these regular polygons have parallel sides? Explain your reasoning.

3. Complete the following for parts (a)–(d).

   - Tell whether it is possible to draw a shape meeting the given conditions. If it is, make a sketch of the shape.

   - If it is possible to make a shape meeting the given conditions, tell whether it is possible to make a different shape that also meets the conditions. If it is, make a sketch of one or more of these different shapes.

   a. A triangle with side lengths of 4 cm, 6 cm, and 9 cm

   b. A triangle with side lengths of 4 cm, 7 cm, and 2 cm

   c. A rectangle with a pair of opposite sides whose lengths are 8 cm

   d. A parallelogram with side lengths of 8 cm, 8 cm, 6 cm, and 6 cm

Explain Your Reasoning

To solve Exercises 1–3, you used basic facts about the ways angle measures and side lengths determine the shapes of polygons.

4. Describe three ways to think about an angle. Discuss some methods for *estimating* angle measures and for accurately *measuring* angles.

5. Suppose you are asked to draw a triangle with three given side lengths.

    a. How can you tell if it is possible to draw a triangle with those side lengths?

    b. If one such triangle is possible, are there other triangles with the same side lengths but different shapes possible?

    c. Why are triangles so useful in building structures?

    d. Sketch a triangle that has both rotation and reflection symmetries.

    e. Sketch a triangle that has only one line of symmetry.

    f. Sketch a triangle that has no symmetries.

6. a. How can you tell if it is possible to draw a quadrilateral given four side lengths? If you can draw one such quadrilateral, can you always draw a different one?

    b. How can you decide whether a given quadrilateral is a square? A rectangle? A parallelogram?

Look Ahead

You will use the properties of angles and polygons you studied in this unit in many future units of *Connected Mathematics*, especially those that deal with perimeter, area, and volume of figures. The side and angle relationships in triangles and quadrilaterals are also applied in many construction and design tasks.

A

acute angle An angle whose measure is less than 90°.

ángulo agudo Ángulo que mide menos de 90°

angle The figure formed by two rays or line segments that have a common vertex. Angles are measured in degrees. The angle at point *A* on the triangle below is identified as angle *BAC* or ∠*BAC*. The sides of an angle are rays that have the vertex as a starting point. Each of the three angles below is formed by the joining of two rays.

ángulo Figura que forman dos rayos o segmentos que tienen en un vértice común. Los ángulos se miden en grados. El ángulo del punto *A* del triángulo representado a continuación se identifica como el ángulo *BAC* o ∠*BAC*. Los lados de un ángulo son rayos que tienen el vértice como punto de partida. Cada uno de los tres ángulos de abajo está formado por la unión de dos rayos.

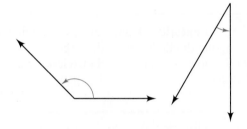
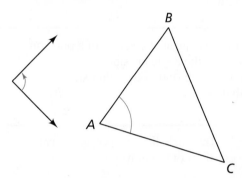

angle sum The sum of all the measures of the interior angles of a polygon.

suma de ángulos Suma de todas las medidas de los ángulos interiores de un polígono.

C

central angle An angle with a vertex at the center of a circle and whose sides are radii of the circle.

ángulo central Ángulo que tiene un vértice en el centro de un círculo y cuyos lados son radios del círculo.

D

degree A unit of measure of angles is also equal to $\frac{1}{360}$ of a complete circle. The angle below measures about 1 degree (1°); 360 of these would just fit around a point and fill in a complete circle; 90 of them make a right angle.

grado Una unidad de medida de ángulos que equivale a $\frac{1}{360}$ de un círculo completo. El ángulo representado a continuación mide aproximadamente un grado (1°); 360 de estos ángulos encajarían alrededor de un punto y llenarían completamente un círculo, mientras que 90 formarían un ángulo recto.

diagonal A line segment connecting two non-adjacent vertices of a polygon. All quadrilaterals have two diagonals, as shown below. The two diagonals of a square are equal in length, and the two diagonals of a rectangle are equal in length. A pentagon has five diagonals. A hexagon has nine diagonals.

diagonal Un segmento de recta que conecta dos vértices no adyacentes de un polígono. Todos los cuadriláteros tienen dos diagonales, como se representa a continuación. Las dos diagonales de un cuadrado tienen longitudes iguales y las dos diagonales de un rectángulo tienen longitudes iguales. Un pentágono tiene cinco diagonales y un hexágono tiene nueve diagonales.

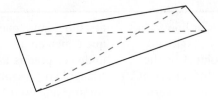

E

equilateral triangle A triangle with all three sides the same length.

triángulo equilátero Un triángulo que tiene tres lados de la misma longitud.

exterior angle An angle at a vertex of a polygon where the sides of the angle are one side of the polygon and the extension of the other side meeting at that vertex.

ángulo exterior Ángulo en el vértice de un polígono donde los lados del ángulo son un lado del polígono y la extensión del otro lado se une en ese vértice.

I

interior angle The angle inside a polygon formed by two adjacent sides of the polygon.

ángulo interior Ángulo dentro de un polígono formado por dos lados adyacentes del polígono.

irregular polygon A polygon which has at least two sides with different lengths or two angles with different measures.

polígono irregular Polígono que tiene al menos dos lados de diferentes longitudes o dos ángulos con diferentes medidas.

isosceles triangle A triangle with two sides the same length.

triángulo isósceles Un triángulo que tiene dos lados de la misma longitud.

L

line of symmetry A line such that if a shape is folded over this line the two halves of the shape match exactly.

eje de simetría Recta por la que si una figura se dobla por ella, sus dos mitades coinciden exactamente.

line segment A line segment consists of two points of a line and all the points between these two points.

segmento de recta Un segmento de recta tiene dos puntos de una recta y todos los puntos entre estos dos puntos.

M

midpoint The point that divides a line segment into two segments of equal length.

punto medio Punto que divide un segmento de recta en dos segmentos de igual longitud.

O

obtuse angle An angle whose measure is greater than 90° and less than 180°.

ángulo obtuso Ángulo cuya medida es mayor de 90° y menor de 180°.

P

parallel lines Lines in a plane that never meet. The opposite sides of a regular hexagon are parallel.

rectas paralelas Rectas en un plano, que nunca se encuentran. Los lados opuestos de un hexágono regular son paralelos. Los polígonos A y B tienen un par de lados opuestos paralelos. Los polígonos C, D y E tienen dos pares de lados opuestos paralelos.

Polygons A and B each have one pair of opposite sides parallel.

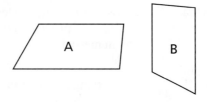

Polygons C, D, and E each have two pairs of opposite sides parallel.

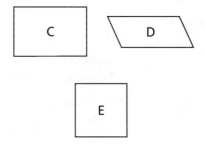

parallelogram A quadrilateral with opposite sides parallel. Both pairs of opposite angles are also equal. In the definition of parallel lines, figure D, rectangle C, and square E are all parallelograms.

paralelogramo Cuadrilátero cuyos lados opuestos son paralelos. Ambos pares de ángulos opuestos también son iguales. En la definición de rectas paralelas, la figura D, el rectángulo C y el cuadrado E son paralelogramos.

perpendicular lines Two lines that intersect to form right angles.

rectas perpendiculares Dos rectas que se intersecan para formar ángulos rectos.

polygon A shape formed by line segments, called *sides*, so that each of the segments meets exactly two other segments, and all of the points where the segments meet are endpoints of the segments.

polígono Figura formada por segmentos de recta, llamados *lados*, de modo que cada uno de los segmentos se junta exactamente con otros dos segmentos, y todos los puntos donde se encuentran los segmentos son extremos de los segmentos.

Polygons

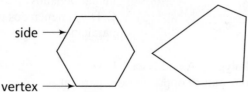

side →

vertex →

Special polygon names use Greek prefixes that tell the number of sides or the number of angles in the polygon.

- triangle: A polygon with 3 sides and angles
- quadrilateral: A polygon with 4 sides and angles
- pentagon: A polygon with 5 sides and angles
- hexagon: A polygon with 6 sides and angles
- heptagon: A polygon with 7 sides and angles
- octagon: A polygon with 8 sides and angles
- nonagon (also called enneagon): A polygon with 9 sides and angles
- decagon: A polygon with 10 sides and angles
- dodecagon: A polygon with 12 sides and angles

Los nombres especiales con que se designan los polígonos provienen de prefijos griegos que indican el número de lados o el número de ángulos del polígono.

- triángulo: polígono con 3 lados y ángulos
- cuadrilátero: polígono con 4 lados y ángulos
- pentágono: polígono con 5 lados y ángulos
- hexágono: polígono con 6 lados y ángulos
- heptágono: polígono con 7 lados y ángulos
- octágono: polígono con 8 lados y ángulos
- nonágono (también llamado eneágono): polígono con 9 lados y ángulos
- decágono: polígono con 10 lados y ángulos
- dodecágono: polígono con 12 lados y ángulos

Q

quadrilateral A polygon with four sides.

cuadrilátero Un polígono de cuatro lados como los que se muestran a continuación.

Quadrilaterals

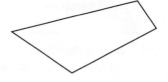

ray A part of a line consisting of a point, called an endpoint, and all the points on the line on one side of the endpoint.

ray Parte de una recta que tiene un punto, llamado extremo, y todos los puntos de la recta están a un lado del extremo.

rectangle A parallelogram with all right angles. Squares are a special type of rectangle.

rectángulo Un paralelogramo con todos los ángulos rectos. Los cuadrados son un tipo especial de rectángulo.

Rectangles

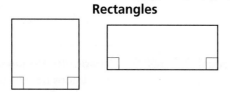

reflection symmetry A shape with reflection symmetry has two halves that are mirror images of each other.

simetría por reflexión Una figura con simetría por reflexión tiene dos mitades que son imágenes reflejas la una de la otra.

regular polygon A polygon that has all of its sides equal and all of its angles equal. The hexagon below is regular, but the pentagon is not regular, because its sides and its angles are not equal.

polígono regular Un polígono que tiene todos los lados y todos los ángulos iguales. El hexágono representado a continuación es regular, pero el pentágono no lo es porque sus lados y sus ángulos no son iguales.

Regular **Not Regular**

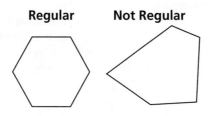

rhombus A quadrilateral that has all sides the same length.

rombo Un cuadrilátero que tiene todos los lados de la misma longitud.

right angle An angle that measures 90°. A rectangle has four right angles.

ángulo recto Un ángulo que mide 90°. Un rectángulo tiene los cuatro ángulos rectos.

right triangle A triangle with one right angle and two acute angles.

triángulo rectángulo Un triángulo que tiene un ángulo recto y dos ángulos agudos.

rotation symmetry A shape has rotation symmetry if it can be rotated less than a full turn about its center point to a position where it looks exactly as it did before it was rotated.

simetría por rotación Una figura tiene simetría por rotación si puede girarse menos de una vuelta completa sobre su centro hasta una posición en la que se vería exactamente igual que antes de girarse.

S

scalene triangle A triangle with no side lengths equal.

triángulo escaleno Triángulo en el cual ninguno de sus lados tiene la misma longitud.

side See *polygon*.

lado Ver *polígono*.

square A rectangle with all sides equal. Squares have four right angles and four equal sides.

cuadrado Rectángulo cuyos lados son iguales. Los cuadrados tienen cuatro ángulos rectos y cuatro lados iguales.

straight angle An angle that measures 180°.

ángulo llano Ángulo que mide 180°.

T

tiling Also called a *tessellation*. The covering of a plane surface with geometric shapes without gaps or overlaps. These shapes are usually regular polygons or other common polygons. The tiling below is made of triangles. You could remove some of the line segments to create a tiling of parallelograms, or remove still more to create a tiling of hexagons. In a tiling, a vertex is a point where the corners of the polygons fit together.

embaldosamiento También llamado *teselado*. Embaldosar es cubrir una superficie plana con figuras geométricas sin dejar espacios o superponer figuras. Estas figuras suelen ser polígonos regulares u otros polígonos comunes. El embaldosamiento representado a continuación está formado por triángulos. Se podrían quitar algunos de los segmentos de recta para crear un teselado de paralelogramos y hasta eliminar otros más para crear un teselado de hexágonos. En un embaldosamiento, un vértice es un punto donde se unen las esquinas de los polígonos.

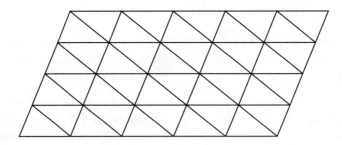

transversal A line that intersects two or more lines. Lines *s* and *t* are transversals.

transversal Recta que interseca dos o más rectas. Las rectas *s* y *t* son transversales.

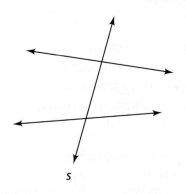

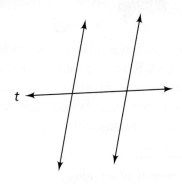

trapezoid A quadrilateral with at least one pair of opposite sides parallel. This definition means that parallelograms are trapezoids.

trapecio Un cuadrilátero que tiene, al menos, un par de lados opuestos paralelos. Esta definición significa que los paralelogramos son trapecios.

Trapezoids

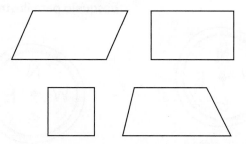

vertex A corner of a polygon. For example, *G*, *H*, *I*, *J*, and *K* are all vertices in the pentagon below. All angles have vertices; for example, in the hexagon below, angle *AFE* has a vertex at *F*.

vértice Las esquinas de un polígono. Por ejemplo, *G*, *H*, *I*, *J* y *K* son vértices del pentágono dibujado a continuación. Todos los ángulos tienen vértices. Por ejemplo, en el hexágono representado a continuación, el ángulo *AFE* tiene el vértice en *F*.

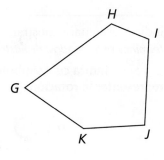

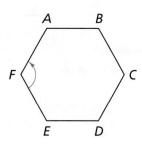

Academic Vocabulary

The following terms are important to your understanding of the mathematics in this unit. Knowing and using these words will help you in thinking, reasoning, representing, communicating your ideas, and making connections across ideas. When these words make sense to you, the investigations and problems will make more sense as well.

I

illustrate To show or present information usually as a drawing or a diagram. You can also illustrate a point using a written explanation.

related terms: present, display

Sample: The needle of a compass is pointing 90 degrees from North. In which direction can the needle be pointing? Make a sketch to illustrate this situation.

The needle could be pointing East, since a needle pointing east would form a 90° angle with North on the compass. The needle can also be pointing West because it also would form a 90° angle with North.

ilustrar Mostrar o presentar información por lo general como un dibujo o un diagrama. También puedes ilustrar un punto usando una explicación escrita.

términos relacionados: presentar, exhibir

Ejemplo: La aguja de una brújula apunta 90 grados desde el Norte. ¿En qué dirección puede estar apuntando la aguja? Haz un bosquejo para ilustrar esta situación.

La aguja podría estar apuntando hacia el Este, puesto que una aguja que apunte al este formaría un ángulo de 90° con el Norte en la brújula. La aguja también puede estar apuntando al Oeste porque también formaría un ángulo de 90° con el Norte.

---

indicate To point out or show.

related terms: demonstrate, show, identify

Sample: Indicate which symbol is used to represent rotation.

The curved arrow is the symbol used to represent rotation. The small circle indicates the degrees of an angle. The dashed line is used to show symmetry.

indicar Apuntar o mostrar.

términos relacionados: demostrar, mostrar, identificar

Ejemplo: Indica cuál símbolo se usa para representar la rotación.

La flecha curvada es el símbolo que se usa para representar la rotación. El círculo pequeño indica los grados de un ángulo. La línea punteada se usa para mostrar simetría.

justify To support your answers with reasons or examples. A justification may include a written response, diagrams, charts, tables, or a combination of these.

related terms: validate, explain, defend, reason

Sample: Tell whether the following statement is true or false. Justify your answer.

All squares are parallelograms.

The statement is true. All squares are parallelograms because all squares have two pairs of parallel sides.

justificar Apoyar tus respuestas con razones o ejemplos. Una justificación puede incluir una respuesta escrita, diagramas, gráficas, tablas o una combinación de éstos.

términos relacionados: validar, explicar, defender, razonar

Ejemplo: Di si la siguiente afirmación es cierta o falsa. Justifica tu respuesta.

Todos los cuadrados son paralelogramos.

La afirmación es cierta. Todos los cuadrados son paralelogramos porque todos los cuadrados tienen dos pares de lados paralelos.

relate To find a connection between two different things

related terms: connect, match

Sample: Tell how the exterior angles of a quadrilateral relate to the interior angles.

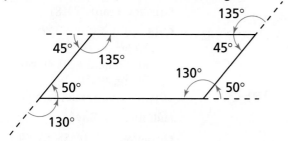

Each pair of interior and exterior angles of the quadrilateral has a sum of 180° because each pair of angles forms a straight angle.

relacionar Hallar una conexión entre dos cosas diferentes.

términos relacionados: conectar, corresponder

Ejemplo: Indica cómo se relacionan los ángulos exteriores de un cuadrilátero con los ángulos interiores.

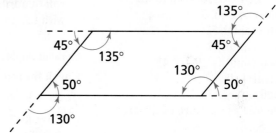

Cada par de ángulos interiores y exteriores del cuadrilátero tiene una suma de 180° porque cada par de ángulos forma un ángulo recto.

sketch To draw a rough outline of something. When a sketch is asked for, it means that a drawing needs to be included in your response.

related terms: draw, illustrate

Sample: Sketch a 30° angle.

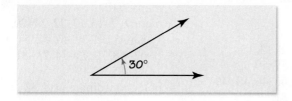

hacer un bosquejo Dibujar un esbozo de algo. Cuando se pide un bosquejo, significa que necesitas incluir un dibujo en tu respuesta.

términos relacionados: dibujar, ilustrar

Ejemplo: Haz un bosquejo de un ángulo de 30°.

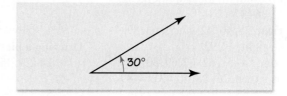

Academic Vocabulary

Index

Index

Acknowledgments

Team Credits

The people who made up the **Connected Mathematics2** team—representing editorial, editorial services, design services, and production services—are listed below. Bold type denotes core team members.

Leora Adler, Judith Buice, Kerry Cashman, Patrick Culleton, Sheila DeFazio, Richard Heater, **Barbara Hollingdale, Jayne Holman,** Karen Holtzman, **Etta Jacobs,** Christine Lee, Carolyn Lock, Catherine Maglio, **Dotti Marshall,** Rich McMahon, Eve Melnechuk, Kristin Mingrone, Terri Mitchell, **Marsha Novak,** Irene Rubin, Donna Russo, Robin Samper, Siri Schwartzman, **Nancy Smith,** Emily Soltanoff, **Mark Tricca,** Paula Vergith, Roberta Warshaw, Helen Young

Additional Credits

Diana Bonfilio, Mairead Reddin, Michael Torocsik, nSight, Inc.

Illustration

Michelle Barbera: 25, 26, 41, 45, 46, 49, 63

Technical Illustration

WestWords, Inc.

Cover Design

tom white.images

Photos

2 t, Dorling Kindersley; **2 m,** Bonnie Kamin/PhotoEdit; **2 b,** Kelly-Mooney Photography/Corbis; **3,** AP Photo/Bizuayehu Tesfaye; **5,** Richard Haynes; **7 t,** Dorling Kindersley; **7 b,** Musee National d'Art Moderne, CentreGeorges Pompidou, Paris/SuperStock; **14,** Mark Chappell/Animals Animals/Earth Scenes; **16 t,** Kevin Schafer/Corbis; **16 b,** M.C. Escher's "Symmetry Drawing E59" © 2004 The M.C. Escher Company - Baarn - Holland. All rights reserved.; **18,** Christie's Images/Corbis; **19 l,** Judith Miller Archive/Dorling Kindersley; **19 r,** Bonnie Kamin/PhotoEdit; **30,** Richard Haynes; **32,** NOAA Photo Library, NOAA Central Library; OAR/ERL/National Severe Storms Laboratory (NSSL); **35,** Spencer Grant/PhotoEdit; **37,** Bettmann/Corbis; **38,** Royalty-Free/Corbis; **40,** Mark Gibson/Index Stock Imagery, Inc.; **49,** Duomo/Corbis; **59,** Jim Cummins/Getty Images, Inc.; **59 inset,** Russ Lappa; **64,** Michelle D. Bridwell/Photo Edit; **66,** Richard Haynes; **70 all,** Russ Lappa; **71,** Kelly-Mooney Photography/Corbis; **73 all,** Russ Lappa; **74,** Russ Lappa; **76,** Pearson Learning; **79,** Raymond Forbes/SuperStock; **81,** Russ Lappa; **83 all,** Getty Images, Inc.

Note: Every effort has been made to locate the copyright owner of the material reprinted in this book. Omissions brought to our attention will be corrected in subsequent editions.

Connected Mathematics 2™

Bits and Pieces II

Using Fraction Operations

Glenda Lappan

James T. Fey

William M. Fitzgerald

Susan N. Friel

Elizabeth Difanis Phillips

Boston, Massachusetts · Glenview, Illinois · Shoreview, Minnesota · Upper Saddle River, New Jersey

Bits and Pieces II

Understanding Fraction Operations

Last season Farmer Sam picked $1\frac{3}{4}$ bushels of tomatoes from his kitchen garden and $14\frac{1}{3}$ bushels from his canning garden. About how many total bushels of tomatoes did he harvest?

Blaine plans to paint a highway stripe that is $\frac{9}{10}$ of a mile long. He is $\frac{2}{3}$ of the way done when he runs out of paint. How long is the stripe he painted?

There are 12 baby rabbits at the pet store. Gabriella has $5\frac{1}{4}$ ounces of parsley to feed the rabbits as treats. She wants to give each rabbit the same amount. How much parsley does each rabbit get?

In *Bits and Pieces I*, you learned what fractions, decimals, and percents mean. In *Bits and Pieces II*, you will investigate situations in which you need to add, subtract, multiply, or divide fractions, such as those described on the previous page. You will decide which operation makes sense in each situation.

Knowing strategies for working with all kinds of numbers is very important. If you take part in developing these strategies, they will make more sense to you, and you will be able to apply them to other situations. You may already know some shortcuts for working with fractions. You can get the most out of this unit by thinking about why those shortcuts, and the strategies you develop with your class, make sense. Remember, it is not enough to get an answer to a problem. The real power is your ability to talk about your ideas and strategies and use them in new situations.

Mathematical Highlights

Understanding Fraction Operations

In *Bits and Pieces II*, you will develop an understanding of and strategies for the four basic arithmetic operations with fractions.

You will learn how to

- Use benchmarks and other strategies to estimate the reasonableness of results of operations with fractions
- Develop ways to model sums, differences, products, and quotients, including the use of areas, fraction strips, and number lines
- Look for rules to generalize patterns in numbers
- Use your knowledge of fractions and equivalence of fractions to develop algorithms for adding, subtracting, multiplying and dividing fractions
- Recognize when addition, subtraction, multiplication, or division is the appropriate operation to solve a problem
- Write fact families to show the inverse relationship between addition and subtraction, and between multiplication and division
- Solve problems using operations on fractions

As you work on the problems in this unit, make it a habit to ask questions about situations that involve fraction operations.

What models or diagrams might be helpful in understanding the situation and the relationships among quantities?

What models or diagrams might help decide which operation is useful in solving a problem?

What is a reasonable estimate for the answer?

Investigation 1

Estimating With Fractions

Sometimes when you need to find an amount, you do not need an exact answer. In these situations, making a reasonable estimate of the answer is good enough. This investigation will help you develop strategies for estimating sums and differences. The sums and differences will involve fractions, as well as decimals.

1.1 Getting Close

Getting Close is a game that will sharpen your estimating skills. In *Bits and Pieces I*, you used *benchmarks* to estimate fractions and decimals. Look at this set of benchmarks.

$$0 \quad \frac{1}{4} \quad \frac{1}{2} \quad \frac{3}{4} \quad 1 \quad 1\frac{1}{4} \quad 1\frac{1}{2} \quad 1\frac{3}{4} \quad 2$$

Which benchmark is $\frac{3}{8}$ nearest? Three-eighths is less than $\frac{1}{2}$, because it is less than $\frac{4}{8}$. Three-eighths is greater than $\frac{1}{4}$, because it is greater than $\frac{2}{8}$. In fact, $\frac{3}{8}$ is exactly halfway between $\frac{1}{4}$ and $\frac{1}{2}$.

Which benchmark is 0.58 nearest? Since $\frac{1}{2}$ is equal to 0.50, 0.58 is greater than $\frac{1}{2}$. You also know that 0.58 is less than $\frac{3}{4}$ or 0.75. So 0.58 is between $\frac{1}{2}$ and $\frac{3}{4}$, but it is closer to $\frac{1}{2}$.

How can you use benchmarks to help you estimate the sum of two fractions? Think about the example below.

$$\frac{1}{2} + \frac{5}{8}$$

- Is the sum between 0 and 1 or between 1 and 2?
- Is the sum closest to 0, to 1, or to 2?

When you play the Getting Close game, you will use benchmarks and other strategies to estimate the sum of two numbers.

Getting Close Rules

Two to four players can play Getting Close.

Materials

- Getting Close game cards (one set per group)
- A set of four number squares (0, 1, 2, and 3) for each player

Playing

1. All players hold their 0, 1, 2, and 3 number squares in their hand.

2. The cards are placed face-down in a pile in the center of the table.

3. One player turns over two game cards from the pile. Each player mentally estimates the sum of the numbers on the two game cards. Each player then selects from their set the number square (0, 1, 2, or 3) closest to their estimate and places it face-down on the table.

4. After each player has played a number square, the players turn their number squares over at the same time.

5. The player whose number square is closest to the actual sum gets the two game cards. If there is a tie, all players who tied get one game card. Players who have tied may take a game card from the deck if necessary.

6. Players take turns turning over the two game cards.

7. When all cards have been used, the player with the most cards wins.

You may find benchmarks, fraction strips, number lines, diagrams, or changing a fraction to a decimal helpful in making estimates. You may discover other ways of thinking that help as well.

Problem 1.1 Using Benchmarks

Play Getting Close several times. Keep a record of the estimation strategies you find useful.

A. 1. Describe or illustrate one estimation strategy that you found useful in the game.

   2. For which pairs was it easy and for which pairs was it hard to estimate the sum? Why?

B. Suppose you played Getting Close with only these game cards:

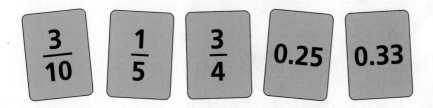

   1. What is the greatest sum possible with any two of the game cards shown?

   2. What is the least sum possible with any two of the game cards shown?

ACE Homework starts on page 10.

Estimating Sums

In this problem, you will see several situations that use fractions and involve estimating sums. There are times when you should overestimate what is needed to make sure you have enough. Other times, you want to underestimate to make sure you do not take or assume too much.

Problem 1.2 Estimating Sums

A. Elaine is making a model of a house that she designed. She wants to put wood molding around two rooms in the model. She measures and finds that she needs $3\frac{1}{4}$ feet of molding for one room and $2\frac{3}{8}$ feet of molding for the other room. She has $5\frac{1}{2}$ feet of molding.

1. Estimate whether she has enough molding.

2. Describe your strategy for estimating the answer.

3. Is your estimate an overestimate or an underestimate of the sum?

B. Elaine asks her granddaughter, Madison, to make curtains for the windows in the two model rooms. The pattern for the first room calls for a $\frac{7}{12}$-yard strip of material. The pattern for the second room calls for a $\frac{5}{8}$-yard strip.

   1. Should Madison underestimate or overestimate the amount of material she needs? Why?

   2. She writes the following computation: $\frac{7}{12} + \frac{5}{8} = \frac{12}{20}$. Use estimation to check whether her computation is reasonable. Explain your thinking.

   3. Madison's friend, Jamar, says that he can write $\frac{7}{12} + \frac{5}{8}$ using the same denominator. He writes $\frac{14}{24} + \frac{15}{24}$ and says, "Now the answer is easy."

   a. What do you think Jamar will give as the sum? Does his thinking make sense?

   b. Is this an exact answer or an estimate?

C. Elaine makes the lace edging that is used to decorate the curtains in the model house. She needs 5 yards of lace for the curtains. She has these lengths of lace on hand:

   $1\frac{1}{3}$ yards $2\frac{5}{6}$ yards $\frac{7}{8}$ yard $\frac{5}{12}$ yard

   1. Should Elaine underestimate or overestimate the amount of lace she has? Why?

   2. Use estimation to tell whether she has enough lace.

   3. Find equivalent fractions with the same denominator to represent the lengths of lace. How does this help you find the actual length of all the lace?

D. Estimate these sums and describe your thinking.

   1. $\frac{2}{3} + \frac{1}{5}$ **2.** $2\frac{1}{3} + 3\frac{2}{3}$ **3.** $\frac{3}{4} + \frac{4}{3}$

ACE Homework starts on page 10.

Applications

For Exercises 1–9, determine whether the number is closest to $0, \frac{1}{2}$, or 1. Explain your reasoning.

1. $\frac{10}{9}$

2. $\frac{9}{16}$

3. $\frac{2}{15}$

4. $\frac{500}{1000}$

5. $\frac{5}{6}$

6. $\frac{48}{100}$

7. 0.67

8. 0.26

9. 0.0009999

For Exercises 10–15, determine whether the sum of the two Getting Close game cards is closest to 0, 1, 2, or 3. Explain.

10. $\frac{7}{8}$ and $\frac{4}{9}$

11. $1\frac{4}{10}$ and 0.375

12. $\frac{2}{5}$ and $\frac{7}{10}$

13. $1\frac{3}{4}$ and $\frac{1}{8}$

14. $1\frac{1}{3}$ and 1.3

15. 0.25 and $\frac{1}{8}$

For Exercises 16–18, you are playing a game called Getting Even Closer. In this game, you have to estimate sums to the nearest $\frac{1}{2}$, or 0.5. Decide if the sum of the two game cards turned up is closest to $0, \frac{1}{2}$, or 1. Explain.

16. $\frac{3}{5}$ and $\frac{1}{10}$

17. $\frac{1}{4}$ and $\frac{1}{10}$

18. $\frac{1}{9}$ and $\frac{1}{8}$

19. Four students were asked the following question: "Can you find two fractions with a sum greater than $\frac{3}{4}$?" Explain whether each student's answer below is correct.

a. $\frac{1}{8} + \frac{2}{4}$

b. $\frac{3}{6} + \frac{2}{4}$

c. $\frac{5}{12} + \frac{5}{6}$

d. $\frac{5}{10} + \frac{3}{8}$

Homework
Help Online
PHSchool.com

For: Help with Exercise 19
Web Code: ame-4119

For Exercises 20–25, find two fractions with a sum that is between the two given numbers.

20. 0 and $\frac{1}{2}$

21. $\frac{1}{2}$ and 1

22. 1 and $1\frac{1}{2}$

23. $1\frac{1}{2}$ and 2

24. 2 and $2\frac{1}{2}$

25. $2\frac{1}{2}$ and 3

26. Many sewing patterns have a $\frac{5}{8}$-inch border for sewing the seam. Is a $\frac{5}{8}$-inch border closest to $0, \frac{1}{2}$, or 1 inch? Explain.

27. Last season Farmer Sam picked $1\frac{3}{4}$ bushels of tomatoes from his kitchen garden and $14\frac{1}{3}$ bushels from his canning garden. About how many total bushels of tomatoes did he harvest?

28. Suppose you mix $\frac{5}{8}$ cup of wheat flour with $1\frac{3}{4}$ cups of white flour. Do you have enough for a recipe that calls for $2\frac{1}{2}$ cups of flour?

29. Soo needs 2 yards of molding to put around the bottom of a stand. He has two pieces of molding: one is $\frac{7}{8}$ yard long and the other is $\frac{8}{7}$ yard long. Estimate whether he has enough molding. Explain.

Go Online
PHSchool.com
For: Multiple-Choice Skills Practice
Web Code: ama-4154

30. Julio is at the grocery store. He has $10.00. Here is a list of the items he would like to buy. Use mental computation and estimation to answer parts (a)–(c).

Milk	$2.47
Eggs	$1.09
Cheese	$1.95
Bread	$0.68
Honey	$1.19
Cereal	$3.25
Avocado	$0.50
Chipotles	$1.29

a. Can Julio buy all the items with the money he has? Explain.

b. If he has only $5.00, what can he buy? Give two possibilities.

c. What different items can Julio buy to come as close as possible to spending $5.00?

Connections

31. The rectangle shown represents $\frac{3}{4}$ of a whole.

   a. Draw a rectangle representing the whole.

   b. Draw a rectangle representing $\frac{5}{4}$ of the whole.

32. The rectangle shown represents 150% of a whole. Draw 100% of the same whole.

33. The beans shown represent $\frac{3}{5}$ of the total beans on the kitchen counter. How many total beans are there on the counter?

34. The following fractions occur so often in our lives that it is useful to quickly recall their decimal and percent equivalents.

$$\frac{1}{2} \quad \frac{1}{3} \quad \frac{1}{4} \quad \frac{2}{3} \quad \frac{3}{4} \quad \frac{1}{6} \quad \frac{1}{5} \quad \frac{1}{8}$$

   a. For each of these important fractions, give the decimal and percent equivalents.

   b. Draw a number line. On your number line, mark the point that corresponds to each fraction shown above. Label each point with its fraction, decimal, and percent equivalent.

35. Multiple Choice Choose the set of decimals that is ordered from least to greatest.

A. 5.603   5.63   5.096   5.67   5.599

B. 5.63   5.67   5.096   5.599   5.603

C. 5.096   5.63   5.67   5.603   5.599

D. 5.096   5.599   5.603   5.63   5.67

36. In which of the following groups of fractions can *all* the fractions be renamed as a whole number of hundredths? Explain your reasoning for each.

a. $\frac{3}{2}, \frac{3}{4}, \frac{3}{5}$

b. $\frac{7}{10}, \frac{7}{11}, \frac{7}{12}$

c. $\frac{2}{5}, \frac{2}{6}, \frac{2}{8}$

d. $\frac{11}{5}, \frac{11}{10}, \frac{11}{20}$

For Exercises 37–40, copy the figure onto your paper. Then, divide the figure into fourths. Shade $\frac{1}{4}$ of the figure.

37.

38.

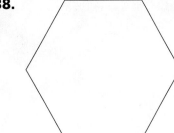

39.

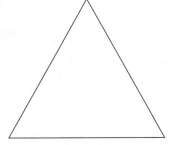

40.

In Exercises 41 and 42, craft paint has spilled on the page, covering part of the fraction strips. Use what is showing to reason about each pair of strips. Find the equivalent fractions indicated by the question marks.

41.

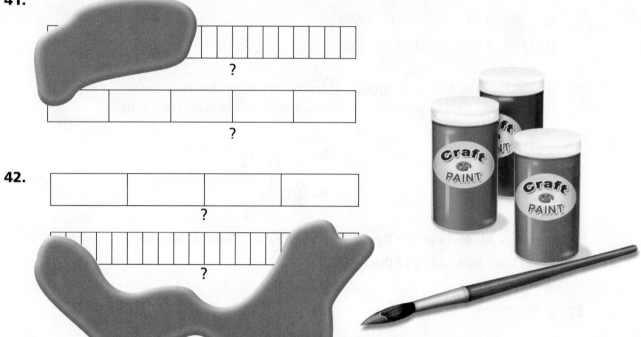

42.

Extensions

For Exercises 43–46, name a fraction in the given interval.

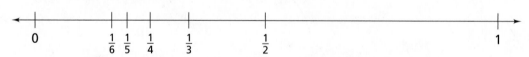

43. between $\frac{1}{3}$ and $\frac{1}{2}$

44. between $\frac{1}{4}$ and $\frac{1}{3}$

45. between $\frac{1}{5}$ and $\frac{1}{4}$

46. between $\frac{1}{6}$ and $\frac{1}{5}$

47. In Exercises 43–46, is it possible to find another fraction in each interval? Why or why not?

Mathematical Reflections 1

In this investigation, you developed strategies for estimating the sum of fractions and decimals. These questions will help you to summarize what you have learned.

Think about your answers to these questions. Discuss your ideas with other students and your teacher. Then write a summary of your findings in your notebook.

1. Describe at least two strategies for estimating fraction sums. Give an example for each strategy. Explain how each strategy is useful.

2. How do you decide whether an overestimate or an underestimate is most helpful? Give examples to help explain your thinking.

Adding and Subtracting Fractions

Knowing how to combine and separate quantities is helpful in understanding the world around you. The mathematical names for combining and separating quantities are *adding* and *subtracting*.

For example, if you own two acres of land and you buy another half-acre lot, you will have $2 + \frac{1}{2}$, or $2\frac{1}{2}$, acres of land. The number sentence that shows this relationship is:

$$2 + \frac{1}{2} = 2\frac{1}{2}$$

The *sum* refers to the $2\frac{1}{2}$ acres of land you own.

If you then sell $\frac{3}{4}$ of an acre of your land, you will own $2\frac{1}{2} - \frac{3}{4}$ acres of land. The number sentence that shows this relationship is:

$$2\frac{1}{2} - \frac{3}{4} = 1\frac{3}{4}$$

The *difference* refers to the $1\frac{3}{4}$ acres of land you will own.

The problems in this investigation require you to add and subtract fractions. As you work, use what you have learned in earlier units and investigations about fractions and finding equivalent fractions. Practice writing number sentences to communicate your strategies for solving the problem.

When Tupelo Township was founded, the land was divided into sections
that could be farmed. Each *section* is a square that is 1 mile long on each
side. In other words, each section is 1 square mile of land. There are
640 acres of land in a square-mile section.

The diagram below shows two sections of land that are *adjacent*, or side by side. Each section is divided among several owners. The diagram shows the part of a section each person owns.

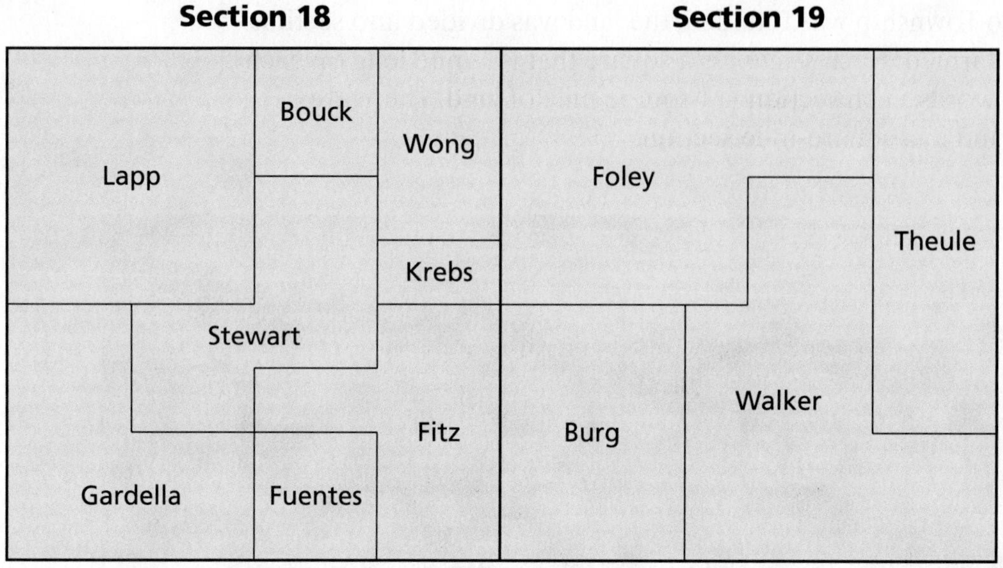

Section 18   **Section 19**

Problem 2.1 Writing Addition and Subtraction Sentences

A. What fraction of a section does each person own? Explain.

B. Suppose Fuentes buys Theule's land. What fraction of a section will Fuentes own? Write a number sentence to show your solution.

C. 1. Find a group of owners whose combined land is equal to $1\frac{1}{2}$ sections of land. Write a number sentence to show your solution.

   2. Find another group of owners whose combined land is equal to $1\frac{1}{2}$ sections of land.

D. 1. Bouck and Lapp claim that when their land is combined, the total equals Foley's land. Write a number sentence to show whether this is true.

   2. Find two other people whose combined land equals another person's land. Write a number sentence to show your answer.

   3. Find three people whose combined land equals another person's land. Write a number sentence to show your answer.

E. How many acres of land does each person own? Explain your reasoning.

F. Lapp and Wong went on a land-buying spree and together bought all the lots of Section 18 that they did not already own. First, Lapp bought the land from Gardella, Fuentes, and Fitz. Then Wong bought the rest.

1. When the buying was completed, what fraction of Section 18 did Lapp own?

2. What fraction of Section 18 did Wong own?

3. Who owned more land? How much more land did he or she own?

 Homework starts on page 24.

2.2 Visiting the Spice Shop

All over the world cooks use spices to add flavor to foods. Because recipe ingredients are often measured using fractions, cooking can involve adding and subtracting fractional quantities.

Reyna owns a spice shop in Tupelo Township. Some of her recipes are shown below.

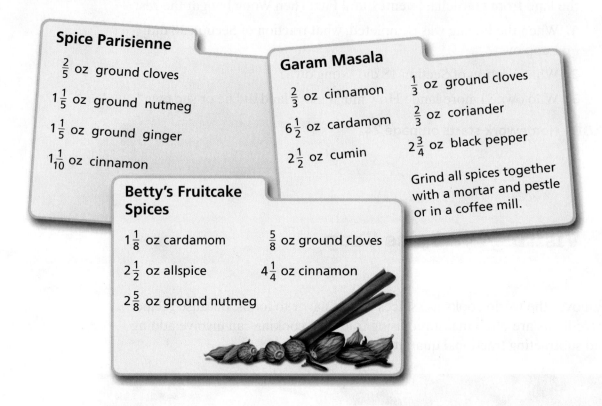

Spice Parisienne

$\frac{2}{5}$ oz ground cloves

$1\frac{1}{5}$ oz ground nutmeg

$1\frac{1}{5}$ oz ground ginger

$1\frac{1}{10}$ oz cinnamon

Garam Masala

$\frac{2}{3}$ oz cinnamon

$6\frac{1}{2}$ oz cardamom

$2\frac{1}{2}$ oz cumin

$\frac{1}{3}$ oz ground cloves

$\frac{2}{3}$ oz coriander

$2\frac{3}{4}$ oz black pepper

Grind all spices together with a mortar and pestle or in a coffee mill.

Betty's Fruitcake Spices

$1\frac{1}{8}$ oz cardamom

$2\frac{1}{2}$ oz allspice

$2\frac{5}{8}$ oz ground nutmeg

$\frac{5}{8}$ oz ground cloves

$4\frac{1}{4}$ oz cinnamon

Problem 2.2 Using Addition and Subtraction

Use number sentences to show your thinking.

A. Latisha buys the spices to make one batch of Spice Parisienne.

1. How many ounces of spice does Latisha buy?

2. a. Suppose she already has the nutmeg at home. How many ounces of spice does she buy?

b. Show a way to determine the answer using subtraction.

B. Ms. Garza buys spices to make one batch of Garam Masala.

1. How many ounces of spice does Ms. Garza buy?

2. a. Suppose she already has enough cinnamon and coriander at home. How many ounces of spice does she buy?

b. Show a way to determine the answer using subtraction.

C. Betty buys spices for her famous fruitcake.

1. How many ounces of spice does Betty buy?

2. Betty makes the fruitcake but forgets the nutmeg! How many ounces of spice does she actually use?

3. Tevin is allergic to cinnamon. If Betty removes cinnamon from the recipe for him, how many ounces of spice does she buy?

D. Use what you have learned to find the value for N that makes each sentence correct.

1. $1\frac{2}{3} + 2\frac{7}{9} = N$

2. $\frac{2}{5} + \frac{1}{4} = N$

3. $2\frac{3}{4} - 1\frac{1}{3} = N$

4. $3\frac{1}{6} - 1\frac{3}{4} = N$

5. $N + \frac{3}{4} = 1\frac{1}{2}$

6. $2\frac{2}{3} - N = 1\frac{1}{4}$

E. Describe a good strategy for adding and subtracting mixed numbers.

ACE Homework starts on page 24.

2.3 Just the Facts

In Problem 2.2, you wrote an addition or subtraction sentence to show a calculation you did. For each addition sentence you write, there are three related number sentences that show the same information.

$$\begin{aligned} \text{addition sentence:}&\quad 2 + 3 = 5 \\ \text{related number sentences:}&\quad 3 + 2 = 5 \\ &\quad 5 - 2 = 3 \\ &\quad 5 - 3 = 2 \end{aligned}$$

These four number sentences form a **fact family.**

You can also create fact families with fractions. For example, $\frac{3}{4} + \frac{1}{8} = \frac{7}{8}$ has these three related number sentences:

$$\frac{1}{8} + \frac{3}{4} = \frac{7}{8}$$

$$\frac{7}{8} - \frac{3}{4} = \frac{1}{8}$$

$$\frac{7}{8} - \frac{1}{8} = \frac{3}{4}$$

You can write this entire fact family using eighths by changing $\frac{3}{4}$ to $\frac{6}{8}$. It looks like this:

$$\frac{6}{8} + \frac{1}{8} = \frac{7}{8}$$

$$\frac{1}{8} + \frac{6}{8} = \frac{7}{8}$$

$$\frac{7}{8} - \frac{6}{8} = \frac{1}{8}$$

$$\frac{7}{8} - \frac{1}{8} = \frac{6}{8}$$

Problem 2.3 Fact Families

A. For each number sentence, write its complete fact family.

   1. $\frac{2}{3} + \frac{5}{9} = \frac{11}{9}$

   2. $\frac{5}{10} - \frac{2}{5} = \frac{1}{10}$

B. For each mathematical sentence, find the value of N. Then write each complete fact family.

   1. $3\frac{3}{5} + 1\frac{2}{3} = N$

   2. $3\frac{1}{6} - 1\frac{2}{3} = N$

   3. $\frac{3}{4} + N = \frac{17}{12}$

   4. $N - \frac{1}{2} = \frac{3}{8}$

C. After writing several fact families, Rochelle claims that subtraction undoes addition. Do you agree or disagree? Explain your reasoning.

D. In the mathematical sentence below, find values for M and N that make the sum exactly 3. Write your answer as a sum that equals 3.

$$\frac{5}{8} + \frac{1}{4} + \frac{2}{3} + M + N = 3$$

ACE Homework starts on page 24.

2.4 Designing Algorithms for Addition and Subtraction

To become skilled in solving problems that involve addition and subtraction of fractions, you need a plan for carrying out computations. In mathematics, a plan, or a series of steps, for doing a computation is called an **algorithm** (AL guh rith um). For an algorithm to be useful, each step should be clear and precise.

In this problem, you develop algorithms for adding and subtracting fractions. You may develop more than one for each computation. You should understand and feel comfortable with at least one algorithm for adding fractions and at least one algorithm for subtracting fractions.

Problem 2.4 Designing Algorithms for Addition and Subtraction

A. 1. Find the sums in each group.

Group 1	Group 2	Group 3
$2\frac{2}{9} + \frac{4}{9}$	$\frac{4}{9} + \frac{1}{3}$	$\frac{1}{8} + \frac{2}{3}$
$\frac{5}{8} + \frac{1}{8}$	$2\frac{1}{2} + \frac{5}{12}$	$\frac{2}{9} + 3\frac{1}{4}$
$\frac{3}{5} + \frac{9}{5}$	$\frac{7}{8} + \frac{1}{2}$	$3\frac{4}{5} + 3\frac{3}{4}$

  2. Describe what the problems in each group have in common.

  3. Make up one new problem that fits in each group.

  4. Write an algorithm that will work for adding *any* two fractions including mixed numbers. Test your algorithm on the problems in the table. If necessary, change your algorithm until you think it will work all the time.

B. 1. Find the differences in each group.

Group 1	Group 2	Group 3
$3\frac{5}{6} - \frac{1}{6}$	$1\frac{3}{4} - \frac{1}{8}$	$3\frac{5}{6} - 1\frac{1}{4}$
$\frac{11}{7} - \frac{1}{7}$	$2\frac{7}{16} - 2\frac{1}{4}$	$\frac{1}{4} - \frac{1}{5}$
$1\frac{2}{3} - \frac{1}{3}$	$6\frac{7}{8} - 3\frac{3}{4}$	$4\frac{3}{5} - \frac{1}{3}$

  2. Describe what the problems in each group have in common.

  3. Make up one new problem that fits in each group.

  4. Write an algorithm that will work for subtracting *any* two fractions, including mixed numbers. Test your algorithm on the problems in the table.

  5. Describe how the subtraction problems below are different from the problems in the subtraction table in part (1).

Group 1	Group 2	Group 3
$1\frac{1}{3} - \frac{2}{3}$	$6\frac{3}{4} - 3\frac{7}{8}$	$3\frac{1}{4} - 1\frac{5}{6}$

  6. If needed, change your algorithm until you think it will work all the time.

C. Use your algorithms for addition and subtraction to find each sum or difference.

  1. $8 - 2\frac{2}{3}$ **2.** $8\frac{2}{3} - 2$ **3.** $2\frac{7}{16} + \frac{4}{9}$ **4.** $1\frac{4}{5} + 1\frac{5}{6} + 1\frac{3}{4}$

ACE Homework starts on page 24.

Applications

Connections

Extensions

Applications

1. The Langstons planted a big garden with flowers to sell to florists.

a. What fraction of the garden is planted with each type of flower?

b. How much more of the garden is planted with lilies than daisies?

c. Suppose the Langstons replace the daisies and irises with lilies. What fraction of the garden would be planted with lilies?

d. Use fractions to explain whether the following sentence is correct or incorrect.

The plots used for growing marigolds and petunias are equivalent to the plot used to grow impatiens.

e. Use fractions to explain whether the following sentence is correct or incorrect.

Marigolds − Begonias = Petunias + Tulips

f. Look at the original garden plan. Find three different combinations of plots that total the fraction of the garden planted with impatiens. Write a number sentence for each combination.

2. A local magazine sells space for ads. It charges advertisers according to the fraction of a page each ad fills.

    a. Advertisers purchase $\frac{1}{8}$ and $\frac{1}{16}$ of a page. What fraction of the page is used for ads?

    b. What fraction of the page remains for other uses? Explain.

3. The Cool Sub Shop is having its grand opening. The owner buys three $\frac{1}{4}$-page ads, four $\frac{1}{8}$-page ads, and ten $\frac{1}{16}$-page ads. What is the total amount of ad space that the owner buys?

Sample Magazine Page

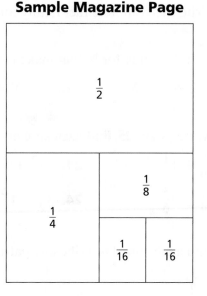

4. A local concert promoter purchases $2\frac{3}{4}$ pages of ads. When one of the concerts is cancelled, the promoter cancels $1\frac{5}{8}$ pages of ads. How much advertising space is the concert promoter actually using?

5. Rico and his friend eat part of a pan of lasagna. Rico eats $\frac{1}{16}$ of the lasagna, and his friend eats $\frac{1}{32}$ of the lasagna. How much of the lasagna is left?

6. Suppose you eat $\frac{3}{4}$ of a pizza and then eat $\frac{1}{8}$ of another pizza of the same size. How much of a whole pizza do you eat altogether?

For Exercises 7–12, find each sum or difference.

7. $8\frac{11}{12} - 2\frac{3}{4}$ **8.** $4\frac{4}{9} + 1\frac{2}{9}$ **9.** $2\frac{1}{8} + 3\frac{3}{4} + 1\frac{1}{2}$

10. $2\frac{7}{9} + 6\frac{1}{3}$ **11.** $11\frac{1}{2} - 2\frac{2}{3}$ **12.** $1\frac{2}{5} + 1\frac{1}{3}$

For: Multiple-Choice Skills Practice
Web Code: ama-4254

13. Find each sum. Describe any patterns that you see.

    a. $\frac{1}{2} + \frac{1}{3}$ **b.** $\frac{2}{4} + \frac{2}{6}$ **c.** $\frac{6}{12} + \frac{4}{12}$

For Exercises 14–17, determine which sum or difference is greater. Show your work.

14. $\frac{2}{3} + \frac{5}{6}$ or $\frac{3}{4} + \frac{4}{5}$ **15.** $\frac{7}{6} - \frac{2}{3}$ or $\frac{3}{5} - \frac{5}{10}$

16. $\frac{1}{4} + \frac{5}{6}$ or $\frac{1}{5} + \frac{7}{8}$ **17.** $\frac{1}{16} + \frac{1}{12}$ or $\frac{5}{4} - \frac{4}{5}$

18. Write the complete fact family for $\frac{1}{16} + \frac{1}{12}$ and for $\frac{5}{4} - \frac{4}{5}$.

19. Find the value for N that makes each number sentence correct.

    a. $\frac{2}{3} + \frac{3}{4} = N$ **b.** $\frac{3}{4} + N = \frac{4}{5}$ **c.** $N - \frac{3}{5} = \frac{1}{4}$

For Exercises 20–25, find each sum or difference.

20. $2\frac{5}{6} + 1\frac{1}{3}$ **21.** $15\frac{5}{8} + 10\frac{5}{6}$ **22.** $4\frac{4}{9} + 2\frac{1}{5}$

23. $6\frac{1}{4} - 2\frac{5}{6}$ **24.** $3\frac{1}{2} - 1\frac{4}{5}$ **25.** $4\frac{1}{3} - \frac{5}{12}$

26. Find each sum. Describe any patterns that you see.

    a. $\frac{1}{2} + \frac{1}{4}$ **b.** $\frac{1}{3} + \frac{1}{6}$ **c.** $\frac{1}{4} + \frac{1}{8}$

    d. $\frac{1}{5} + \frac{1}{10}$ **e.** $\frac{1}{6} + \frac{1}{12}$ **f.** $\frac{1}{7} + \frac{1}{14}$

27. Tony works at a pizza shop. He cuts two pizzas into eight equal sections each. Customers then eat $\frac{7}{8}$ of each pizza. Tony says that $\frac{7}{8} + \frac{7}{8} = \frac{14}{16}$, so $\frac{14}{16}$ of all the pizza was eaten. Is Tony's addition correct? Explain.

Homework Help Online
PHSchool.com
For: Help with Exercise 27
Web Code: ame-4227

Connections

28. Suppose you select a number in the interval from $\frac{1}{2}$ to $\frac{3}{4}$ and a number in the interval from $\frac{3}{4}$ to $1\frac{1}{4}$. What is the least their sum can be? What is the greatest their sum can be? Explain your reasoning. (Note: The numbers $\frac{1}{2}$ and $\frac{3}{4}$ are included in the interval from $\frac{1}{2}$ to $\frac{3}{4}$.)

29. One number is near the benchmark $\frac{1}{4}$, and another is near the benchmark $1\frac{1}{2}$. Estimate their sum. Explain.

For Exercises 30–35, find a value for N that will make the sentence true.

30. $\frac{3}{12} = \frac{N}{8}$ **31.** $\frac{N}{4} = \frac{6}{8}$ **32.** $\frac{1}{2} = \frac{N}{12}$

33. $\frac{N}{12} = \frac{2}{3}$ **34.** $\frac{N}{8} = \frac{14}{16}$ **35.** $\frac{5}{12} = \frac{10}{N}$

In Exercises 36–38, paint has spilled on the page, covering part of the fraction strips. Use what is showing to reason about each set of strips. Find the equivalent fractions indicated by the question marks.

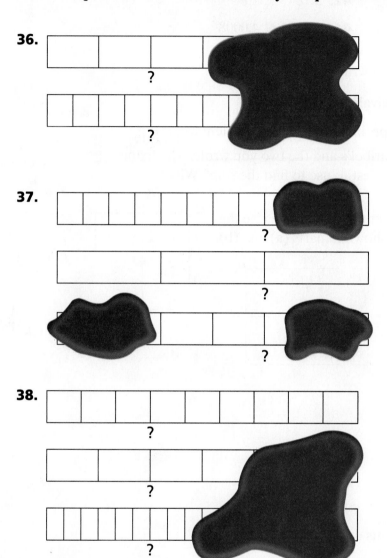

36.

37.

38.

For Exercises 39 and 40, use the map of Tupelo Township from Problem 2.1.

39. Multiple Choice Choose the combination of landowners who together own exactly one hundred percent of a section.

 A. Burg, Lapp, Wong, Fuentes, and Bouck

 B. Burg, Lapp, Fuentes, Bouck, Wong, Theule, and Stewart

 C. Lapp, Fitz, Foley, and Walker

 D. Walker, Foley, Fitz, and Fuentes

40. Find two different combinations of landowners whose land is equal to 1.25 sections of land. Write number sentences to show your solutions.

Investigation 2 Adding and Subtracting Fractions   **27**

Copy each pair of numbers in Exercises 41–44. Insert <, >, or = to make a true statement.

41. 18.156 ■ 18.17

42. 3.184 ■ 31.84

43. 5.78329 ■ 5.78239

44. 4.0074 ■ 4.0008

45. When solving $\frac{7}{15} + \frac{2}{10}$, Maribel writes $\frac{70}{150} + \frac{30}{150}$.

   a. Show why $\frac{70}{150} + \frac{30}{150}$ is equivalent to $\frac{7}{15} + \frac{2}{10}$.

   b. Write two more addition problems that are equivalent to $\frac{7}{15} + \frac{2}{10}$.

   c. Of the three problems, Maribel's and the two you wrote, which one do you think will be the easiest to use to find the sum? Why?

46. The model at the right represents $\frac{1}{3}$ of a whole. Use the model to name the amounts shown in parts (a) and (b).

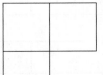

   a.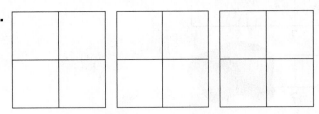

   b.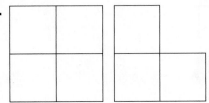

47. The following model represents one whole.

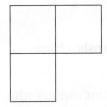

   a. Draw a picture to represent $1\frac{1}{3} + \frac{1}{6}$.

   b. Draw a picture to represent $2\frac{2}{3} - \frac{4}{3}$.

Extensions

48. *The Spartan* magazine wants to charge $160 for each full page of advertising.

   a. Develop a pricing plan to show the cost for each size ad shown below. Explain.

$$\frac{1}{32}\text{ page, }\ \frac{1}{16}\text{ page, }\ \frac{1}{8}\text{ page, }\ \frac{1}{4}\text{ page, }\ \frac{1}{2}\text{ page, }\ 1\text{ page}$$

   b. Use the pricing plan you developed. What is the bill for the Cool Sub Shop if the owner purchases three $\frac{1}{4}$-page ads, four $\frac{1}{8}$-page ads, and a $\frac{1}{16}$-page ad?

   c. The senior class is raising money for their senior trip. They have $80 to spend on advertising. Geraldo says they can purchase two $\frac{1}{8}$-page ads and four $\frac{1}{16}$-page ads with their money. According to your pricing plan in part (a), is he correct? Explain.

   d. Use your pricing plan from part (a). Find four different sets of ad sizes that the senior class can purchase for $80. Show why your answers are correct.

49. a. Find a number for each denominator to make the sentence true. If necessary, you may use a number more than once.

$$\frac{1}{\blacksquare} - \frac{1}{\blacksquare} = \frac{1}{\blacksquare}$$

   b. Find another set of numbers that works.

50. It takes 8 people to clear an acre of weeds in 4 hours.

   a. How many acres can 16 people clear in 4 hours?

   b. How many acres can 2 people clear in 4 hours?

   c. How many people are needed to clear 3 acres in 4 hours?

   d. How many people are needed to clear 3 acres in 2 hours?

51. The sixth-grade students at Cleveland Middle School are selling popcorn as a fundraiser. They keep track of their progress using a number line like the one below:

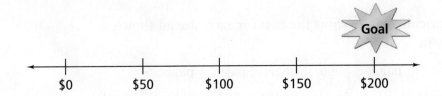

After Day 2, the students have not sold enough popcorn to make up for the money they spent getting started. Ms. Johnson suggests they change their number line to look like this:

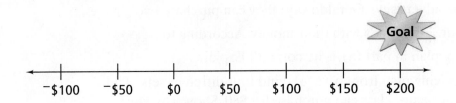

a. The students then plot this point to show their progress:

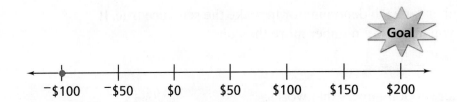

How much money have the sixth-graders lost?

b. After Day 4, the sixth-graders are doing better. They have lost a total of $25. Mark this point on a copy of the number line.

c. After Day 6, the sixth-graders are breaking even. This means they are no longer losing any money, but they are not gaining any money either. Mark their progress on your number line.

d. At the end of the fundraiser, the sixth-graders' number line looks like the one below. How much money have they raised?

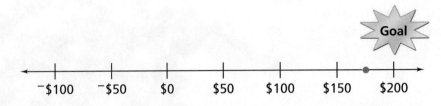

e. What fraction of their goal did they raise after they broke even?

Mathematical Reflections 2

In this investigation you explored ways to add and subtract fractions. These questions will help you to summarize what you have learned.

Think about your answers to these questions. Discuss your ideas with other students and your teacher. Then write a summary of your findings in your notebook.

1. Suppose you are helping a student who has not studied fractions. What is the most important thing you can say about adding or subtracting fractions?

2. Describe at least two things that you have to think about when you add or subtract with mixed numbers. Choose things that you do *not* need to think about when you add or subtract fractions.

3. Use an example to show how addition and subtraction of fractions are related in fact families.

Multiplying With Fractions

Sometimes, instead of adding or subtracting fractions, you need to multiply them. For example, suppose you take inventory at the sporting goods store where you work. There are $13\frac{1}{2}$ boxes of footballs in the stock room, and there are 12 footballs in a full box. How can you find the total number of footballs without opening all the boxes? This situation requires multiplication.

In this investigation, you will relate what you already know about multiplication to situations involving fractions. Remember, to make sense of a situation you can draw a model or change a fraction to an equivalent form. You can also estimate to see if your answer makes sense.

3.1 How Much of the Pan Have We Sold?

Paulo and Shania work the brownie booth at the school fair. Sometimes, they have to find a fractional part of another fraction.

How much is $\frac{1}{3}$ of $\frac{2}{3}$?

Problem 3.1 A Model for Multiplication

All the pans of brownies are square. A pan of brownies costs \$12. You can buy any fractional part of a pan of brownies and pay that fraction of \$12. For example, $\frac{1}{2}$ of a pan costs $\frac{1}{2}$ of \$12.

A. Mr. Williams asks to buy $\frac{1}{2}$ of a pan that is $\frac{2}{3}$ full.

Model of a Brownie Pan

1. Use a copy of the brownie pan model shown at the right. Draw a picture to show how the brownie pan might look before Mr. Williams buys his brownies.

2. Use a different colored pencil to show the part of the brownies that Mr. Williams buys. Note that Mr. Williams buys *a part of a part* of the brownie pan.

3. What fraction of a whole pan does Mr. Williams buy? What does he pay?

B. Aunt Serena buys $\frac{3}{4}$ of another pan that is half full.

1. Draw a picture to show how the brownie pan might look before Aunt Serena buys her brownies.

2. Use a different colored pencil to show the part of the brownies that Aunt Serena buys.

3. What fraction of a whole pan does Aunt Serena buy? How much did she pay?

C. When mathematicians write $\frac{1}{2}$ of $\frac{1}{4}$, they mean the operation of multiplication, or $\frac{1}{2} \times \frac{1}{4}$. When you multiply a fraction by a fraction, you are finding "a part of a part." Think of each example below as a brownie-pan problem in which you are buying part of a pan that is partly full—a part of a part.

1. $\frac{1}{3} \times \frac{1}{4}$ **2.** $\frac{1}{4} \times \frac{2}{3}$ **3.** $\frac{1}{3} \times \frac{3}{4}$ **4.** $\frac{3}{4} \times \frac{2}{5}$

D. Use estimation to decide if each product is greater than or less than 1. To help, use the "of" interpretation for multiplication. For example, in part (1), think "$\frac{5}{6}$ of $\frac{1}{2}$."

1. $\frac{5}{6} \times \frac{1}{2}$ **2.** $\frac{5}{6} \times 1$ **3.** $\frac{5}{6} \times 2$ **4.** $\frac{3}{7} \times 2$

5. $\frac{3}{4} \times \frac{3}{4}$ **6.** $\frac{1}{2} \times \frac{9}{3}$ **7.** $\frac{1}{2} \times \frac{10}{7}$ **8.** $\frac{9}{10} \times \frac{10}{7}$

ACE Homework starts on page 40.

In *Bits and Pieces I*, you used thermometers to show what fraction of a fundraising goal had been met. These thermometers are like number lines. You mark thermometers in the same way you mark number lines to show parts of parts and to name the resulting piece. The fundraising thermometers can help you make sense of the number lines you will use in this problem.

One sixth-grade class raises $\frac{2}{3}$ of their goal in four days. They wonder what fraction of the goal they raise each day on average. To figure this out, they find $\frac{1}{4}$ of $\frac{2}{3}$. One student makes the drawings shown below:

Goal

$\frac{1}{3}$ $\frac{2}{3}$

Goal

$\frac{1}{4}$ of $\frac{2}{3}$

Goal

?

Getting Ready for Problem 3.2

The student above divides the fraction of the goal $\left(\frac{2}{3}\right)$ that is met in four days into fourths to find the length equal to $\frac{1}{4}$ of $\frac{2}{3}$. To figure out the new length, the student divides the whole thermometer into pieces of the same size.

What part of the whole thermometer is $\frac{1}{4}$ of $\frac{2}{3}$?

How would you represent $\frac{1}{4} \times \frac{2}{3}$ on a number line?

How would you represent $\frac{3}{4} \times \frac{2}{3}$ on a number line?

A. 1. For parts (a)–(d), use estimation to decide if the product is greater than or less than $\frac{1}{2}$.

    a. $\frac{1}{3} \times \frac{1}{2}$ **b.** $\frac{2}{3} \times \frac{1}{2}$ **c.** $\frac{1}{8} \times \frac{4}{5}$ **d.** $\frac{5}{6} \times \frac{3}{4}$

  2. Solve parts (a)–(d) above. Use the brownie-pan model or the number-line model.

  3. What patterns do you see in your work for parts (a)–(d)?

  4. For part (b) above, do each of the following.

    a. Write a word problem where it makes sense to use the brownie-pan model to solve the problem.

    b. Write a word problem where it makes sense to use the number-line model to solve the problem.

B. Solve the following problems. Write a number sentence for each.

  1. Seth runs $\frac{1}{4}$ of a $\frac{1}{2}$-mile relay race. How far does he run?

  2. Mali owns $\frac{4}{5}$ of an acre of land. She uses $\frac{1}{3}$ of it for her dog kennel. How much of an acre is used for the kennel?

  3. Blaine drives the machine that paints stripes along the highway. He plans to paint a stripe that is $\frac{9}{10}$ of a mile long. He is $\frac{2}{3}$ of the way done when he runs out of paint. How long is the stripe he painted?

C. What observations can you make from Questions A and B that help you write an algorithm for multiplying fractions?

D. Ian says, "When you multiply, the product is greater than each of the two numbers you are multiplying: $3 \times 5 = 15$, and 15 is greater than 3 and 5." Libby disagrees. She says, "When you multiply a fraction by a fraction, the product is less than each of the two fractions you multiplied." Who is correct and why?

ACE Homework starts on page 40.

3.3 Modeling More Multiplication Situations

In this problem, you will work with multiplication situations that use fractions, whole numbers, and mixed numbers. It is helpful to estimate first to see if your answer makes sense.

Getting Ready for Problem 3.3

Estimate each product to the nearest whole number (1, 2, 3, . . .).

$$\frac{1}{2} \times 2\frac{9}{10} \qquad 1\frac{1}{2} \times 2\frac{9}{10} \qquad 2\frac{1}{2} \times \frac{4}{7} \qquad 3\frac{1}{4} \times 2\frac{11}{12}$$

Will the actual product be greater than or less than your whole number estimate?

Problem 3.3 Modeling More Multiplication Situations

For each question:

- Estimate the answer.
- Create a model or a diagram to find the exact answer.
- Write a number sentence.

A. The sixth-graders have a fundraiser. They raise enough money to reach $\frac{7}{8}$ of their goal. Nikki raises $\frac{3}{4}$ of this money. What fraction of the goal does Nikki raise?

B. A recipe calls for $\frac{2}{3}$ of a 16-ounce bag of chocolate chips. How many ounces are needed?

C. Mr. Flansburgh buys a $2\frac{1}{2}$-pound wheel of cheese. His family eats $\frac{1}{3}$ of the wheel. How much cheese have they eaten?

D. Peter and Erin run the corn harvester for Mr. McGreggor. They harvest about $2\frac{1}{3}$ acres each day. They have only $10\frac{1}{2}$ days to harvest the corn. How many acres of corn can they harvest for Mr. McGreggor?

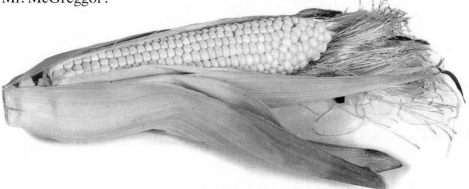

ACE Homework starts on page 40.

3.4 Changing Forms

You have developed some strategies for modeling multiplication and finding products involving fractions. This problem will give you a chance to further develop your strategies. Before you begin a problem, you should always ask yourself: "About how large will the product be?"

Getting Ready for Problem 3.4

Yuri and Paula are trying to find the following product.

$$2\frac{2}{3} \times \frac{1}{4}$$

Yuri says that if he rewrites $2\frac{2}{3}$, he can use what he knows about multiplying fractions. He writes:

$$\frac{8}{3} \times \frac{1}{4}$$

Paula asks, "Can you do that? Are those two problems the same?"

What do you think about Yuri's idea? Are the two multiplication problems equivalent?

A. Use what you know about equivalence and multiplying fractions to first estimate, and then determine, the following products.

1. $2\frac{1}{2} \times 1\frac{1}{6}$ **2.** $3\frac{4}{5} \times \frac{1}{4}$ **3.** $\frac{3}{4} \times 16$

4. $\frac{5}{3} \times 2$ **5.** $1\frac{1}{3} \times 3\frac{6}{7}$ **6.** $\frac{1}{4} \times \frac{9}{4}$

B. Choose two problems from Question A. Draw a picture to prove that your calculations make sense.

C. Takoda answers Question A part (1) by doing the following:

$$\left(2 \times 1\frac{1}{6}\right) + \left(\frac{1}{2} \times 1\frac{1}{6}\right)$$

1. Do you think Takoda's strategy works? Explain.

2. Try Takoda's strategy on parts (2) and (5) in Question A. Does his strategy work? Why or why not?

D. For parts (1)–(3), find a value for N so that the product of $1\frac{1}{2} \times N$ is:

1. between 0 and $1\frac{1}{2}$ **2.** $1\frac{1}{2}$ **3.** between $1\frac{1}{2}$ and 2

4. Describe when a product will be less than each of the two factors.

5. Describe when a product will be greater than each of the two factors.

ACE Homework starts on page 40.

3.5 Writing a Multiplication Algorithm

Recall that an algorithm is a reliable mathematical procedure. You have developed algorithms for adding and subtracting fractions. Now you will develop an algorithm for multiplying fractions.

Problem 3.5 Writing a Multiplication Algorithm

A. 1. Find the products in each group below.

Group 1	Group 2	Group 3
$\frac{1}{3} \times \frac{3}{4}$	$2 \times 1\frac{7}{8}$	$3\frac{2}{3} \times 1\frac{1}{2}$
$\frac{1}{4} \times \frac{2}{5}$	$\frac{2}{5} \times 12$	$2\frac{1}{4} \times 2\frac{5}{6}$
$\frac{2}{3} \times \frac{5}{7}$	$6 \times 1\frac{3}{8}$	$1\frac{1}{5} \times 2\frac{2}{3}$

2. Describe what the problems in each group have in common.

3. Make up one new problem that fits in each group.

4. Write an algorithm that will work for multiplying *any* two fractions, including mixed numbers. Test your algorithm on the problems in the table. If necessary, change your algorithm until you think it will work all the time.

B. Use your algorithm to multiply.

1. $\frac{5}{6} \times \frac{3}{4}$ **2.** $1\frac{2}{3} \times 12$ **3.** $\frac{14}{3} \times \frac{10}{3}$ **4.** $\frac{2}{5} \times 1\frac{1}{2}$

C. Find each product. What pattern do you see? Give another example that fits your pattern.

1. $\frac{7}{8} \times \frac{8}{7}$ **2.** $\frac{1}{9} \times \frac{9}{1}$ **3.** $1\frac{2}{3} \times \frac{3}{5}$ **4.** $11 \times \frac{1}{11}$

ACE Homework starts on page 40.

Did You Know?

When you reverse the placement of the numbers in the numerator and the denominator, a new fraction is formed. This new fraction is the **reciprocal** of the original. For example, $\frac{7}{8}$ is the reciprocal of $\frac{8}{7}$, and $\frac{12}{17}$ is the reciprocal of $\frac{17}{12}$, or $1\frac{5}{12}$. Notice that the product of a fraction and its reciprocal is 1.

Applications

1. Greg buys $\frac{2}{5}$ of a square pan of brownies that has only $\frac{7}{10}$ of the pan left.

   a. Draw a picture of how the brownie pan might look before and after Greg buys his brownies.

   b. What fraction of a whole pan does Greg buy?

2. Ms. Guerdin owns $\frac{4}{5}$ acre of land in Tupelo Township. She wants to sell $\frac{2}{3}$ of her land to her neighbor.

   a. What fraction of an acre does she want to sell? Draw pictures to illustrate your thinking.

   b. Write a number sentence that can be used to solve the problem.

3. Find each answer and explain how you know.

   a. Is $\frac{3}{4} \times 1$ greater than or less than 1?

   b. Is $\frac{3}{4} \times \frac{2}{3}$ greater than or less than 1?

   c. Is $\frac{3}{4} \times \frac{2}{3}$ greater than or less than $\frac{2}{3}$?

   d. Is $\frac{3}{4} \times \frac{2}{3}$ greater than or less than $\frac{3}{4}$?

4. **a.** Use a brownie-pan model to show whether finding $\frac{2}{3}$ of $\frac{3}{4}$ of a pan of brownies means the same thing as finding $\frac{3}{4}$ of $\frac{2}{3}$ of a pan of brownies.

   b. If the brownie pans are the same size, how do the final amounts of brownies compare in the situations in part (a)?

   c. What does this say about $\frac{2}{3} \times \frac{3}{4}$ and $\frac{3}{4} \times \frac{2}{3}$?

5. Find each product. Describe any patterns that you see.

   a. $\frac{1}{2}$ of $\frac{1}{3}$ **b.** $\frac{1}{2}$ of $\frac{1}{4}$ **c.** $\frac{1}{2}$ of $\frac{2}{3}$ **d.** $\frac{1}{2}$ of $\frac{3}{4}$

6. Mrs. Mace's class is planning a field trip, and $\frac{3}{5}$ of her students want to go to Chicago. Of those who want to go to Chicago, $\frac{2}{3}$ say they want to go to Navy Pier. What fraction of the class wants to go to Navy Pier?

7. Min Ji uses balsa wood to build airplane models. After completing a model, she has a strip of balsa wood measuring $\frac{7}{8}$ yard left over. Shawn wants to buy half of the strip from Min Ji. How long is the strip of wood Shawn wants to buy?

8. Aran has a fruit roll-up for a snack. He gives half of it to Jon. Jon then gives Kiona $\frac{1}{3}$ of his part. How much of the fruit roll-up does each person get?

9. In Vashon's class, three fourths of the students are girls. Four fifths of the girls in Vashon's class have brown hair.

   a. What fraction represents the girls in Vashon's class with brown hair?

   b. How many students do you think are in Vashon's class?

10. Find each product.
    a. $\frac{1}{3}$ of $\frac{2}{3}$ **b.** $\frac{5}{6}$ of 3   **c.** $\frac{2}{3}$ of $\frac{5}{6}$ **d.** $\frac{2}{5}$ of $\frac{5}{8}$

11. Estimate each product. Explain.
    a. $\frac{2}{3} \times 4$ **b.** $2 \times \frac{2}{3}$ **c.** $2\frac{1}{2} \times \frac{2}{3}$

12. Esteban is making turtle brownies. The recipe calls for $\frac{3}{4}$ bag of caramel squares. The bag has 24 caramel squares in it.

  a. How many caramel squares should Esteban use to make one batch of turtle brownies?

  b. Esteban decides to make two batches of turtle brownies. Write a number sentence to show how many bags of caramel squares he will use.

13. Isabel is adding a sun porch onto her house. She measures and finds that covering the entire floor requires 12 rows with $11\frac{1}{3}$ tiles in each row. Write a number sentence to show how many tiles Isabel will use to cover the floor.

14. Judi is making a frame for her little sister's drawing. The wood strip for the frame is 1 inch wide. She allows two extra inches of wood for each corner. If the square is $11\frac{3}{8}$ inches on a side, how much wood should Judi buy?

15. Find each product. Look for patterns to help you.

  a. $\frac{1}{3} \times 18$ **b.** $\frac{2}{3} \times 18$ **c.** $\frac{5}{3} \times 18$ **d.** $1\frac{2}{3} \times 18$

16. Write a number sentence for each situation. (Assume that the fractions are all less than 1.)

  a. a fraction and a whole number with a whole number product

  b. a fraction and a whole number with a product less than 1

  c. a fraction and a whole number with a product greater than 1

  d. a fraction and a whole number with a product between $\frac{1}{2}$ and 1

Homework Help Online
PHSchool.com
For: Help with Exercise 16
Web Code: ame-4316

17. Bonnie and Steve are making snack bags for their daughter's field hockey team. They put $\frac{3}{4}$ cup of pretzels, $\frac{2}{3}$ cup of popcorn, $\frac{1}{3}$ cup of peanuts, and $\frac{1}{4}$ cup of chocolate chips in each bag.

   a. If they want to make 12 bags, how much of each ingredient do they need?

   b. Bonnie decides that she would like to make snack bags for her card club. There are 15 people in the card club. How much of each ingredient will she need?

18. a. When Sierra gets home from school, $\frac{3}{4}$ of a sandwich is left in the refrigerator. She cuts the part remaining into three equal parts and eats two of them. What fraction of the whole sandwich did she eat?

   b. Write a number sentence to show your computation.

19. Mr. Jablonski's class is making fudge for a bake sale. He has a recipe that makes $\frac{3}{4}$ pound of fudge. There are 21 students in the class and each one makes one batch of fudge for the bake sale. How many pounds of fudge do the students make?

20. Carolyn is making cookies. The recipe calls for $1\frac{3}{4}$ cups of brown sugar. If she makes $2\frac{1}{2}$ batches of cookies, how much brown sugar will she need?

For Exercises 21–29, use your algorithm for multiplying fractions to determine each product.

21. $\frac{5}{12} \times 1\frac{1}{3}$

22. $\frac{2}{7} \times \frac{7}{8}$

23. $3\frac{2}{9} \times \frac{7}{3}$

24. $2\frac{2}{5} \times 1\frac{1}{15}$

25. $10\frac{3}{4} \times 2\frac{2}{3}$

26. $1\frac{1}{8} \times \frac{4}{7}$

27. $\frac{11}{6} \times \frac{9}{10}$

28. $\frac{9}{4} \times 1\frac{1}{6}$

29. $\frac{5}{2} \times \frac{8}{11}$

Go Online
PHSchool.com

For: Multiple-Choice Skills Practice
Web Code: ama-4354

Applications

30. Multiple Choice Choose the number that, when multiplied by $\frac{4}{7}$, will be greater than $\frac{4}{7}$.

A. $\frac{1}{7}$ B. $\frac{7}{7}$ C. $\frac{17}{7}$ D. $\frac{4}{7}$

31. Multiple Choice Choose the number that, when multiplied by $\frac{4}{7}$, will be less than $\frac{4}{7}$.

F. $\frac{1}{7}$ G. $\frac{7}{7}$ H. $\frac{17}{7}$ J. $\frac{8}{7}$

32. Multiple Choice Choose the number that, when multiplied by $\frac{4}{7}$, will be exactly $\frac{4}{7}$.

A. $\frac{1}{7}$ B. $\frac{7}{7}$ C. $\frac{17}{7}$ D. $\frac{4}{7}$

33. a. How many minutes are in 1 hour?

b. How many minutes are in $\frac{1}{2}$ hour?

c. How many minutes are in 0.5 hour?

d. How many minutes are in 0.1 hour?

e. How many minutes are in 1.25 hours?

f. How many hours are in 186 minutes? Express this as a mixed number and as a decimal.

34. A magazine advertises stained glass sun catchers. The ad says that the actual sun catcher is $1\frac{3}{4}$ times the size shown in the picture. Mrs. Inman wants to know how tall the actual sun catcher is. She gets a ruler and measures the sun catcher in the picture. If the sun catcher in the picture is $1\frac{3}{8}$ inches high, how tall is the actual sun catcher?

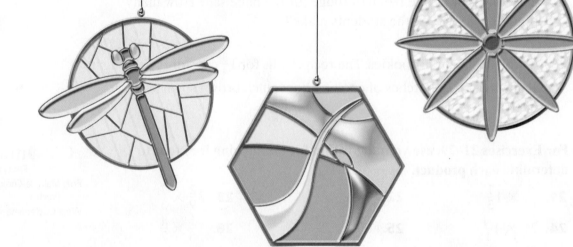

35. Violeta and Mandy are making beaded necklaces. They have several beads in various colors and widths. As they design patterns to use, they want to figure out how long the final necklace will be. Violeta and Mandy have the following bead widths to work with.

Widths of Beads

Bead	Width
Trade Neck	$\frac{1}{4}$ inch
Medium Rosebud	$\frac{3}{8}$ inch
Large Rosebud	$\frac{7}{16}$ inch

a. If Mandy uses 30 Trade Neck beads, 6 medium Rosebud beads, and 1 large Rosebud bead, how long will her necklace be?

b. Violeta would like to make a 16-inch necklace by alternating medium and large Rosebud beads. She only has 8 medium Rosebud beads. If she uses 8 medium Rosebud beads and 8 large Rosebud beads, will her necklace be 16 inches long?

Connections

36. Here is a multiplication-division fact family:

$$4 \times 5 = 20 \qquad 5 \times 4 = 20 \qquad 20 \div 4 = 5 \qquad 20 \div 5 = 4$$

For each number sentence, write a multiplication-division fact family.

a. $3 \times 6 = 18$ **b.** $16 \times 3 = 48$ **c.** $1\frac{1}{2} \times 7 = 10\frac{1}{2}$

d. $15 \div 3 = 5$ **e.** $100 \div 20 = 5$ **f.** $15 \div 1\frac{1}{2} = 10$

37. Roshaun and Lea go to an amusement park. Lea spends $\frac{1}{2}$ of her money, and Roshaun spends $\frac{1}{4}$ of his money. Is it possible for Roshaun to have spent more money than Lea? Explain your reasoning.

38. Bianca and Yoko work together to mow the lawn. Suppose Yoko mows $\frac{5}{12}$ of the lawn and Bianca mows $\frac{2}{5}$ of the lawn. How much lawn still needs to be mowed?

39. Joe and Ashanti need $2\frac{2}{5}$ bushels of apples to make applesauce. Suppose Joe picks $1\frac{5}{6}$ bushels of apples. How many more bushels need to be picked?

For Exercises 40–45, calculate each sum or difference.

40. $2\frac{2}{3} + 3\frac{5}{6}$

41. $2\frac{8}{10} + 2\frac{4}{5} + 1\frac{1}{2}$

42. $4\frac{3}{10} + 2\frac{2}{6}$

43. $5\frac{5}{8} - 2\frac{2}{3}$

44. $6\frac{7}{10} - 3\frac{4}{5}$

45. $8 - 3\frac{14}{15}$

46. Three students multiply $6 \times \frac{1}{5}$. Their answers are $\frac{6}{5}$, 1.2, and $1\frac{1}{5}$. Match each answer to the strategy described below that is most likely to produce it. Explain.

  a. Fala draws six shapes, each representing $\frac{1}{5}$, and fits them together.

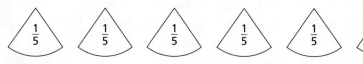

  b. Bri writes $\frac{6}{1} \times \frac{1}{5}$.

  c. Hiroshi writes 6×0.2.

47. Multiple Choice Linda is making bows to put on wreaths. Each bow uses $2\frac{1}{3}$ yards of ribbon. A spool of ribbon contains 15 yards of ribbon. Choose the number of whole bows she can make from one spool.

  F. 6 **G.** 7 **H.** 12 **J.** 35

Extensions

48. Find each product.

  a. $\frac{2}{3} \times \frac{1}{2} \times \frac{3}{4}$

  b. $\frac{5}{8} \times \frac{1}{2} \times \frac{2}{3}$

49. Multiple Choice Choose the best answer for the number of square tiles needed to make a rectangle that is $4\frac{1}{3}$ tiles long by $\frac{1}{2}$ tile wide.

  A. $2\frac{1}{3}$ **B.** $2\frac{1}{6}$ **C.** 2 **D.** $2\frac{1}{4}$

Mathematical Reflections 3

In this investigation, you explored situations that required you to multiply fractions. You also developed an algorithm for multiplying fractions. These questions will help you summarize what you have learned.

Think about your answers to these questions. Discuss your ideas with other students and your teacher. Then write a summary of your findings in your notebook.

1. Describe and illustrate your algorithm for multiplying fractions. Explain how you use the algorithm when you multiply fractions by fractions, fractions by mixed numbers, and fractions by whole numbers.

2. When you multiply two whole numbers, neither of which is zero, your answer is always equal to or greater than each of the factors. For example, $3 \times 5 = 15$, and 15 is greater than the factors 3 and 5. Use an example to help explain the following statement.

   When you multiply a fraction less than 1 by another fraction less than 1, your answer is always less than either factor.

3. Explain and illustrate what "of" means when you find a fraction *of* another number. What operation is implied by the word?

Dividing With Fractions

In earlier investigations of this unit, you learned to use addition, subtraction, and multiplication of fractions in a variety of situations. There are times when you also need to divide fractions. To develop ideas about when and how to divide fractions, let's review the meaning of division in problems involving only whole numbers.

Getting Ready for Problem **4.1**

Students at Lakeside Middle School raise funds to take a field trip each spring. In each of the following fundraising examples, explain how you recognize what operation(s) to use. Then write a number sentence to show the required calculations.

- The 24 members of the school swim team get dollar-per-mile pledges for a swim marathon they enter. The team goal is to swim 120 miles. How many miles should each swimmer swim?

- There are 360 students going on the field trip. Each school bus carries 30 students. How many buses are needed?

- The school band plans to sell 600 boxes of cookies. There are 20 members in the band. How many boxes should each member sell to reach the goal if each sells the same number of boxes?

Compare your number sentences and reasoning about these problems with classmates. Decide which are correct and why.

4.1 Preparing Food

There are times when the amounts given in a division situation are not whole numbers but fractions. First, you need to understand what division of fractions means. Then you can learn how to calculate quotients when the divisor or the dividend, or both, is a fraction.

When you do the division $12 \div 5$, what does the answer mean?

The answer should tell you how many fives are in 12 wholes. Because there is not a whole number of fives in 12, you might write:

$$12 \div 5 = 2\frac{2}{5}$$

Now the question is, what does the *fractional part* of the answer mean?

The answer means you can make 2 fives and $\frac{2}{5}$ *of another five.*

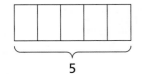 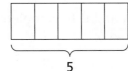 

Suppose you ask, "How many $\frac{3}{4}$'s are in 14?" You can write this as a division problem, $14 \div \frac{3}{4}$.

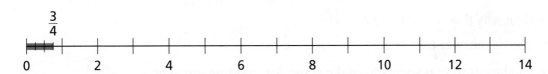

Can you make a whole number of $\frac{3}{4}$'s out of 14 wholes?

If not, what does the fractional part of the answer mean?

As you work through the problems in this investigation, keep these two questions in mind.

  What does the answer to a division problem mean?

  What does the fractional part of the answer to a division problem mean?

Problem 4.1 Dividing a Whole Number by a Fraction

Use written explanations or diagrams to show your reasoning for each part. Write a number sentence showing your calculation(s).

A. Naylah plans to make small cheese pizzas to sell at a school fundraiser. She has nine bars of cheese. How many pizzas can she make if each pizza needs the given amount of cheese?

1. $\frac{1}{3}$ bar   **2.** $\frac{1}{4}$ bar   **3.** $\frac{1}{5}$ bar

4. $\frac{1}{6}$ bar   **5.** $\frac{1}{7}$ bar   **6.** $\frac{1}{8}$ bar

B. Frank also has nine bars of cheese. How many pizzas can he make if each pizza needs the given amount of cheese?

1. $\frac{1}{3}$ bar   **2.** $\frac{2}{3}$ bar   **3.** $\frac{3}{3}$ bar   **4.** $\frac{4}{3}$ bar

5. The answer to part (2) is a mixed number. What does the fractional part of the answer mean?

C. Use what you learned from Questions A and B to complete the following calculations.

1. $12 \div \frac{1}{3}$ **2.** $12 \div \frac{2}{3}$ **3.** $12 \div \frac{5}{3}$

4. $12 \div \frac{1}{6}$ **5.** $12 \div \frac{5}{6}$ **6.** $12 \div \frac{7}{6}$

7. The answer to part (3) is a mixed number. What does the fractional part of the answer mean in the context of cheese pizzas?

D. 1. Explain why $8 \div \frac{1}{3} = 24$ and $8 \div \frac{2}{3} = 12$.

     2. Why is the answer to $8 \div \frac{2}{3}$ exactly half the answer to $8 \div \frac{1}{3}$?

E. Write an algorithm that seems to make sense for dividing any whole number by any fraction.

F. Write a story problem that can be solved using $12 \div \frac{2}{3}$. Explain why the calculation matches the story.

ACE   **Homework starts on page 55.**

4.2 Fundraising Continues

While figuring prizes for the games at their fundraiser, students and teachers face more fraction problems!

Use written explanations or diagrams to show your reasoning for each part.
Write a number sentence showing your calculation(s).

A. Ms. Li brings peanuts to be shared equally by members of groups
winning each game. How much of a pound of peanuts will each student
get in the given situations?

   1. Four students share $\frac{1}{2}$ pound of peanuts.

   2. Three students share $\frac{1}{4}$ pound of peanuts.

   3. Two students share $\frac{1}{5}$ pound of peanuts.

B. A popcorn store donates its different-sized boxes of popcorn for use as
prizes at a team competition. How much popcorn does each team
member get in the given situations?

   1. A two-person team shares a $\frac{3}{4}$-pound box of popcorn equally.

   2. A four-person team shares a $\frac{7}{8}$-pound box of popcorn equally.

   3. A four-person team shares a $1\frac{1}{2}$-pound box of popcorn equally.
     (Remember $1\frac{1}{2} = \frac{3}{2}$.)

C. Find each quotient and explain which model you used.

   1. $\frac{1}{2} \div 4$ **2.** $\frac{3}{2} \div 2$

   3. $\frac{2}{5} \div 3$ **4.** $\frac{4}{5} \div 4$

D. What algorithm makes sense for dividing any fraction by any whole
number?

E. Write a story problem that can be solved by $\frac{8}{3} \div 4$. Explain why the
calculation matches the story.

ACE | **Homework starts on page 55.**

4.3 Summer Work

In Problems 4.1 and 4.2, you developed ways of thinking about and solving division problems involving a whole number and a fraction. In the next problem, the questions involve division of a fraction by another fraction.

Problem 4.3 Dividing a Fraction by a Fraction

Rasheed and Ananda have summer jobs at a ribbon company. Answer the questions below. Use written explanations or diagrams in each to show your reasoning. Write a number sentence to show your calculation(s).

A. Rasheed takes a customer order for ribbon badges. It takes $\frac{1}{6}$ yard to make a ribbon for a badge. How many ribbon badges can he make from the given amounts of ribbon? Describe what each fractional part of an answer means.

1. $\frac{1}{2}$ yard

2. $\frac{3}{4}$ yard

3. $2\frac{2}{3}$ yards (Remember $2\frac{2}{3} = \frac{8}{3}$.)

B. Ananda is working on an order for bows. She uses $\frac{2}{3}$ yard of ribbon to make one bow. How many bows can Ananda make from each of the following amounts of ribbon?

1. $\frac{4}{5}$ yard   **2.** $1\frac{3}{4}$ yards   **3.** $2\frac{1}{3}$ yards

C. Solve each of the following examples as if they were ribbon problems.

1. $\frac{3}{4} \div \frac{2}{3}$ **2.** $1\frac{3}{4} \div \frac{1}{2}$ **3.** $2\frac{3}{4} \div \frac{3}{4}$

D. What algorithm makes sense for dividing any fraction by any fraction?

E. To solve $\frac{3}{4} \div \frac{2}{5}$, Elisha writes, "$\frac{3}{4} \div \frac{2}{5}$ is the same as $\frac{15}{20} \div \frac{8}{20}$. So the answer to $\frac{3}{4} \div \frac{2}{5}$ is the same as $15 \div 8$."

1. Is Elisha's first claim, that $\frac{3}{4} \div \frac{2}{5}$ is the same as $\frac{15}{20} \div \frac{8}{20}$, correct?

2. Is his second claim, that the answer to $\frac{3}{4} \div \frac{2}{5}$ is the same as $15 \div 8$, correct?

3. Use Elisha's method to solve $\frac{3}{5} \div \frac{1}{3}$. Does the method give a correct solution?

ACE Homework starts on page 55.

4.4 Writing a Division Algorithm

You are ready now to develop an algorithm for dividing fractions. To get started, you will break division problems into categories and write steps for each kind of problem. Then you can see whether there is one "big" algorithm that will solve them all.

Problem 4.4 Writing a Division Algorithm

A. 1. Find the quotients in each group below.

Group 1	Group 2	Group 3	Group 4
$\frac{1}{3} \div 9$	$12 \div \frac{1}{6}$	$\frac{5}{6} \div \frac{1}{12}$	$5 \div 1\frac{1}{2}$
$\frac{1}{6} \div 12$	$5 \div \frac{2}{3}$	$\frac{3}{4} \div \frac{3}{4}$	$\frac{1}{2} \div 3\frac{2}{3}$
$\frac{3}{5} \div 6$	$3 \div \frac{2}{5}$	$\frac{9}{5} \div \frac{1}{2}$	$3\frac{1}{3} \div \frac{2}{3}$

2. Describe what the problems in each group have in common.

3. Make up one new problem that fits in each group.

4. Write an algorithm that works for dividing *any* two fractions, including mixed numbers. Test your algorithm on the problems in the table. If necessary, change your algorithm until you think it will work all the time.

B. Use your algorithm to divide.

1. $9 \div \frac{4}{5}$ **2.** $1\frac{7}{8} \div 3$ **3.** $1\frac{2}{3} \div \frac{1}{5}$ **4.** $2\frac{5}{6} \div 1\frac{1}{3}$

C. Here is a multiplication-division fact family for whole numbers:

$5 \times 8 = 40$ $8 \times 5 = 40$ $40 \div 5 = 8$ $40 \div 8 = 5$

1. Complete this multiplication-division fact family for fractions.

$$\frac{2}{3} \times \frac{4}{5} = \frac{8}{15}$$

2. Check the division answers by using your algorithm.

D. For each number sentence, find a value for N that makes the sentence true. If needed, use fact families.

1. $\frac{2}{3} \div \frac{4}{5} = N$ **2.** $\frac{3}{4} \div N = \frac{7}{8}$ **3.** $N \div \frac{1}{4} = 3$

ACE Homework starts on page 55.

Applications

1. The Easy Baking Company makes muffins. Some are small and some are huge. There are 20 cups of flour in the packages of flour they buy. How many muffins can be made from a package of flour if each takes the following amounts of flour?

   a. $\frac{1}{4}$ cup   **b.** $\frac{2}{4}$ cup   **c.** $\frac{3}{4}$ cup

   d. $\frac{1}{10}$ cup   **e.** $\frac{2}{10}$ cup   **f.** $\frac{7}{10}$ cup

   g. $\frac{1}{7}$ cup   **h.** $\frac{2}{7}$ cup   **i.** $\frac{6}{7}$ cup

   j. Explain how the answers for $20 \div \frac{1}{7}$, $20 \div \frac{2}{7}$, and $20 \div \frac{6}{7}$ are related. Show why this makes sense.

2. Find each quotient.

   a. $6 \div \frac{3}{5}$ **b.** $5 \div \frac{2}{9}$ **c.** $3 \div \frac{1}{4}$ **d.** $4 \div \frac{5}{8}$

3. For parts (a)–(c), do the following steps:

   - Draw pictures or write number sentences to show why your answer is correct.

   - If there is a remainder, tell what the remainder means for the situation.

   a. Bill is making 22 small pizzas for a party. He has 16 cups of flour. Each pizza crust takes $\frac{3}{4}$ cup of flour. Does he have enough flour?

   b. There are 12 baby rabbits at the pet store. The manager lets Gabriella feed vegetables to the rabbits as treats. She has $5\frac{1}{4}$ ounces of parsley today. She wants to give each rabbit the same amount. How much parsley does each rabbit get?

   c. It takes $18\frac{3}{8}$ inches of wood to make a frame for a small snapshot. Ms. Jones has 3 yards of wood. How many frames can she make?

4. Find each quotient. Describe any patterns that you see.

    a. $5 \div \frac{1}{4}$ **b.** $5 \div \frac{1}{8}$ **c.** $5 \div \frac{1}{16}$

5. Maria uses $5\frac{1}{3}$ gallons of gas to drive to work and back four times.

    a. How many gallons of gas does Maria use in one round trip to work?

    b. Maria's car gets 28 miles to the gallon. How many miles is her round trip to work?

6. Anoki is in charge of giving prizes to teams at a mathematics competition. With each prize, he also wants to give each member of the team an equal amount of mints. How much will each team member get if Anoki has the given amounts of mints?

    a. $\frac{1}{2}$ pound of mints for 8 students

    b. $\frac{1}{4}$ pound of mints for 4 students

    c. $\frac{3}{4}$ pound of mints for 3 students

    d. $\frac{4}{5}$ pound of mints for 10 students

    e. $1\frac{1}{2}$ pounds of mints for 2 students

7. Multiple Choice Nana's recipe for applesauce makes $8\frac{1}{2}$ cups. She serves the applesauce equally among her three grandchildren. How many cups of applesauce will each one get?

    A. $\frac{3}{2}$ cups   **B.** $25\frac{1}{2}$ cups   **C.** $\frac{9}{6}$ cups   **D.** Not here

8. Divide. Draw a picture to prove that each quotient makes sense.

    a. $\frac{4}{5} \div 3$ **b.** $1\frac{2}{3} \div 5$ **c.** $\frac{5}{3} \div 5$

9. Multiple Choice Which of the following diagrams represents $4 \div \frac{1}{3}$?

  F. 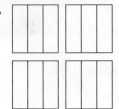   **G.**    **H.**   **J.**

10. Multiple Choice Which of the following diagrams represents $\frac{1}{3} \div 4$?

A.

B.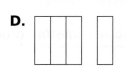

C.

D.

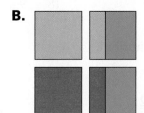

11. A latte (LAH tay) is the most popular coffee drink at Antonio's Coffee Shop.

Antonio makes only one size latte, and he uses $\frac{1}{3}$ cup of milk to make each drink. For parts (a)–(c), find:

● How many lattes he can make with the amount of milk given.

● What the remainder means, if there is one.

a. $\frac{7}{9}$ cup   **b.** $\frac{5}{6}$ cup   **c.** $3\frac{2}{3}$ cups

12. Write a story problem that can be solved using $1\frac{3}{4} \div \frac{1}{2}$. Explain why the calculation matches your story.

For: Help with Exercise 12
Web Code: ame-4412

13. Find each quotient.

a. $\frac{5}{6} \div \frac{1}{3}$ **b.** $\frac{2}{3} \div \frac{1}{9}$ **c.** $1\frac{1}{2} \div \frac{3}{8}$

14. Is each quotient greater than or less than 1? Explain.

a. $\frac{7}{9} \div \frac{1}{9}$ **b.** $\frac{2}{3} \div \frac{1}{9}$ **c.** $\frac{1}{18} \div \frac{1}{9}$ **d.** $1 \div \frac{1}{9}$

Go Online
PHSchool.com

For: Multiple-Choice Skills Practice

Web Code: ama-4454

For Exercises 15–20, find the quotient.

15. $10 \div \frac{2}{3}$ **16.** $5 \div \frac{3}{4}$ **17.** $\frac{6}{7} \div 4$

18. $\frac{3}{10} \div 2$ **19.** $\frac{2}{5} \div \frac{1}{3}$ **20.** $2\frac{1}{2} \div 1\frac{1}{3}$

21. For Exercises 15 and 17 above, write a story problem to fit the computation.

Write a complete multiplication-division fact family.

22. $\frac{2}{3} \times \frac{5}{7} = \frac{10}{21}$ **23.** $\frac{3}{4} \div 1\frac{1}{2} = \frac{1}{2}$

Connections

24. Mr. Delgado jogs $2\frac{2}{5}$ km on a trail and then sits down to wait for his friend Mr. Prem. Mr. Prem has jogged $1\frac{1}{2}$ km down the trail. How much farther will Mr. Prem have to jog to reach Mr. Delgado?

25. Toshi has to work at the car wash for 3 hours. So far, he has worked $1\frac{3}{4}$ hours. How many more hours before he can leave work?

For Exercises 26–29, find each sum or difference. Then, give another fraction that is equivalent to the answer.

26. $\frac{9}{10} + \frac{1}{5}$ **27.** $\frac{5}{6} + \frac{7}{8}$ **28.** $\frac{2}{3} + 1\frac{1}{3}$ **29.** $12\frac{5}{6} - 8\frac{1}{4}$

30. Every fraction can be written in many equivalent forms. For example, $\frac{12}{15}$ is equivalent to $\frac{24}{30}$. For each fraction, find two equivalent fractions. One fraction should have a numerator greater than the one given. The other fraction should have a numerator less than the one given.

    a. $\frac{4}{6}$ **b.** $\frac{10}{12}$ **c.** $\frac{12}{9}$ **d.** $\frac{8}{6}$

Find each product.

31. $\frac{2}{7} \times \frac{1}{3}$ **32.** $\frac{3}{4} \times \frac{7}{8}$ **33.** $1\frac{1}{2} \times \frac{1}{3}$ **34.** $4\frac{2}{3} \times 2\frac{3}{4}$

35. The marks on each number line are spaced so that the distance between two consecutive marks is the same. Copy each number line and label the marks.

a.

b.

c.

d.

    e. Explain how you determined what the labels should be.

36. By what number should you multiply to get 1 as the product?

    a. $2 \times \blacksquare = 1$ **b.** $\frac{1}{2} \times \blacksquare = 1$ **c.** $3 \times \blacksquare = 1$

    d. $\frac{1}{3} \times \blacksquare = 1$ **e.** $\blacksquare \times \frac{2}{3} = 1$ **f.** $\frac{3}{4} \times \blacksquare = 1$

    g. $\blacksquare \times \frac{5}{2} = 1$ **h.** $1\frac{1}{4} \times \blacksquare = 1$ **i.** $\frac{7}{12} \times \blacksquare = 1$

37. Find the missing numbers in each pair. What is the relationship between each pair?

a. $3 \div \blacksquare = 9$

$3 \times \blacksquare = 9$

b. $3 \div \blacksquare = 12$

$3 \times \blacksquare = 12$

c. $2\frac{1}{2} \div \blacksquare = 5$

$2\frac{1}{2} \times \blacksquare = 5$

38. Use the cartoon to answer the questions below.

a. How many slices of the pizza will have olives?

b. How many slices of the pizza will be plain?

c. What fraction of the pizza will have onions and green peppers?

Extensions

39. DonTae says that when you want to find out how many quarters are in some whole number of dollars, you should divide the number of dollars by $\frac{1}{4}$. Vanna says that you need to multiply the number of dollars by 4. With whom do you agree? Why?

40. Find a value for N that makes the sentence true. Don't forget fact families.

a. $N \times \frac{1}{5} = \frac{2}{15}$

b. $N \div \frac{1}{5} = \frac{2}{3}$

c. $\frac{1}{2} \times N = \frac{1}{3}$

d. $\frac{1}{5} \div N = \frac{1}{3}$

e. $1\frac{3}{4} \div N = \frac{1}{4}$

f. $2\frac{2}{3} \div N = 8$

41. Use the table below to solve parts (a)–(e).

Measurement	Equivalent Measurement
1 cup	16 tablespoons
1 quart	4 cups
1 quart	2 pints
1 gallon	4 quarts
1 tablespoon	3 teaspoons

a. Brian is missing his measuring cup. He needs to measure out $\frac{1}{2}$ cup of vegetable oil. How many tablespoons should he use?

b. How many teaspoons does Brian need to use to measure out $\frac{1}{2}$ cup of vegetable oil?

c. What fraction of a quart is $\frac{1}{2}$ cup?

d. What fraction of a gallon is $\frac{1}{2}$ cup?

e. Suppose you need to measure out exactly one gallon of water. The only measuring cups you have are $\frac{1}{2}$ cup, 1 cup, and 1 pint. Which measuring cup would you use? How would you make sure you had exactly one gallon?

Mathematical Reflections 4

In this investigation, you developed strategies for dividing with fractions. You developed algorithms that can be used to divide any two fractions or mixed numbers. These questions will help you to summarize what you have learned.

Think about your answers to these questions. Discuss your ideas with other students and your teacher. Then write a summary of your findings in your notebook.

1. Explain your algorithm for dividing two fractions. Demonstrate your algorithm with an example for each situation.

    - a whole number divided by a fraction
    - a fraction divided by a whole number
    - a fraction divided by a fraction
    - a mixed number divided by a fraction

2. Explain why the following example can be solved using division.

    A local coffee house donates $2\frac{2}{3}$ pounds of gourmet coffee beans to be sold at a local fundraiser. The people running the fundraiser decide to package and sell the coffee beans in $\frac{1}{2}$-pound packages. How many $\frac{1}{2}$-pound packages can they make?

3. How is the quotient of $20 \div \frac{1}{5}$ related to the quotient of $20 \div \frac{3}{5}$? Explain.

Looking Back and Looking Ahead

The problems in this unit helped you develop strategies for estimating and computing with fractions. You learned how to identify situations that call for computation with fractions. You developed algorithms for adding, subtracting, multiplying, and dividing fractions. You learned how to solve problems with fractions. Use what you have learned to solve the following examples.

For: Vocabulary Review Puzzle
Web Code: amj-4051

Use Your Understanding: Fraction Operations

1. The Scoop Shop sells many types of nuts. Jayne asks for this mix:

   $\frac{1}{2}$ pound peanuts $\frac{1}{6}$ pound hazelnuts

   $\frac{1}{3}$ pound almonds $\frac{3}{4}$ pound cashews

   $\frac{1}{4}$ pound pecans

   a. Nuts cost $5.00 per pound. What is Jayne's bill?

   b. What fraction of the mix does each kind of nut represent?

   c. Diego does not like cashews, so he asks for Jayne's mix without the cashews. What is his bill?

   d. Kalli is making small bowls of nuts for a party. Each bowl uses $\frac{1}{4}$ cup of nuts. Kalli has $3\frac{3}{8}$ cups of nuts. How many bowls can she make?

2. Shaquille likes dried fruit. He wants a mix of peaches, cherries, pineapple chunks, and apple rings. The following chart shows how much The Scoop Shop has of each fruit and how much of each fruit Shaquille orders.

The Scoop Shop's Stock	Shaquille's Order
$1\frac{1}{2}$ pounds dried peaches	$\frac{1}{3}$ of the stock
$\frac{4}{5}$ pound dried cherries	$\frac{1}{2}$ of the stock
$\frac{3}{4}$ pound dried pineapple chunks	$\frac{2}{3}$ of the stock
$2\frac{1}{4}$ pounds dried apple rings	$\frac{3}{5}$ of the stock

a. How many pounds of dried fruit does Shaquille order?

b. Dried fruit cost $5.00 per pound. What is Shaquille's bill?

Explain Your Reasoning

When you use mathematical calculations to solve a problem or make a decision, it is important to be able to support each step in your reasoning.

3. What operations did you use to find the cost of the nuts in Jayne's mix?

4. How did you find the fraction of the mix for each kind of nut?

5. $4 \div \frac{1}{3} = 12$ and $4 \div \frac{2}{3} = 6$. Why is the second answer half of the first?

6. Use the following problems to show the steps involved in algorithms for adding, subtracting, multiplying, and dividing fractions. Be prepared to explain your reasoning.

a. $\frac{5}{6} + \frac{1}{4}$ b. $\frac{3}{4} - \frac{2}{3}$ c. $\frac{2}{5} \times \frac{3}{8}$ d. $\frac{3}{8} \div \frac{3}{4}$

Look Ahead

The ideas and techniques you have used in this unit will be applied and expanded in future units of *Connected Mathematics*, in other mathematics work in school, and in your future work. Fractions are used in measuring and calculating quantities of all kinds—from length, area, and volume to time, money, test scores, and weights.

English/Spanish Glossary

A

algorithm A set of rules for performing a procedure. Mathematicians invent algorithms that are useful in many kinds of situations. Some examples of algorithms are the rules for long division or the rules for adding two fractions. The following algorithm was written by a middle-grade student:

To add two fractions, first change them to equivalent fractions with the same denominator. Then add the numerators and put the sum over the common denominator.

algoritmo Un conjunto de reglas para realizar un procedimiento. Los matemáticos inventan algoritmos que son útiles en muchos tipos de situaciones. Algunos ejemplos de algoritmos son las reglas para una división larga o las reglas para sumar dos fracciones. El siguiente es un algoritmo escrito por un estudiante de un grado intermedio.

Para sumar dos fracciones, primero transfórmalas en fracciones equivalentes con el mismo denominador. Luego suma los numeradores y coloca la suma sobre el denominador común.

B

benchmark A "nice" number that can be used to estimate the size of other numbers. For work with fractions, $0, \frac{1}{2}$, and 1 are good benchmarks. We often estimate fractions or decimals with benchmarks because it is easier to do arithmetic with them, and estimates often give enough accuracy for the situation. For example, many fractions and decimals—such as $\frac{37}{50}, \frac{5}{8}$, 0.43, and 0.55—can be thought of as being close to $\frac{1}{2}$. You might say $\frac{5}{8}$ is between $\frac{1}{2}$ and 1 but closer to $\frac{1}{2}$, so you can estimate $\frac{5}{8}$ to be about $\frac{1}{2}$. We also use benchmarks to help compare fractions. For example, we could say that $\frac{5}{8}$ is greater than 0.43 because $\frac{5}{8}$ is greater than $\frac{1}{2}$ and 0.43 is less than $\frac{1}{2}$.

punto de referencia Un número "bueno" que se puede usar para estimar el tamaño de otros números. Para trabajar con fracciones, $0, \frac{1}{2}$ y 1 son buenos puntos de referencia. Por lo general estimamos fracciones o decimales con puntos de referencia porque nos resulta más fácil hacer cálculos aritméticos con ellos, y las estimaciones suelen ser bastante exactas para la situación. Por ejemplo, muchas fracciones y decimales, como por ejemplo $\frac{37}{50}, \frac{5}{8}$, 0.43 y 0.55, se pueden considerar como cercanos a $\frac{1}{2}$. Se podría decir que $\frac{5}{8}$ está entre $\frac{1}{2}$ y 1, pero más cerca de $\frac{1}{2}$, por lo que se puede estimar que $\frac{5}{8}$ es alrededor de $\frac{1}{2}$. También usamos puntos de referencia para ayudarnos a comparar fracciones. Por ejemplo, podríamos decir que $\frac{5}{8}$ es mayor que 0.43, porque $\frac{5}{8}$ es mayor que $\frac{1}{2}$ y 0.43 es menor que $\frac{1}{2}$.

denominator The number written below the line in a fraction. In the fraction $\frac{3}{4}$, 4 is the denominator. In the part-whole interpretation of fractions, the denominator shows the number of equal-sized parts into which the whole has been split.

denominador El número escrito debajo de la línea en una fracción. En la fracción $\frac{3}{4}$, 4 es el denominador. En la interpretación de partes y enteros de fracciones, el denominador muestra el número de partes iguales en que fue dividido el entero.

equivalent fractions Fractions that are equal in value, but may have different numerators and denominators. For example, $\frac{2}{3}$ and $\frac{14}{21}$ are equivalent fractions. The shaded part of this rectangle represents both $\frac{2}{3}$ and $\frac{14}{21}$.

fracciones equivalentes Fracciones de igual valor, que pueden tener diferentes numeradores y denominadores. Por ejemplo, $\frac{2}{3}$ y $\frac{14}{21}$ son fracciones equivalentes. La parte sombreada de este rectángulo representa tanto $\frac{2}{3}$ como $\frac{14}{21}$.

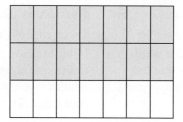

fact family A set of related addition-subtraction sentences or multiplication-division sentences. For example, the set of numbers 3, 5, and 15 are part of this multiplication-division fact family:

$$3 \times 5 = 15 \qquad 5 \times 3 = 15$$
$$15 \div 5 = 3 \qquad 15 \div 3 = 5$$

If you have one fact from a family, you can use the addition-subtraction or multiplication-division relationship to write the three related facts that are also part of the family. For example, with $2 + 3 = 5$, you can use the relationship between addition and subtraction to write the related number sentences $3 + 2 = 5, 5 - 3 = 2$, and $5 - 2 = 3$.

familia de datos Conjunto de oraciones de suma y resta o de multiplicación y división relacionadas. Por ejemplo, el grupo de números 3, 5 y 15 son parte de esta familia de datos de multiplicación y división:

$$3 \times 5 = 15 \qquad 5 \times 3 = 15$$
$$15 \div 5 = 3 \qquad 15 \div 3 = 5$$

Si tienes un dato de una familia, puedes usar la relación entre la suma y la resta, y entre la multiplicación y división para escribir los tres datos relacionados que también son parte de la familia. Por ejemplo, con $2 + 3 = 5$, puedes usar la relación entre la suma y la resta para escribir las oraciones numéricas relacionadas $3 + 2 = 5, 5 - 3 = 2$ y $5 - 2 = 3$.

numerator The number written above the line in a fraction. In the fraction $\frac{5}{8}$, 5 is the numerator. When you interpret the fraction $\frac{5}{8}$ as a part of a whole, the numerator 5 tells that the fraction refers to 5 of the 8 equal parts.

numerador El número escrito sobre la línea en una fracción. En la fracción $\frac{5}{8}$, 5 es el numerador. Cuando interpretas una fracción como $\frac{5}{8}$ como parte de un entero, el numerador 5 te dice que la fracción se refiere a 5 de 8 partes iguales.

reciprocal A factor by which you multiply a given number so that their product is 1. For example, $\frac{3}{5}$ is the reciprocal of $\frac{5}{3}$, and $\frac{5}{3}$ is the reciprocal of $\frac{3}{5}$ because $\frac{3}{5} \times \frac{5}{3} = 1$. Note that the reciprocal of $1\frac{2}{3}$ is $\frac{3}{5}$ because $1\frac{2}{3} \times \frac{3}{5} = 1$.

número recíproco Un factor por el cual multiplicas un número dado de manera que su producto sea 1. Por ejemplo, $\frac{3}{5}$ es el número recíproco de $\frac{5}{3}$, y $\frac{5}{3}$ es el número recíproco de $\frac{3}{5}$, porque $\frac{3}{5} \times \frac{5}{3} = 1$. Fíjate que el recíproco de $1\frac{2}{3}$ es $\frac{3}{5}$, porque $1\frac{2}{3} \times \frac{3}{5} = 1$.

unit fraction A fraction with a numerator of 1. For example, in the unit fraction $\frac{1}{13}$, the part-whole interpretation of fractions tells us that the whole has been split into 13 equal-sized parts, and that the fraction represents the quantity of 1 of those parts.

fracción de unidad Una fracción con numerador 1. Por ejemplo, en la fracción de unidad $\frac{1}{13}$, la interpretación de fracciones de una parte entera nos indica que el entero ha sido dividido en 13 partes iguales y que la fracción representa la cantidad 1 de esas partes.

Academic Vocabulary

The following terms are important to your understanding of the mathematics in this unit. Knowing and using these words will help you in thinking, reasoning, representing, communicating your ideas, and making connections across ideas. When these words make sense to you, the investigations and problems will make more sense as well.

E

explain To give facts and details that make an idea easier to understand. Explaining can involve a written summary supported by a diagram, chart, table, or a combination of these.

related terms: analyze, clarify, describe, justify, tell

Sample: Explain why the answer to $12 \div \frac{3}{4}$ is one third the answer to $12 \div \frac{1}{4}$.

> Because $\frac{3}{4} = 3 \times \frac{1}{4}$, it takes three $\frac{1}{4}$s to make every $\frac{3}{4}$. There are forty-eight $\frac{1}{4}$s in 12, but there are only sixteen $\frac{3}{4}$s in 12.

explicar Dar hechos y detalles que hacen que una idea sea más fácil de comprender. Explicar puede implicar un resumen escrito apoyado por un diagrama, una gráfica, una tabla o una combinación de éstos.

términos relacionados: analizar, aclarar, describir, justificar, decir

Ejemplo: Explica por qué la respuesta a $12 \div \frac{3}{4}$ es un tercio de la respuesta a $12 \div \frac{1}{4}$.

> Porque $\frac{3}{4} = 3 \times \frac{1}{4}$, se requieren tres $\frac{1}{4}$ para formar cada $\frac{3}{4}$. Hay cuarenta y ocho $\frac{1}{4}$ en 12, pero sólo hay dieciséis $\frac{3}{4}$ en 12.

M

model To represent a situation using pictures, diagrams, or number sentences.

related terms: represent, demonstrate

Sample: Yolanda has one half of an apple pie. She eats one third of the half pie. Model this situation using a number sentence or a picture.

> I can write one third as $\frac{1}{3}$ and half as $\frac{1}{2}$, so one third of one half can be written as $\frac{1}{3} \times \frac{1}{2}$. Because $\frac{1}{3} \times \frac{1}{2} = \frac{1}{6}$, she eats $\frac{1}{6}$ of the entire pie.
> I can also divide a whole fraction strip into halves, then divide each half into thirds.
>
> | $\frac{1}{2}$ | $\frac{1}{2}$ |
> | $\frac{1}{6}$ | $\frac{1}{6}$ | $\frac{1}{6}$ | $\frac{1}{6}$ | $\frac{1}{6}$ | $\frac{1}{6}$ |
>
> Yolanda eats $\frac{1}{6}$ of the entire pie.

hacer modelos Representar una situación usando imágenes, diagramas u oraciones numéricas.

términos relacionados: representar, demostrar

Ejemplo: Yolanda tiene una mitad de una tarta de manzana. Se come un tercio de la mitad de la tarta. Haz un modelo de esta situación usando una oración numérica o una imagen.

> Puedo escribir un tercio como $\frac{1}{3}$ y la mitad como $\frac{1}{2}$, así que un tercio de una mitad puede escribirse como $\frac{1}{3} \times \frac{1}{2}$. Debido a que $\frac{1}{3} \times \frac{1}{2} = \frac{1}{6}$, ella se come $\frac{1}{6}$ de la tarta entera.
> También puedo dividir una tira de fracciones entera en mitades, luego divido cada mitad en tercios.
>
> | $\frac{1}{2}$ | $\frac{1}{2}$ |
> | $\frac{1}{6}$ | $\frac{1}{6}$ | $\frac{1}{6}$ | $\frac{1}{6}$ | $\frac{1}{6}$ | $\frac{1}{6}$ |
>
> Yolanda se come $\frac{1}{6}$ de la tarta entera.

reason To think through using facts and information.

related terms: think, examine, logic

Sample: **To find the number of $\frac{1}{2}$-cup servings in 6 cups, Jenni says it is necessary to multiply 6 by $\frac{1}{2}$. Zach says that 6 must be divided by $\frac{1}{2}$ to find the number of servings. With whom do you agree? Explain how you reasoned.**

> I agree with Zach because you want to know how many halves there are in 6. This question is answered by division: $6 \div \frac{1}{2} = 12$. Multiplying 6 by $\frac{1}{2}$ separates it into 2 equal parts of 3 each. That is not what is asked for in the question.

razonar Considerar usando hechos e información.

términos relacionados: pensar, examinar, lógica

Ejemplo: **Para hallar el número de porciones de $\frac{1}{2}$ taza en 6 tazas, Jenni dice que es necesario multiplicar 6 por $\frac{1}{2}$. Zach dice que 6 debe dividirse entre $\frac{1}{2}$ para hallar el número de porciones. ¿Con quién estás de acuerdo? Explica cómo hiciste tu razonamiento.**

> Estoy de acuerdo con Zach porque se desea saber cuántas mitades hay en 6. Esta pregunta se responde por división: $6 \div \frac{1}{2} = 12$. Multiplicar 6 por $\frac{1}{2}$ lo separa en 2 partes iguales de 3 cada una. Esto no es lo que se pide en la pregunta.

---

recall To remember a fact quickly.

related terms: remember, recognize

Sample: **Mateo wants to add 0.3 to $\frac{1}{2}$. What can you recall about $\frac{1}{2}$ or 0.3 that will help him find the sum? Explain.**

> I recall that $\frac{1}{2}$ is equivalent to the decimal 0.5. When both numbers are in decimal form, they can be added easily. Mateo can add $0.5 + 0.3$ to get 0.8.
>
> I also recall that 0.3 is the same as $\frac{3}{10}$ and $\frac{1}{2}$ is equivalent to $\frac{5}{10}$. Mateo can add $\frac{3}{10} + \frac{5}{10}$ to get $\frac{8}{10}$ which is the same as 0.8.

recordar Acordarse rápido de un hecho.

términos relacionados: acordarse, reconocer

Ejemplo: **Mateo desea sumar 0.3 a $\frac{1}{2}$. ¿Qué puedes recordar sobre $\frac{1}{2}$ o 0.3 que le ayudará a hallar la suma? Explica tu respuesta.**

> Recuerdo que $\frac{1}{2}$ es equivalente al decimal 0.5. Cuando ambos números están en forma decimal, pueden sumarse con facilidad. Mateo puede sumar $0.5 + 0.3$ para obtener 0.8.
>
> También recuerdo que 0.3 is igual a $\frac{3}{10}$ y $\frac{1}{2}$ es equivalente a $\frac{5}{10}$. Mateo puede sumar $\frac{3}{10} + \frac{5}{10}$ para obtener $\frac{8}{10}$, que es igual a 0.8.

Index

Index

Acknowledgments

Team Credits

The people who made up the **Connected Mathematics2** team—representing editorial, editorial services, design services, and production services—are listed below. Bold type denotes core team members.

Leora Adler, Judith Buice, Kerry Cashman, Patrick Culleton, Sheila DeFazio, Richard Heater, **Barbara Hollingdale, Jayne Holman,** Karen Holtzman, **Etta Jacobs,** Christine Lee, Carolyn Lock, Catherine Maglio, **Dotti Marshall,** Rich McMahon, Eve Melnechuk, Kristin Mingrone, Terri Mitchell, **Marsha Novak,** Irene Rubin, Donna Russo, Robin Samper, Siri Schwartzman, **Nancy Smith,** Emily Soltanoff, **Mark Tricca,** Paula Vergith, Roberta Warshaw, Helen Young

Additional Credits

Diana Bonfilio, Mairead Reddin, Michael Torocsik, nSight, Inc.

Technical Illustration

WestWords, Inc.

Cover Design

tom white.images

Photos

2 t, Courtesy of JCL Equipment Co. Inc.; **2 b,** GK Hart/Vikki Hart/Getty Images, Inc.; **3,** Ed Young/Corbis; **7,** Richard Haynes; **8,** Syracuse Newspapers/The Image Works; **17,** PhotoDisc/PictureQuest; **19,** Paul Hardy/Corbis; **22,** Richard Haynes; **29,** E.R. Degginger/Bruce Coleman, Inc.; **32,** Richard Haynes; **35,** Courtesy of JCL Equipment Co. Inc.; **37,** Russ Lappa; **41,** L. Clarke/Corbis; **43,** Tony Freeman/PhotoEdit; **48,** Tony Freeman/PhotoEdit; **51 l,** Dorling Kindersley; **51 r,** Royalty-Free/Corbis; **52,** Ed Scott/AGE Fotostock; **55,** GK Hart/Vikki Hart/Getty Images, Inc.; **58,** Eric Bean/Getty Images, Inc.; **60,** ©2001, Hilary B. Price. Distributed by King Features Syndicate, Inc.; **61,** Silver Burdett Ginn; **63,** Russ Lappa

Connected Mathematics 2

Covering and Surrounding

Two-Dimensional Measurement

$$P = 2 \times (\ell + w)$$

Glenda Lappan
James T. Fey
William M. Fitzgerald
Susan N. Friel
Elizabeth Difanis Phillips

PEARSON

Boston, Massachusetts · Glenview, Illinois · Shoreview, Minnesota · Upper Saddle River, New Jersey

Covering and Surrounding

Two-Dimensional Measurement

Suppose you are building a playhouse. How much carpeting do you need to cover the floor? How much molding (used to protect the bases of walls) do you need around the edges of the floor?

Suppose you need to make sails shaped as triangles and parallelograms for a schooner (SKOON ur). What measurements must you make to find how much cloth you need for the sails?

Suppose a piece of rope wraps around Earth. Rope is added to make the entire rope 3 feet longer. The new rope circles Earth exactly the same distance away from the surface at all points. How far is the new rope from Earth's surface?

You can describe the size of something in many different ways. You can use words such as long, short, thin, wide, big, or small to give a general description of size. Suppose you want to be more specific. You can use numbers with units of measurement, such as centimeters, inches, or square feet.

All these questions involve size. In this unit you will learn mathematical ideas and techniques that can help you answer questions about size.

Mathematical Highlights

In *Covering and Surrounding,* you will explore areas and perimeters of figures, especially quadrilaterals, triangles, and circles.

You will learn how to

- Use area and relate area to *covering* a figure
- Use perimeter and relate perimeter to *surrounding* a figure
- Analyze what it means to measure area and perimeter
- Develop strategies for finding areas and perimeters of rectangular and non-rectangular shapes
- Discover relationships between perimeter and area, including that one can vary while the other stays fixed
- Analyze how the area of a triangle and the area of a parallelogram are related to the area of a rectangle
- Develop formulas and procedures, stated in words or symbols, for finding areas and perimeters of rectangles, parallelograms, triangles, and circles
- Develop techniques for estimating the area and perimeter of an irregular figure
- Recognize situations in which measuring perimeter or area will help answer practical questions

As you work on the problems in this unit, ask yourself questions about situations that involve area and perimeter.

How do I know whether area or perimeter are involved?

What attributes of a shape are important to measure?

What am I finding when I find area and when I find perimeter?

What relationships involving area or perimeter, or both, will help solve the problem?

How can I find the area and perimeter of a regular or irregular shape? Is an exact answer required?

Investigation 1

Designing Bumper Cars

Most people enjoy the rides at amusement parks and carnivals, from merry-go-rounds and Ferris wheels to roller coasters and bumper cars.

Suppose a company called Midway Amusement Rides (MARS for short) builds rides for amusement parks and carnivals. To do well in their business, MARS designers have to use mathematical thinking.

1.1 Designing Bumper-Car Rides

Bumper cars are a popular ride at amusement parks and carnivals. Bumper cars ride on a smooth floor with bumper rails all around it. MARS makes their bumper-car floors from 1 meter-by-1 meter square tiles. The bumper rails are built from 1-meter sections.

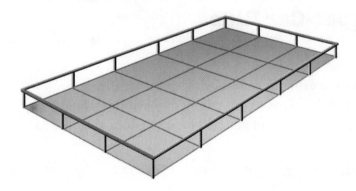

Problem 1.1 Understanding Area and Perimeter

When a customer sends an order, the designers at MARS first use square tiles to model possible floor plans. MARS has received the customer orders below. Experiment with square tiles and then sketch some designs for the customer to consider.

A. Badger State Shows in Wisconsin requests a bumper-car ride with 36 square meters of floor space and 26 meters of rail sections. Sketch two or three floor plans for this request.

B. Lone Star Carnivals in Texas wants a bumper-car ride that covers 36 square meters of floor space and has lots of rail sections. Sketch two or three possible floor plans for this customer.

C. Two measures tell you important facts about the size of the bumper-car floor plans you have designed. The number of tiles needed to cover the floor is the **area.** The number of rail sections needed to surround the floor is the **perimeter.**

1. What are the area and perimeter of this bumper-car floor plan?

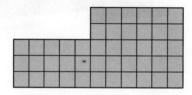

2. Which measure, perimeter or area, do you think better describes the *size* of a bumper-car floor plan? Why?

ACE Homework starts on page 10.

1.2 Pricing Bumper-Car Rides

When it is time to prepare the estimates or bills for customers, the designers at MARS turn over the plans to the billing department. The company charges $25 for each rail section and $30 for each floor tile.

Problem 1.2 Finding Area and Perimeter

The Buckeye Amusement Company in Ohio wants some sample floor plans and cost estimates for bumper-car rides. The designers come up with these bumper-car floor plans.

bumper-car tile: ☐ 1 m
1 m

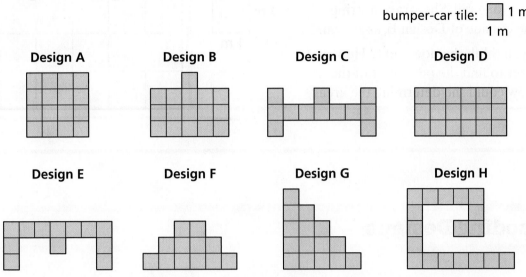

Design A Design B Design C Design D

Design E Design F Design G Design H

A. Find the area and perimeter for each design. Record your data in a table such as the one started at the right.

Design	Area	Perimeter	Cost
A	▪	▪	▪
B	▪	▪	▪

B. Use the data in your table.

   1. Which designs can be made from the same number of floor tiles?

   2. Choose a set of designs that can be made from the same number of floor tiles. What is the perimeter of each design?

   3. In the designs with the same floor area, which design costs the most? Which design costs the least? Why?

C. 1. Rearrange the tiles in Design H to form a rectangle. Can you make more than one rectangle using the same number of tiles? If so, are the perimeters of the rectangles the same? Explain.

   2. Design B and Design D have the same perimeter. Can you rearrange Design B to make Design D? Explain.

D. 1. The Buckeye Amusement Company said that it is willing to pay between $1,000 and $2,000 for a bumper-car ride. Design two possible floor plans. Find the area, perimeter, and cost for each.

   2. Suppose you were the manager. Which design would you choose? Why?

ACE Homework starts on page 10.

A student is tired of counting the individual rail sections around the outside of each bumper-car track. She starts to think of them as one long rail. She wraps a string around the outside of Design B, as shown.

What do you think she does next? How does this help her to find the perimeter of the figure? How could she determine the area?

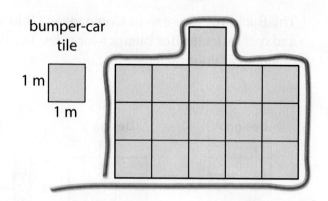

bumper-car tile

1 m

1 m

1.3 Decoding Designs

The Portland Community Events Council is planning its annual summer festival. The council asks for bids from different traveling carnival shows. Each carnival show sends descriptions of the rides they offer.

Problem 1.3 Finding Area and Perimeter of Rectangles

The council wants to have a bumper-car ride in the shape of a rectangle at the festival.

A. American Carnival Company sends Designs I, II and III. The Fun Ride Company sends Designs IV and V (on the next page).

  1. What is the area of each design? Explain how you found the area.

  2. What is the perimeter of each design? Explain how you found the perimeter.

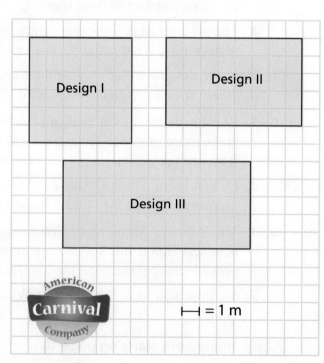

Design I

Design II

Design III

American Carnival Company

⊢⊣ = 1 m

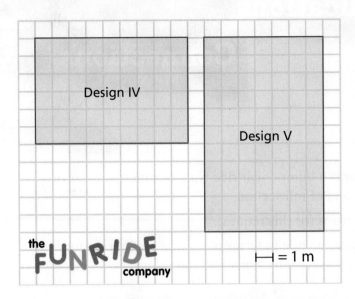

B. One carnival company sends the rectangular floor plan below. Find the area and the perimeter of this floor plan.

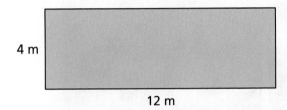

4 m

12 m

C. Another carnival company sends a description rather than a diagram. They describe the ride as a rectangle that is 17 meters by 30 meters.

1. What is the area of this floor plan?

2. What is the perimeter of this floor plan?

D. The dimensions of a rectangle are called **length** and **width.** Length can be represented using ℓ and width can be represented using w.

1. Using ℓ for length and w for width, write a rule for finding the perimeter of a rectangle.

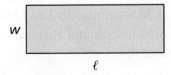

w

ℓ

2. Using ℓ for length and w for width, write a rule for finding the area of a rectangle.

ACE Homework starts on page 10.

Applications

1. Coney Island Park wants a bumper-car ride with 24 square meters of floor space and 22 meters of rail section.

   a. Sketch some floor plans for this request.

   b. Describe the bumper-car ride in terms of its area and perimeter. Report what each measure tells you about the ride.

 **Did You Know?**

Bumper cars came from the Dodgem, a rear-steering car invented by Max and Harold Stoeher of Methuen, Massachusetts. The Dodgem's popularity drew the attention of cousins Joseph and Robler Lusse, who made roller coaster parts in their Philadelphia machine shop.

The Lusses knew that people like to bump into each other, and also want to choose who to bump. So they worked on designs that let a bumper car go from forward to reverse without going through neutral. They filed the first of 11 patents in 1922 for their bumper car.

Go Online
PHSchool.com
For: Information about bumper cars
Web Code: ame-9031

For Exercises 2–5, experiment with tiles or square grid paper. Sketch each answer on grid paper.

2. Draw two different shapes with an area of 16 square units. What is the perimeter of each shape?

3. Draw two different shapes with a perimeter of 16 units. What is the area of each shape?

4. Draw two different shapes with an area of 6 square units and a perimeter of 12 units.

5. Draw two different shapes with an area of 15 square units and a perimeter of 16 units.

6. Use this design for parts (a) and (b).

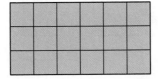

   a. If possible, draw a figure with the same area, but with a perimeter of 20 units. If this is not possible, explain why.

   b. If possible, draw a figure with the same area, but with a perimeter of 28 units. If this is not possible, explain why.

7. These designs have an area of 12 square meters. Are the perimeters the same? Explain how you decided.

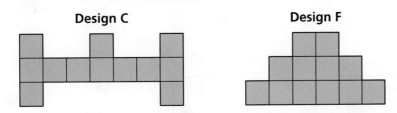

8. Copy the design below onto grid paper. Add six squares to make a new design with a perimeter of 30 units. Explain how the perimeter changes as you add tiles to the figure.

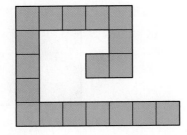

For Exercises 9–12, each unit length represents 12 feet. Find the area and perimeter of each floor plan.

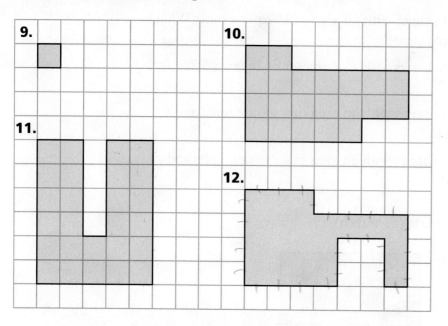

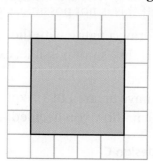

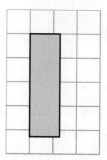

For Exercises 13–20, find the area and perimeter of each shaded rectangle.

13.

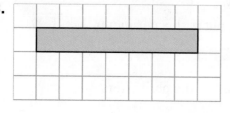

14.

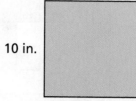

15.

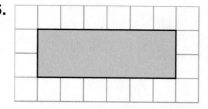

16.

17. 2 cm

14 cm

18.

10 in.

10 in.

19.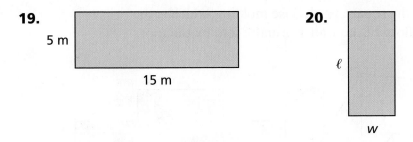

5 m

15 m

20.

ℓ

w

21. Copy and complete the table. Sketch each rectangle and label its dimensions.

Rectangle Area and Perimeter

Rectangle	Length	Width	Area	Perimeter
A	5 in.	6 in.	◼	◼
B	4 in.	13 in.	◼	◼
C	$6\frac{1}{2}$ in.	8 in.	◼	◼

For Exercises 22 and 23, find the area and perimeter of each figure. Figures are not drawn to scale.

22.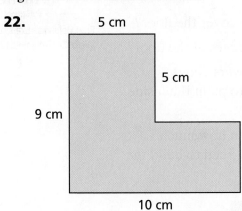

5 cm

5 cm

9 cm

10 cm

23.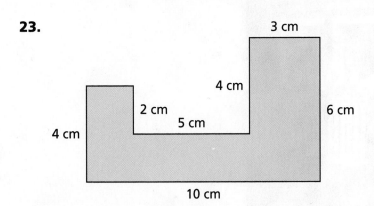

3 cm

4 cm

2 cm

5 cm

4 cm

6 cm

4 cm

10 cm

24. Carpet is usually sold by the square yard. Base molding, which is the strips of wood along the floor of the wall, is usually sold by the foot.

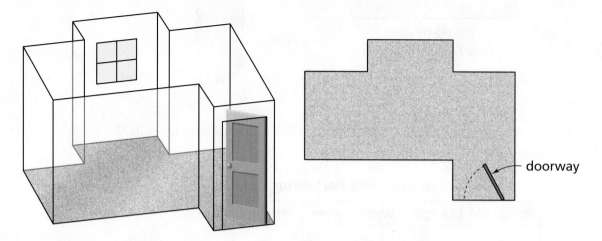

doorway

   a. Describe a method you could use to compute the cost of carpet for the room sketched here.

   b. Describe a method you could use to compute the cost of base molding around the base of the walls of this room.

25. Karl and Rita are building a playhouse for their daughter. The floor of the playhouse will be a rectangle that is 6 feet by $8\frac{1}{2}$ feet.

For: Help with Exercise 25
Web Code: ame-5125

   a. How much carpeting do Karl and Rita need to cover the floor?

   b. How much molding do they need around the edges of the floor?

   c. The walls will be 6 feet high. A pint of paint covers about 50 square feet. How much paint do they need to paint the inside walls? Explain.

   d. Make your own plan for a playhouse. Figure out how much carpeting, wood, paint, and molding you would need to build the playhouse.

26. MARS sells a deluxe model of bumper-car rides for $95 per square foot. Most rides require about 100 square feet per bumper car. One ride design is a rectangle that is 40 feet by 120 feet.

   a. How much does it cost to buy this design without cars?

   b. What is the maximum number of cars this design can have?

27. Chuck and Ruth think that you can find the perimeter of a rectangle if you know its length and width. They each write a rule for finding the perimeter P in terms of the length ℓ and the width w. Is either rule correct? Explain your reasoning.

$$\text{Chuck's rule: } P = (2 \times \ell) + (2 \times w)$$
$$\text{Ruth's rule: } P = 2 \times (\ell + w)$$

Connections

28. Multiple Choice How many square feet are in one square yard?

   A. 1   **B.** 3   **C.** 9   **D.** 27

29. Describe a flat surface in your home or classroom with an area of about one square foot. Describe another one with an area of about one square yard.

30. Which measure is greater? Or are the measures the same? Explain.

   a. one square yard or one square foot

   b. 5 feet or 60 inches

   c. 12 meters or 120 centimeters

   d. 12 yards or 120 feet

   e. 50 centimeters or 500 millimeters

   f. one square meter or one square yard

31. Sketch all the rectangles with whole-number dimensions for each area on grid paper.

   a. 18 square units   **b.** 25 square units   **c.** 23 square units

   d. Explain how the factors of a number are related to the rectangles you sketched for parts (a)–(c).

32. Find each product.

   a. $4\frac{1}{4} \times 7\frac{2}{5}$ **b.** $12\frac{1}{2} \times 4$ **c.** $10\frac{5}{8} \times 2\frac{1}{4}$ **d.** $\frac{15}{6} \times \frac{7}{12}$

33. The product of two numbers is 20.

    a. Suppose one number is $2\frac{1}{2}$. What is the other number?

    b. Suppose one number is $1\frac{1}{4}$. What is the other number?

    c. Suppose one number is $3\frac{1}{3}$. What is the other number?

34. Midge and Jon are making a pan of brownies. They use a 10 inch-by-10 inch baking pan. They want to cut the brownies into equal-sized pieces. For each possibility, give the dimensions of one piece. Sketch the cuts you would make to get the given number of brownies.

    a. 25 pieces   **b.** 20 pieces   **c.** 30 pieces

35. a. What is the area of the bottom of the largest brownie from parts (a)–(c) of Exercise 34?

    b. What is the area of the bottom of the smallest brownie from parts (a)–(c) of Exercise 34?

36. A football field is a rectangle 100 yards long and 50 yards wide (not counting the end zones).

    a. What is the area of the football field in square yards? What is the perimeter in yards?

    b. What is the area of the football field in square feet? What is the perimeter in feet?

    c. John's classroom measures 20 feet by 25 feet. About how many classrooms will fit on one football field?

37. One soccer field is a rectangle 375 feet long and 230 feet wide.

  a. What is the area of the soccer field in square feet? What is the perimeter in feet?

  b. What is the area of the soccer field in square yards? What is the perimeter in yards?

  c. Jamilla's classroom measures 15 feet by 25 feet. About how many classrooms will fit on this soccer field?

38. Copy and complete the table for rectangles with an area of 20 square feet.

Rectangle Dimensions

Length (ft)	Width (ft)
20	1
10	2
5	4
$2\frac{1}{2}$	8
■	■
■	■

Extensions

39. A group of students is finding the perimeters of rectangles whose lengths and widths are whole numbers. They notice that all the perimeters are even numbers. Is this always true? Explain why or why not.

40. Design a rectangle with an area of 18 square centimeters such that its length is twice its width.

41. Suppose you know the perimeter of a rectangle. Can you find its area? Explain why or why not.

42. How many rectangular tiles are needed to cover this floor?

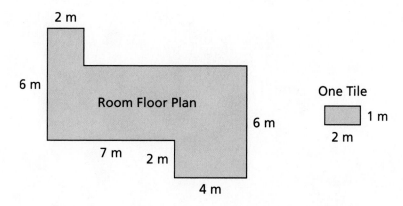

Mathematical Reflections 1

In this investigation, you examined the areas and perimeters of figures made from square tiles. You found that some arrangements of tiles have large perimeters and other arrangements of the same tiles have smaller perimeters. You also found an efficient way to find the area and perimeter of a rectangle. These questions will help you to summarize what you have learned.

Think about your answers to these questions. Discuss your ideas with other students and your teacher. Then write a summary of your findings in your notebook.

1. Explain what area and perimeter of a figure refer to.

2. Is it possible for two shapes to have the same area but different perimeters? Explain your answer using words and drawings.

3. Describe how you can find the area of a rectangle if you know its length and width. Explain why this method works.

4. Describe how you can find the perimeter of a rectangle if you know its length and width. Explain why this method works.

Investigation 2

Changing Area, Changing Perimeter

Whether you make a floor plan for a bumper-car ride or a house, there are many options.

You should consider the cost of materials and the use of a space to find the best possible plan. In Investigation 1, you saw that floor plans with the same area could have different perimeters. Sometimes you want the largest, or *maximum*, possible area or perimeter. At other times, you want the smallest, or *minimum*, area or perimeter.

This investigation explores these two kinds of problems. You will find the maximum and minimum perimeter for a fixed area. You will also find the maximum and minimum area for a fixed perimeter. *Fixed* area or perimeter means that the measurement is given and does not change.

2.1 Building Storm Shelters

Sometimes, during a fierce winter storm, people are stranded in the snow, far from shelter. To prepare for this kind of emergency, parks often provide shelters at points along major hiking trails. Because the shelters are only for emergency use, they are designed to be simple buildings that are easy to maintain.

The rangers in a national park want to build several storm shelters. The shelters must have 24 square meters of rectangular floor space.

A. Experiment with different rectangles that have whole-number dimensions. Sketch each possible floor plan on grid paper. Record your data in a table such as the one started below. Look for patterns in the data.

Shelter Floor Plans

Length	Width	Perimeter	Area
1 m	24 m	50 m	24 sq. m

B. Suppose the walls are made of flat rectangular panels that are 1 meter wide and have the needed height.

1. What determines how many wall panels are needed, area or perimeter? Explain.

2. Which design would require the most panels? Explain.

3. Which design would require the fewest panels? Explain.

C. 1. Use axes like the ones below to make a graph for various rectangles with an area of 24 square meters.

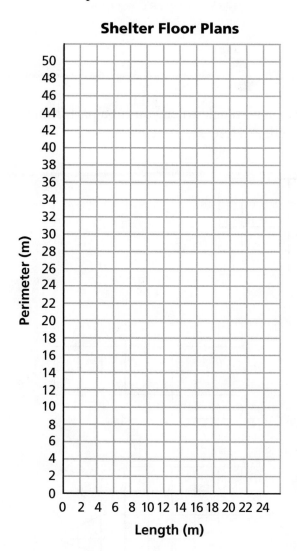

Shelter Floor Plans

2. Describe the graph. How do the patterns that you observed in your table show up in the graph?

D. 1. Suppose you consider a rectangular floor space of 36 square meters with whole-number side lengths. Which design has the least perimeter? Which has the greatest perimeter? Explain your reasoning.

2. In general, describe the rectangle with whole-number dimensions that has the greatest perimeter for a fixed area. Which rectangle has the least perimeter for a fixed area?

ACE **Homework starts on page 26.**

2.2 Stretching the Perimeter

Getting Ready for Problem 2.2

What happens to the perimeter of a rectangle when you cut a part from it and slide that part onto another edge? Here are some examples.

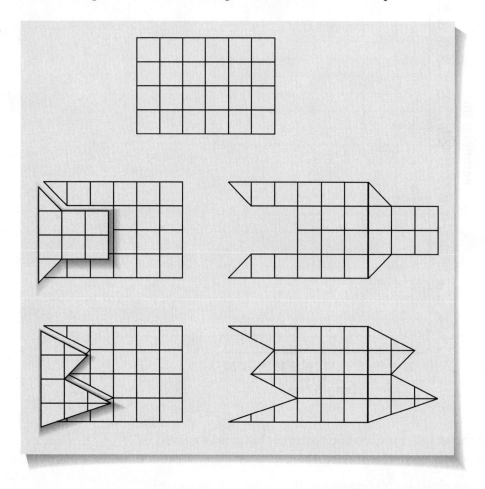

Think about whether you can use this technique to make nonrectangular shapes from a 4-by-6 rectangle to make a larger perimeter.

Draw a 4-by-6 rectangle on grid paper, and cut it out.

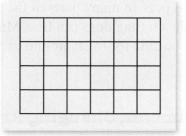

Starting at one corner, cut an interesting path to an adjacent corner.

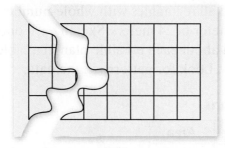

Tape the piece you cut off to the opposite edge, matching the straight edges.

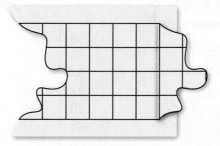

A. Estimate the area and the perimeter of your new figure.

B. Is the perimeter of the new figure greater than, the same as, or less than the perimeter of a 4-by-6 rectangle?

C. Is the area of the new figure greater than, the same as, or less than the area of a 4-by-6 rectangle?

D. Talecia asks, "Wait a minute! Can't you find the perimeter if you know the area of a figure?" How would you answer Talecia?

E. Can you make a figure with an area of 24 square units that has a longer perimeter than the one you made? Explain your answer.

ACE Homework starts on page 26.

2.3 Fencing in Spaces

Americans have over 61 million dogs as pets. In many parts of the country, particularly in cities, there are laws against letting dogs run free. Many people build pens so their dogs can get outside for fresh air and exercise.

Problem 2.3 Constant Perimeter, Changing Area

Suppose you want to help a friend build a rectangular pen for her dog. You have 24 meters of fencing, in 1-meter lengths, to build the pen.

A. 1. Use tiles or grid paper to find all rectangles with whole-number dimensions that have a perimeter of 24 meters. Sketch each one on grid paper. Record your data about each possible plan in a table such as the one started below. Look for patterns in the data.

Dog Pen Floor Plans

Length	Width	Perimeter	Area
1 m	11 m	24 m	11 sq. m

2. Which rectangle has the least area? Which rectangle has the greatest area?

B. 1. Make a graph from your table, using axes similar to those at the right.

2. Describe the graph. How do the patterns that you saw in your table show up in the graph?

3. Compare this graph to the graph you made in Problem 2.1.

C. Suppose you have 36 meters of fencing. Which rectangle with whole-number dimensions has the least area? Which rectangle has the greatest area?

D. In general, describe the rectangle that has the least area for a fixed perimeter. Which rectangle has the greatest area for a fixed perimeter?

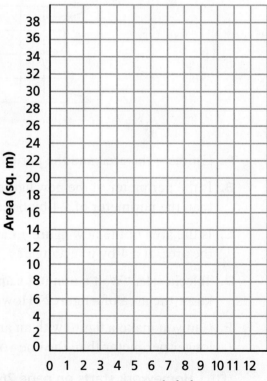

Dog Pen Floor Plans

ACE Homework starts on page 26.

2.4 Adding Tiles to Pentominos

Shapes that are not rectangles can also be made from tiles. A *pentomino* (pen TAWM in oh) is a shape made from five identical square tiles connected along their edges. Turning or flipping a pentomino does not make a different pentomino, so these two figures are considered the same.

 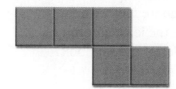

In this problem, you will add tiles to a pentomino and examine its area and perimeter.

Problem 2.4 Increasing Area and Perimeter

Make this pentomino with your tiles:

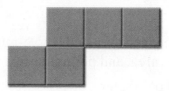

A. Add tiles to the pentomino to make a new figure with a perimeter of 18 units. Draw the new figure on grid paper. Show where you added tiles to the pentomino.

B. What is the fewest number of tiles you can add to the pentomino to make a new figure with a perimeter of 18 units? Draw the new figure, showing where you would add tiles to the pentomino.

C. What is the greatest number of tiles you can add to the pentomino to make a new figure with a perimeter of 18 units? Draw the new figure, showing where you would add tiles to the pentomino.

ACE Homework starts on page 26.

Applications

1. Nu is designing a rectangular sandbox. The bottom is 16 square feet. Which dimensions require the least amount of material for the sides of the sandbox?

2. Alyssa is designing a garage with a rectangular floor area of 240 square feet.

   a. List the length and width in feet of all the possible garages Alyssa could make. Use whole-number dimensions.

   b. Which rectangles are reasonable for a garage floor? Explain.

In Exercises 3–5, the area of a rectangle is given. For each area, follow the steps below.

   a. Sketch all the rectangles with the given area and whole-number side lengths. Record the length, width, area, and perimeter in a table.

   b. Sketch a graph of the length and perimeter.

   c. Describe how you can use the table and graph to find the rectangle with the greatest perimeter and the rectangle with the least perimeter for Exercise 3.

3. 30 square meters

4. 20 square meters

5. 64 square meters

6. The graph shows the lengths and perimeters for rectangles with a fixed area and whole-number dimensions.

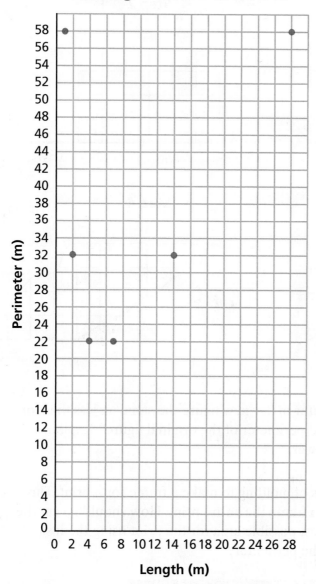

Rectangles With a Fixed Area

a. What is the perimeter of a rectangle with a length of 2 meters? What is its width?

b. Describe the rectangle that has the greatest perimeter represented in the graph above.

c. Describe the rectangle that has the least perimeter represented in the graph above.

d. What is the fixed area? Explain how you found your answer.

7. Billie drew a 4-by-6 rectangle on grid paper. She started at an edge and cut a path to the opposite corner. Then she slid the piece onto the opposite edge, making the straight edges match.

Step 1

Step 2

Step 3

Step 4

Are the area and perimeter of her new figure the same as, less than, or greater than the area and perimeter of the original figure? Explain how you found your answer.

8. Niran has 72 centimeters of molding to make a frame for a print. This is not enough molding to frame the entire print. How should he cut the molding to give the largest possible area for the print using the inside edge of the molding as the perimeter?

9. The graph below shows the whole-number lengths and areas for rectangles with a fixed perimeter.

For: Help with Exercise 9
Web Code: ame-5209

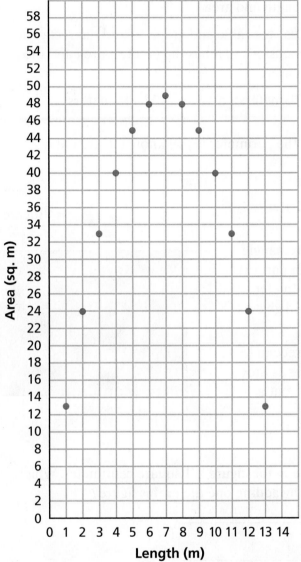

a. What is the area of a rectangle with a length of 2 meters? What is its width?

b. Describe the rectangle that has the greatest area represented in the graph above.

c. Describe the rectangle that has the least area represented in the graph above.

d. What is the fixed perimeter? Explain.

In Exercises 10–12, the perimeter of a rectangle is given. For each perimeter, follow the steps below.

    a. Sketch all the rectangles with the given perimeter and whole-number side lengths. Record the length, width, area, and perimeter in a table.

    b. Sketch a graph of the length and area.

    c. Describe how you can use the table and graph to find the rectangle with whole-number dimensions that has the greatest area and the rectangle with the least area.

10. 8 meters   **11.** 20 meters   **12.** 15 meters

13. Diego says, "You can find the perimeter if you know the area of a rectangle." Do you agree?

14. a. Find the perimeter and area of the blue rectangle.

    b. On grid paper, draw a rectangle with the same area as in part (a), but with a different perimeter. Label its dimensions and give its perimeter.

    c. On grid paper, draw a rectangle with the same perimeter as the rectangle you just drew, but a different area. Label its dimensions and give its area.

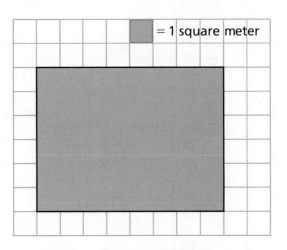

= 1 square meter

15. Multiple Choice Each tile in this figure is 1 square centimeter. Which result is impossible to get by adding one tile to this figure?

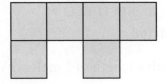

    A. Increase the area by 1 square centimeter and the perimeter by 1 centimeter.

    B. Increase the area by 1 square centimeter and the perimeter remains the same.

    C. Increase the area by 1 square centimeter and decrease the perimeter by 2 centimeters.

    D. Increase the area by 1 square centimeter and the perimeter by 2 centimeters.

Connections

16. a. The floor area of a rectangular storm shelter is 65 square meters, and its length is $6\frac{1}{2}$ meters. What is the width of the storm shelter?

b. What is its perimeter?

c. A one-meter wall panel costs \$129.99. Use benchmarks to estimate the total cost of the wall panels for this four-sided shelter.

Go Online
PHSchool.com
For: Multiple-Choice Skills Practice
Web Code: ama-5254

17. Multiple Choice The area of a storm shelter is 24 square meters. The length is $5\frac{1}{3}$ meters. What is the width of the storm shelter in meters?

F. $4\frac{1}{2}$ **G.** $4\frac{1}{3}$ **H.** $4\frac{1}{4}$ **J.** $4\frac{1}{5}$

18. These sketches show rectangles without measurements or grid background. Use a centimeter ruler to make any measurements you need to find the perimeter and area of each figure.

a.

b.

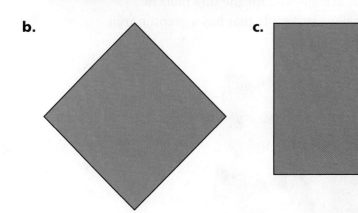

c.

19. Find the area and perimeter of each rectangle.

a.

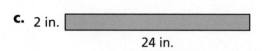

3 cm

10 cm

b.

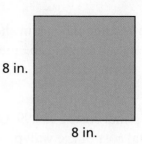

8 in.

8 in.

c. 2 in.

24 in.

20. Suppose fractional side lengths are allowed for the storm shelters in Problem 2.1. Is it possible to have a rectangle that has a smaller perimeter than the rectangles in your table? Explain.

21. Multiple Choice The perimeter of a dog pen is 24 meters. The length is $5\frac{1}{3}$ meters. What is the width of the dog pen in meters?

A. 6

B. $6\frac{1}{3}$

C. $6\frac{2}{3}$

D. 7

22. Suppose fractional side lengths are allowed for the dog pens in Problem 2.3. Is it possible to have a rectangle that has a greater area than the rectangles in your table? Explain.

23. The diagram below represents a field next to Sarah's house. Each small square shows a space that is one foot on each side.

   a. How many feet of fencing will Sarah need to enclose the field?

   b. Each box of grass seed seeds an area of 125 square feet. How many boxes of seed will Sarah need to seed the field? Explain.

   c. Sarah decides to include some flower and vegetable plots in the field, as well as a swing and a sandbox for her children. On grid paper, make a design for Sarah with these items. Give the area and the dimensions of each part of your design.

   d. How many boxes of grass seed will she need to seed the new design?

   e. What fraction of the area of the field can be covered with 1 box of grass seed?

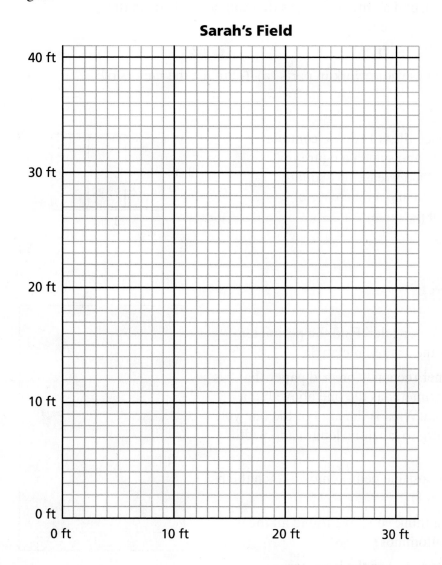

Sarah's Field

24. Four people can be seated for dinner at a card table, one person on each side. With two card tables put together, six people can be seated.

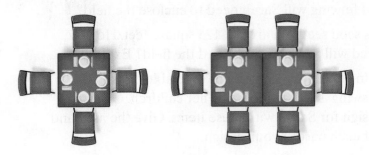

How would you arrange 36 card tables to make a rectangular banquet table that seats the greatest number of people? Explain.

25. For parts (a)–(c), find all the rectangles that can be made from the given number of square tiles.

a. 60   **b.** 61   **c.** 62

d. How can you use your work in parts (a)–(c) to list the factors of 60, 61, and 62?

26. In the figure, each tile is 1 square centimeter. Remove one tile and sketch a figure that would represent a decrease of 1 square centimeter of area and an increase of 2 centimeters of perimeter.

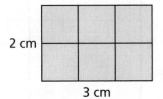

Extensions

27. a. Use a centimeter ruler. Find the perimeter and area of the shaded rectangle.

    b. Draw another rectangle on grid paper that has the same perimeter as the one above but a different area. What is the area of the one you drew? Be sure to label the length and width.

28. a. Find all the possible pentominos. Sketch them on grid paper.

    b. Why do you think you have found all the possible pentominos?

    c. Which pentomino has the least perimeter? Which pentomino has the greatest perimeter?

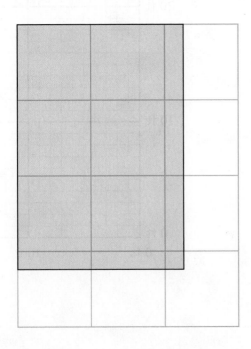

29. Suppose a square sheet of paper has a perimeter of 1 meter.

   a. What is the length of each side (in meters)?

   b. Suppose you fold the square sheet in half. What new shape would you have? What would the lengths of the shape's four sides be in meters? What would the perimeter be?

   c. Suppose you fold over the top $\frac{1}{4}$ of the square. What new shape do you have? What are the lengths of the shape's four sides in meters? What is the perimeter?

   d. Suppose you fold over only the top $\frac{1}{8}$ of the square. What new shape do you have? What are the lengths of the shape's four sides in meters? What is the perimeter?

   e. What do you predict for the perimeter of the shape if you fold over $\frac{1}{16}$ of the square?

Mathematical Reflections 2

In this investigation, you examined how shapes with the same perimeter can have different areas and how shapes with the same area can have different perimeters. These questions will help you to summarize what you have learned.

Think about your answers to these questions. Discuss your ideas with other students and your teacher. Then write a summary of your findings in your notebook.

1. **a.** Of all rectangles with whole-number dimensions that have a given area, how would you describe the one that has the least perimeter?

   b. Of all rectangles with whole-number dimensions that have a given area, how would you describe the one that has the greatest perimeter?

2. **a.** Of all rectangles with whole-number dimensions that have a given perimeter, how would you describe the one that has the least area?

   b. Of all rectangles with whole-number dimensions that have a given perimeter, how would you describe the one that has the greatest area?

Measuring Triangles

You can find the area of a figure by drawing it on a grid (or covering it with a transparent grid) and counting squares, but this can be very time consuming. In Investigation 1, you found a rule for finding the area of a rectangle without counting squares. In this investigation, you will look for rules for finding the area of triangles using what you know about rectangles.

3.1 Triangles on Grids

Getting Ready for Problem 3.1

A square centimeter is 1 centimeter by 1 centimeter. It has an area of 1 square centimeter. Sketch a square centimeter such as the one here.

1 cm²

1 cm

1 cm

- Draw one diagonal to form two triangles.
- What is the area of each triangle?
- Is the perimeter of one of the triangles greater than, less than, or equal to 3 centimeters?

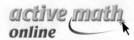

active math
online

For: Areas and Perimeters
of Shapes and Images
Activity
Visit: PHSchool.com
Web Code: amd-5303

A. On the next page, six triangles labeled A–F are drawn on a centimeter grid.

   1. Find the perimeter of each triangle.

   2. Describe the strategies you used for finding the perimeters.

   3. Find the area of each triangle.

   4. Describe the strategies you used for finding the areas.

B. Look at triangles A–F again. Draw the smallest possible rectangle on the grid lines around each triangle.

   1. Find the area of each rectangle. Record your data in a table with columns labeled for the triangle name, the area of the rectangle, and the area of the triangle.

   2. Use the data in your table. Compare the area of the rectangle and the area of the triangle. Describe a pattern that tells how the two are related.

C. Use your results from Question B. Write a rule to find the area of a triangle.

ACE Homework starts on page 44.

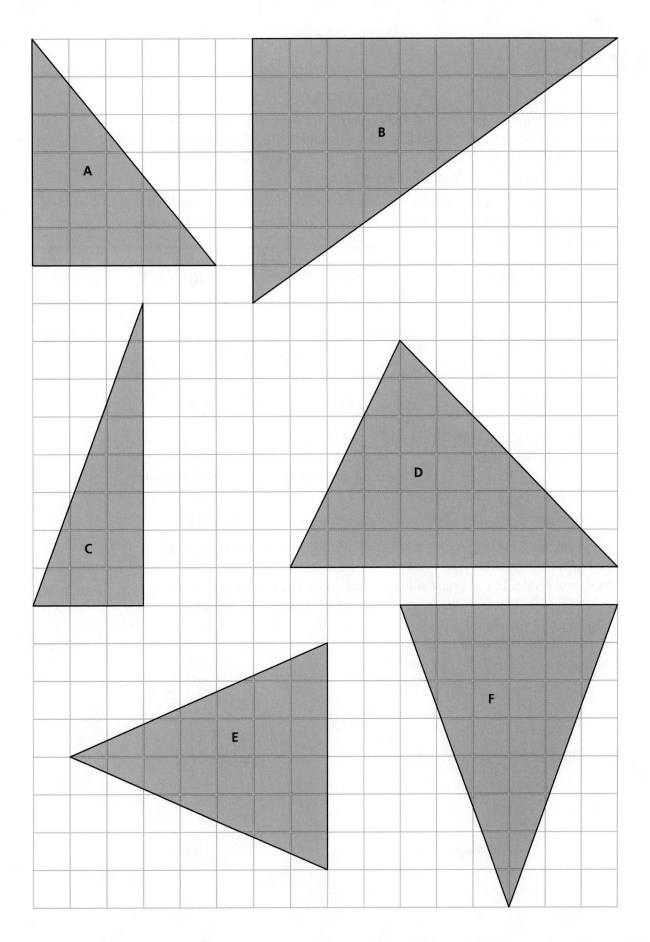

Base and height are two words that describe triangles. The **base** of a triangle can be any one of the sides of the triangle. "Base" also refers to the length of the side you choose as the base. The **height** of a triangle is the perpendicular distance from the top vertex to the base.

You can think of the height of a triangle as the distance a rock would fall if you dropped it from the top vertex of the triangle straight down to the line that the base is on.

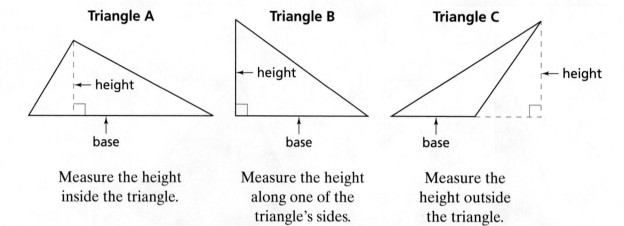

Triangle A   **Triangle B**   **Triangle C**

Measure the height inside the triangle.

Measure the height along one of the triangle's sides.

Measure the height outside the triangle.

The side you identify as the base also determines what the height is.

Look at triangle A again. Suppose you turn triangle A so it rests on its shortest side. The shortest side of the triangle becomes the base. The height is measured outside and to the left of the triangle.

Suppose you turn triangle A again. The second longest side becomes the base. The height is measured outside and to the right of the triangle.

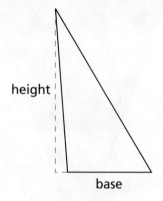

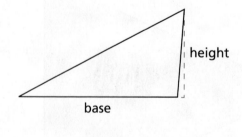

In this problem, you are going to explore how changing the position or orientation of a triangle affects the base, height, and area of a triangle.

Problem 3.2 Identifying Base and Height

A. Cut out copies of Triangles 1 and 2. Position each triangle on centimeter grid paper.

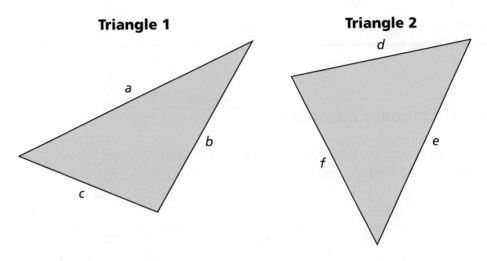

Triangle 1

Triangle 2

1. Label the base and height of each triangle.

2. Find the area of each triangle. Explain how you found the area. Include any calculations that you do.

B. Find a second way to place each triangle on the grid paper.

1. Label the base and height of each triangle in its new position.

2. Find the area of each triangle. Explain how you found the area. Include any calculations that you do.

C. Does changing which side you label the base change the area of the triangle? Explain.

D. When finding the area of a triangle, are there advantages or disadvantages to choosing a particular base and its corresponding height? Explain.

ACE **Homework starts on page 44.**

Sometimes the word "family" is used to describe relationships among objects.

For example, if Tamarr says that $\frac{1}{2}$, $\frac{2}{4}$, $\frac{3}{6}$, and $\frac{4}{8}$ form a "family" of fractions, what might she mean?

This problem challenges you to make a triangle "family" on a coordinate grid. As you make the triangles described in the problem, think about why they are called a triangle family.

Problem 3.3 Triangle Families

On a grid like the one below, draw a segment 6 centimeters long. Use this segment as a base for each triangle described in Question A. Draw each triangle on a separate grid.

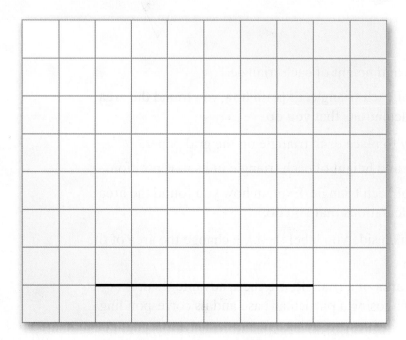

A. 1. Sketch a right triangle with a height of 4 centimeters.

2. Sketch a different right triangle with a height of 4 centimeters.

3. Sketch an isosceles triangle with a height of 4 centimeters.

4. Sketch a scalene triangle with a height of 4 centimeters.

5. Find the area of each triangle that you made.

B. 1. What do these four triangles have in common?

2. Why do you think these four triangles can be called a triangle family?

C. Use grid paper to make a new triangle family that has a different base and height than the one you have already made. What are the base, height, and area of your triangle family?

 Homework starts on page 44.

3.4 Designing Triangles Under Constraints

In this problem, use your knowledge about triangles to draw triangles that meet given conditions, or constraints.

Problem 3.4 Designing Triangles Under Constraints

For each description, draw two triangles that are *not* congruent (same shape, same size) to each other. If you can't draw a second triangle, explain why. Make your drawings on centimeter grid paper.

A. The triangles each have a base of 5 centimeters and a height of 6 centimeters. Suppose you draw two different triangles. Do they have the same area?

B. The triangles each have an area of 15 square centimeters. Suppose you draw two different triangles. Do they have the same perimeter?

C. The triangles each have sides of length 3 centimeters, 4 centimeters, and 5 centimeters. Suppose you draw two different triangles. Do they have the same area?

D. The triangles are right triangles and each have a 30° angle. Suppose you draw two different triangles. Do they have the same area? Do they have the same perimeter?

 Homework starts on page 44.

Applications

For Exercises 1–6, calculate the area and perimeter of each triangle.
Briefly explain your reasoning for Exercises 1, 4, and 5.

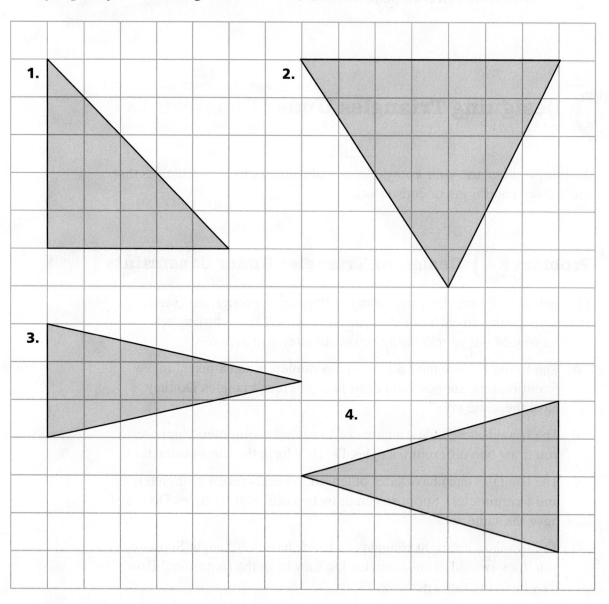

1.

2.

3.

4.

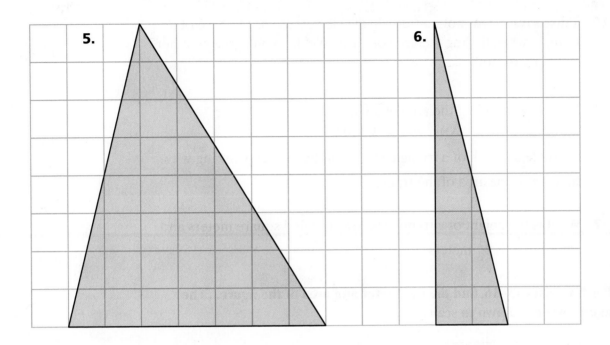

5.

6.

7. Find the area of each figure. (The figures are not drawn to scale.)

Go Online
PHSchool.com

For: Multiple-Choice Skills
   Practice
Web Code: ama-5354

a.

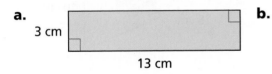

3 cm

13 cm

b.

3 cm

5 cm

c.

8 m

10 m

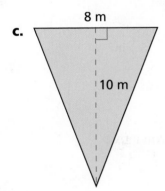

d.

12.2 ft

7 ft

10 ft

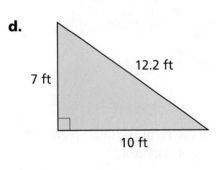

8. Vashon said that if you used 7 feet as the base for the triangle in Exercise 7(d), you would calculate the same area as you did when you used the 10-foot base. Do you agree with him? Explain.

9. For each triangle in Problem 3.1, find a base and corresponding height.

  a. Use these values to find the area of each triangle.

  b. Compare these areas to the answers you got in Problem 3.1. What do you notice?

Investigation 3 Measuring Triangles   **45**

10. Talisa says it does not matter which side you use as the base of a triangle when finding the area of a triangle. Do you agree with her? Why or why not?

11. Melissa was finding the area of a triangle when she wrote:
$$\text{Area} = \tfrac{1}{2} \times 3 \times 4\tfrac{1}{2}$$

 a. Make a sketch of a triangle she might have been working with.

 b. What is the area of the triangle?

12. What is the height of a triangle whose area is 4 square meters and whose base is $2\tfrac{1}{2}$ meters?

For Exercises 13–16, find the perimeter and area of the figure. (The figures are not drawn to scale.)

13.
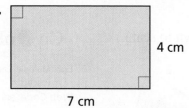
4 cm
7 cm

14.
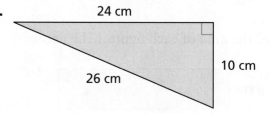
24 cm
26 cm
10 cm

15.
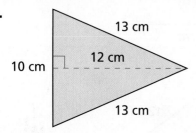
13 cm
12 cm
10 cm
13 cm

16.
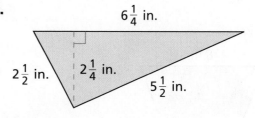
$6\tfrac{1}{4}$ in.
$2\tfrac{1}{2}$ in.
$2\tfrac{1}{4}$ in.
$5\tfrac{1}{2}$ in.

17. Keisha says these right triangles have different areas. Do you agree with her? Why or why not?

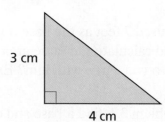
4 cm
3 cm
3 cm
4 cm

For Exercises 18–20, find the area of the triangle.

18.
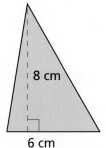
8 cm

6 cm

19.
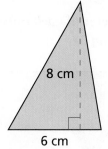
8 cm

6 cm

20.
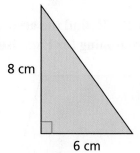
8 cm

6 cm

21. Tomas said that scalene, isosceles, and right triangles have different areas because they look different. Marlika disagrees and says that if they have the same base and the same height, their areas will be the same. Do you agree with Tomas or Marlika? Why?

22. Multiple Choice What is the best statement about this family of triangles?

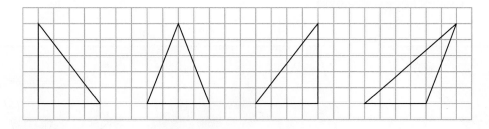

A. They each have the same base length.

B. They each have the same area.

C. They each have interior angles totaling 180°.

D. All the above statements are true.

For Exercises 23–25, draw two triangles that are not congruent to each other for each description. If you can't draw a second triangle, explain why. Make your drawings on centimeter grid paper.

23. The triangles each have a base of 8 centimeters and a height of 5 centimeters. Suppose you draw two different triangles. Do they have the same area?

24. The triangles each have an area of 18 square centimeters. Suppose you draw two different triangles. Do they have the same perimeter?

25. The triangles each have sides of length 6 centimeters, 8 centimeters, and 10 centimeters. Suppose you draw two different triangles. Do they have the same area?

For: Help with Exercises 23–25
Web Code: ame-5323

Connections

For Exercises 26–31, find the area and perimeter of each polygon. Briefly explain your reasoning for Exercises 27, 30, and 31.

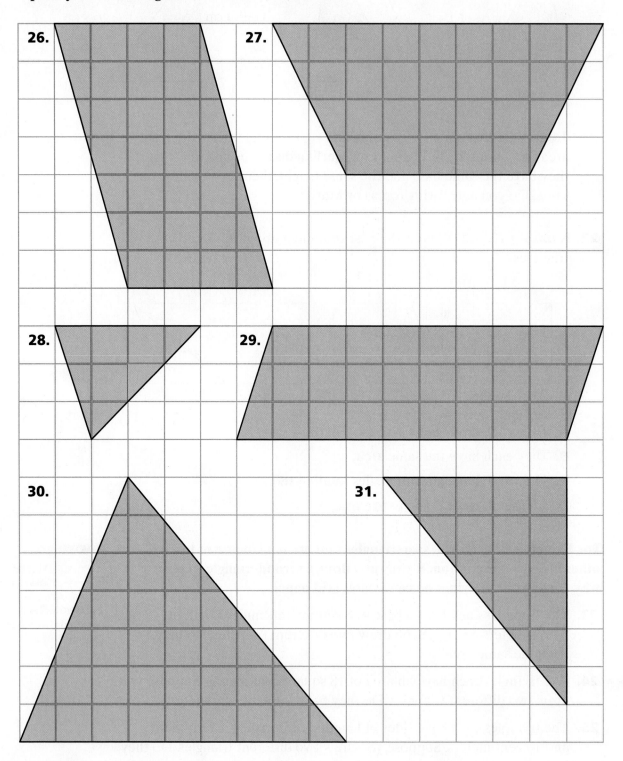

32. A schooner (SKOON ur) is a sailing ship with two or more masts. The sails of a schooner have interesting shapes. Many sails are triangular or can be made by putting two or more triangles together.

a. Look at the sails on the schooner above. For each sail that is visible, sketch the sail and show how it can be made from one or more triangles.

b. For each sail in part (a), what measurements would you have to make to find the amount of cloth needed to make the sail?

33. Multiple Choice Portland Middle School students are submitting designs for a school flag. The area of each region of the flag and its color must accompany the design.

10 cm

In this design, an isosceles triangle is drawn inside a square with sides that are 10 centimeters long. What is the area of the shaded region inside the square but outside the triangle?

F. 100 cm² **G.** 50 cm² **H.** 25 cm² **J.** 10 cm²

34. The garden club is making glass pyramids to sell as terrariums (tuh RAYR ee um; a container for a garden of small plants). They need to know how much glass to order.

The four faces (sides) of the terrarium are isosceles triangles. Each triangle has a base of 42 centimeters and a height of 28 centimeters. The square bottom of the terrarium is also glass. How much glass is needed for each terrarium?

For Exercises 35–38, a game company decides to experiment with new shapes for dartboards. For each problem, subdivide the shape into the given regions. Explain your strategies.

35. a square with four regions representing
$\frac{1}{10}$ of the area, $\frac{1}{5}$ of the area,
$\frac{3}{10}$ of the area, and $\frac{2}{5}$ of the area

36. an equilateral triangle with four regions,
each representing $\frac{1}{4}$ of the area

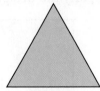

37. a rectangle with four regions representing $\frac{1}{3}$ of the area, $\frac{1}{6}$ of the area, $\frac{3}{12}$ of the area, and $\frac{1}{4}$ of the area

38. a rectangle with four regions representing $\frac{1}{2}$ of the area, $\frac{1}{4}$ of the area, $\frac{3}{16}$ of the area, and $\frac{1}{16}$ of the area

Extensions

39. Multiple Choice Which diagram would make a pyramid when folded along the dashed lines? (A pyramid is the shape shown in Exercise 34.)

A.

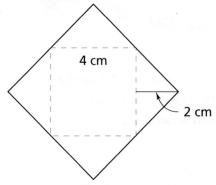

4 cm

2 cm

B.

$2\frac{1}{2}$ cm $2\frac{1}{2}$ cm

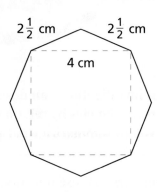

4 cm

C.

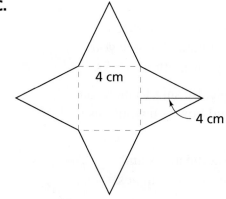

4 cm

4 cm

D.

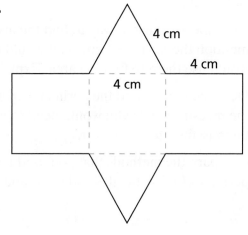

4 cm

4 cm

4 cm

40. Explain how you could calculate the area and perimeter of this regular hexagon.

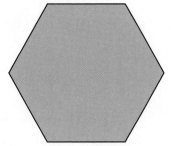

Mathematical Reflections 3

In your work in this investigation, you discovered strategies for finding the areas and perimeters of triangles by relating them to rectangles. These questions will help you to summarize what you have learned.

Think about your answers to these questions. Discuss your ideas with other students and your teacher. Then write a summary of your findings in your notebook.

1. Describe an efficient way to find the area of a triangle. Be sure to mention the measurements you would need to make and how you would use them to find the area. Explain why your method works.

2. Describe how to find the perimeter of a triangle. Be sure to mention the measurements you would need to make and how you would use them to find the perimeter.

3. Compare the methods that you used for finding the areas and perimeters of rectangles and areas and perimeters of triangles.

Investigation 4

Measuring Parallelograms

In this unit, you have developed ways to find the area and perimeter of rectangles and of triangles. In this investigation you will develop ways to find the area and perimeter of parallelograms.

When you work with rectangles, you use measurements like length and width. For triangles, you use the side lengths, the base, and the height. Like triangles, parallelograms are often described by measures of side length, base, and height.

4.1 Finding Measures of Parallelograms

As you work with parallelograms, remember what you know about triangles and look for ways to relate these two figures.

Here are three parallelograms with the base and height of two parallelograms marked. What do you think the *base* and the *height* of a parallelogram mean? How do you mark and measure the base and height of the third figure?

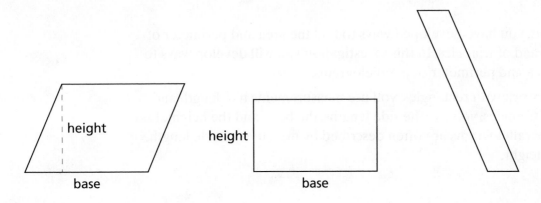

Problem 4.1 Finding Measures of Parallelograms

Six parallelograms labeled A–F are drawn on the centimeter grid on the next page.

A. 1. Find the perimeter of each parallelogram.

2. Describe a strategy for finding the perimeter of a parallelogram.

B. 1. Find the area of each parallelogram.

2. Describe the strategies you used to find the areas.

ACE Homework starts on page 60.

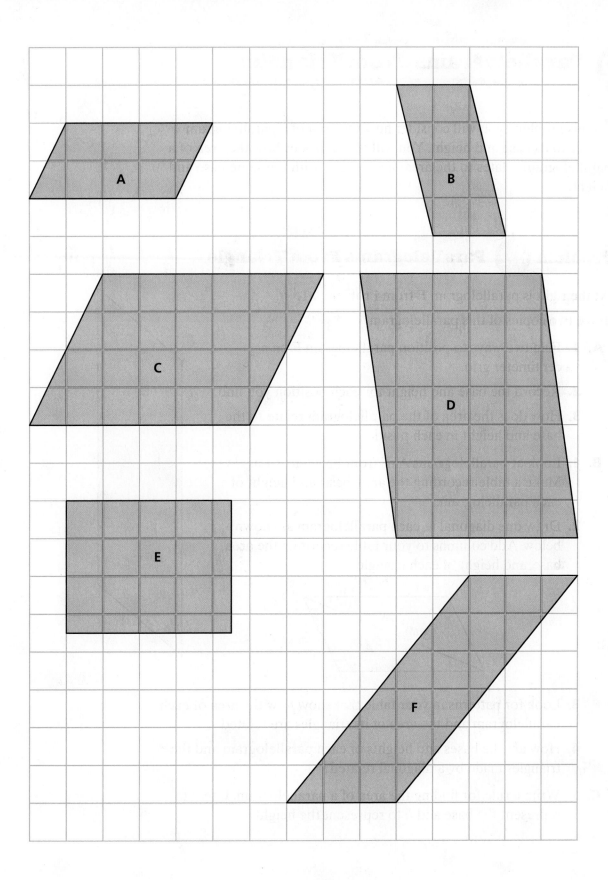

4.2 Parallelograms From Triangles

In this problem, you will consider how the area of a parallelogram relates to its base and height. You will also consider how the area of a parallelogram relates to the area of a triangle with the same base and height.

Problem 4.2 Parallelograms From Triangles

At the right is parallelogram F from Problem 4.1.

Trace two copies of this parallelogram.

A. 1. Find two ways to position parallelogram F on a centimeter grid.

   2. Record the base and height for each position you find.

   3. How does the area of the parallelogram relate to the base and height in each position?

B. 1. Look at parallelograms A–F from Problem 4.1 again. Make a table recording the area, base, and height of each parallelogram.

   2. Draw one diagonal in each parallelogram as shown below. Add columns to your table recording the area, base, and height of each triangle.

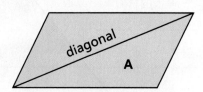

   3. Look for patterns in your table that show how the area of each parallelogram and the area of its triangles are related.

   4. How are the bases and heights of each parallelogram and the triangles made by a diagonal related?

C. 1. Write a rule for finding the area of a parallelogram. Use *b* to represent the base and *h* to represent the height.

2. Use your rule to find the area of this parallelogram. Make any measurements you need in centimeters.

ACE Homework starts on page 60.

4.3 Designing Parallelograms Under Constraints

Now you can draw parallelograms that meet given conditions. Sometimes you will be able to draw more than one parallelogram that satisfies the constraints given.

Problem 4.3 Designing Parallelograms Under Constraints

For each description, draw two figures that are *not* congruent (same shape, same size) to each other. If you can't draw a second figure, explain why. Make your drawings on centimeter grid paper.

A. The rectangles each have an area of 18 square centimeters. If you can draw two different rectangles, do they have the same perimeter?

B. The rectangles are each 3 centimeters by 8 centimeters. If you can draw two different rectangles, do they have the same area?

C. The parallelograms each have a base of 7 centimeters and a height of 4 centimeters. If you can draw two different parallelograms, do they have the same area?

D. The parallelograms each have all 6-centimeter side lengths. If you can draw two different parallelograms, do they have the same area?

E. The parallelograms each have an area of 30 square centimeters. If you can draw two different parallelograms, do they have the same perimeter?

ACE Homework starts on page 60.

4.4 Parks, Hotels, and Quilts

Now that you know how to find the area of rectangles, triangles, and parallelograms, here are some problems to test your skills.

Problem 4.4 Finding Areas and Perimeters

A. The Luis Park District set aside a rectangular section of land to make a park. After talking with students, the park district decides to make an area for skateboarding, an area with playground equipment, and an area with a basketball court, as shown.

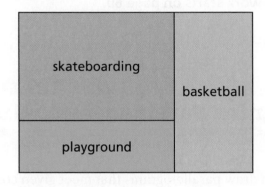

1. A fence surrounds the skateboarding area that takes up $\frac{2}{3}$ of the length and $\frac{2}{3}$ of the width of the park. What fraction of the area of the park does the skateboarding area occupy?

2. The basketball court is 35 feet by 60 feet. Use this information and what you know about the skateboarding area to find the area and the perimeter of the playground area.

B. The Luxor Hotel in Las Vegas is built in the shape of a pyramid. When you look at the pyramid from the outside, each face (side) of the pyramid is a glass equilateral triangle.

1. Each face is an equilateral triangle with a base that is 646 feet and a height that is approximately $559\frac{9}{20}$ feet. Sketch a face of the pyramid. Label the base and height.

2. Estimate the area of the glass used to cover one triangular face.

3. If lights are strung along the three edges of one triangular face, how many feet of lights are needed?

C. Quilters use shapes such as triangles, squares, rectangles, and parallelograms when designing quilts. This is a pattern of a 10 inch-by-10 inch quilt square on inch grid paper.

├────┤ = 1 inch

1. Each parallelogram in the quilt is made from how many square inches of fabric?

2. How many square inches of fabric are used to make the small red squares in the quilt square?

3. The squares and the parallelograms will be sewn onto white fabric. How many square inches of the white fabric will be visible?

ACE Homework starts on page 60.

Applications

For Exercises 1–7, find the area and perimeter of each parallelogram. Give a brief explanation of your reasoning for Exercises 2, 6, and 7.

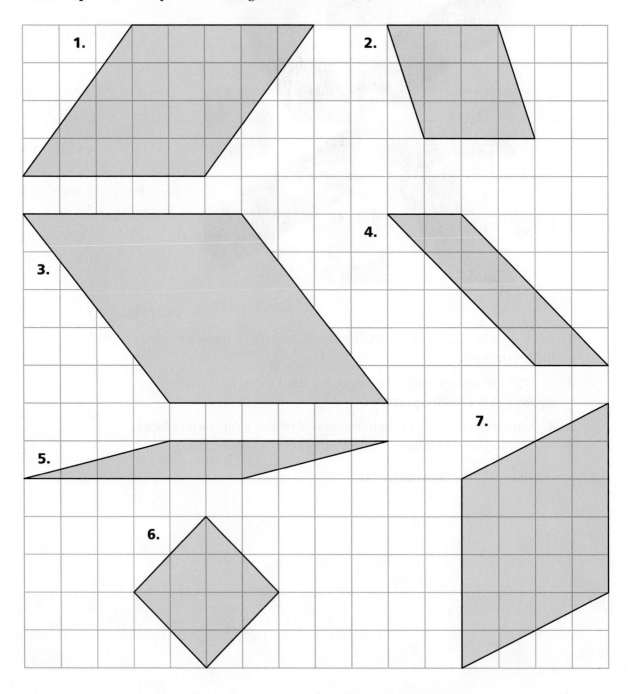

8. On the grid is a family of parallelograms.

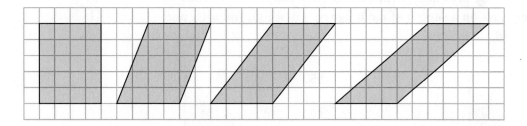

a. Find the base, height, and area of each of the parallelograms.

b. What patterns do you see?

c. Why do you think they are called a family of parallelograms?

For Exercises 9–13, find the area and perimeter of each figure. (Figures are not drawn to scale.)

Go Online
PHSchool.com
For: Multiple-Choice Skills
Web Code: ama-5454

9.

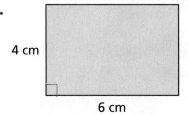

4 cm

6 cm

10.

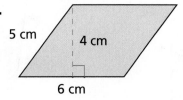

5 cm

4 cm

6 cm

11.

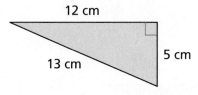

12 cm

13 cm

5 cm

12.

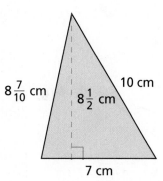

$8\frac{7}{10}$ cm

$8\frac{1}{2}$ cm

10 cm

7 cm

13.

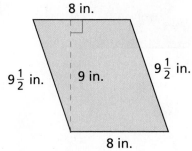

8 in.

$9\frac{1}{2}$ in.

9 in.

$9\frac{1}{2}$ in.

8 in.

For Exercises 14–19, make the measurements (in centimeters) that you need to find the area and perimeter of each shape. Write your measurements on a sketch of each figure. Then find the area and perimeter of each shape.

14.

15.

16.

17.

18.

19.

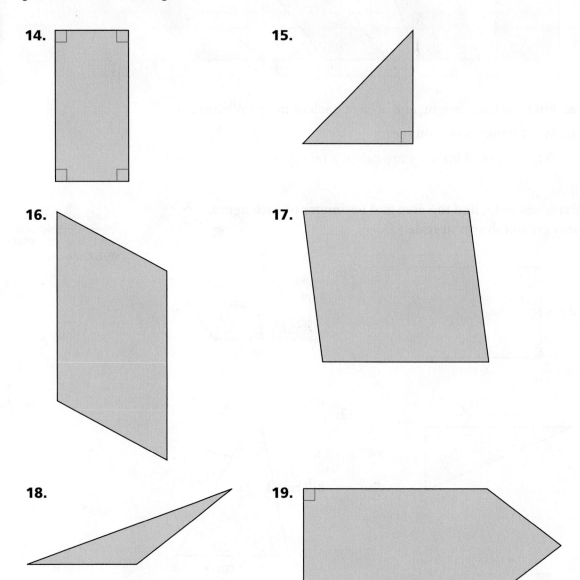

20. Denzel decides the shape of Tennessee is approximately that of a parallelogram, as shown below.

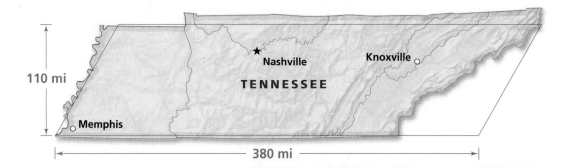

a. Use the distances shown to estimate the area of Tennessee.

b. The actual area of Tennessee is 41,217 square miles. How does your estimate compare to the actual area? Explain.

21. Explain why these three parallelograms have the same area.

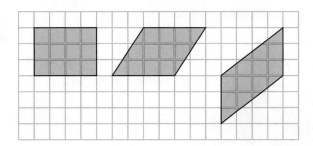

For Exercises 22–27:
   a. Sketch the described parallelogram.
   b. Label its base and height.
   c. Explain whether you can draw more than one parallelogram that will meet the given conditions.

22. The base is 8 cm and the perimeter is 28 cm.

23. The base is $4\frac{1}{2}$ cm and the area is 27 cm².

24. A non-rectangular parallelogram has a base of 10 cm and a height of 8 cm.

25. The base is 6 cm and the area is 30 cm².

26. The area is 24 cm².

27. The perimeter is 24 cm.

28. a. An equilateral triangle can be divided into equal-sized triangles using lines parallel to the opposite sides. The lines connect two midpoints. How many parallelograms can you find in the figure?

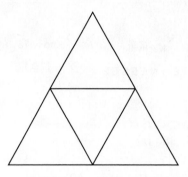

   b. Suppose the area of the large triangle is 16 square units. What is the area of each of the parallelograms?

29. Akland Middle School plans to make a flowerbed in front of the administration building. The plan involves one main parallelogram surrounded by four small parallelograms as shown.

For: Help with Exercise 29
Web Code: ame-5429

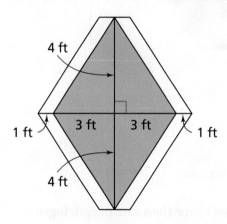

   a. How many square feet is the area of each of the four small parallelograms?

   b. How many square feet is the area of the main parallelogram?

30. Mr. Lee wants to install ceiling tiles in his recreation room. The room is 24 feet by 18 feet. Each ceiling tile is 2 feet by 3 feet. How many ceiling tiles will he need?

31. The Lopez family bought a plot of land in the shape of a parallelogram. It is 100 feet wide (across the front) and 200 feet deep (the height). Their house covers 2,250 square feet of land. How much land is left for grass?

Connections

32. Multiple Choice Which set of numbers is ordered from greatest to least?

A. $0.215, 0.23, 2.3, \frac{2}{3}$

B. $\frac{2}{3}, 0.215, 0.23, 2.3$

C. $\frac{2}{3}, 0.23, 0.215, 2.3$

D. $2.3, \frac{2}{3}, 0.23, 0.215$

33. Rectangles made from Polystrips can easily tilt out of shape into another parallelogram.

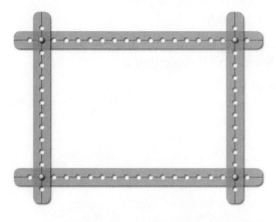 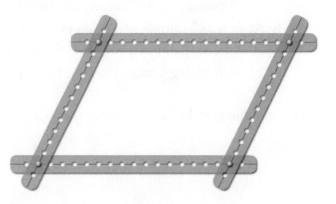

    a. Suppose a rectangle made of Polystrips tilts out of shape with the sides staying the same length. How will the angles, area, and perimeter of the new figure compare to the original?

    b. What relationships among the sides and angles of rectangles are also true of parallelograms?

34. Multiple Choice Two quadrilaterals are congruent. Which statement is correct?

    F. They have the same area, but may have different perimeters.

    G. They have the same perimeters, but may have different areas.

    H. They may have different perimeters and different areas.

    J. They have the same area and the same perimeter.

35. Give two examples of a pair of congruent quadrilaterals.

36. Rapid City is having its annual citywide celebration. The city wants to rent a bumper-car ride. The pieces used to make the floor are 4 foot-by-5 foot rectangles. The ride covers a rectangular space that is 40 feet by 120 feet.

    a. How many rectangular floor pieces are needed?

    b. The ride costs $20 per floor piece and $10 per bumper car. How much would it cost Rapid City to rent the floor and the bumper cars? (You will need to decide how many bumper cars will be appropriate.)

Extensions

37. You saw earlier that in some parallelograms and triangles, the height is outside the shape being measured.

    a. Sketch an example of a parallelogram with the height outside the parallelogram. Explain why the area of the parallelogram can still be calculated by multiplying the base times the height.

    b. Sketch an example of a triangle with the height outside the triangle. Explain why the area of the triangle can still be calculated by multiplying $\frac{1}{2}$ times the base times the height.

38. Find the area and perimeter of the figure.

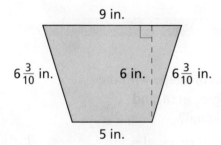

9 in.

$6\frac{3}{10}$ in.   6 in. $6\frac{3}{10}$ in.

5 in.

39. A trapezoid is a polygon with at least two opposite edges parallel. Use these six trapezoids. Make a table to summarize what you find in parts (a) and (c).

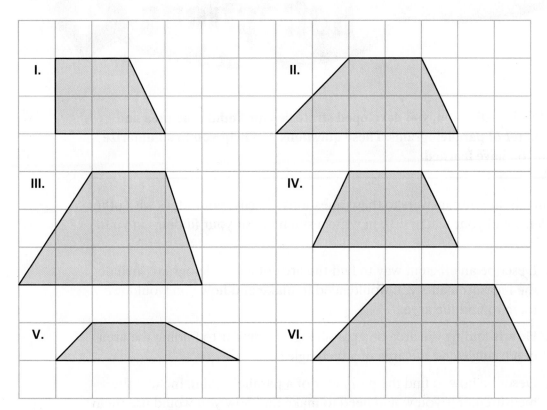

a. Without counting all the squares, find the area of each trapezoid.

b. Summarize your method for part (a) with a rule or a description.

c. Find the perimeter of each trapezoid.

d. Summarize your method for part (c) with a rule or a description.

Mathematical Reflections 4

In this investigation, you developed strategies for finding the area and perimeter of parallelograms. These questions will help you to summarize what you have learned.

Think about your answers to these questions. Discuss your ideas with other students and your teacher. Then write a summary of your findings in your notebook.

1. Describe an efficient way to find the area of a parallelogram. Include the measurements you would need to make and how you would use them to find the area.

2. How is finding the area of a parallelogram similar to finding the area of a triangle and the area of a rectangle?

3. Describe how to find the perimeter of a parallelogram. Include the measurements you would need to make and how you would use them to find the perimeter.

4. How is finding the perimeter of a parallelogram like finding the perimeter of a triangle and the perimeter of a rectangle?

Measuring Irregular Shapes and Circles

It is not hard to find the area and perimeter of shapes made from straight lines. These shapes include rectangles, triangles, and parallelograms. But measuring the area and perimeter of shapes made from curved lines is not always as easy.

You encounter circles every day in tools, toys, vehicles, bottle caps, compact discs, coins, and so on. Irregular shapes are also all around you. The shorelines and the shapes of lakes and islands are usually curvy, or irregular. Cartographers, or mapmakers, often work with irregular shapes such as those of the islands that form the state of Hawaii.

Because you do not have rules for finding areas and perimeters of shapes with curved edges, you can only estimate. You will develop good estimating skills to compare areas. You will then find more accurate ways to measure the area and the perimeter of some shapes with curved edges.

5.1 Measuring Lakes

Geographers must know the scale of the picture to estimate the area and perimeter of a lake from a picture.

To estimate perimeter, they can

- Lay a string around the lake's shoreline in the picture of the lake.
- Measure the length of the string.
- Scale the answer.

To estimate area, they can

- Put a transparent grid over the picture of the lake.
- Count the number of unit squares needed to cover the picture.
- Use the scale of the picture to tell what the count means.

The state Parks and Recreations Division bought a property containing Loon Lake and Ghost Lake. Park planners will develop one lake for swimming, fishing, and boating. The other lake will be used as a nature preserve for hiking, camping, and canoeing. Planners have to think about many things when deciding how to use a lake. The perimeter, area, and shape of the lake influence their decisions.

Scale pictures for Loon Lake and Ghost Lake are on the grid.

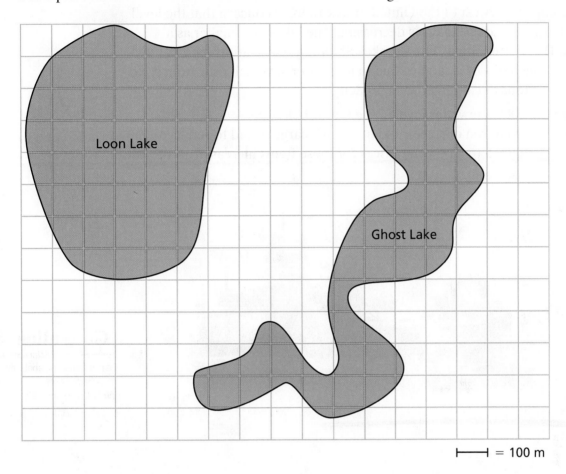

⊢——⊣ = 100 m

A. Estimate the area and perimeter of Loon Lake and Ghost Lake.

B. Which lake is larger? Explain your reasoning.

C. Use your estimates to answer the questions. Explain your answers.

1. Naturalists claim that water birds need long shorelines for nesting and fishing. Which lake will better support water birds?

2. Sailboaters and waterskiers want a lake with room to cruise. Which lake works better for boating and skiing?

3. Which lake has more space for lakeside campsites?

4. Which lake is better for swimming, boating, and fishing? Which lake is better for the nature preserve?

D. 1. Is your estimate of the area of each lake more or less than the actual area of that lake? Explain.

2. How could you get a more accurate estimate?

ACE **Homework starts on page 78.**

Did You Know?

In the upper Midwest of the United States, there is concern that the level of water in the Great Lakes is decreasing. The lakes get smaller as a result. The United States Great Lakes Shipping Association reports that for every inch of lost clearance due to low water, a vessel loses from 90 to 115 metric tons of cargo-carrying capacity.

In the year 2000, the water level in the Great Lakes decreased. Carriers that transported iron ore, coal, and other raw cargoes had to reduce their carrying load by 5 to 8 percent. Prices for these items increased as a result.

Go Online
PHSchool.com

For: Information about the Great Lakes
Web Code: ame-9031

5.2 Surrounding a Circle

The most popular shape for pizzas is a circle. The size of a pizza is usually given by its diameter. The **diameter** of a circle is any line segment from a point on a circle through the center to another point on the circle.

Radius, area, and circumference are also useful for describing the size of a circle. A **radius** is any line segment from the center of a circle to a point on the circle.

Circumference means perimeter in the language of circles. It is the distance around the circle. And, of course, area is a measure of how many square units it takes to exactly cover the region inside the circle.

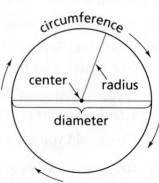

As you work with circular objects in this investigation, look for connections among a circle's diameter, radius, area, and circumference.

Getting Ready for Problem 5.2

Many pizza restaurants sell small, medium, and large pizzas. Of course, the prices are different for the three sizes.

● How do pizza makers determine the price of a pizza? Do you think a large pizza is usually the best buy?

In addition to pricing pizza, pizza makers also need to look for new ways to sell pizzas. One innovation is a pizza with cheese baked into the rim of the crust. To determine the price of these new pizzas, the pizza maker needs to know the length of the rim for each pizza. The length of the rim of crust is the circumference of the pizza.

Problem 5.2 Finding Circumference

When you want to find out if measurements are related, looking at patterns from many examples will help.

A. Use a tape measure or string to measure the circumference and diameter of several different circular objects. Record your results in a table with columns for the object, diameter, and circumference.

B. Study your table. Look for patterns and relationships between the circumference and the diameter. Test your ideas on some other circular objects.

   1. Can you find the circumference of a circle if you know its diameter? If so, how?

   2. Can you find the diameter of a circle if you know its circumference? If so, how?

ACE Homework starts on page 78.

In the last problem, you found a pattern that was helpful in finding the circumference of a circle.

Do you think there is a similar pattern for finding the area of a circle?

A pizzeria decides to sell three sizes of its new pizza. A small pizza is 9 inches in diameter, a medium is 12 inches in diameter, and a large is 15 inches in diameter.

The owner surveyed her lunch customers to find out what they would be willing to pay for a small pizza. She found that $6 was a fair price for a 9-inch pizza with one topping. Based on this price, the owner wants to find fair prices for 12- and 15-inch pizzas with one topping. She uses the scale models of the different size pizzas on grid paper shown below.

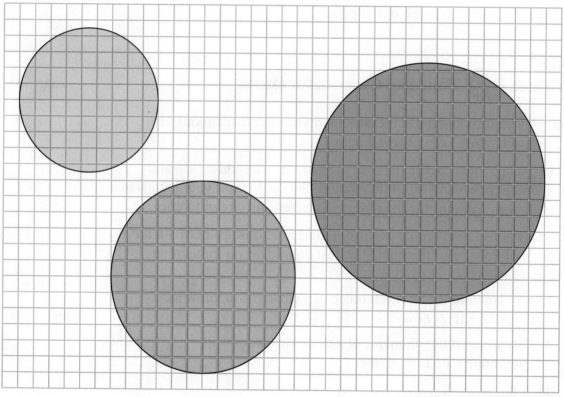

⊢⊣ = 1 inch

Problem 5.3 Exploring Area and Circumference

A. Find as many different ways as you can to estimate the area of the pizzas. For each method, give your estimate for the area and describe how you found it.

B. Copy the table and record each pizza's size, diameter, radius, circumference, and area in a table.

Size	Diameter	Radius	Circumference	Area
Small	■	■	■	■
Medium	■	■	■	■
Large	■	■	■	■

C. Examine the data in the table and your strategies for finding area. Describe any shortcuts that you found for finding the area of a circle.

D. In your opinion, should the owner of the pizzeria base the cost of a pizza on area or on circumference? Explain.

ACE Homework starts on page 78.

You have discovered that the circumference of a circle is a little more than three times the diameter. There is a special name given to this number.

In 1706, William Jones used the Greek letter for π (also written as **pi,** and pronounced "pie") to represent this number. He used the symbol to stand for the distance around a circle with a diameter of 1 unit.

As early as 2000 B.C., the Babylonians knew that π was more than 3. Their estimate for π was $3\frac{1}{8}$. By the fifth century, Chinese mathematician Tsu Chung-Chi wrote that π was somewhere between 3.1415926 and 3.1415927. From 1436 to 1874, the known value of π went from 14 places past the decimal point to 707 places.

We have used computers to calculate millions more digits. Mathematicians have shown that π cannot be expressed as a fraction with whole numbers in the numerator and denominator. Numbers having decimal representations that never come out "even" and have no repeating pattern are called *irrational numbers*.

Go Online
PHSchool.com
For: Information about pi
Web Code: ame-9031

3.141592653589793238462643383279502884197169399

5.4 "Squaring" a Circle

Earlier you developed formulas for the area of triangles and parallelograms by comparing them to rectangles. Now you can find out more about the area of circles by comparing them to squares.

Problem 5.4 Finding Area

A portion of each circle is covered by a shaded square. The length of a side of the shaded square is the same length as the radius of the circle. We call such a square a "radius square."

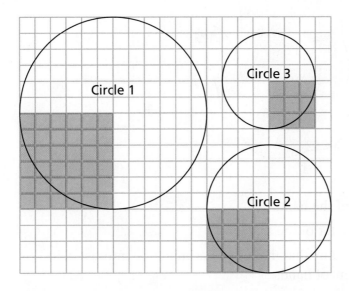

A. How many radius squares does it take to cover the circle? (You can cut out radius squares, cover the circle and see how many it takes to cover.)

Record your data in a table with columns for circle number, radius, area of the radius square, area of the circle, and number of radius squares needed.

B. Describe any patterns and relationships you see in your table that will allow you to predict the area of the circle from its radius square. Test your ideas on some other circular objects.

C. How can you find the area of a circle if you know the radius?

D. How can you find the radius of a circle if you know the area?

ACE Homework starts on page 78.

Applications

1. This is a tracing of a baby's hand on grid paper.

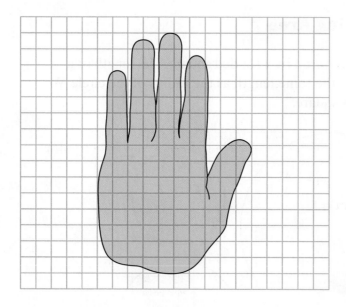

a. Estimate the area of the hand.

b. Estimate the perimeter of the hand.

c. Explain how a company that makes gloves might be interested in areas and perimeters of hands.

d. Suppose the baby's hand had been traced with its fingers spread as far apart as possible. How would this affect the area? Explain.

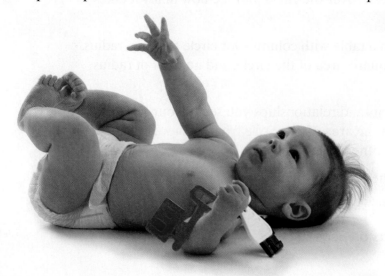

2. This is a tracing of a foot on centimeter grid paper.

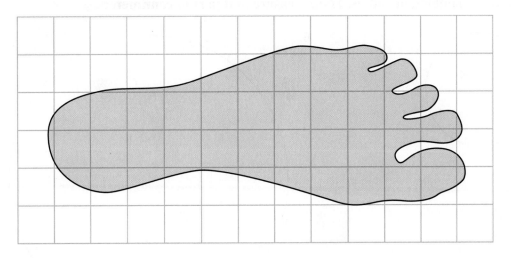

    a. Estimate the area of the foot.

    b. Estimate the perimeter of the foot.

    c. Explain how a company that makes shoes might be interested in areas and perimeters of feet.

For Exercises 3 and 4, use this map of Lake Okeebele and a centimeter grid transparency or grid paper.

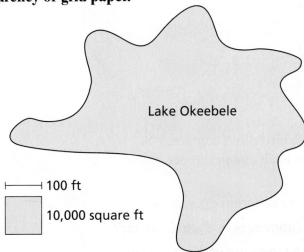

Lake Okeebele

├────┤ 100 ft

☐ 10,000 square ft

3. A developer plans to build houses around Lake Okeebele. Most of his customers want to buy about 100 feet of lakefront. How many lots can the developer build around the lake? Explain your answer.

4. The buyers want to know whether the lake has shrunk or grown over time. The developer found in the county records that the lake covered 500,000 square feet in 1920. What is happening to the lake? Give evidence to support your answer.

For Exercises 5–8, identify the part of the circle drawn in red as its circumference, diameter, or radius. Then measure that part in centimeters.

5.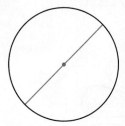

6.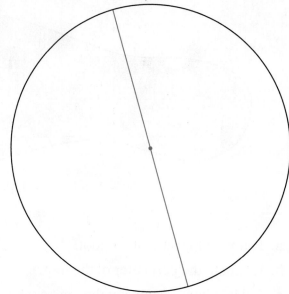

7.

8.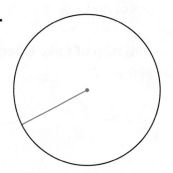

9. Measure the diameter of each circle in Exercises 5–8. Use this measurement to find each circumference.

10. Trace this circle and draw three different diameters.

   a. What is the measure, in centimeters, of each diameter?

   b. What can you say about the measure of diameters in a circle?

   c. Estimate the circumference of this circle using the diameter measurements you found.

11. Trace this circle and draw three different radii (RAY dee eye, the plural for radius).

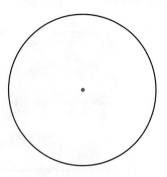

   a. What is the measure, in centimeters, of each radius?

   b. What can you say about the measure of the radii in the same circle?

   c. Estimate the circumference of this circle using the radius measurements you found.

12. Terrell says that when you know the radius of a circle, you can find the diameter by doubling the radius. Do you agree? Why or why not?

13. Enrique says that when you know the diameter of a circle you can find the radius. How does he find the measure of a radius if he knows the measure of the diameter? Give an example in your explanation.

14. **Multiple Choice** A soft-drink can is about 2.25 inches in diameter. What is its circumference?

   A. 3.53 in.   **B.** 3.97 in.^{2} **C.** 7.065 in.   **D.** 14.13 in.

15. Best Crust Pizzeria sells three different sizes of pizza. The small size has a radius of 4 inches, the medium size has a radius of 5 inches, and the large size has a radius of 6 inches.

   a. Make a table with these headings. Fill in the table. Explain how you found the area of the pizzas.

Best Crust Pizzeria

Pizza Size	Diameter (in.)	Radius (in.)	Circumference (in.)	Area (in.²)
Small	■	■	■	■
Medium	■	■	■	■
Large	■	■	■	■

   b. Jamar claims the area of a pizza is about $0.75 \times (\text{diameter})^2$. Is he correct? Explain.

For Exercises 16–20, some common circular objects are described by giving their radius or diameter. Explain what useful information (if any) you would get from calculating the area or circumference of the object.

16. $4\frac{5}{8}$-inch-diameter compact disc

17. 21-inch-diameter bicycle wheel

18. 12-inch-diameter water pipe

19. lawn sprinkler that sprays a 15-meter-radius section of lawn

20. Ferris wheel

21. Pick one of the objects from Exercises 16–20 and write a problem about it. Be sure to give the answer to your problem.

For Exercises 22–25, you may want to make scale drawings on grid paper to help find the missing measurements.

22. Derek's dinner plate has a diameter of about 9 inches. Find its circumference and area.

23. A bicycle wheel is about 26 inches in diameter. Find its radius, circumference, and area.

24. The spray from a lawn sprinkler makes a circle 40 feet in radius. What are the approximate diameter, circumference, and area of the circle of lawn watered?

25. A standard long-play record has a 12-inch diameter; a compact disc has a $4\frac{5}{8}$-inch diameter. Find the radius, circumference, and area of each.

26. A rectangular lawn has a perimeter of 36 meters and a circular exercise run has a circumference of 36 meters. Which shape will give Rico's dog more area to run? Explain.

27. The swimming pool below is a rectangle with a semicircle at one end. What are the area and perimeter of the pool?

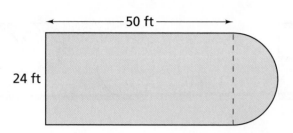

For each figure in Exercises 28–33, estimate the area in square centimeters and the perimeter or circumference in centimeters.

Go Online
PHSchool.com

For: Multiple-Choice Skills Practice
Web Code: ama-5554

28.

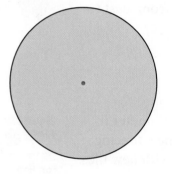

29.

30.

31.

32.

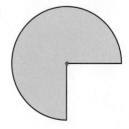

33.

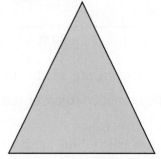

For Exercises 34 and 35, use these figures, which are drawn to scale.

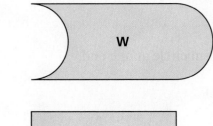
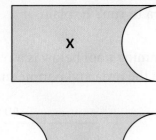
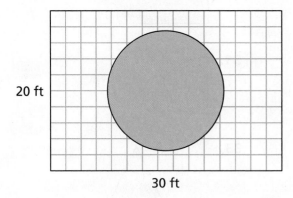

34. **Multiple Choice** Which answer has the figures in order from least to greatest area?

   F. W, X, Y, Z

   G. Z, X, W or Y

   H. Y, X, Z or W

   J. Z, Y, X, W

35. **Multiple Choice** Which answer has the figures in order from least to greatest perimeter?

   A. W, X, Y, Z

   B. Z, X, W or Y

   C. Y, X, Z or W

   D. Z, Y, X, W

36. The Nevins want to install a circular pool with a 15-foot diameter in their rectangular patio. The patio will be surrounded by new fencing and the patio area surrounding the pool will be covered with new tiles.

Homework Help Online PHSchool.com

For: Help with Exercise 36
Web Code: ame-5536

   a. How many feet of fencing are needed to enclose the patio?

   b. How much plastic is needed to cover the pool if there is a 1-foot overhang?

   c. How many feet of plastic tubing are needed to fit around the edge of the pool?

   d. How many square feet of the patio will be covered with tiles?

37. A group of students submitted these designs for a school flag. The side length of each flag is 6 feet. Each flag has two colors. How much of each color of material will be needed?

a.
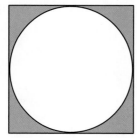

b.
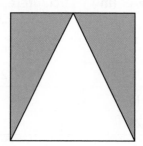

38. This circular dartboard has three circles with the same center. (These are called *concentric circles*.) The diameter of the largest circle is 20 inches. The diameters of the inner circles decrease by 4 inches as you move from the largest to the smallest. Each of the circular bands is a different color with different points assigned to it. Find the area of each circular band.

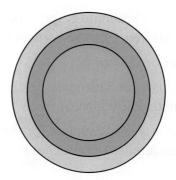

Connections

39. Explain which measurements would be useful in describing the size of each article of clothing. How would you make each measurement?

   a. belts   **b.** jeans   **c.** hats   **d.** shirts

40. The table shows the diameter and circumference of the three circular pizzas. The diameters of two other pizzas are listed.

Diameter (in.)	Circumference (in.)
9	28.27
12	37.70
15	47.12
18	■
21	■

   a. Find the circumference of the two other pizzas.

   b. Make a coordinate graph with diameter on the horizontal axis and circumference on the vertical axis.

   c. Describe the graph.

   d. What is a good estimate for the circumference of a pizza with a diameter of 20 inches?

   e. What is a good estimate for the diameter of a pizza with a circumference of 80 inches?

For Exercises 41–46, do each calculation. Explain how each number expression relates to the area and perimeter problems in this unit.

41. 2×10.5

42. $(4.25)^2 \times 3.14$

43. $\frac{1}{2} \times 15.25 \times 7.3$

44. $1\frac{3}{5} \times 2\frac{1}{4}$

45. $(2 \times 8) + (2 \times 10)$

46. $7\frac{1}{2} \times 3.14$

Extensions

47. List some events in everyday life that involve irregular shapes. Describe some features of the shapes that might be important to measure. Explain your answers.

48. The diameter of Earth is approximately 41,900,000 feet along the equator. If a 6-foot-tall man walked around Earth, how much farther would his head move than his feet?

49. a. Suppose a piece of rope wraps around Earth. Then the rope is cut, and rope is added to make the entire rope 3 feet longer. Suppose the new rope circles the earth exactly the same distance away from the surface at all points. How far is the new rope from Earth's surface?

b. A piece of rope is wrapped around a person's waist. Then rope is added to make it 3 inches longer. How far from the waist is the rope if the distance is the same all around?

c. Compare the results in parts (a) and (b).

Mathematical Reflections 5

In this investigation, you discovered strategies for finding the area and circumference of a circle. You examined relationships between the circumference and diameter of a circle and between the area and radius of a circle. You also used grids to find accurate estimates of the area and perimeter of irregular shapes. These questions will help you to summarize what you have learned.

Think about your answers to these questions. Discuss your ideas with other students and your teacher. Then write a summary of your findings in your notebook.

1. Describe how you can find the circumference of a circle by measuring its radius or its diameter.

2. Describe how you can find the area of a circle by measuring its radius or its diameter.

3. Describe how you can, with reasonable accuracy, find the area and perimeter of an irregular shape such as a lake or an island.

4. What does it mean to measure the area of a shape? What kinds of units are appropriate for measuring area? Why?

5. What does it mean to measure the perimeter or circumference of a shape? What kinds of units are appropriate for measuring perimeter or circumference? Why?

Unit Project

Plan a Park

The City Council of Roseville is planning to build a park for families in the community. Your job is to design a park to submit to the City Council for consideration. You will need to make an argument for why your design should be chosen. Use what you know about parks and what you learned from this unit to prepare your final design.

Part 1: The Design

Your design should satisfy the following constraints:

- The park is rectangular with dimensions 120 yards by 100 yards.
- About half of the park consists of a picnic area and a playground. These sections need not be located together.
- The picnic area contains a circular flower garden. There also is a garden in at least one other place in the park.
- There are trees in several places in the park. Young trees will be planted, so your design should show room for the trees to grow.
- The park must appeal to families. There should be more than just a picnic area and a playground.

- rectangular (120 yd by 100 yd)
- picnic area and playground
- circular flower garden in picnic area
- another garden
- trees
- family interest

Part 2: Write a Report

Your design package should be neat, clear, and easy to follow. Draw and label your design in black and white. In addition to a scale drawing of your design for the park, your project should include a report that gives:

1. the size (dimensions) of each item (include gardens, trees, picnic tables, playground equipment, and any other item in your design).

2. the amount of land needed for each item and the calculations you used to determine the amount of land needed

3. the materials needed (include the amount of each item needed and the calculations you did to determine the amounts)
   - each piece of playground equipment
   - fencing
   - picnic tables
   - trash containers
   - the amount of land covered by concrete or blacktop (so the developers can determine how much cement or blacktop will be needed)
   - other items

Extension Question

Write a letter to the City Council. Explain why they should choose your design for the park. Justify the choices you made about the size and quantity of items in your park.

Looking Back and Looking Ahead

Unit Review

Working on problems in this unit helped you to understand area and perimeter. You learned

- efficient strategies for estimating and calculating the area and perimeter of figures such as triangles, rectangles, parallelograms, and circles
- to investigate the relationship between area and perimeter of simple polygons

For: Vocabulary Review Puzzle
Web Code: amj-5051

Use Your Understanding: Area and Perimeter

Test your understanding and skill in working with area and perimeter on these problems.

1. The diagram shows a hexagon drawn on a centimeter grid.

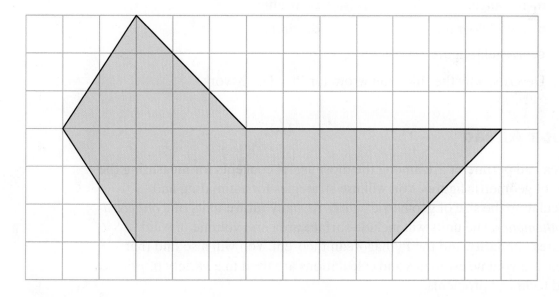

   a. Find the area of the hexagon.

   b. Describe two different strategies for finding the area.

2. The Nevins' living room floor is a square 20 feet by 20 feet. It is covered with wood. They have carpeted a quarter-circle region as shown.

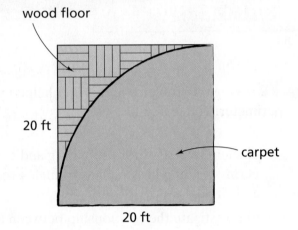

wood floor

20 ft

carpet

20 ft

a. What is the area of the uncovered wood, to the nearest square foot?

b. A 1-quart can of floor wax covers 125 square feet of wood flooring. How many cans of floor wax are needed to wax the uncovered wood?

c. A special finishing trim was placed along the curved edge of the carpet. How much trim, to the nearest tenth of a foot, was needed?

Explain Your Reasoning

3. Give a rule for finding the area and perimeter of each figure.

a. rectangle
b. triangle
c. parallelogram
d. circle
e. irregular figure

4. Describe why the rules you wrote for Problem 3 work.

Look Ahead

Area and perimeter are among the most useful concepts for measuring the size of geometric figures. You will use strategies for estimating and calculating the size of geometric figures in many future units of *Connected Mathematics*. The units will include surface area and volume of solid figures, similarity, and the Pythagorean theorem. You will also find that area and volume estimates and calculations are used in a variety of practical and technical problems.

A

area The measure of the amount of surface enclosed by the boundary of a figure. To find the area of a figure, you can count how many unit squares it takes to cover the figure. You can find the area of a rectangle by multiplying the length by the width. This is a shortcut method for finding the number of unit squares it takes to cover the rectangle. If a figure has curved or irregular sides, you can estimate the area. Cover the surface with a grid and count whole grid squares and parts of grid squares. When you find the area of a shape, write the units, such as square centimeters (cm^2), to indicate the unit square that was used to find the area.

área La medida de la cantidad de superficie encerrada por los límites de una figura. Para hallar el área de una figura, puedes contar cuántas unidades cuadradas se requieren para cubrir la figura. Puedes hallar el área de un rectángulo multiplicando el largo por el ancho. Esto es un método más corto para hallar el número de unidades cuadradas requeridas para cubrir el rectángulo. Si una figura tiene lados curvos o irregulares, puedes estimar el área. Para ello, cubre la superficie con una cuadrícula y cuenta los cuadrados enteros y las partes de cuadrados en la cuadrícula. Cuando halles el área de una figura, escribe las unidades, como centímetros cuadrados (cm^2), para indicar la unidad cuadrada que se usó para hallar el área. El área del cuadrado representado a continuación es de 9 unidades cuadradas y el área del rectángulo es de 8 unidades cuadradas.

 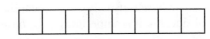

A = 9 square units   A = 8 square units

B

base See *linear dimensions.*

base Ver *dimensiones lineales.*

C

circle A two-dimensional object in which every point is the same distance from a point called the *center.* Point C is the center of this circle.

círculo Un objeto bidimensional en el que cada punto está a la misma distancia de un punto llamado el *centro.* El punto C es el centro del siguiente círculo.

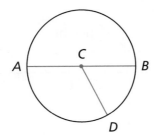

circumference The distance around (or perimeter of) a circle. It takes slightly more than three diameters to match the circumference of a circle. More formally, the circumference of a circle is pi (π) times the diameter of the circle.

circunferencia La distancia alrededor de un círculo (o su perímetro). Se requiere apenas más de tres diámetros para representar la circunferencia de un círculo. Más formalmente, la circunferencia de un círculo es pi (π) multiplicado por el diámetro del círculo.

D

diameter A segment that goes from one point on a circle through the center of the circle to another point on the circle. Also, diameter is used to indicate the length of this segment. In the definition of *circle* above, segment *AB* is a diameter.

diámetro Un segmento que va desde un punto en un círculo, pasando por el centro hasta otro punto en el círculo. La longitud de este segmento también se llama "diámetro". En la definición de *círculo* de más arriba, el segmento *AB* es un diámetro.

H

height See *linear dimensions.*

altura Ver *dimensiones lineales.*

L

length See *linear dimensions.*

largo Ver *dimensiones lineales.*

linear dimensions Linear measurements, such as length, width, base, and height, which describe the size of figures. The longest dimension or the dimension along the bottom of a rectangle is usually called the *length,* and the other dimension is called the *width,* but it is not incorrect to reverse these labels. The word *base* is used when talking about triangles and parallelograms. The *base* is usually measured along a horizontal side, but it is sometimes convenient to think of one of the other sides as the base. For a triangle, the *height* is the perpendicular distance from a vertex opposite the base to the line containing the base. For a parallelogram, the height is the perpendicular distance from a point on the side opposite the base to the base. You need to be flexible when you encounter these terms, so you are able to determine their meanings from the context of the situation.

dimensiones lineales Medidas lineales, como el largo, el ancho, la base y la altura, que describen el tamaño de las figuras. La dimensión más larga o la dimensión a lo largo de la parte inferior de un rectángulo generalmente se llama *largo* y la otra dimensión se llama *ancho,* pero no es incorrecto invertir estos nombres. La palabra *base* se usa cuando se habla de triángulos y de paralelogramos. La *base* se mide a lo largo de un lado horizontal, pero a veces es conveniente pensar en uno de los otros lados como la base. En un triángulo, la *altura* es la distancia perpendicular desde el vértice opuesto de la base hasta la base. En un paralelogramo, la altura es la distancia perpendicular desde un punto en el lado opuesto de la base hasta la base. Tienes que ser flexible cuando te encuentres con estos términos para que puedas determinar su significado dentro del contexto de la situación.

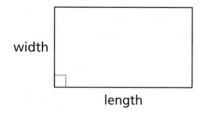

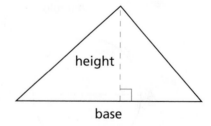

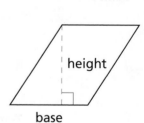

perimeter The measure of the distance around a figure. Perimeter is a measure of length. To find the perimeter of a figure, you count the number of unit lengths it takes to surround the figure. When you find the perimeter of a shape, write the units (such as centimeters, feet, or yards) to indicate the unit that was used to find the perimeter. The perimeter of the square below is 12 units, because 12 units of length surround the figure. The perimeter of the rectangle is 18 units. Notice that the rectangle has a larger perimeter, but a smaller area, than the square.

perímetro La medida de la distancia alrededor de una figura. El perímetro es una medida de longitud. Para hallar el perímetro de una figura, cuentas el número de unidades de longitud que se requieren para rodear la figura. Cuando halles el perímetro de una figura, escribe las unidades (como, por ejemplo, centímetros, pies o yardas) para indicar la unidad que se usó para hallar el perímetro. El perímetro del cuadrado de abajo es de 12 unidades, porque 12 unidades de longitud rodean la figura. El perímetro del rectángulo es de 18 unidades. Observa que el rectángulo tiene un perímetro más largo, pero un área más pequeña, que el cuadrado.

P = 12 units

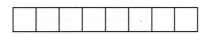

P = 18 units

perpendicular lines Lines that meet at right angles. The length and width of a rectangle are perpendicular to each other and the base and height of a triangle are perpendicular to each other. In diagrams, perpendicular lines are often indicated by drawing a small square where the lines meet.

rectas perpendiculares Rectas que se encuentran en ángulos rectos. El largo y el ancho de un rectángulo son perpendiculares entre sí, y la base y la altura de un triángulo son perpendiculares entre sí. En los diagramas, las rectas perpendiculares generalmente se indican dibujando un pequeño cuadrado donde se unen las rectas.

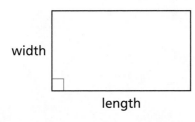

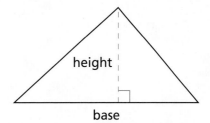

pi (π) The mathematical name for the ratio of a circle's circumference to its diameter. This ratio is the same for every circle, and is approximately equal to 3.1416.

pi (p) El nombre matemático para la razón entre la circunferencia de un círculo y su diámetro. Esta razón es la misma para cada círculo y es aproximadamente igual a 3.1416.

radius A segment from the center of a circle to a point on the circle. The length of this segment is also called the radius. The radius is half of the diameter. *CD* is one radius of the circle below. The plural of radius is radii. All the radii of a circle have the same length.

radio Un segmento desde el centro de un círculo hasta un punto en el círculo. La longitud de este segmento también se llama radio. El radio es la mitad del diámetro. *CD* es un radio del círculo de abajo. Todos los radios de un círculo tienen la misma longitud.

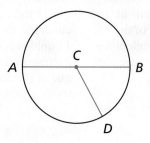

width See *linear dimensions*.

ancho Ver *dimensiones lineales*.

Academic Vocabulary

The following terms are important to your understanding of the mathematics in this unit. Knowing and using these words will help you in thinking, reasoning, representing, communicating your ideas, and making connections across ideas. When these words make sense to you, the investigations and problems will make more sense as well.

experiment To try in several different ways to gather information.
related terms: explore, examine, discover

Sample: **Experiment to see if you can draw an isosceles, a right, and an equilateral triangle with the same base length.**

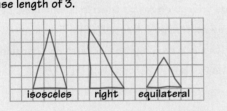

I can draw all three types of triangles with a base length of 3.

experimentar Intentar recopilar información en varias formas diferentes.
términos relacionados: explorar, examinar, descubrir

Ejemplo: **Experimenta para ver si puedes dibujar un triángulo isósceles, un triángulo rectángulo y un triángulo equilátero con la misma longitud de base.**

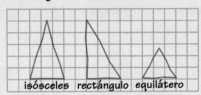

Puedo dibujar los tres tipos de triángulos con una longitud de base de 3.

explain To give facts and details that make an idea easier to understand. Explaining can involve a written summary supported by a diagram, chart, table, or a combination of these.
related terms: clarify, describe, justify

Sample: **Is it possible to increase the area of a rectangle without increasing its perimeter? Explain.**

I can increase the area of a rectangle from 8 square units to 9 without increasing the perimeter of 12.

explicar Dar hechos y detalles que hacen que una idea sea más fácil de comprender. Explicar puede implicar un resumen escrito apoyado por un diagrama, una gráfica, una tabla o una combinación de éstos.
términos relacionados: aclarar, describir, justificar, decir

Ejemplo: **¿Es posible aumentar el área de un rectángulo sin aumentar su perímetro? Explica tu respuesta.**

Puedo aumentar el área de un rectángulo de 8 unidades cuadradas a 9 sin aumentar el perímetro de 12 unidades.

identify To match a definition or a description to an object or to recognize something and be able to name it.

related terms: name, find, recognize, locate

Sample: Identify the triangles shown below that have the same area. Explain.

A.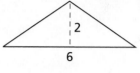

B.

C.

D.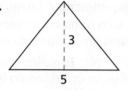

> Triangles A and B have the same area. The area of triangle A is $\frac{1}{2}(2)(6) = 6$. The area of triangle B is $\frac{1}{2}(3)(4) = 6$. The area of triangle C is 2, and the area of triangle D is 7.5.

identificar Relacionar una definición o una descripción con un objeto, o bien, reconocer algo y ser capaz de nombrarlo.

términos relacionados: nombrar, hallar, reconocer, localizar

Ejemplo: Identifica los triángulos mostrados a continuación que tengan la misma área. Explica tu respuesta.

A.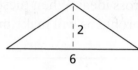

B.

C.

D.

> Los triángulos A y B tienen la misma área. El área del triángulo A es $\frac{1}{2}(2)(6) = 6$. El área del triángulo B es $\frac{1}{2}(3)(4) = 6$. El área del triángulo C es 2, y el área del triángulo D es 7.5.

summarize To go over or review the most important points.

related terms: explain, demonstrate, present

Sample: Summarize what you know about isosceles, right, and equilateral triangles.

> An isosceles triangle has at least 2 sides with equal lengths. A right triangle has one right angle. An equilateral triangle is a triangle with 3 equal side lengths.
>
>
>
> isosceles   right   equilateral

resumir Repasar o revisar los puntos más importantes.

términos relacionados: explicar, demostrar, presentar

Ejemplo: Resume lo que sepas sobre los triángulos isósceles, los triángulos rectángulos y los triángulos equiláteros.

> Un triángulo isósceles tiene al menos 2 lados con longitudes iguales. Un triángulo rectángulo tiene un ángulo recto. Un triángulo equilátero es un triángulo con 3 lados de longitudes iguales.
>
>
>
> triángulo isósceles   triángulo rectángulo   triángulo equilátero

Index

Index

Index

Acknowledgments

Team Credits

The people who made up the **Connected Mathematics 2** team—representing editorial, editorial services, design services, and production services—are listed below. Bold type denotes core team members.

Leora Adler, Judith Buice, Kerry Cashman, Patrick Culleton, Sheila DeFazio, Richard Heater, **Barbara Hollingdale, Jayne Holman,** Karen Holtzman, **Etta Jacobs,** Christine Lee, Carolyn Lock, Catherine Maglio, **Dotti Marshall,** Rich McMahon, Eve Melnechuk, Kristin Mingrone, Terri Mitchell, **Marsha Novak,** Irene Rubin, Donna Russo, Robin Samper, Siri Schwartzman, **Nancy Smith,** Emily Soltanoff, **Mark Tricca,** Paula Vergith, Roberta Warshaw, Helen Young

Additional Credits

Diana Bonfilio, Mairead Reddin, Michael Torocsik, nSight, Inc.

Illustration

Michelle Barbera: 43, 50, 69, 76

Technical Illustration

WestWords, Inc.

Cover Design

tom white.images

Photos

2 t, James Lafayette/Index Stock Imagery, Inc.; **2 m,** Sherman Hines/Masterfile; **2 b,** NASA Goddard Space Flight Center; **3,** Larry Dunmire/SuperStock; **5,** Digital Vision/SuperStock; **10,** Seth Wenig/Corbis; **14,** James Lafayette/Index Stock Imagery, Inc.; **16,** David Young-Wolff/ PhotoEdit; **19,** GoodShoot/SuperStock; **20,** Jim DuFresne/Lonely Planet Images; **26,** Pixtal/AGE Fotostock; **28,** Vincent Van Gogh/The Bridgeman Art Library/Getty Images, Inc.; **32,** Koichi Kamoshida/Getty Images, Inc.; **38,** Pat O'Hara/Corbis; **49,** Sherman Hines/Masterfile; **53,** Richard Haynes; **58,** B.S.P.I./Corbis; **65,** Liane Cary/AGE Fotostock; **70,** Greg Stott/Masterfile; **72,** Dennis MacDonald/PhotoEdit; **75,** Lawrence Migdale; **78,** Jo Foord/Dorling Kindersley; **82,** David Young-Wolff/PhotoEdit; **87,** NASA Goddard Space Flight Center; **89,** Richard Haynes

Data Sources

Did You Know on page 10 is from A Short History of Bumper Cars from AUTOMOBILE MAGAZINE Copyright © 2005 PRIMEDIA Magazines, Inc. All rights reserved.

Introductory paragraph on page 24 is from "Pet Incidence Trend Report" Copyright © 2003 Pet Food Institute. Used with permission of the Pet Food Institute, Washington D.C.

Effect on Water Level Decreasing on Ship Carrying Capacity on page 72 from THE UNITED STATES GREAT LAKES SHIPPING ASSOCIATION. Copyright © 2004 United States Great Lakes Shipping Association. All rights reserved.

William Jones Used the Pi Symbol in 1706 on page 76 from A HISTORY OF MATHEMATICS, 2ND EDITION by Carl B. Boyer. Copyright © 1991 John Wiley & Sons, Inc.

Babylonian pi history on page 76 is from "pi." Encyclopedia Britannica. 2005. Encyclopedia Britannica Online. 15 Aug. 2005 and from A HISTORY OF PI, 3RD EDITION by Peter Beckmann. Copyright © 1974 St. Martin's Press.

Tsu Chun-Chi discovering the value of Pi on page 76 from A HISTORY OF MATHEMATICS, 2ND EDITION by Carl B. Boyer. Copyright © 1991 John Wiley & Sons, Inc.

Note: Every effort has been made to locate the copyright owner of the material reprinted in this book. Omissions brought to our attention will be corrected in subsequent editions.

Connected Mathematics 2™

Bits and Pieces III

Computing With Decimals and Percents

Glenda Lappan

James T. Fey

William M. Fitzgerald

Susan N. Friel

Elizabeth Difanis Phillips

PEARSON

Boston, Massachusetts · Glenview, Illinois · Shoreview, Minnesota · Upper Saddle River, New Jersey

Bits and Pieces III

Computing With Decimals and Percents

Shing is helping his brother, Chi, with his math homework. Shing says that to multiply a number by 10, you just add a zero to it. What do you think he means? Is he correct? What mistake do you think Chi might make when he tries to use Shing's rule?

Mrs. Doran takes her three grandchildren out to lunch. Each grandchild orders a meal that costs $2.95. What is the cost of the three meals?

★ Kids' Menu ★

Chicken Nuggets . . $2.95
P.B. & J. $2.95
Hot Dog $2.95
Mac & Cheese $2.95

Lisa buys a hat for $27.00 that originally cost $36.00. What percent has the hat been marked down?

In *Bits and Pieces II*, you studied the operations of addition, subtraction, multiplication, and division with fractions. In this unit, you will study the same operations with decimals. You will need to decide which operation makes sense in each situation.

Knowing how to estimate and to compute with all kinds of numbers is important. You already know about working with fractions and with whole numbers. In this unit, you will use what you know to make sense of, and find shortcuts for, computing with decimal numbers.

You will then use all of this knowledge to develop strategies for working with percents in everyday situations.

Remember, finding the right answers is only one part of your work in math. You must also be able to make sense of and describe your strategies for finding these answers.

Mathematical Highlights

Computing With Decimals and Percents

In *Bits and Pieces III,* you will learn how to perform and make sense of the four operations (+, −, ×, ÷) on decimal numbers. You will improve your understanding and skill in working with percents.

You will learn how to

- Use your knowledge of fractions to learn about operating on decimals
- Estimate the results of operations on decimals
- Use your knowledge of place value in working with decimals
- Know when to use each operation in a situation involving decimals
- Recognize real-world situations where people often choose to use decimals instead of common fractions
- Develop algorithms for solving a variety of types of percent problems

As you work on problems in this unit, ask yourself questions about situations that involve decimals and percents:

What is the whole (unit) in this situation?

How big are the numbers in this problem?

About how large will the sum be?

About how large will the difference be?

About how large will the product be?

About how large will the quotient be?

How do these decimals compare to fractions that I know?

Why are percents useful in this problem?

Investigation 1

Decimals—More or Less!

In this unit you will consider everyday situations in which decimals are used. For example, you can measure a person's height using inches or centimeters, and then record the results as a decimal. So, 66 inches is 5.5 feet, and 102 cm is 1.02 meters. You can measure the time it takes a person to run a race, and then record the results. You can also use decimals to find the cost of items that you buy at the store.

1.1 About How Much?

When you are working with decimals, it is helpful to use what you know about fractions. Here is a number line labeled with some of the fraction and decimal benchmarks you learned about in *Bits and Pieces I*.

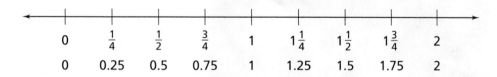

These benchmarks are useful when you are estimating with decimals. For example, you can use a benchmark to quickly estimate the total amount of a bill.

Tat Ming estimates total cost as he adds items to his cart in the grocery store. He wants to make sure he has enough money to pay the cashier. He puts the following items in his cart:

Chips	$2.79	Salsa	$1.99	Ground Beef	$3.12
Cheese	$1.29	Jalapeños	$0.45		

- Estimate the total cost and tell what you think he might be making for his friends!

- Tat Ming has only $10.00. From your estimate, does he have enough money? How confident are you of your answer?

As you work with decimals in this unit, estimate before you start the calculations. This will help you to know what answer to expect. If your estimate and your answer are not close, you may have made a mistake in calculating, even if you are using a calculator.

Problem 1.1 Estimating With Decimals

For each situation decide which operation to use. Then use benchmarks and other strategies to estimate the sum or difference.

A. Nick is going to Big Thrifty Acres to spend the $20 he got for a birthday present. His mom offers to pay the sales tax for him. He cannot spend more than $20. As he walks through the store, he has to estimate the total cost of all the items he wants to buy.

1. Nick chooses a game that costs $6.89. About how much money will be left if he buys the game?

2. Nick finds some other things he would like to have. He finds a CD on sale for $5.99, a package of basketball cards for $2.89, a bag of peanuts for $1.59, and a baseball hat for $4.29. Does Nick have enough money to buy everything he wants?

3. In this situation, would you overestimate or underestimate? Why?

4. Nick decides to spend $10 and save the rest for another time. What can Nick buy from the items he wants to come as close as possible to spending $10?

B. Maria is saving to buy a new bicycle. The price for the bike she wants is $129.89. She has saved $78 from babysitting. She owes her brother $5. Her grandmother gives her $25 for her birthday. She expects another $10 or $12 from babysitting this weekend. She empties her piggy bank and finds $13.73. Should she plan to buy the bike next week? Why or why not?

C. What strategies do you find useful in estimating sums and differences with decimals?

ACE **Homework starts on page 13.**

1.2 Adding and Subtracting Decimals

Perhaps something like the following happened to you.

Getting Ready for Problem 1.2

Sally Jane and her friend Zeke buy snacks at Quick Shop. They pick out a bag of pretzels for $0.89 and a half-gallon of cider for $1.97. The cash register in the express lane is broken and the clerk says the bill (before taxes) is $10.87.

- Do you agree? If not, explain what the clerk probably did wrong.

It looks like the Quick Shop clerk does not know about place value! For example, in the numbers 236.5 and 23.65, the 2, 3, 6, and 5 mean different things because the decimal point is in a different place. The chart below shows the two numbers and the place value for each digit.

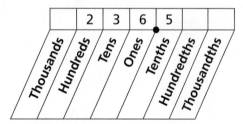
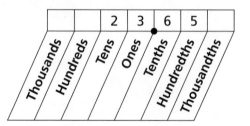

- Why is it an error for the clerk to add the 8 in the price of the pretzels to the 1 in the price of the cider?

Here is a situation that uses decimals but does not involve money. Use what you know about measurement and place value to help you think about the problems.

Every year, students at Memorial High School volunteer to clean local highway roadsides. Each club or team at the school is assigned a section of highway to clean.

One member of a club measures out each member's part of the section of highway using a trundle wheel. A trundle wheel can measure distances in thousandths of a mile.

A. Solve each problem. Write a mathematical sentence using decimal notation to show your computation. Record your sentence in a table like the one below. You will add to your table in Problem 1.3.

Person	Number Sentence (decimal notation)	(Leave this column blank for Problem 1.3)
Carmela		

1. Carmela signed up to clean 1.5 miles for the cross-country team. It starts to rain after she has cleaned 0.25 of a mile. How much does she have left to clean?

2. Pam cleans 0.25 of a mile for the chorus and cleans another 0.375 of a mile for the math club. How much does she clean altogether?

3. Jim, a member of the chess club, first cleans 0.287 of a mile. He later cleans another 0.02 of a mile. How much of a mile does he clean altogether?

4. Teri doesn't notice that she finished her section of highway until she is 0.005 of a mile past her goal of 0.85 of a mile. She claims she cleaned nine tenths of a mile. Is she correct? Explain.

B. 1. Explain what place value has to do with adding and subtracting decimals.

2. Use your ideas about place value and adding and subtracting decimals to solve the following problems.

   a. 27.9 + 103.2   **b.** 0.45 + 1.2

   c. 2.011 + 1.99   **d.** 34.023 − 1.23

   e. 4.32 − 1.746   **f.** 0.982 − 0.2

ACE **Homework starts on page 13.**

1.3 Using Fractions to Add and Subtract Decimals

To add or subtract decimals, you have to be sure to only add or subtract digits that have the same place value. You can make sure by writing addition and subtraction problems in column form and lining up the decimal points.

You can use your knowledge of fractions to see why this strategy for adding or subtracting decimals works. Remember that decimals can be written as fractions with 10; 100; 1,000; 10,000; etc. as denominators. Revisit the Quick Shop problem and think of the money amounts as fractions.

Getting Ready for Problem 1.3

Remember that Sally Jane and her friend Zeke went to Quick Shop to buy snacks. They picked out a bag of pretzels for $0.89 and a half-gallon of cider for $1.97.

$$0.89 = \frac{89}{100}$$

$$1.97 = \frac{197}{100}$$

So the total cost is $\frac{89}{100} + \frac{197}{100} = \frac{286}{100} = 2.86$.

How is this like thinking of the cost in pennies and then finally writing the sum in dollars?

Problem 1.3 Using Fractions to Add and Subtract Decimals

A. Write the decimal numbers in parts (1)–(4) in fraction form with denominators of 10, 100, 1000, etc. Then add or subtract the fractions. Write a number sentence in fraction notation that shows your computation. Add it to your table in Problem 1.2.

   1. Carmela signed up to clean 1.5 miles for the cross-country team. It starts to rain after she has cleaned 0.25 of a mile. How much does she have left to clean?

   2. Pam cleans 0.25 of a mile for the chorus and cleans another 0.375 of a mile for the math club. How much does she clean altogether?

3. Jim, a member of the chess club, first cleans 0.287 of a mile. He later cleans another 0.02 of a mile. How much of a mile does he clean altogether?

4. Teri doesn't notice that she finished her section of highway until she is 0.005 of a mile past her goal of 0.85 of a mile. She claims she cleaned nine tenths of a mile. Is she correct? Explain.

B. Use your table to compare your sentences in Problem 1.3A to those you wrote in Problem 1.2A. How does the fraction method help explain why you can line up the decimals and add digits with the same place values to find the answer?

C. Fraction benchmarks are a useful way to estimate in decimal situations. For parts (1)–(6), write a number sentence using fraction benchmarks to estimate the sum or difference.

1. $1.199 + 2.02$ **2.** $1.762 + 6.9$ **3.** $0.243 + 0.7$

4. $3.724 - 0.49$ **5.** $6.899 - 2.9$ **6.** $7.5097 - 1.008$

ACE Homework starts on page 13.

1.4 Decimal Sum and Difference Algorithms

You have looked at how place value and fraction addition and subtraction can help you make sense of adding and subtracting decimals. You can use those ideas to describe an algorithm for adding and subtracting decimals.

Problem 1.4 Decimal Sum and Difference Algorithms

A. Use your experiences adding and subtracting decimals in money and measurement situations. Describe an algorithm for adding and subtracting decimal numbers.

B. In *Bits and Pieces II*, you learned about fact families. Here is an addition-subtraction fact family that uses fractions:

$$\frac{1}{2} + \frac{1}{3} = \frac{5}{6} \qquad \frac{1}{3} + \frac{1}{2} = \frac{5}{6} \qquad \frac{5}{6} - \frac{1}{2} = \frac{1}{3} \qquad \frac{5}{6} - \frac{1}{3} = \frac{1}{2}$$

    1. Write the complete addition-subtraction fact family for
       $0.02 + 0.103 = 0.123$.

    2. Write the complete addition-subtraction fact family for
       $1.82 - 0.103 = 1.717$.

C. Find the value of N that makes the mathematical sentence correct. Fact families might help.

    1. $63.2 + 21.075 = N$ **2.** $44.32 - 4.02 = N$

    3. $N + 2.3 = 6.55$ **4.** $N - 6.88 = 7.21$

D. 1. Explain how you can solve the problem $4.27 - 2\frac{1}{8}$ by changing $2\frac{1}{8}$ to a decimal.

    2. Explain how you can solve the problem $4.27 - 2\frac{1}{8}$ by changing 4.27 to a fraction.

ACE **Homework starts on page 13.**

Applications

For Exercises 1–6, tell whether the number is closest to 0, $\frac{1}{2}$, or 1.
Explain your reasoning.

1. 0.07

2. 1.150

3. 0.391

4. 0.0999

5. 0.99

6. 0.599

7. Billie goes to the fabric store to buy material and other items she
needs for a project. She has $16.95 to spend. The material costs $8.69.
A container of craft glue costs $1.95. A package of craft paper is $4.29.

a. Estimate how much it will cost to buy the material, glue, and craft
paper.

b. Did you overestimate or underestimate? Explain.

c. Billie also finds a package of ribbon that costs $2.89. Based on your
estimate in part (a), how much more money does she need if she
buys the ribbon? Explain.

Add or subtract.

8. 3.42 + 5.8

9. 5.012 + 0.93

10. 10.437 + 4.0034

11. 0.403 + 0.07

12. 5.2 − 0.12

13. 4.54 − 2.9

14. 0.095 − 0.0071

15. 2.057 − 1.99

16. 10.91 − 1.068

For: Multiple-Choice Skills
Practice
Web Code: ama-6154

17. Ms. Palkowski cleans 0.125 of a mile of highway for a group of teachers
and then 0.4 of a mile for the science club. How much does she clean
altogether?

18. Multiple Choice Which is correct?

A.
$$\begin{array}{r} 81.9 \\ + \ 0.62 \\ \hline 88.1 \end{array}$$

B.
$$\begin{array}{r} 81.9 \\ + \ 0.62 \\ \hline 82.52 \end{array}$$

C.
$$\begin{array}{r} 81.9 \\ + \ 0.62 \\ \hline 8.81 \end{array}$$

D.
$$\begin{array}{r} 81.9 \\ + \ 0.62 \\ \hline 0.881 \end{array}$$

19. Estimate using fraction benchmarks.

   a. 2.43 + 1.892   **b.** 4.694 − 1.23   **c.** 12.92 + 3.506 − 6.18

20. Gregory walks 1.8 miles from his home to school. Halfway between his home and school there is a music store. This morning, he wants to stop at the store before school. Right now he is 0.36 miles away from home.

   a. How much more does he need to walk, in miles, to get to the store?

   b. How many miles does he have left to walk to school?

21. Christopher, Tim, Lee, and Dwayne are running in a 4 × 100-meter relay race. Christopher runs his stretch in 12.35 seconds, Tim takes 13.12 seconds, and Lee takes 11.91. If the team wants to break the school record of 48.92 seconds, how fast will Dwayne have to run?

22. Karen, Lou, and Jeff each bought a miniature tree. They measured the height of their trees once a month over the five months from December to April.

Miniature Tree Height (m)					
	December	**January**	**February**	**March**	**April**
Karen's Tree	0.794	0.932	1.043	1.356	1.602
Lou's Tree	0.510	0.678	0.84	1.34	1.551
Jeff's Tree	0.788	0.903	1.22	1.452	1.61

   a. Who had the tallest tree at the beginning?

   b. Whose tree was the tallest at the end of April?

   c. Whose tree grew fastest during the first month?

   d. Whose tree grew by the most from December to April?

Add or subtract.

23. $\frac{4}{5} + \frac{3}{4}$ **24.** $2\frac{3}{5} + \frac{3}{8}$ **25.** $1\frac{2}{3} + 3\frac{5}{6}$

26. $\frac{8}{3} - \frac{4}{5}$ **27.** $1\frac{4}{5} - \frac{1}{2}$ **28.** $4\frac{2}{8} - 1\frac{3}{4}$

29. Rewrite Exercises 23–28 with decimal numbers and find the results of the operations using the decimal equivalents of the numbers. Compare your decimal answers to the fraction answers.

30. Solve. Then write the complete addition-subtraction fact family.

 a. $22.3 + 31.65 = N$ **b.** $18.7 - 4.24 = N$

31. Add.

 a. $4.9 + 3\frac{3}{4}$ **b.** $91.678 + 2.34 + 12.001$ **c.** $2.75 + 3\frac{2}{5}$

32. Find the value of N that makes the mathematical sentence correct. Use fact families to help you.

 a. $2.3 + N = 3.42$ **b.** $N - 11.6 = 3.75$

33. Find the missing numbers.

 a.

$$
\begin{array}{r}
36.03 \\
+ \quad\rule{1cm}{0.3cm} \\
\hline
45.218
\end{array}
$$

 b.

$$
\begin{array}{r}
\rule{1cm}{0.3cm} \\
+ \quad 0.488 \\
\hline
13.762
\end{array}
$$

 c. $0.45 + N + 0.4 = 2.62$ **d.** $75.4 - 10.801 + N = 77.781$

34. Place decimal points in 102 and 19 so that the sum of the two numbers is 1.21.

35. Place decimal points in 34, 4, and 417 so that the sum of the three numbers is 7.97.

36. Place decimal points in 431 and 205 so that the difference between the two numbers is 16.19.

Connections

37. Which of the numbers is the greatest? How do you know?

    81.9   81.90   81.900

Homework Help Online
PHSchool.com

For: Help with Exercise 37
Web Code: ame-6137

38. Multiple Choice Which group of decimals is ordered from least to greatest?

    A. 5.6, 5.9, 5.09, 5.96, 5.139

    B. 0.112, 1.012, 1.3, 1.0099, 10.12

    C. 2.8, 2.109, 2.72, 2.1, 2.719

    D. 0.132, 0.23, 0.383, 0.3905, 0.392

39. Find the missing lengths. Then find the perimeter of the figure. (All units are in inches.)

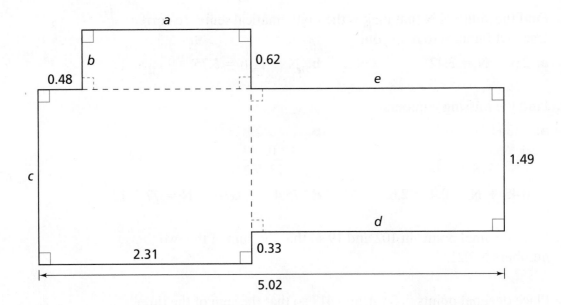

For Exercises 40–43, name the geometric figures and find their perimeters. (All units are in inches. The figures are not drawn to scale.)

40.

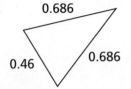

41.

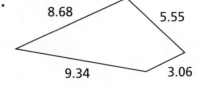

42.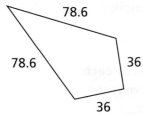

78.6

78.6   36

36

43.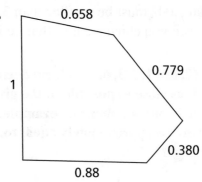

0.658

0.779

1

0.380

0.88

44. The perimeter of a parallelogram is 15.42 cm. The length of one of its sides is 2.93 cm. What are the lengths of its other sides?

Find the measures of the missing angles.

45.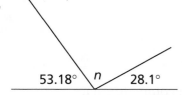

53.18°   *n*   28.1°

46.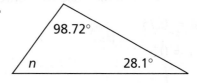

98.72°

n   28.1°

Extensions

47. a. In order to add 3 dollars and 35 cents to 5 dollars and 78 cents, you can write each amount as a decimal. Since 3.35 + 5.78 = 9.13, the total is 9 dollars and 13 cents.

Now consider adding time values in a similar way. For example, can you add 2 hours and 45 minutes to 3 hours and 57 minutes by using decimal numbers (2.45 + 3.57)? Explain.

b. Consider length measurements. You can add 13 meters and 47 centimeters to 4 meters and 72 centimeters using decimal numbers. Since 13.47 + 4.72 = 18.19, the total length is 18 meters and 19 centimeters.

Suppose you want to add 3 feet and 7 inches to 5 feet 6 inches. Can you apply the same idea so that you add 3.7 to 5.6 to get the total length? Explain.

48. Mark says that 3.002 must be smaller than 3.0019 since 2 is smaller than 19. How can you convince him that he is wrong?

For Exercises 49–52, use 1, 2, 3, or 4 to form decimal numbers so that each sum or difference is as close as possible to the given number. You may use the same digit twice in one number. For example, you may write 0.33. The symbol ≈ means "is approximately equal to."

49. $0.\blacksquare\blacksquare + 0.\blacksquare\blacksquare \approx \frac{1}{3}$

50. $0.\blacksquare\blacksquare - 0.\blacksquare\blacksquare \approx 0.125$

51. $0.\blacksquare\blacksquare - 0.\blacksquare\blacksquare \approx \frac{2}{7}$

52. $0.\blacksquare\blacksquare + 0.\blacksquare\blacksquare \approx 0.9$

For Exercises 53 and 54, use 1, 2, 3, or 4 to form decimal numbers so that each calculation is correct. You may use the same digit twice in one number.

53. $0.\blacksquare\blacksquare + 0.\blacksquare\blacksquare = 0.75$

54. $0.\blacksquare\blacksquare - 0.\blacksquare\blacksquare = 0.3$

55. Use the numbers 2, 9, 7, and 4 only once in each part to complete each decimal.

   a. Write the greatest possible number of the form $3.\blacksquare\blacksquare\blacksquare\blacksquare$.

   b. Write the least possible number of the form $3.\blacksquare\blacksquare\blacksquare\blacksquare$.

   c. Write all the possible numbers of the form $3.\blacksquare\blacksquare\blacksquare\blacksquare$ that are greater than 3.795.

   d. Write all the possible numbers of the form $3.\blacksquare\blacksquare\blacksquare\blacksquare$ that are less than 3.73 but greater than 3.4399.

56. Use the fact that there are 16 ounces in a pound to answer parts (a)–(d).

   a. How many pounds are in 256 ounces?

   b. How many ounces are in 0.125 pound?

   c. How many ounces are in 3.375 pounds?

   d. How many pounds are in 17 ounces? Express this as a mixed number and as a decimal.

57. Julie has a bread recipe that calls for 1.75 pounds of flour.

    a. She wants to make this recipe three times. How much flour does she need?

    b. She has no flour at home. How many 5-pound bags of flour should she buy to make the recipe three times?

    c. A ton is 2,000 pounds. Estimate how many loaves of bread she could make with a ton of flour.

58. Will likes to keep track of his friends on road clean-up day. He thinks of himself as being at 0 on the number line below. Friends who are on the road ahead of him he pictures to the right on a number line. Friends who are on the road behind him he pictures to the left.

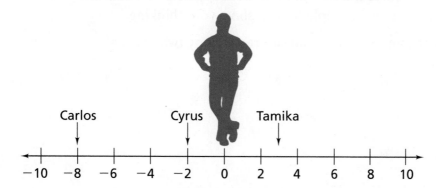

Sample   Tamika is 3 km ahead, at +3. Cyrus is 2 km behind, at −2. We read "+3" as "positive three" and "−2" as "negative 2."

    a. Justin is 3 km behind Will. Mark his position on a copy of the number line above.

    b. Carlos is at the location shown on the number line. Is Carlos ahead of or behind Will? By how many kilometers?

    c. Write three more numbers that show locations behind Will.

    d. Write three numbers that show locations ahead of Will.

Mathematical Reflections 1

In this investigation you looked at situations involving measurement data and money written as decimals. You found strategies for estimating addition or subtraction involving decimals. You used your understanding of fractions and place value to develop algorithms for adding and subtracting decimals. The following questions will help you summarize what you have learned.

Think about your answers to these questions. Discuss your ideas with other students and your teacher. Then write a summary of your findings in your notebook.

1. Describe one strategy that you found helpful in estimating sums or differences of decimals. Explain why it was helpful to you.

2. How does interpreting decimals as fractions help you make sense of adding and subtracting decimals? Use an example to help show your thinking.

3. How does the place value interpretation of decimals help you add and subtract decimals? Use an example to help show your thinking.

4. Describe an algorithm for adding and subtracting any two decimal numbers.

Investigation

Decimal Times

Here are two everyday situations in which you could multiply decimals.

- How many square feet of carpet do you need to carpet an 11.5 by 12.5 foot room?

- One soccer ball costs $16.79. You buy four soccer balls. How can you find the total cost?

In this investigation you will develop strategies for multiplying decimal numbers. Estimating can help you decide whether a product is reasonable. Changing the form of a number from a fraction to a decimal, or a decimal to a fraction, can help you estimate or find an exact answer.

2.1 Relating Fraction and Decimal Multiplication

You know you can write decimals as fractions. You can also write fractions as decimals. For example, to write $\frac{2}{5}$ as a decimal, first rewrite it as the equivalent fraction $\frac{4}{10}$. Then write $\frac{4}{10}$ as the decimal 0.4.

The grid on the left below is a tenths grid with one strip shaded. This strip represents $\frac{1}{10}$, or 0.1. On the right, the strip representing 0.1 is divided into 10 squares. The single square with darker shading is $\frac{1}{10}$ *of* $\frac{1}{10}$, or 0.1 × 0.1.

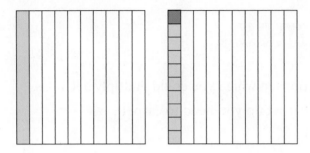

You can extend the horizontal lines to make a hundredths grid. This shows that $\frac{1}{10}$ *of* $\frac{1}{10}$ is one square out of one hundred squares, which is $\frac{1}{100}$, or 0.01 of the whole.

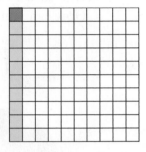

This makes sense because decimals are just fractions written in a different notation. You know that $0.63 = \frac{63}{100}$ and that $0.0063 = \frac{63}{10,000}$. Fraction multiplication can help you with decimal multiplication.

Getting Ready for Problem 2.1

To find the product of 0.3 × 2.3, you can use equivalent fractions.

$$0.3 = \frac{3}{10} \text{ and } 2.3 = 2\frac{3}{10} \text{ or } \frac{23}{10}, \text{ so } 0.3 \times 2.3 = \frac{3}{10} \times \frac{23}{10}$$

- What is the product written as a fraction?
- What is the product written as a decimal?
- How can knowing the product as a fraction help you write the product in decimal form?

Problem 2.1 Relating Fraction and Decimal Multiplication

A. On the next page are some multiplication situations that happen at the Apple-A-Day fruit stand. For each situation, do the following:

- Estimate the product.
- Write the decimals in fraction notation with denominators of 10, 100, 1000, etc.
- Find the exact answer and compare it to your estimate.

1. Ajay buys 1.7 pounds of Red Delicious apples on sale for $0.50 a pound. What is his bill?

   2. Kelly buys 0.4 of a pound of Granny Smith apples on sale for $0.55 a pound. What is her bill?

   3. Chayton buys Northern Spy apples for his mother's pie. He buys 3.2 pounds at $1.10 a pound. What is his bill?

   4. The Apple-A-Day roadside fruit stand sells bunches of wildflowers. The seller wraps each bunch in a sheet of paper with dimensions of 1.5 feet by 1.5 feet. What is the area of the paper?

B. Why does it make sense to use multiplication to solve the situations in Question A?

C. 1. When one factor in a multiplication problem is greater than 1, is the product greater or less than the other factor? Explain.

   2. When one factor is less than 1, is the product greater or less than the other factor?

ACE Homework starts on page 28.

2.2 Missing Factors

Suppose you put decimal points into 125×5 to make the problem 1.25×0.5.

- How is the product of 125×5 related to the product of 1.25×0.5?
- Does writing the problem as $\frac{125}{100} \times \frac{5}{10}$ help?

Problem 2.2 Missing Factors

A. Use what you know about fraction multiplication and place value.

    1. What number times 6 gives the product 0.36?

    2. What number times 0.9 gives the product 2.7?

    3. What number times 1.5 gives the product 0.045?

    4. What strategies did you use to solve these problems?

B. Use what you know about decimal multiplication and place value.

    1. Find two numbers with a product of 1,344.

    2. Find two numbers with a product of 134.4.

    3. Find two numbers with a product of 0.1344.

    4. What strategies did you use to solve these problems?

C. 1. What number times 0.3 gives the product 9?

    2. What number times 0.12 gives the product 24?

    3. What strategies did you use to solve these problems?

ACE Homework starts on page 28.

2.3 Finding Decimal Products

Sometimes you don't need to know an actual product. Estimation can help you find an amount that is reasonable.

Sometimes an estimate can help you decide if a computation is correct.

Sometimes an estimate can help you decide where to place the decimal point in an actual product.

Look at two different estimation strategies for the problem 2.1×1.4.

Jose rounded to whole numbers and fractions: $2 \times 1\frac{1}{2} = 3$

Rosa only rounded one number: $2 \times 1.4 = 2.8$

- Are both estimates reasonable? Which estimate is closer to the actual answer?

Problem 2.3 Finding Decimal Products

A. Estimate each product. Describe how you found your estimate.

1. 0.9×3.4 **2.** 4.92×0.5

3. 0.22×0.301 **4.** 23.87×6.954

B. Julia says that sometimes she uses estimation to decide where to place the decimal in an actual product.

With the problem 0.9×1.305, a reasonable estimate is $1 \times 1.3 = 1.3$. Even 1×1 is a good estimate. I think that the actual product is a little more than 1. When I multiply $9 \times 1,305$ I get 11,745, so I know the actual product is 1.1745.

1. How did Julia use her estimate to find the actual product of 1.1745?

2. Use Julia's estimation strategy to find the product N.

a. $31.2 \times 2.1 = N$

b. If $6,946 \times 28 = 194,488$, then $694.6 \times 2.8 = N$.

ACE **Homework starts on page 28.**

2.4 Factor–Product Relationships

Understanding our place value system depends on knowing about **powers of ten.** The numbers 10; 100; 1,000; 10,000; and so on are powers of ten. You can write these numbers as $10, 10 \times 10, 10 \times 10 \times 10$, and so on OR as $10, 10^2, 10^3 \ldots$.

Our place value system is centered around the units place (ones). A number that is one place to the left of the units place has a value ten times larger. For example, in the number 77, the 7 on the right represents 7 and the 7 on the left represents 7×10, or 70.

As we move to the right we divide by powers of ten.

7 ones

$7 \div 10 \div 10$, OR $7 \div 100$, OR $\frac{7}{100}$

7.77

$7 \div 10$, OR $\frac{7}{10}$

Problem 2.4 Factor–Product Relationships

Estimate before you find an exact answer to the questions below.

A. Record the products in each set in an organized way. Describe any patterns that you see.

Set A	Set B	Set C
21 × 100	2.1 × 100	0.21 × 100
21 × 10	2.1 × 10	0.21 × 10
21 × 1	2.1 × 1	0.21 × 1
21 × 0.1	2.1 × 0.1	0.21 × 0.1
21 × 0.01	2.1 × 0.01	0.21 × 0.01
21 × 0.001	2.1 × 0.001	0.21 × 0.001

B. In a decimal multiplication problem, there is a relationship between the number of decimal places in the factors and the number of decimal places in the product.

   1. Use your answers to Question A to summarize what you think the decimal place relationship is.

   2. Test the relationship on these two problems:

   a. 4.5×0.9 **b.** 0.004×0.12

   3. a. Write the two problems in part (2) as fractions. Find the product using fraction multiplication.

   b. How does fraction multiplication support the relationship you tested in part (2)?

C. Describe an algorithm you can use to multiply any two decimal numbers.

D. 1. Find the following products using the fact that $21 \times 11 = 231$.

   a. 2.1×11 **b.** 2.1×1.1

   c. 2.1×0.11 **d.** 2.1×0.011

   e. 0.21×11 **f.** 0.021×1.1

   g. 0.021×0.11 **h.** 0.21×0.011

   2. Test the algorithm you wrote in Question C on the problems.

ACE   **Homework starts on page 28.**

Applications

Estimate each product.

1. 2.95 × 14.7   **2.** 0.491 × 120.2   **3.** 12.45 × 0.93

4. 0.52 × 18.3   **5.** 1.262 × 7.94   **6.** 0.82 × 0.302

For Exercises 7–12, estimate each product. Then find the exact product using fraction multiplication.

7. 0.6 × 0.8   **8.** 2.1 × 1.45   **9.** 3.822 × 5.2

10. 0.9 × 1.305   **11.** 5.13 × 2.9   **12.** 4.17 × 6.72

13. Sweety's Ice Cream Shop sells ice cream by weight. They charge $2.95 per pound. Suppose your dish of ice cream weighs 0.42 pounds. How much will your ice cream cost?

14. Aaron plans to buy new flooring for his rectangular office. His office is 7.9 meters by 6.2 meters.

     a. How many square meters of floor space does his office have?

     b. Suppose flooring costs $5.90 per square meter. How much will the new flooring cost for Aaron's office?

15. Multiple Choice Which of the products is greater than 1?

     A. 2.4 × 0.75   **B.** 0.66 × 0.7   **C.** 9.8 × 0.001   **D.** 0.004 × 0.8

16. What number times 9 gives each product?

     a. 45   **b.** 4.5   **c.** 0.45

Find the value of N.

17. 3.2 × N = 0.96   **18.** 0.7 × N = 0.042   **19.** N × 3.21 = 9.63

20. Multiple Choice Which of the products is the greatest?

     F. 0.6 × 0.4   **G.** 0.06 × 0.04

     H. 0.06 × 0.4   **J.** 0.6 × 0.04

21. Tom plants corn in 0.4 of his vegetable garden. Of the corn section, 0.75 is early sweet corn and the rest is later-maturing sweet corn.

   a. What part of his garden does Tom plant in early corn? What part does he plant in late corn?

   b. Tom's garden covers 8 acres. How many acres of early corn does he have? How many acres of late corn does he have?

22. Ali sometimes finds it easier to estimate products by using the fractional equivalent of decimal numbers. What do you think he said for the missing numbers below?

"In estimating 0.52×18.3, 0.52 is about 0.5, which as a fraction is the same as ▦. And, I can round 18.3 to 18. So, ▦ of ▦ is ▦."

"For 1.262×7.94, I can round the numbers to 1.25×8. Then, 1.25 as a fraction is the same as ▦. Since ▦ of 8 is 8, and ▦ of 8 is 2, the estimate is $8 + 2$, or 10."

23. Ali's classmate, Ahmed, estimates for 0.82×0.302 as follows:

"0.82×0.302 is very close to 0.8×0.3. But, the result of 0.8×0.3 is related to 8×3, which is 24. Since each of 0.8 and 0.3 has only one decimal place, so will their product. The result of 0.8×0.3 should be about 2.4."

Ali immediately said:

"This can't be true. Since both 0.82 and 0.302 are less than 1, their product must also be less than 1. It can't be 2.4!"

Who is right? Where did the other person make his mistake?

24. Suppose you estimate the product 0.153×3.4.

   a. Is the result greater than 0.153 or less than 0.153? Why?

   b. Is the result greater than 3.4 or less than 3.4? Why?

25. Suppose you estimate the product 57.132×0.682.

    a. Is the result greater than 57.132 or less than 57.132? Why?

    b. Is the result greater than 0.682 or less than 0.682? Why?

26. Suppose you estimate the product 0.372×0.134.

    a. Is the result greater than 0.372 or less than 0.372? Why?

    b. Is the result greater than 0.134 or less than 0.134? Why?

27. Use the number sentence $78 \times 12 = 936$ to find each product.

    a. 7.8×1.2 **b.** 7.8×0.12

    c. 7.8×0.012 **d.** 0.78×1.2

    e. 0.078×1.2 **f.** 0.0078×1.2

28. Use the number sentence $145 \times 326 = 47{,}270$ to help you solve the following problems.

    a. $1.45 \times 32.6 = \blacksquare$ **b.** $0.326 \times 1{,}450 = \blacksquare$

    c. $\blacksquare \times 32.6 = 472.7$ **d.** $0.0145 \times \blacksquare = 47.27$

29. Use the number sentence $35 \times 123 = 4{,}305$ to help you solve the following problems.

    a. $3.5 \times 123 = \blacksquare$ **b.** $0.35 \times 123 = \blacksquare$

    c. $1.23 \times 0.35 = \blacksquare$ **d.** $3.5 \times \blacksquare = 43.05$

    e. $\blacksquare \times 12.3 = 4.305$ **f.** $3.5 \times 1.23 = \blacksquare$

30. Explain how the number of decimal places in the factors of a decimal multiplication problem relates to the number of decimal places in the product.

31. Explain how you can find the product of 2.7×4.63 if your calculator screen is damaged and does not display numbers with decimals in them.

32. Find each product.

    a. 1.32×10 **b.** 1.32×100

    c. $1.32 \times 1{,}000$ **d.** $1.32 \times 10{,}000$

    e. 12.45×10 **f.** 12.45×100

    g. $12.45 \times 1{,}000$ **h.** $12.45 \times 10{,}000$

Go Online
PHSchool.com

For: Multiple-Choice Skills
    Practice
Web Code: ame-6254

33. Ten-year-old Chi learned a lot of math from his older brother, Shing. One day, Shing tells him that when you multiply a number by 10, "you just add a zero."

a. With Shing's idea in his mind, Chi says, "To find 10×20, I just add a zero. So, $20 + 0 = 20$." How would you correct him?

b. After Chi realizes that "adding zero" actually means "putting an extra zero at the end," he says,

"10×0.02 equals 0.020 by putting the extra zero at the end."

Is he right this time? How would you rephrase "putting an extra zero at the end" in case the other number is a decimal number? Explain why your suggestion works.

c. How can you find the result of multiplying by 100; 1,000; or 10,000 using a similar strategy?

Connections

Multiply.

34. $\frac{7}{3} \times \frac{4}{9}$

35. $\frac{2}{5} \times 15$

36. $3 \times \frac{4}{9}$

37. $2\frac{2}{3} \times \frac{1}{2}$

38. $4 \times 2\frac{2}{3}$

39. $1\frac{1}{2} \times 2.3$

40. Midge wants to buy a carpet for her new room. She finds three carpets that she likes, but they are different sizes and have different prices. She writes down the information about their sizes and prices so that she can decide at home.

Carpet Comparison

Carpet	Length (m)	Width (m)	Price (per m²)
A	5.09	4.32	$15.89
B	5.86	3.85	$13.85
C	5.95	3.75	$14.59

a. Which carpet is the longest?

b. Which carpet has the greatest area?

c. What is the total cost of each carpet? Which carpet costs the most? Which carpet costs the least?

Find the area of each shape.

41.

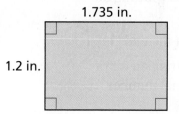

1.735 in.

1.2 in.

42.

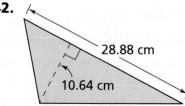

28.88 cm

10.64 cm

Homework Help Online
PHSchool.com
For: Help with Exercises 41–44
Web Code: ame-6241

43.

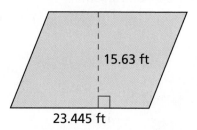

15.63 ft

23.445 ft

44.

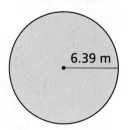

6.39 m

45. Find a length and a width for a rectangle with each given area.

a. 56 ft²　　　　**b.** 5.6 ft²　　　　**c.** 0.56 ft²

Extensions

Find the products.

46. $1.2 \times \frac{31}{40}$　　　**47.** $0.45 \times 1.7 \times 0.34$　　　**48.** $0.14 \times 74.3 \times 2.125$

49. a. Write a fraction equivalent to $\frac{3.7}{23}$ without decimals.

b. Write a fraction equivalent to $\frac{1.6}{4}$ without decimals.

c. Use your equivalent fractions from parts (a) and (b) to find the product of $\frac{3.7}{23} \times \frac{1.6}{4}$.

50. Fill in the blanks and put a decimal point where needed to make the calculation complete.

$$
\begin{array}{r}
152\blacksquare \\
\times \quad \blacksquare.9 \\
\hline
1371\blacksquare \\
+ \quad 3\blacksquare48 \\
\hline
4\blacksquare.196
\end{array}
$$

51. Tanisha and Belinda found estimates for the product of 5.2×100.4 in two different ways:

Tanisha said: "I round 5.2 to 5. I multiply 5×100.4 because I know that 5×0.4 is 2. So, my estimation is $500 + 2$, or 502."

Belinda said: "I prefer to round 100.4 to 100 and find 5.2×100 instead. Moving the decimal point two places to the right, I find the estimation as 520."

Without finding the exact result of 5.2×100.4, can you tell whose estimation is closer to the exact answer?

52. Explain why you do not have to align the decimal points when multiplying two decimal numbers.

53. a. Find the area of the square.   **b.** Find the area of each piece within the larger square.

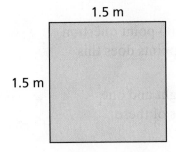

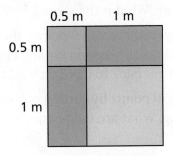

c. Explain how the values you obtained in part (b) are related to your answer to part (a).

54. This morning, Janet was feeling very sleepy toward the end of class when her teacher multiplied two decimal numbers and got 24.9344. Later, when Janet looked at her notebook, she realized that she forgot to put the decimal points of the two numbers in her notebook. Here is what she had written:

a. Where do you think the decimal points should be in the factors?

b. Is there more than one possibility? Explain.

55. On some television game shows, players can lose points for wrong answers. For example, if a player starts with 0 points and gets a 100-point question wrong, he or she has −100 (read as "negative one hundred") points.

a. Suppose a player starts with 0 points and gets three 50-point questions wrong. What is the score?

b. Suppose a player starts with 50 points and gets three 100-point questions wrong. What is the score?

c. Suppose a player starts with 0 points, then gets a 100-point question right and a 200-point question wrong. How many points does this player need to get back to 0 points?

d. A player has 150 points by getting one question right and one question wrong. What are the possible point values of these questions?

Mathematical Reflections 2

In this investigation, you solved problems that involved multiplication of decimals. You looked at the fractional notation of decimals as a way to help you develop strategies for multiplying decimals. You also found patterns in decimal multiplication problems that help you predict the number of decimal places in the answer. The following questions will help you summarize what you have learned.

Think about your answers to these questions. Discuss your ideas with other students and your teacher. Then write a summary of your findings in your notebook.

1. Describe an algorithm for multiplying any two decimal numbers. Use an example to show why your algorithm works.

2. Describe two strategies that you can use to estimate decimal products. Use number sentences to show how your strategies work.

Investigation 3

The Decimal Divide

In this investigation, you will use what you learned about fraction division in *Bits and Pieces II* to make sense of decimal division. You will estimate a solution to a division problem and you will learn to divide decimals.

3.1 Deciphering Decimal Situations

Use what you know about decimal, fraction, and whole number operations to find solutions for each problem.

Problem 3.1 Deciphering Decimal Situations

A. In a grocery store, all of the scales measure in decimals. Explain or draw diagrams to show your reasoning for the following situations.

   1. Ricardo buys 3.2 ounces of a sliced Italian ham called prosciutto (pruh SHOO toh) to make sandwiches. Each sandwich uses one 0.4-ounce slice of prosciutto. How many sandwiches can he make?

   2. Ms. Difanis buys 11.6 pounds of hamburger for a cookout. How many quarter-pound (0.25) burgers can she make?

   3. Write a number sentence that shows the operations you would use to find your solutions in parts (1) and (2).

   4. The answer to part (2) is not a whole number. What does the answer mean?

B. Examine each situation. Decide what operation to use and then estimate the size of the answer.

   1. Ashley eats five 5.25-ounce slices of watermelon in a contest at the picnic. How many ounces of watermelon does she eat?

   2. Stacey needs $39.99 for a pair of sneakers. She has $22.53 in her savings and a $15 check from babysitting. Can she buy the shoes?

   3. Li Ming's allowance for transportation is $12.45. How many times can she ride the bus if it costs $0.75 a trip?

ACE Homework starts on page 43.

3.2 The Great Equalizer: Common Denominators

Each number in a division problem has a name to help us communicate. The number you are dividing by is the **divisor.** The number into which you are dividing is the **dividend.** The answer is the **quotient.**

$$18 \div 3 = 6$$
$$\text{dividend} \div \text{divisor} = \text{quotient}$$

Remember that there are three ways to write a division problem:

Number Sentence: $22 \div 88$ Fraction: $\frac{22}{88}$ Long Division: $88\overline{)22}$

You know that decimals can be thought of as fractions. You can use what you already know about dividing fractions to help you figure out a way to divide decimals.

Getting Ready for Problem 3.2

- What does the division $3.25 \div 0.5$ mean?
- What is a reasonable estimate for $3.25 \div 0.5$?

To find the answer to $3.25 \div 0.5$, think of the decimals as fractions.

$$3.25 \div 0.5 = \frac{325}{100} \div \frac{5}{10}$$
$$= \frac{325}{100} \div \frac{50}{100}$$

This is the same as 325 hundredths $\div$ 50 hundredths $= 6\frac{1}{2}$, or 6.5.

- Why does the quotient to $\frac{325}{100} \div \frac{50}{100}$ equal $325 \div 50$?
- What does the answer to the division mean?

Problem 3.2 Using Common Denominators to Divide Decimals

A. Estimate each quotient. Write each dividend and divisor in fraction form with common denominators. Use fraction division.

    1. 4.2 ÷ 2.1   **2.** 16.1 ÷ 2.3   **3.** 0.44 ÷ 0.08

B. 1. Rewrite the problems in each set below as fraction division problems with common denominators.

Set 1	Set 2	Set 3
46.4 ÷ 5.8	28.8 ÷ 1.8	175 ÷ 12.5
4.64 ÷ 0.58	2.88 ÷ 18	1.75 ÷ 0.125

    2. Write the whole number division problem that corresponds to each problem you wrote in part (1).

    3. Without solving, decide if the problems within each set lead to the same quotient. Explain.

    4. Solve the problems and check your predictions.

C. Luis thinks that he can use long division with decimals just as he does with whole numbers. He writes 78.5 ÷ 9.1 as $9.1\overline{)78.5}$, but he does not know what to do with the decimals.

    1. Use fractions to represent Luis' dividend and divisor.

    2. Replace the division problem with an easier division problem that has the same answer. Check that the answer is the same.

D. Describe how to rewrite a decimal division problem so that the division is easier and the answer is the same. Check your ideas by solving these division problems.

    1. $15\overline{)375}$

    2. 3.75 ÷ 0.15

    3. 37.5 ÷ 0.015

ACE Homework starts on page 43.

3.3 Exploring Dividing Decimals

You have explored several different situations involving decimal division. You will use your ideas to describe a way to do decimal division.

Problem 3.3 Exploring Dividing Decimals

A. 1. Solve each division problem.

    a. $5.5\overline{)27.5}$ **b.** $550\overline{)2{,}750}$ **c.** $0.055\overline{)0.275}$

    d. Write another division problem that belongs to this set.

2. Do these problems all have the same solution? Why or why not?

    a. $55\overline{)27.5}$ **b.** $5.5\overline{)2{,}750}$ **c.** $0.55\overline{)0.275}$

B. Write a word problem for $1.75 \div 0.5$. Explain what the dividend, divisor, and quotient mean in your problem.

C. 1. Write the complete multiplication-division fact family for $0.84 \div 0.06 = 14$.

2. Find the value of N. Writing a fact family may help.

    a. $N \div 0.8 = 3.5$ **b.** $2.75 \div N = 5.5$

D. Five science lab teams measure the height of a plant at the end of week 1 and week 2. See their measurements below.

Week	Team 1	Team 2	Team 3	Team 4	Team 5
1	3.4 cm	3.25 cm	3.3 cm	3.5 cm	3.35 cm
2	7.95 cm	7.8 cm	8 cm	8.15 cm	8.2 cm

1. All the teams measured the same plant. Why are the measurements different?

2. Find the mean (average) of the teams' measurements for each week.

3. Using each week's mean, how much did the plant grow from the first week to the second week?

ACE Homework starts on page 43.

In *Bits and Pieces I,* you learned that you can express any fraction with a whole number numerator and a whole number denominator as a decimal by dividing the numerator by the denominator.

$\frac{1}{2} = 0.5$ $\frac{1}{4} = 0.25$

$\frac{1}{3} = 0.333333\ldots$ $\frac{1}{11} = 0.090909\ldots$

This is a repeating decimal.

The fractions $\frac{1}{2}$ and $\frac{1}{4}$ have decimal representations that end or terminate. Decimals like these are called **terminating decimals.** Notice that $\frac{1}{3}$ and $\frac{1}{11}$ have decimal representations that repeat over and over. Decimals like these are called **repeating decimals.**

You know that decimals are easy to write as fractions with 10, 100, 1000, etc. in the denominator.

$$0.23 = \frac{23}{100} \qquad\qquad 0.7 = \frac{7}{10} \qquad\qquad 0.070 = \frac{70}{1000}$$

You can see that fractions with 10, 100, 1000, etc. in their denominators have terminating decimal forms.

- Why do fractions like $\frac{1}{2}$ and $\frac{1}{4}$ also have terminating decimal forms?
- Are there fractions equivalent to $\frac{1}{2}$ and $\frac{1}{4}$ that have 10, 100, 1000, etc. as their denominators?

A. Write each fraction as a decimal. Tell whether the decimal is terminating or repeating. If it is repeating, tell which digits repeat.

1. $\frac{2}{5}$ **2.** $\frac{3}{8}$ **3.** $\frac{5}{6}$ **4.** $\frac{35}{10}$ **5.** $\frac{8}{99}$

6. For the fractions in parts (1)–(5) that have terminating decimal forms, try to find an equivalent fraction that has 10, 100, 1000, etc. as the denominator.

B. 1. Find two other fractions that have a terminating decimal form.

2. For each fraction you found in part (1), write three fractions that are equivalent.

3. Find the decimal form for the fractions you found in part (2).

4. What do you notice about the decimal form for a set of equivalent fractions?

C. Find a fraction that is equivalent to each of the following terminating decimals.

1. 0.35   **2.** 2.1456   **3.** 89.050   **4.** 2.14560

5. Explain how your answers in part (2) and part (4) compare.

D. 1. Find three fractions that have repeating decimal forms.

2. Can you find an equivalent form for any of these fractions that has 10, 100, 1000, etc. in the denominator? Why or why not?

E. Describe any differences in the forms of repeating and terminating decimals that you have found.

ACE **Homework starts on page 43.**

Applications

For Exercises 1–4, decide what operation is needed to answer the question. Explain.

1. Akiko's dog has three puppies. They weigh 2.6 pounds, 2.74 pounds, and 3.1 pounds. How much more does the heaviest puppy weigh than the lightest puppy?

2. Angie is making wreaths to sell at a craft show. She has 6.5 yards of ribbon. Each wreath has a bow made from $1\frac{1}{3}$ yards of ribbon. How many bows can she make?

3. Mrs. Doran has three grandchildren. She takes them to lunch where kids' meals are $2.95 each. How much will the three kids' meals cost?

4. Loren is putting brick along both edges of the 21-meter walkway to his house. Each brick is 0.26 meters long. Loren is placing the bricks end to end. How many bricks does he need?

★ Kids' Menu ★

Chicken Nuggets . . $2.95
P.B. & J. $2.95
Hot Dog $2.95
Mac & Cheese $2.95

5. Draw a diagram to show how to find the solution to 2.6 ÷ 0.4. Explain what the quotient means.

6. Will the quotient in each be greater than or less than 1? Explain.

   a. 19.36 ÷ 3.893
   b. 0.962 ÷ 0.3
   c. 5.3 ÷ 11.07
   d. 0.072 ÷ 0.09

For Exercises 7–12, write the decimals as fractions. Then find each quotient.

7. 4.5 ÷ 0.9
8. 0.6 ÷ 0.12
9. 1.2 ÷ 0.5
10. 0.18 ÷ 0.03
11. 22.5 ÷ 1.5
12. 3.42 ÷ 0.19

13. Find the quotient of 22.4 ÷ 0.5 and describe what the quotient means.

14. Explain how finding the quotient of 401 ÷ 5 can help you find the quotient of 40.1 ÷ 0.5.

Compute each quotient.

15. $12.012 \div 5.6$

16. $45.13 \div 0.125$

17. $1.2 \div 4.8$

18. $1.99 \div 10$

For: Multiple-Choice Skills Practice

Web Code: ama-6354

For Exercises 19 and 20, compute the quotients. Look for patterns in your answers.

19. **a.** $36 \div 12$ **b.** $3.6 \div 12$ **c.** $3.6 \div 1.2$

  d. $3.6 \div 0.12$ **e.** $3.6 \div 120$ **f.** $0.36 \div 0.012$

20. **a.** $124 \div 32$ **b.** $1,240 \div 320$ **c.** $12,400 \div 3,200$

  d. $12,400 \div 3.2$ **e.** $1.24 \div 3.2$ **f.** $1.24 \div 0.32$

21. **a.** Find the quotient of $0.37 \div 10$.

  b. How is the quotient similar to 0.37? How is it different?

  c. Divide the quotient from part (a) by 10. How is the quotient similar to 0.37, and how is it different?

  d. In general, what do you think happens to a decimal number when you divide it by 10?

22. **a.** Write two related problems with the same answer as $48 \div 12$. Explain.

  b. Write two related problems with the same answer as $4.8 \div 0.12$.

Find the value of N, and then write the complete multiplication-division fact family.

23. $0.42 \div N = 0.6$

24. $N \div 0.5 = 6.4$

25. Find the decimal equivalent for each of these fractions:

  a. $\frac{2}{6}$ **b.** $\frac{13}{39}$ **c.** $\frac{5}{15}$

  d. Describe the relationship between the fractions and their decimal equivalents.

26. Find the decimal equivalent for each fraction or mixed number:

  a. $\frac{11}{9}$ **b.** $1\frac{6}{27}$

  c. Describe the relationship between the fraction or mixed number and its decimal equivalents.

27. a. Copy the table below, and write each fraction as a decimal.

Fraction	Decimal
$\frac{1}{9}$	■
$\frac{2}{9}$	■
$\frac{3}{9}$	■
$\frac{4}{9}$	■
$\frac{5}{9}$	■
$\frac{6}{9}$	■
$\frac{7}{9}$	■
$\frac{8}{9}$	■

b. Describe the pattern you see in your table.

c. Use the pattern to write decimal representations for each of these fractions. Use your calculator to check your answers.

   i. $\frac{9}{9}$ **ii.** $\frac{10}{9}$ **iii.** $\frac{15}{9}$

d. What fraction is equivalent to each of these decimals? Note that $1.222\ldots$ can be written as $1 + 0.22\ldots$.

   i. $1.2222\ldots$ **ii.** $2.7777\ldots$

Connections

28. For parts (a)–(d), copy the number line and label the marks.

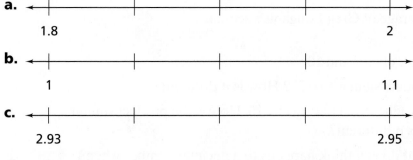

a. 1.8   2

b. 1   1.1

c. 2.93   2.95

d. 1.99   2.01

e. Explain your strategy for parts (a)–(d).

29. Multiple Choice Which quotient is greater than 1?

A. $\frac{1}{4} \div \frac{3}{8}$ **B.** $\frac{19}{5} \div 5$ **C.** $1\frac{2}{3} \div 2\frac{2}{9}$ **D.** $3 \div \frac{19}{7}$

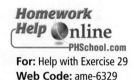
Homework Help Online
PHSchool.com
For: Help with Exercise 29
Web Code: ame-6329

30. For parts (a)–(c), use the table. Give evidence to support your conclusions. You may want to make a table of the differences between each pair of consecutive years.

Men's Springboard Diving		
Year	Winner (country)	Score
1960	Gary Tobian (USA)	170
1964	Kenneth Stizberger (USA)	150.9
1968	Bernie Wrightson (USA)	170.15
1972	Vladimir Vasin (USSR)	594.09
1976	Phil Boggs (USA)	619.52
1980	Aleksandr Portnov (USSR)	905.02
1984	Greg Louganis (USA)	754.41
1988	Greg Louganis (USA)	730.8
1992	Mark Lenzi (USA)	676.53
1996	Ni Xiong (CHINA)	701.46
2000	Ni Xiong (CHINA)	708.72
2004	Bo Peng (CHINA)	787.38

a. Between what consecutive Olympic years did the greatest change in winning score occur?

b. Between what consecutive Olympic years did the next greatest change in winning score occur?

c. Between what consecutive Olympic years did the least change in winning score occur?

d. What is the average of Greg Louganis's scores?

31. a. Find the product of 0.37 and 10.

b. How is the product similar to 0.37? How is it different?

c. Multiply the product from part (a) by 10. How is the product similar to 0.37? How is it different?

d. In general, what do you think happens to a decimal number when you multiply it by 10?

32. a. Give four different ways to label the unlabeled marks on the number line.

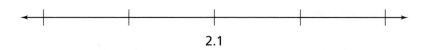

2.1

b. Find the mean of the five numbers in each of your answers in part (a). Do you see a pattern?

c. Can you label the unlabeled marks on the number line in part (a) so that the sum of the five numbers will be 10? Explain.

33. The area of a circle is 2.0096 square inches. Use 3.14 as an approximation for the number π.

a. What is the diameter of this circle?

b. What is the circumference of this circle?

Extensions

34. Leah filled her gas tank at the start of a trip and noted that her mileage indicator read 15,738.1 miles. When her mileage indicator read 16,167.6, she needed gas again. It took 18.2 gallons of gas to fill the tank. About how many miles did her car go on each gallon of gas?

35. Explore the decimal representations of fractions with a denominator of 99. Try $\frac{1}{99}, \frac{2}{99}, \frac{3}{99}$, and so on. What patterns do you see?

36. Explore the decimal representations of fractions with a denominator of 999. Try $\frac{1}{999}, \frac{2}{999}, \frac{3}{999}$, and so on. What patterns do you see?

Use the patterns you discovered in Exercises 35 and 36 to write fractions for these decimal representations.

37. 0.05050505 . . .

38. 0.45454545 . . .

39. 0.045045045 . . .

40. 10.121212 . . .

Each of the shapes in Exercises 41–43 has the same area as the area of the rectangle.

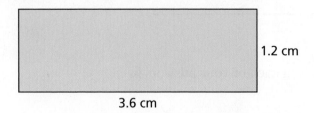

1.2 cm

3.6 cm

Use this information to find the length marked by *n*.

41.

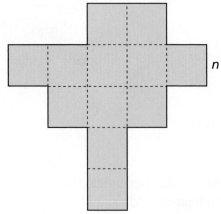

n

42.

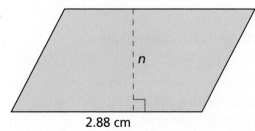

n

2.88 cm

43.

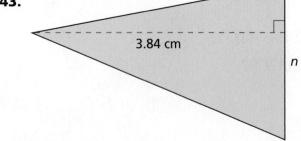

3.84 cm

n

Mathematical Reflections 3

In this investigation, you looked at the relationship between division of fractions and division of decimals. You also looked at patterns in decimal divisions that give the same answers. Finally, you looked at patterns in terminating and repeating decimal representations of fractions. The following questions will help you review and organize what you have learned.

Think about your answers to these questions. Discuss your ideas with other students and your teacher. Then write a summary of your findings in your notebook.

1. Describe a way to write a division problem that has the same answer as a given decimal division problem but has a whole number dividend and divisor. Use an example to help explain.

2. Describe an algorithm for dividing decimals. Tell why you think the algorithm works.

3. Explain how you can tell if a fraction has a terminating or a repeating decimal form.

Investigation 4

Using Percents

When a store has a sale, you see advertisements for discounts. The discounts are usually given in percents (20% off, 30% off, etc.). Percents are helpful in many situations involving money. Discounts, taxes, and tips are all described with percents. Understanding how to compute and use these percents can make you a smarter consumer.

4.1 Determining Tax

Remember that a percent is a special way of representing a fraction (or rate) with a denominator of 100. You can think of percent as meaning "out of 100."

Most states have a sales tax. A sales tax of 6% means that for every dollar an item costs, a person needs to pay an additional six hundredths of a dollar, which is 6 cents, or $0.06, for taxes:

$$\$1.00 + (6\% \text{ of } \$1.00) = \$1.00 + \$0.06 = \$1.06$$

Or, since $1.00 is 100 pennies:

$$100 \text{ pennies} + (6\% \text{ of } 100 \text{ pennies}) = 100 \text{ pennies} + 6 \text{ pennies}$$
$$= 106 \text{ pennies}$$
$$= \$1.06$$

You can use this same type of reasoning with other sales tax problems.

States, and sometimes counties and cities, establish sales tax for certain goods and services. Some states have a higher sales tax than others.

- What is the sales tax in your area?
- How does it compare to the taxes in other parts of the country?

Problem 4.1 Determining Tax

A. Jill wants to buy a CD that is priced at $7.50. The sales tax is 6%. What will be the total cost of the CD? Try to find more than one way to solve this problem. Be prepared to explain the different methods you find.

B. Using a sales tax of 6%, find the total cost for each item.

  1. a $2.00 magazine   **2.** a $5.00 book on dogs

  3. a $0.50 comic book

C. Use a sales tax of 7%. Find the total cost for each item in Question B.

D. Use what you have learned to solve these problems.

  1. Alexis bought a CD player. She does not remember the price, but she does know that the 6% sales tax came to $4.80. What was the price of the CD player? Explain your reasoning.

  2. Frank buys a new video game. The 5% sales tax is $0.75. What is the price of the game? Explain.

ACE **Homework starts on page 55.**

4.2 Computing Tips

You have developed some strategies for computing a sales tax and finding the total cost. As you work on Problem 4.2, look for more shortcuts and strategies for solving problems involving taxes and tips.

At most restaurants, customers pay their server a tip for providing good service. A typical tip is 15% to 20% of the price of the meal. Some people calculate the tip based on the price of the meal before the tax is added. Others base the tip on the total cost after the tax is added.

Try to find more than one way to solve the problems. Be prepared to explain the different methods you used.

A. Have each member of your group use the menu shown to make up a lunch order. Write a list of all the items ordered by your group.

Larry's Lunch Place

Lunch Specials

Roast Turkey.................................3.95
Slices of turkey breast, savory dressing, homemade gravy, and cranberry sauce

Veggie Quesadilla.........................3.95
Whole-wheat tortillas stuffed with tomatoes, roasted peppers, and three kinds of cheese

Chicken Tenders...........................4.50
Strips of all-white-meat chicken baked to a golden brown, served with a baked potato, coleslaw, and barbeque sauce

Larry's Famous Burgers

**Quarter Pound
Hamburger Platter**.......................3.30

**Quarter Pound
Cheeseburger Platter**...................3.60

Larry's Special.............................4.35
Two patties, with crisp lettuce, Larry's own sauce, and cheese on a specially baked bun

Seafood

Shrimp Cocktail...........................6.95
Tender steamed shrimp served on ice with tangy cocktail sauce

Fish and Chips............................4.45
Three deep-fried fillets with french fries, coleslaw, and tartar sauce

Baked Meatloaf...........................3.95
Tasty homestyle meatloaf with mixed green salad

Spaghetti with Tomato Sauce......3.25
A generous portion of pasta with zesty sauce, parmesan cheese, and garlic bread

Grilled Chicken Breast..................5.25
Served over rice with lemon parsley sauce, crisp lettuce, tomato slices, and whole wheat rolls (low cholesterol)

Desserts

Fresh Strawberry Pie....................1.89
With frozen yogurt.................................2.25
Chocolate Cake............................1.50
With ice cream..1.95

Beverages

Coffee, Regular or Decaffeinated........80
Hot or Iced Tea.....................................80
White or Chocolate Milk....................99
Lemonade..99
Soft Drinks...99
Orange Juice.......................................99
Hot Chocolate.....................................99
Root Beer Float.................................1.99

1. Find the total bill for food and tax for your group. Use a sales tax of 6%.

2. How much will you leave for the tip? (The tip must be between 15% and 20%.)

3. Your group members decide to share the cost of the meal equally. What is each person's share of the cost, including the tip?

B. Many people use benchmarks for determining tips. Gil explains his strategy: "I always figure out 10% of the bill, and then I use this information to calculate a 15% or 20% tip."

1. Find 10% and 5% of $20.00. How are the two percents related?

2. Find 10% and 20% of $24.50. How are the two percents related?

3. Find 10% of $17.35. Use this to find 15% and 20% of $17.35. Explain.

C. The sales tax in Kadisha's state is 5%. Kadisha says she computes a 15% tip by multiplying the tax shown on her bill by three. For a bill with a tax charge of $0.38, Kadisha's tip is $0.38 \times 3 = 1.14.

Garden Cafe

ITEM	AMOUNT
Food	$7.55
5% Tax	.38
TOTAL	$7.93

1. Why does Kadisha's method work?

2. Use a similar method to compute a 20% tip. Explain.

D. When people leave a 15% or 20% tip, they often round up to the nearest multiple of 5 or 10 cents. For example, in Question C, Kadisha might leave a tip of $1.15 rather than $1.14.

1. If Kadisha always rounds up, what is a 20% tip on her bill?

2. Omar always leaves a 20% tip based on the meal price before tax is added. Find a meal price for which Omar leaves a tip of $1.00 after rounding up to the nearest multiple of 5 or 10 cents.

3. Marlene always leaves a 15% tip based on the meal price before tax. Find a meal price for which Marlene leaves a tip of $4.50 after rounding up to the nearest multiple of 5 or 10 cents.

4. Customers leave Jerome $2.50 as a tip for service. The tip is 20% of the total bill for their food. How much is the bill?

ACE Homework starts on page 55.

4.3 Finding Bargains

At Loud Sounds Music, CDs are regularly priced at $15.95, and CD singles are regularly priced at $3.45. Every day this month, the store is offering a discount on all CDs and CD singles.

Problem 4.3 Using Discounts

Jeremy goes to Loud Sounds. He discovers that if he buys two or more items today, he can save 20% on each item.

A. Suppose Jeremy buys a CD and a CD single. The store adds a 6.5% sales tax on the discounted price. How much does Jeremy spend?

B. Jeremy thinks he can buy six CD singles for less money than the cost of one CD single and a CD. Is he correct? Explain your reasoning.

C. Mr. Fernandes wants to take advantage of the day's 20% special to add to his CD collection. There are 15 CDs he wants to buy.

   1. What is the total amount of the discount he will receive?

   2. Suppose the discount is only 1%. What total discount amount would Mr. Fernandes receive on the 15 CDs?

   3. What is the relationship between 1% and 20% of the cost?

   4. How can you use what you found out above to find a 16% discount on the cost of the 15 CDs? Can you find another way to compute 16%? Explain your methods and how they are related.

D. 1. At another music store, Rita gets a $12 discount off a purchase of $48. What percent discount does she get?

   2. Masako has a $25-off coupon on a purchase of $100 or more at a department store. She buys a jacket with a price tag of $125. What percent off does she get on her purchase?

   3. Describe how you answered parts (1)–(2). Explain why your method works.

ACE Homework starts on page 55.

Applications

1. Find three examples of percents used in the real world. Newspapers, magazines, radio, and television are good places to look. Write down each example, or cut it out and tape it to your paper. For each example, describe how percents are used and what they mean.

2. Hot dogs at a carnival cost $0.99 each plus 7% tax. What is the total cost for one hot dog?

3. Jason stops at a ball-toss game at the carnival. The sign reads, "Three balls for 50 cents or six balls for 80 cents." What percent does he save by buying one set of six balls instead of two sets of three balls?

4. A class conducts a survey of 1,000 students.

   a. The survey reveals that 20% of the students speak Spanish. How many students is this?

   b. 6% of the students have forgotten their locker combinations at some time. How many students is this?

   c. Of the sixth-grade students surveyed, 12% bring their lunches to school. Suppose 24 sixth-graders do this. How many sixth-graders are at the school?

5. a. Arif and Keisha go to a restaurant for dinner. Their meals total $13.75. The sales tax is 5%. How much tax is added to the bill?

   b. They want to leave a 15% tip based on the bill and the tax combined. How much should they leave? Explain.

   c. Arif ordered a more expensive meal than Keisha. After tax and tip are figured, he decides he should pay $3 more than Keisha. How much should each pay?

6. Jen and Sarah go to lunch at the Green Grill. Their meal totals $28. The sales tax is 6%.

   a. What is the total cost with the tax?

   b. They want to leave a 20% tip based on the total cost before the tax. How much tip should they leave?

   c. Describe two strategies that Jen and Sarah can use to figure the amount of the tip.

For: Multiple-Choice Skills Practice
Web Code: ama-6454

7. Marilyn carries a tip calculator card with her. It lists the amounts for 15% and 20% tips on whole dollar values up to $100. Her daughter notices a pattern. She says, "For each dollar the cost increases, the tips in the 15% column increase $0.15."

   a. Explain why this pattern occurs for 15% tip values.

   b. What is the amount of increase for each dollar increase in the 20% tip column?

   c. The tip calculator card only goes up to $100. How can you use the card if your restaurant bill totals $325?

8. The Science Supply Store is having a sale. All graduated cylinders are 25% off. Mrs. Delmar buys four graduated cylinders that were originally $8 each and six that were originally $9.50 each.

   a. How much money will Mrs. Delmar save?

   b. What percent of the original price will Mrs. Delmar pay?

   c. Suppose the sales tax is 4%. What is Mrs. Delmar's total cost?

The local boutique is having a sale on hats. All regular-priced hats are 20% off. Shirley, Lisa, and Sandy each find a hat to buy.

   9. Shirley's beach hat was originally $24.95. What is the sale price?

   10. Sandy finds a sun visor that was originally $12.50. What is the sale price?

   11. Lisa finds a hat that is already marked down. The price tag shows that the original price was $36. The marked-down price is $27. What percent has the hat been marked down? Explain.

12. a. Inline skates are on sale for 35% off the regular price. What fraction off is this discount?

b. The original price of one pair of inline skates is $124.99. What is the sale price?

c. A tax of 5% is computed on the sale price. What is the total cost of the inline skates?

Connections

13. Theo does $\frac{3}{10}$ of his homework. What percent is equal to $\frac{3}{10}$? What percent does Theo still have left to do?

14. Multiple Choice In a survey, 75% of 400 parents said they give their children fruit as a snack. How many parents of those surveyed is this?

A. 150 **B.** 200 **C.** 225 **D.** 300

15. If $2.4 \div 0.2 = 12$, is $2.4 \div 0.5$ greater than or less than 12? Explain.

16. If $0.25 \times 0.8 = 0.2$, is $0.25 \div 0.8$ greater than or less than 0.2?

17. A certain bean plant grows 15% of its height each day. Express this percent as a decimal.

18. Multiple Choice Ike's Bikes requires 25% of the cost as a down payment for a new mountain bike. What fraction of the cost is this percent?

F. $\frac{9}{35}$ **G.** $\frac{5}{21}$ **H.** $\frac{8}{32}$ **J.** $\frac{7}{24}$

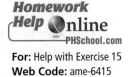

For: Help with Exercise 15
Web Code: ame-6415

19. Four friends order a square pizza. Marisa says she isn't very hungry and only wants 10% of the pizza. Tomarr is very hungry and says he will eat 50% of the pizza. Jon says he will eat 35%, and Kwan says she will eat 15%. Is this possible? Explain your reasoning.

20. The Running Shoe Company advertises that they will award prizes for 1% of the total number of entries in a contest. They receive 1,600 entries. How many prizes do they award?

In Exercises 21 and 22, a paint spill covers up part of the fraction strips. Use what is showing to reason about each set of strips and to find fractions equivalent to those marked.

21.

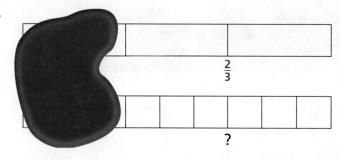

22.

Find numbers that will make each sentence true. There may be more than one solution. If so, show at least two solutions.

23. $\frac{4}{9} = \frac{\blacksquare}{\blacksquare}$ **24.** $\frac{\blacksquare}{\blacksquare} = \frac{3}{5}$ **25.** $\frac{\blacksquare}{3} = \frac{8}{\blacksquare}$ **26.** $\frac{5}{\blacksquare} = \frac{\blacksquare}{18}$

Extensions

27. Write a percent problem that involves discounts on food, cars, books, clothes, or other items. Solve your problem.

28. You are shopping in Chicago, Illinois, where the state sales tax is $6\frac{1}{4}\%$. You purchase a $5.00 map of the city. What is your total cost?

29. Carrie buys a pair of jeans that cost $32.00. The local sales tax is $2\frac{1}{2}\%$ and the state sales tax is 5%.

Now Only **$32.00**

    a. What is the amount of each tax?

    b. What is the total cost of the jeans?

30. In January the news reported an inflation rate of 4%. In February, the news reported that inflation had increased by 10% since the January report. What does that mean? What is the new rate of inflation?

For Exercises 31 and 32, copy the number line (including all the labeled marks). Mark each number line at 1. Rewrite each fraction, including 1, as a decimal and a percent.

31.

       0            $\frac{3}{4}$

32.

       0                   $\frac{5}{3}$

33. Copy the percent bar below. Mark it carefully to show the location of 100%.

0%   120%

34. Each year the Mannel Department Store has a big end-of-summer sale. At the sale, they give customers an additional 25% off on all marked-down merchandise.

a. A beach towel had an original price of $22. It was marked down 10%. What is the final price, after the additional 25% discount?

b. A patio table and four chairs originally cost $350. They were marked down 50%. What is the final cost of the table and chairs with the additional discount?

Find numbers that will make each sentence true.

35. $\frac{1}{3} = \frac{\blacksquare}{9} = \frac{\blacksquare}{6}$ **36.** $\frac{\blacksquare}{18} = \frac{8}{12} = \frac{4}{\blacksquare}$ **37.** $\frac{3}{\blacksquare} = \frac{12}{\blacksquare} = \frac{9}{\blacksquare}$ **38.** $\frac{\blacksquare}{3} = \frac{\blacksquare}{21} = \frac{\blacksquare}{6}$

39. In Exercises 35–38, which sentences have more than one possible answer? Why?

40. A box of macaroni and cheese says that it makes 25% more than the regular box. If a regular box makes three cups of macaroni and cheese, how many cups will this box make?

Mathematical Reflections 4

In this investigation you solved problems that involved finding percents of numbers. You computed discounts, sale prices, tips, and sales tax. The following questions will help you summarize what you have learned.

Think about your answers to these questions. Discuss your ideas with other students and your teacher. Then write a summary of your findings in your notebook.

1. Explain how to find the sales tax on a purchase and calculate the final bill. Use an example.

2. Describe a procedure for finding the price of a discounted item if you know the percent of the discount.

3. **a.** Explain a process for finding 17% of a number if you know 1% and 5% of the number.

   b. Give five other percents of a number that are easy to find if you know 1% and 5% of the number.

4. Describe how to find the cost of a purchase if you know the percent of the tax and the amount of the sales tax on the purchase.

5. How can you find the percent one number is of another? For example, what percent of 35 is 7?

More About Percents

In *Bits and Pieces I*, you changed numbers in fraction or decimal form to percent form. In the last investigation, you built on this to find an amount given as a percent of a total. For example, you started with the price of an item and the percent discount offered on the item, and you computed how much money you would save.

Now you will face similar situations, but you will be given different pieces of information.

5.1 Clipping Coupons

Newspapers often have coupons for discounts on many different things. One coupon for shampoo is shown.

The regular price for the shampoo is $5.00. Alicia wants to figure out what percent discount this is. She thinks about the problem this way:

> "I need to find what percent $1.50 is of $5.00. I can think of these amounts in pennies. The fraction I want to represent as a percent is $\frac{150}{500}$, which is equivalent to $\frac{30}{100}$. This means that the discount is 30%!"

A. What percent discount do you get with this coupon? Try to find more than one way to solve this problem. Be prepared to explain your methods.

75¢ OFF

BACK TO SCHOOL SPECIAL

Any two spiral-bound notebooks

Regular price	**$3.00**
With coupon	**$2.25**

Not valid with any other offer.

B. Estimate each percent discount for the sales below. Explain.

1.

MOVIE

Regular price: **$8.50**
Today only: **$8.00**

TICKET

2.

BIG SALE ON
BINOCULARS!

Regular price:......$29.50
Now pay just:......**$17.70**

C. The 25% discount on a skateboard is $24.75. What is the cost without the discount?

D. The 15% discount on a sweater is $6.75. What is the original cost?

ACE Homework starts on page 67.

Sometimes you have to figure out whether you have enough money in your pocket to buy an item that you want. Suppose you go out to dinner with friends and put all of your money together. What can you buy?

Problem 5.2 Solving Percent Problems

A. Your group has $60 altogether for pizza. The tax is 5% and you want to leave a 15% tip on the price of the food before sales tax. What is the maximum amount your group can spend and not go over $60? Explain your reasoning. Show any diagrams you make to help figure out the answer.

B. You and your friends go out to eat again. This time you have $80 altogether. The tax is 7% and you want to leave an 18% tip. What is the maximum amount your group can spend and not go over $80? Explain. Show any diagrams you make to help figure out the answer.

C. To celebrate your election to the student council, your grandparents take you shopping. You have a 20%-off coupon. The cashier takes 20% off the $68.79 bill. Your grandmother remembers that she has an additional coupon for 10% off. The cashier takes the 10% off what the cash register shows. Does this result in the same amount as 30% off the original bill? Explain.

ACE Homework starts on page 67.

Circle graphs, or pie charts, are special kinds of graphs used to show how a whole (100%) is divided into several categories. They are often used to survey data. For example, dog and cat owners who said their pets had bad breath were asked, "Which of these methods do you use most frequently to take care of your pet's bad breath?" Here are the results:

**Owner Solutions for
Bad Breath in Pets**

	Dog Owners	Cat Owners
Toothpaste	54%	53%
Mouthwash	16%	14%
Dental floss	7%	24%
Other	23%	9%
Total	100%	100%

Notice that the total of each column in the table is 100%.

Now, here are the results displayed in two pie charts.

**Owner Solutions for
Bad Breath in Dogs**

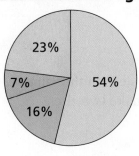

**Owner Solutions for
Bad Breath in Cats**

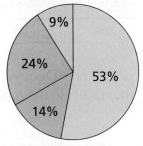

 Toothpaste 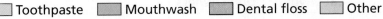 Mouthwash Dental floss Other

Study the circle graphs below. Use what you know about angle measures, circles, and percents to figure out how they were made. Then work on the questions below.

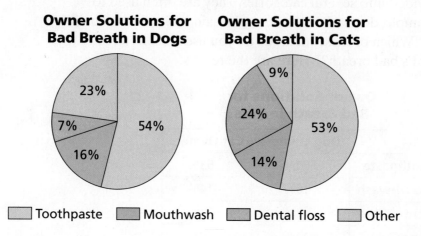

Owner Solutions for Bad Breath in Dogs

Owner Solutions for Bad Breath in Cats

☐ Toothpaste   ☐ Mouthwash   ☐ Dental floss   ☐ Other

A. Private investigators and crime-lab technicians were asked, "Would you say your job is exciting?" Use the results in the table to make two circle graphs.

	Crime-Lab Technicians	Private Investigators
Yes	40%	75%
No	60%	25%
Total	100%	100%

B. 1. Cat and dog owners were asked, "Does your pet sleep in the same room with you?" Use the results in the table to make two circle graphs.

	Cat Owners	Dog Owners
Yes	73%	47%
No	27%	53%
Total	100%	100%

2. How do the answers of the cat owners and dog owners compare?

ACE | Homework starts on page 67.

Applications

Solve Exercises 1–4, and then show how you found your answer.

1. What is 5% of 40?

2. What is 22% of 220?

3. 5 is what percent of 40?

4. 75 is what percent of 80?

5. **Multiple Choice** What is 75% of 80?

   A. 20   **B.** 40   **C.** 60   **D.** 75

6. **Multiple Choice** 22 is what percent of 220?

   F. 10%   **G.** 22%   **H.** 44%   **J.** 198%

7. A music store reported 15 sales for every 100 people who visited the store last year. What percent of the visitors bought something?

8. As part of a probability activity, Roberto is counting the occurrence of different letters in a paragraph in his biology book. In the first 1,000 letters, he finds 50 b's. What percent of the letters are b's?

9. Estimate what percent discount Ling will receive if she buys the microscope kit advertised below. Explain.

MICROSCOPE KITS

Customers usually pay..... **$7.95**
Students save by paying only.................. **$6.76**

10. The auto shop class conducted a survey to determine which math teacher's car was the most popular with the students. These were the results:

a. What percent of the votes did Mr. Alberto's car receive? Explain.

b. What percent of the votes did Ms. Dole's car receive?

c. One student said Ms. Grant's car received 48% of the votes. Is he correct? Explain.

Math Teacher	Student Votes
Ms. Grant	48
Ms. Dole	35
Mr. Alberto	12
Ms. Bock	75

11. Juan, Makayla, and Sam belong to an after-school group. They joined the group at different times after the beginning of school. The chart shows their attendance so far at the various events, including meetings, held by the group.

Attendance Since Joining Group

Member	Events Attended	Total Events Held
Juan	20	30
Makayla	11	18
Sam	7	12

a. Suppose the attendance pattern of all three students remains about the same for the next 30 events. Who will have the highest percent of attendance at the 30 events? Explain.

b. There are 120 events planned for the rest of the year. How many would you expect each of the students to attend if they keep the same percent of attendance? Explain.

12. Three children put their money together to buy their parents a present. Together they have $91. If the state sales tax is 4%, what is the maximum amount of money they can spend on the gift?

13. You and your friends are going out to eat. You decide to pool your money and order several dishes and appetizers to share. You have $75 altogether. If the tax is 5% and you want to leave a 15% tip (on the price before tax), what is the maximum you can spend?

14. Violeta is shopping. She has a coupon for 20% off her total purchase. The tax is 5%.

   a. Violeta has $60 to spend. How much of this can she use (after the discount is figured) and still have enough to pay the tax?

   b. Violeta realizes that she has extra money to pay the tax and can spend the entire $60 on merchandise. Use the original cost of the merchandise before the 20% is taken off. How much can the total amount to? Explain.

15. **a.** Dog and cat owners were asked, "How often do you feed your pet?" Make two circle graphs of the results shown in the table.

Feeding Times for Pets		
Time of Day	Cat Owners	Dog Owners
Night only	4%	2%
Morning only	6%	10%
Morning and night	42%	46%
Anytime	48%	42%
Total	100%	100%

   b. Compare the feeding patterns of dog owners to cat owners.

   c. Suppose the radius of each circle graph is 6 cm. Find the area of the "Morning only" section of each circle graph.

Connections

16. In a survey of 100 dog owners about their pets' habits, 39% said that their dogs eat bugs. How many dog owners surveyed said this?

17. In a survey of 80 students, 40% said they had a savings account of their own. How many students surveyed said this?

18. Suppose 300 tarantula owners were surveyed, and 26% said they let their spiders crawl on them. How many tarantula owners surveyed said this?

19. In a survey of 80 student artists, 6% said they had sold at least one of their works of art. How many students surveyed said this?

20. It is Crazy Coupon Day at the school store. At each counter students are given a coupon to use on any item at that counter. For each of the following items, compute the percent of discount.

  a. $5.00 off a $25 item

  b. $2.50 off a $20 item

  c. $8.00 off a $160 item

  d. If you know the discount and the price, how do you find the percent discount that the coupon gives?

21. A sugarless gum company used to state:

Homework
Help **online**
PHSchool.com
For: Help with Exercise 21
Web Code: ame-6521

"Nine out of ten dentists surveyed recommended sugarless gum for their patients who chew gum."

Sketch a circle graph showing the percent of dentists who recommended sugarless gum for their patients who chewed gum and the percent of dentists who did not.

22. The chart below shows the percent of various reasons for moving.

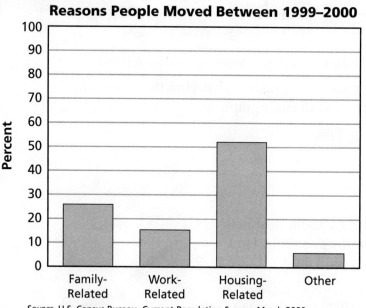

Source: U.S. Census Bureau, Current Population Survey, March 2000

  a. Sketch a circle graph of the data in the chart and label each section.

  b. Which representation of the data would you use to argue that most people surveyed moved for housing-related reasons? Explain.

Extensions

For Exercises 23–28, find numbers that make each sentence true.

23. $\dfrac{6}{\blacksquare} = \dfrac{18}{\blacksquare} = \dfrac{\blacksquare}{20}$ **24.** $\dfrac{12}{\blacksquare} = \dfrac{\blacksquare}{36} = \dfrac{\blacksquare}{12}$ **25.** $\dfrac{\blacksquare}{8} = \dfrac{16}{\blacksquare} = \dfrac{\blacksquare}{4}$

26. $\dfrac{2}{3} < \dfrac{\blacksquare}{9}$ **27.** $\dfrac{2}{3} = \dfrac{\blacksquare}{9}$ **28.** $\dfrac{2}{3} > \dfrac{\blacksquare}{9}$

29. 80 is 40% of what number? Explain.

30. 220 is 20% of what number? Explain.

31. When people are allowed to choose more than one answer to a survey question, the percents for the categories may add to more than 100%. For example, in one survey people were asked why they owned a pet. They were allowed to mark off more than one reason, so the percents add to more than 100%. Here are the results.

Reasons People Give for Owning Pets

Reason	Dog Owners	Cat Owners
Love/Companionship	88%	93%
Security	39%	0%
Protection	35%	0%
Entertainment	26%	33%
Catching Rodents	0%	16%
Breeding (to make money)	16%	6%
Children Grown/Spouse Died	4%	10%
Total	208%	158%

When percents add to more than 100%, you can make a bar graph to show the information.

a. Make bar graphs to display the data shown in the table. Before you make your bar graphs, think about these questions:

- What kinds of data will you display in your graphs?
- What will you show on the horizontal axis (the *x*-axis)?
- What will you show on the vertical axis (the *y*-axis)?
- What scale will you use for the *y*-axis?

b. Write a paragraph comparing the responses of dog owners to cat owners in this survey.

32. Copy machines use percents to enlarge and reduce the size of copies.

a. The picture below has been enlarged to 200% with a copy machine. Suppose you want to return this enlarged copy to its original size. What percent should you enter on the copy machine?

b. Suppose you have a copy that is reduced to 50% of its original size. In order to return it to its original size, what percent should you enter into the copy machine?

c. A copy is $1\frac{1}{2}$ times the size of the original. What percent should you enter in a copy machine to return it to its original size?

d. A copy is $\frac{3}{4}$ of its original size. What percent should you enter in a copy machine to return it to its original size?

Mathematical Reflections 5

In this investigation you studied situations for which you need to find the percent one number is of another number so that you could describe the situation or compare it to another situation. The following questions will help you summarize what you have learned.

Think about your answers to these questions. Discuss your ideas with other students and your teacher. Then write a summary of your findings in your notebook.

1. Describe at least two ways to find what percent one number is of another. Use an example to help explain why each method works.

2. Describe how to find what the original cost is if you know the amount and the percent of the discount. Use an example to explain your method.

3. Suppose you have a fixed amount of money to spend and you have to pay a percent of it for tax. How do you find the amount you can spend so that you will have enough for the purchase and for the tax? Use an example to explain your strategy.

4. Describe how to make a circle graph. Use an example to explain your strategy.

Unit Project

Ordering From a Catalog

Buying things from catalogs is something that families do frequently. But you might not ever have been the family member that filled out the order form. This project gives you a chance to show what you have learned about decimals and percents as you dream about things that you would love to order from a favorite catalog.

Part 1:

Choose a catalog and fill out the order form provided on the next page. Be sure that you correctly compute the taxes and figure the shipping costs for your items. Information on what the shipping costs are will be in your catalog. You also need to know the sales tax on merchandise in your state.

Steps in Filling Out the Order

Step 1:

1. Find three different items you would like to order from a catalog. Each item must cost at least $10. In your report, include a picture or sketch of the items. Tape or glue the picture of the item and its description, or draw a picture of the item and write out its description. Include the price with your picture or drawing.

Step 2:

2. Complete the attached order form as if you were ordering your three items from the C. M. Project catalog.

Record all the work you do to calculate the amounts for shipping and tax.

3. a. Choose one of the items you ordered. List the item with a brief description and give its price. Then answer these questions:

   b. What would this item cost if it were on sale for 25% off? Show how you found your answer.

   c. What would the item cost if it were on sale for $\frac{1}{3}$ off? Show how you found your answer.

4. Suppose another catalog has your first item listed for $5 less than the price you have listed. A third catalog has your item marked down 20%. If shipping charges and sales tax are the same, which is the better deal for you, and why?

Part 2:

5. Uri got $125 for his twelfth birthday and is going to use your catalog to order three items. Uri's state has a tax rate of 6%. Assume that the shipping costs are 9% of the cost before tax.

   a. Find the most that the three items can cost, before tax and shipping, so that Uri has enough money to order the items. Show your work and explain your reasoning.

   b. Find three items in the catalog that use up as much of Uri's birthday money as possible. Remember the sales tax and shipping charges.

C.M. Project Catalog Order Form

Item	Size	Qty.	Price
		Subtotal	
		Shipping	
		Tax	
		Total	

Looking Back and Looking Ahead

Unit Review

Go Online
PHSchool.com

For: Vocabulary Review
Puzzle
Web Code: amj-6051

Working on the problems in this unit helped you to develop strategies for estimating and for computing with decimals and percents. You learned how to

- relate operations on decimals to the same operations on common fractions

- use place value ideas to look for patterns in answers to computation problems

- use your knowledge of whole numbers, fractions, decimals, and percents to find shortcuts for some computations (algorithms)

Use Your Understanding: Decimals and Percents

The National Football League (NFL™) has developed an algorithm for rating the passing performance of any player who attempts a pass during a season. Since the quarterback position requires passing, the system is most often used to rate quarterback performance.

Four categories are used in a passer rating:

    percent of passes completed

    average yards gained per pass

    percent of passes for touchdowns

    percent of passes intercepted

Use the algorithm and data on the next page to find the passing performance of the three highest-rated quarterbacks of the 2003 NFL regular season.

Passer Rating Formula

- Calculate the percent of completed passes, or pass completions out of pass attempts. Subtract 30 from the percent, then multiply by 0.05.
- Calculate the average yards gained per pass, or pass yardage out of pass attempts. Subtract 3 from the average and multiply by 0.25.
- Calculate the percent of touchdown passes, or touchdown passes out of pass attempts. Multiply the percent by 0.2.
- Calculate the percent of interceptions, or interceptions out of pass attempts. Multiply the percent by 0.25. Subtract the product from 2.375.
- Determine the overall passer rating. Find the sum of the values from steps 1–4. Divide the sum by 6 and multiply by 100.

1. a. Calculate the passer rating for each quarterback.

2003 NFL Quarterback Statistics

Player	Pass Attempts	Passes Completed	Pass Yardage	Passes For Touchdowns	Passes Intercepted
Steve McNair	400	250	3,215	24	7
Peyton Manning	566	379	4,267	29	10
Daunte Culpepper	454	295	3,479	25	11

b. Which quarterback has the highest passer rating?

2. A local department store has scratch-off coupons that offer shoppers a discount of 5%, 10%, 15%, and 25% off any item.

a. What are the least and the greatest possible costs, including a 6% sales tax, for a shirt listed at $24.99?

b. Yoshi decides to buy the $24.99 shirt in blue, yellow, and brown. At the checkout counter, he scratches the coupon to find a 15% discount. What does he actually pay, including the 6% sales tax, for the three shirts?

c. The store conducted a survey to find out whether the scratch-off coupons had influenced customers to buy. At the end of the day, they tallied the results.

- Would have purchased the items without the coupon: 556
- Were strongly influenced by the coupon: 378
- Were somewhat influenced by the coupon: 137

What percent of customers were influenced in any way by the coupon?

Explain Your Reasoning

When you use mathematical calculations to solve a problem or make a decision, it is important to be able to justify each step in your reasoning.

3. Describe an algorithm for each of the following operations on decimals: addition, subtraction, multiplication, division.

4. Use the algorithms from Question 3 to solve the following problems. Show your steps.

a. 23.4 + 17.42

b. 43.09 − 17.62

c. 3.51 × 1.2

d. 11.7 ÷ 3

5. Explain the general procedures you use to answer these questions about percents. Give specific numerical examples.

a. How do you find the percent equivalent to a given decimal?

b. How do you find what percent one number is of another?

c. How do you find a given percent of a number?

Look Ahead

There are many everyday situations and many mathematical contexts that use decimals and percents. You will use the algorithms and concepts developed in this unit in most of the future *Connected Mathematics* units you work on. You will encounter decimals and percents in algebra, geometry, measurement, statistics, and many other areas. Some of the units where you will apply this reasoning include *Filling and Wrapping, Stretching and Shrinking,* and *Data Distributions.*

D

dividend The name for the number into which you are dividing in a division problem. For example, 26.5 is the dividend in the problem 26.5 ÷ 4.

dividendo Nombre del número que divides en un problema de división. Por ejemplo, 26.5 es el dividendo en el problema 26.5 ÷ 4.

divisor The name for the number you are dividing by in a division problem. For example, 4 is the divisor in the problem 26.5 ÷ 4.

divisor Nombre del número por el que divides en un problema de división. Por ejemplo, 4 es el divisor en el problema 26.5 ÷ 4.

P

powers of ten Numbers of the form 10, 10 × 10, 10 × 10 × 10 . . . or 10; 100; 1,000; 10,000 . . . or 10, 10^2, 10^3 . . . .

potencias de diez Números en la forma 10, 10 × 10, 10 × 10 × 10 . . . ó 10; 100; 1,000; 10,000 . . . ó 10, 10^2, 10^3 . . . .

Q

quotient The name for the answer to a division problem. For example, 6.625 is the quotient to 26.5 ÷ 4.

cociente Nombre del resultado de un problema de división. Por ejemplo, 6.625 es el cociente de 26.5 ÷ 4.

R

repeating decimal A decimal with a pattern of digits that repeats over and over, such as 0.3333333 . . . and 0.73737373 . . . . Repeating decimals are rational numbers.

decimal periódico Un decimal con un patrón de dígitos que se repite una y otra vez, por ejemplo, 0.3333333 . . . y 0.73737373 . . . . Los decimales periódicos son números racionales.

T

terminating decimal A decimal with a representation that ends, or terminates, such as 0.5 or 0.125. Terminating decimals are rational numbers.

decimal finito Un decimal con una representación que termina, como 0.5 ó 0.125. Los decimales finitos son números racionales.

Academic Vocabulary

The following terms are important to your understanding of the mathematics in this unit. Knowing and using these words will help you in thinking, reasoning, representing, communicating your ideas, and making connections across ideas. When these words make sense to you, the investigations and problems will make more sense as well.

D

describe To explain or tell in detail. A written description can contain facts and other information needed to communicate your answer. A diagram or a graph may also be included.
related terms: express, explain, illustrate

Sample: Describe the difference between a terminating decimal and a repeating decimal.

> A repeating decimal repeats a number or a set of numbers over and over again, for example $\frac{1}{3}$ is $0.\overline{3}$. A terminating decimal is a decimal that does not repeat a number or set of numbers, for example $\frac{2}{5}$ is 0.4.

describir Explicar o decir con detalle. Una descripción escrita puede contener hechos y otra información necesaria para comunicar tu respuesta. También se puede incluir un diagrama o una gráfica.
términos relacionados: expresar, explicar, ilustrar

Ejemplo: Describe la diferencia entre un decimal finito y un decimal periódico.

> Un decimal periódico repite un número o un conjunto de números una y otra vez, por ejemplo $\frac{1}{3}$ es $0.\overline{3}$. Un decimal finito es un decimal que no repite un número o conjunto de números, por ejemplo $\frac{2}{5}$ es 0.4.

E

estimate To find an approximate answer that is relatively close to an exact amount.
related terms: approximate, guess

Sample: Jonathan takes $10.00 with him to lunch. He orders a chicken sandwich for $1.99, a side salad for $1.79, a yogurt for $1.29, and a soda for $0.99. Estimate the total cost for Jonathan's lunch and the amount of change he should receive from $10.00.

> I used benchmarks to make my estimate. The sandwich is close to $2.00, the salad $1.75, the yogurt $1.25, and the soda $1.00.
>
>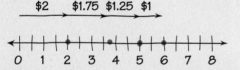
>
> The total cost of the lunch is about $6.00. Since $10.00 − $6.00 = $4.00, he should receive about $4.00 in change.

estimar Hallar una respuesta aproximada que esté relativamente cerca de una cantidad exacta.
términos relacionados: aproximar, conjeturar

Ejemplo: Jonathan tiene $10.00 para el almuerzo. Ordena un sándwich de pollo por $1.99, una ensalada pequeña por $1.79, un yogurt por $1.29 y un refresco por $0.99. Estima el costo total del almuerzo de Jonathan y el cambio que debería recibir por $10.00.

> Usé puntos de referencia para hacer mi estimado. El sándwich costó cerca a $2.00, la ensalada a $1.75 y el refresco a $1.00.
>
>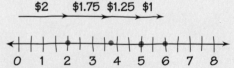
>
> El costo total del almuerzo es de alrededor a $6.00. Puesto que $10.00 − $6.00 = $4.00, él debe recibir alrededor de $4.00 de cambio.

explain To give facts and details that make an idea easier to understand. Explaining can involve a written summary supported by a diagram, chart, table, or a combination of these.

related terms: describe, show, justify, tell, present

Sample: Using a 6% sales tax, explain how to find the total cost for a pack of tennis balls priced at $10.00.

> To find the sales tax, change 6% to 0.06. Then multiply the price of the tennis balls by 0.06. $10 × 0.06 = $0.60. Add this to the cost of the tennis balls. $10 + $0.60 = $10.60.

explicar Dar hechos y detalles que hacen que una idea sea más fácil de comprender. Explicar puede implicar un resumen escrito apoyado por hechos, un diagrama, una gráfica, una tabla o una combinación de éstos.

términos relacionados: describir, mostrar, justificar, decir, presentar

Ejemplo: Usando un impuesto sobre ventas de 6%, explica cómo hallar el costo total de un paquete de pelotas de tenis que cuesta $10.00.

> Para hallar el impuesto sobre ventas, cambio 6% a 0.06. Luego multiplica el precio de las pelotas de tenis por 0.06. $10 × 0.06 = $0.60. Suma esto al costo de las pelotas de tenis. $10 + $0.60 = $10.60.

F

find To calculate or determine.

related terms: solve, locate

Sample: Find the value of *N*. Writing a fact family may help.

$$4.5 \div N = 9$$

> I first wrote down the fact family.
> $4.5 \div N = 9$ $4.5 \div 9 = N$ $9 \times N = 4.5$
> I then found the quotient of $4.5 \div 9$. Since $4.5 \div 9 = 0.5$, $N = 0.5$.

hallar Calcular o determinar.

términos relacionados: resolver, localizar

Ejemplo: Halla el valor de *N*. Escribir una familia de operaciones puede ayudar.

$$4.5 \div N = 9$$

> Primero escribí la familia de operaciones.
> $4.5 \div N = 9$ $4.5 \div 9 = N$ $9 \times N = 4.5$
> Luego hallé el cociente de $4.5 \div 9$. Puesto que $4.5 \div 9 = 0.5$, $N = 0.5$.

U

use To draw upon given information to help you determine something else.

related terms: utilize, employ

Sample: Consider the following fractions and their decimal representations.

$\frac{1}{9} = 0.1111111...$ $\frac{2}{9} = 0.2222222...$ $\frac{3}{9} = 0.3333333...$

Use the pattern you see to write decimal representations for $\frac{7}{9}$ and $\frac{8}{9}$.

> When the denominator is 9, the digit in the numerator repeats in the decimal representation. Therefore, $\frac{7}{9} = 0.7777777777...$ and $\frac{8}{9} = 0.8888888888...$.

usar Recurrir a información dada para ayudarte a determinar algo más.

términos relacionados: utilizar, emplear

Ejemplo: Considera las siguientes fracciones y sus representaciones decimales.

$\frac{1}{9} = 0.1111111...$ $\frac{2}{9} = 0.2222222...$ $\frac{3}{9} = 0.3333333...$

Usa el patrón que ves para escribir las representaciones decimales para $\frac{7}{9}$ y $\frac{8}{9}$.

> Cuando el denominador es 9, el dígito en el numerador se repite en la representación decimal. Por lo tanto, $\frac{7}{9} = 0.7777777777...$ y $\frac{8}{9} = 0.8888888888...$.

Index

Addition, 5–12, 20
    ACE, 13–19
    algorithm, 12, 20, 77
    estimation, 5–7
    of decimals, 7–12, 13–15, 17–19, 33
    of fractions, 15

Algebra
    algorithm 4, 12, 20, 35, 49, 76, 78
    difference 4, 6, 7, 11, 15, 18
    dividend 38, 39, 49
    divisor 38, 39, 49
    equivalent 15, 21, 29, 33, 41, 42, 44, 58
    factor 23, 27, 34
    horizontal axis 71
    interpret 20
    mathematical sentence 9, 12
    multiple 53
    notation 9
    number line 3, 4, 19, 45, 47, 59
    number sentence 10, 11, 30, 35, 36, 38
    operation 4, 6, 15, 27, 36, 37, 43, 76, 78
    product 4, 22–30, 32–35, 45, 77
    quotient 4, 38, 40, 43–45
    solve 9, 12, 15, 23, 24, 30, 39, 40
    strategy 3, 6, 7, 10, 20, 21, 24, 31, 35, 45, 51, 56, 73, 76
    sum 4, 6, 7, 15, 18, 47, 77
    vertical axis 71
    x-axis 71
    y-axis 71

Algorithm, 75–77
    for adding decimals, 12, 20, 77
    for dividing decimals, 49, 77
    for multiplying decimals, 27, 35, 77
    for subtracting decimals, 12, 20, 77

Angle 17

Area model, 16–17, 32–33, 48

Bar graph, making, 71

Benchmark
    decimal, 5–6, 11, 29
    fraction, 5, 11, 14
    percent, 53

Check for reasonableness, 21–22, 24–25, 28, 33, 38–39

Circle graph, 65–66, 69–70, 73
    making, 66, 69–70

Common denominators, 38–39

Comparing decimals, 16, 28, 32

Comparing fractions, 22, 46

Concrete model, *see* **Model**

Coupons, 62–64, 69–70

Data 20, 70

Decimals, 5–12, 20, 21–27, 35, 36–42, 49
    ACE, 13–19, 28–34, 43–48
    adding, 7–12, 13–15, 17–19, 33
    addition and subtraction algorithms for, 12, 20, 77
    benchmarks, 5–6, 11, 29
    comparing, 16, 28, 32
    converting to and from fractions, 12, 15, 20, 21–22, 27, 29, 33, 35, 38–39, 41–42, 43–45, 47, 49
    converting to and from percents, 50, 57, 60, 62, 77
    dividing with, 28–29, 36–40, 43–44, 47, 57, 77, 78
    division algorithm for, 49, 77
    equivalent, 38, 44
    estimating with, 5–7, 11, 13–14, 20, 21–26, 28–30, 33, 35, 37, 38–39
    fractions and, 10–12
    multiplication algorithm for, 27, 35, 77
    multiplying, 21–25, 27, 28–34, 35, 46, 57, 77, 78
    ordering, 16, 18–19, 28, 32
    and place value, 7–9, 17, 20, 24, 26
    repeating, 41–42, 49, 79
    subtracting, 7–12, 13–15, 17–18, 77, 78
    terminating, 41–42, 49, 79

Denominator 10, 22, 39, 41, 42, 47, 50

Difference 4, 6, 7, 11, 15, 18

Discounts, 54, 60–63, 73, 75
    ACE, 56, 58, 67

Dividend, 38, 79

Divisor, 38, 79

Division, 36–42, 59
    ACE, 43–48
    algorithm, 49, 77
    dividend, 38, 79
    divisor, 38, 79
    pattern, 44, 49
    quotient, 38, 43–44, 79
    with common denominators, 38–39
    with decimals, 28–29, 36–40, 43–44, 47, 57
    with fractions, 38–39

Equivalent decimals, 38, 44

Equivalent fractions, 22, 33, 38, 41–42, 44, 58, 60, 62, 71

Estimation
    ACE, 13–14, 28–30, 33
    and addition, 5–7
    overestimating, 13
    underestimating, 13
    with decimals, 5–7, 11, 13–14, 20, 21–26, 28–30, 33, 35, 37, 38–39
    with fractions, 21

Fact families, 12, 15, 40, 44

Factors, 23–27
    missing, 23–24

Fraction strips, 58

Fractions
    ACE, 14–15, 29, 31–33, 43–45, 47, 57–58, 71
    adding, 15
    benchmarks, 5, 11, 14
    comparing, 22, 46
    converting to and from decimals, 12, 15, 20, 21–22, 27, 29, 33, 35, 38–39, 41–42, 43–45, 47, 49
    converting to and from percents, 50, 57–58, 60, 62
    decimals and, 10–12
    dividing, 38–39
    equivalent, 22, 33, 38, 41–42, 44,

Index

Acknowledgments

Team Credits

The people who made up the **Connected Mathematics 2** team—representing editorial, editorial services, design services, and production services—are listed below. Bold type denotes core team members.

Leora Adler, Judith Buice, Kerry Cashman, Patrick Culleton, Sheila DeFazio, Richard Heater, **Barbara Hollingdale, Jayne Holman,** Karen Holtzman, **Etta Jacobs,** Christine Lee, Carolyn Lock, Catherine Maglio **Dotti Marshall,** Rich McMahon, Eve Melnechuk, Kristin Mingrone, Terri Mitchell, **Marsha Novak,** Irene Rubin, Donna Russo, Robin Samper, Siri Schwartzman, **Nancy Smith,** Emily Soltanoff, **Mark Tricca,** Paula Vergith, Roberta Warshaw, Helen Young

Additional Credits

Diana Bonfilio, Mairead Reddin, Michael Torocsik, nSight,Inc.

Technical Illustration

WestWords, Inc.

Cover Design

tom white.images

Photos

2 t, Michael Newman/PhotoEdit; **2 b,** Susan Findlay/Masterfile; **3,** Lee Foster/Lonely Planet Images; **5,** Ronnie Kaufman/Corbis; **6,** David Young-Wolff/PhotoEdit; **8,** Jeff Greenberg/Omni Photo Communications, Inc.; **11,** Mark Gibson/Index Stock Imagery, Inc.; **14,** Lori Adamski Peek/Getty Images, Inc.; **19,** David Young-Wolff/PhotoEdit; **23,** Tony Freeman/ PhotoEdit; **25,** Richard Haynes; **31,** Michael Newman/PhotoEdit; **36,** Warren Lynch/Getty Images, Inc.; **37,** Creatas/PictureQuest; **39,** Richard Haynes; **46,** AP Photo/Mark Humphrey; **50,** Tony Freeman/PhotoEdit; **54,** Dennis MacDonald/AGE Fotostock; **56,** Susan Findlay/Masterfile; **57,** C Squared Studios/PictureQuest; **62,** Dorling Kindersley; **69,** Geoff Dann/Dorling Kindersley; **72 both,** Creatas/Alamy; **76,** Photodisc/Getty Images, Inc.

Data Sources

NFL® and passer rating categories on page 76 are Copyright © NFL Enterprises LLC. Used by permission of the National Football League Properties (NFLP).

NFL®, passer rating formula, and 2003 quarterback statistics on page 77 are Copyright © NFL Enterprises LLC. Used by permission of the National Football League Properties (NFLP).

Note: Every effort has been made to locate the copyright owner of the material reprinted in this book. Omissions brought to our attention will be corrected in subsequent editions.

Connected Mathematics 2

How Likely Is It?

Understanding Probability

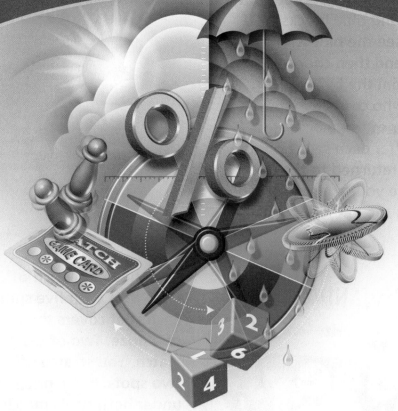

Glenda Lappan

James T. Fey

William M. Fitzgerald

Susan N. Friel

Elizabeth Difanis Phillips

PEARSON

Boston, Massachusetts · Glenview, Illinois · Shoreview, Minnesota · Upper Saddle River, New Jersey

How Likely Is It?

Understanding Probability

You are on a game show. The host is holding a bucket with red, yellow, and blue blocks. You cannot see the blocks. Guess a color and then choose a block from the bucket. A player who correctly predicts the color of the block wins $500. After each selection, the block is returned to the bucket. What are your chances of winning the game?

You have a scratch-off prize card with five spots. Each spot covers the name of a prize. Two of the prizes match. You scratch off only two spots. If the prize under both spots match, you win. How likely is it that you will win?

Some people can curl their tongues into a "U" shape. Other people can't. What are the chances that a person can curl her or his tongue?

How do you make decisions? Suppose you are deciding whether to wear a raincoat. Would you ask "How likely is it that it will rain today?" Suppose you are deciding whether to buy a raffle ticket. Would you ask "What are the chances that I will win the raffle?" These questions ask about the probability that an event will occur.

Finding probabilities can help you understand past events. They can also help you make decisions about future events. In this unit, you will look at questions that involve probability, including the three questions on the opposite page.

Mathematical Highlights

Understanding Probability

In *How Likely Is It?*, you will explore concepts related to chance, or probability. You will analyze situations that have uncertain outcomes.

You will learn how to

- Use probabilities to predict what will happen over the long run
- Use the concepts of *equally likely* and *not equally likely*
- Analyze a game to see if it is fair (Does each player have an equal chance of winning?)
- Build two kinds of probability models:
  (1) Gather data from experiments (experimental probability)
  (2) Analyze possible outcomes (theoretical probability)
- Understand that experimental probabilities are better estimates of theoretical probabilities when they are based on larger numbers of trials
- Develop strategies for finding both experimental and theoretical probabilities
- Interpret statements of probability to make decisions and answer questions

As you work on the problems of this unit, make it a habit to ask questions about situations that involve probability and uncertainty:

What are the possible outcomes that can occur for the event in this situation?

How can I determine the experimental probability of each of the outcomes?

Is it possible to determine the theoretical probability of each of the outcomes? If so, what are these probabilities?

How can I use the probabilities to answer questions or make decisions about this situation?

A First Look at Chance

Decisions, decisions, decisions! You make decisions every day. You choose what to wear, with whom to have lunch, what to do after school, and maybe what time to go to bed.

You make some decisions without even thinking. For example, you may automatically eat the same breakfast cereal each morning. You base other decisions on how you feel at a given time. If you are in the mood to laugh, you might decide to meet a friend with a good sense of humor.

To make some decisions, you consider the chance, or likelihood, that something will happen. You may listen to the weather forecast to decide whether you will wear a raincoat to school. In some cases, you may even let chance make a decision for you, such as when you roll a number cube to see who goes first in a game.

A number cube shows the numbers 1, 2, 3, 4, 5, and 6 on its faces.

1.1 Choosing Cereal

Getting Ready for Problem 1.1

- What are the chances of getting a 2 when you roll a number cube? Are you more likely to roll a 2 or a 6? How can you decide?

- The weather forecaster says the chance of rain tomorrow is 40%. What does this mean? Should you wear a raincoat?

- When you toss a coin, what are the chances of getting tails? If you toss seven tails in a row, are you more likely to get heads or tails on the next toss?

Kalvin always has cereal for breakfast. He likes Cocoa Blast cereal so much that he wants it every morning. Kalvin's mother wants him to eat Health Nut Flakes at least some mornings because it is more nutritious than Cocoa Blast.

Kalvin and his mother have found a fun way to choose which cereal he will have for breakfast. Each morning in June, Kalvin tosses a coin. If the coin lands on heads, he will have Cocoa Blast. If the coin lands on tails, he will have Health Nut Flakes.

Predict how many days in June Kalvin will eat Cocoa Blast.

Problem 1.1 Finding Probabilities With a Coin

A. 1. Conduct an experiment to test your prediction. Toss a coin 30 times (one for each day in June). Record your results in a table such as the one shown with 30 rows:

Coin Toss Results

Day	Result of Toss (H or T)	Number of Heads So Far	Fraction of Heads So Far	Percent of Heads So Far
1	■	■	■	■
2	■	■	■	■

2. As you add more data, what happens to the percent of tosses that are heads?

B. Work with your teacher and your classmates to combine the results from all the groups.

  1. What percent of the total number of tosses for your class is heads?

  2. As your class adds more data, what happens to the percent of tosses that are heads?

  3. Based on what you found for June, how many times do you expect Kalvin to eat Cocoa Blast in July? Explain your reasoning.

C. Kalvin's mother tells him that the chance of a coin showing heads when he tosses it is $\frac{1}{2}$. Does this mean that every time he tosses a coin twice he will get one head and one tail? Explain.

 ACE Homework starts on page 13.

1.2 Tossing Paper Cups

Kalvin really loves Cocoa Blast. He wants to find something else to toss that will give him a better chance of eating the cereal each morning. He looks through a cupboard and finds a package of paper cups. He wonders if a paper cup is a good thing to toss.

Because Kalvin wants to eat Cocoa Blast cereal more of the time, he needs to determine if the cup lands in one position more often than another. If so, he will ask to toss a paper cup instead of a coin.

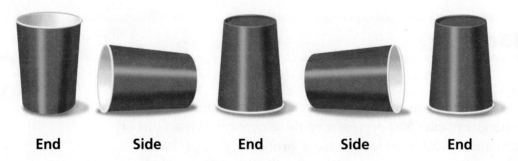

End   Side   End   Side   End

Which of the landing positions, end or side, should Kalvin use to represent Cocoa Blast? (Remember, he wants to eat Cocoa Blast as often as possible.)

Problem 1.2 Finding More Probabilities

A. Conduct an experiment to test your prediction about how a paper cup lands. Toss a paper cup 50 times. Make a table to record your data.

B. Use your results to answer the following questions:

   1. For what fraction of your 50 tosses did the cup land on one of its ends? What percent is this?

   2. For what fraction of your 50 tosses did the cup land on its side? What percent is this?

   3. Do the landing positions *end* and *side* have the same chance of occurring? If not, which is more likely? Explain.

   4. Which of the cup's landing positions should Kalvin use to represent Cocoa Blast? Explain your reasoning.

C. Combine the data from all the groups in your class. Based on these data, would you change your answers to Question B, parts (3) and (4), above? Explain.

D. Kalvin's mom agrees to let him use a cup to decide his cereal each morning. On the first morning, the cup lands on its end. On the second morning, it lands on its side. Kalvin says, "This cup isn't any better than the coin. It lands on an end 50% of the time!" Do you agree or disagree with Kalvin? Explain.

ACE Homework starts on page 13.

1.3 One More Try

In the last two problems, you conducted experiments and found the chances of particular results. You represented these chances as fractions or percents. The mathematical word for chance is **probability**. A probability that you find by conducting an experiment and collecting data is called an **experimental probability**.

Suppose you toss a paper cup 50 times, and it lands on its side 31 times. Based on these data, the experimental probability that the cup will land on its side is $\frac{31}{50}$. Each toss of the cup is called a *trial*.

Use the ratio below to find experimental probability.

$$\frac{\text{number of favorable trials}}{\text{total number of trials}}$$

Favorable trials are the trials in which the desired result occurs. To find the probability of a cup landing on its side, count each time the cup lands on its side as a favorable trial.

You can write "the probability of the cup landing on its side" as P(side). In the experiment just described,

$$P(\text{side}) = \frac{\text{number of times cup landed on its side}}{\text{number of times cup was tossed}} = \frac{31}{50}.$$

Kalvin has come up with one more way to use probability to decide his breakfast cereal. This time, he tosses two coins.

- If the coins match, he gets to eat Cocoa Blast.

Match

Match

- If the coins do not match, he eats Health Nut Flakes.

No Match

Suppose his mother agrees to let him use this method. How many days in June do you think Kalvin will eat Cocoa Blast?

A. 1. Conduct an experiment by tossing a pair of coins 30 times. Keep track of the number of times the coins *match* and the number of times a *no-match* occurs.

 2. Based on your data, what is the experimental probability of getting a match? Of getting a no-match?

B. Combine your data with your classmates' data.

 1. Find the experimental probabilities for the combined data. Compare these probabilities with the probabilities in Question A.

 2. Based on the class data, do you think a match and a no-match have the same chance of occurring? Explain.

C. Think about the possible results when you toss two coins.

 1. In how many ways can a match occur?

 2. In how many ways can a no-match occur?

 3. Based on the number of ways each result can occur, do a match and a no-match have the same chance of occurring? Explain.

D. Kalvin's friend Asta suggests that he toss a thumbtack. If it lands on its side, he eats Cocoa Blast. If it lands on its head, he eats Health Nut Flakes. She says they must first experiment to find the probabilities involved. Asta does 11 tosses. Kalvin does 50 tosses. Here are the probabilities they find based on their experiments:

 Asta: $P(\text{heads}) = \frac{6}{11}$ Kalvin: $P(\text{heads}) = \frac{13}{50}$

 Which result do you think better predicts the thumbtack landing on its head when tossed? Explain.

ACE Homework starts on page 13.

1.4 Analyzing Events

Kalvin finds a coin near a railroad track. It looks flat and a little bent, so he guesses it has been run over by a train. He decides to use this unusual coin to choose his breakfast cereal during November. By the end of the month, he has had Health Nut Flakes only seven times. His mother is suspicious of the coin. She wonders if the coin is fair.

- Why do you think Kalvin's mother is suspicious of the coin?

- What do you think it means for a coin to be "fair"?

Kalvin's mother explains why she is suspicious. "With a fair coin, heads and tails are **equally likely.** This means that you have the same chance of getting heads as tails." Kalvin is not sure what his mother means by "equally likely," so she uses an example to help explain.

"Suppose each person in our family writes his or her name on a card and puts the card in a hat. If you mix up the cards and pull one out, each name is equally likely to be picked. But suppose I put my name in the hat ten times. Then, the names are not equally likely to be picked. My name has a greater chance of being chosen."

A. The table below lists several actions and possible results. In each case, decide whether the possible results are equally likely and explain. For actions 5–7, start by listing all the possible results.

Action	**Possible Results**
1. You toss an empty juice can.	The can lands on its side, the can lands upside down, or the can lands right side up.
2. A baby is born.	The baby is a boy or the baby is a girl.

3. A baby is born.	The baby is right-handed or the baby is left-handed.
4. The Pittsburgh Steelers play a football game.	The Steelers win, the Steelers lose, or the Steelers tie.
5. You roll a six-sided number cube.	_____
6. You guess an answer on a true/false test.	_____
7. In basketball, you attempt a free throw.	_____

B. For which of the actions in Question A did you find the results to be equally likely? Does this mean that the probability of each result is $\frac{1}{2}$ (or 50%)? Explain.

C. Describe an action for which the results are equally likely. Then, describe an action for which the results are *not* equally likely.

ACE Homework starts on page 13.

Applications

Go Online
PHSchool.com

For: Multiple-Choice Skills
Practice
Web Code: ama-7154

1. a. Miki tosses a coin 50 times and the coin shows heads 28 times. What fraction of the 50 tosses is heads? What percent is this?

   b. Suppose the coin is fair, and Miki tosses it 500 times. About how many times can she expect it to show heads? Explain your reasoning.

2. Suppose Kalvin tosses a coin to determine his breakfast cereal every day. He starts on his twelfth birthday and continues until his eighteenth birthday. About how many times would you expect him to eat Cocoa Blast cereal?

3. Kalvin tosses a coin five days in a row and gets tails every time. Do you think there is something wrong with the coin? How can you find out?

4. Len tosses a coin three times. The coin shows heads every time. What are the chances the coin shows tails on the next toss? Explain.

5. Is it possible to toss a coin 20 times and have it land heads up 20 times? Is this likely to happen? Explain.

6. Kalvin tosses a paper cup once each day for a year to determine his breakfast cereal. Use your results from Problem 1.2 to answer the following.

   a. How many times do you expect the cup to land on its side? On one of its ends?

   b. How many times a month do you expect Kalvin to eat Cocoa Blast? How many times a year? Explain.

7. Dawn tosses a pawn from her chess set five times. It lands on its base four times and on its side only once.

Andre tosses the same pawn 100 times. It lands on its base 28 times and on its side 72 times. Based on their data, if you toss the pawn one more time, is it more likely to land on its base or its side? Why?

8. Kalvin flips a small paper cup 50 times and a large paper cup 30 times. The table below displays the results of his experiments. Based on this data, should he use the small cup or the large cup to determine his breakfast each morning? Explain.

For: Help with Exercise 8
Web Code: ame-7108

Paper Cup Toss Results

Where Cup Lands	Small Paper Cup	Large Paper Cup
Side	39 times	22 times
One of Its Ends	11 times	8 times

9. Kalvin's sister Kyla finds yet another way for him to pick his breakfast. She places one blue marble and one red marble in each of two bags. She says that each morning he can choose one marble from each bag. If the marbles are the same color, he eats Cocoa Blast. If not, he eats Health Nut Flakes. Explain how selecting one marble from each of the two bags and tossing two coins are similar.

10. Brooke and Jake have to decide who will take out the garbage. Jake suggests they toss two coins. If at least one head comes up, Brooke takes out the garbage. If no heads come up, Jake takes out the garbage. Should Brooke agree to Jake's proposal? Why or why not?

For Exercises 11–15, decide whether the possible results are equally likely. Explain.

Action	Possible Results
11. Your phone rings at 9:00 P.M.	The caller is your best friend, the caller is a relative, or the caller is someone else.
12. You check the temperature in your area tomorrow morning.	The temperature is 30°F or higher, or the temperature is below 30°F.
13. You spin the pointer once.	The pointer lands on yellow, the pointer lands on red, or the pointer lands on blue.

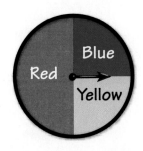

Action	Possible Results
14. You find out how many car accidents occurred in your city or town yesterday.	There were fewer than five accidents, there were exactly five accidents, or there were more than five accidents.
15. You choose a card from a standard deck of playing cards (with no jokers).	The card is a spade, the card is a heart, the card is a diamond, or the card is a club.

For Exercises 16 and 17, first list all the possible results for each action. Then, decide whether the results are equally likely.

16. You choose a block from a bag containing one red block, three blue blocks, and one green block.

17. You try to steal second base during a baseball game.

18. For parts (a)–(f), give an example of a result that would have a probability near the percent given.

    a. 0%   **b.** 25%   **c.** 50%

    d. 75%   **e.** 80%   **f.** 100%

Connections

19. Colby rolls a number cube several times. She records the result of each roll and organizes her data in the table below.

Number Cube Results

Number	Times the Number is Rolled
1	卌 l
2	卌 llll
3	卌 l
4	卌 lll
5	卌 卌 l
6	卌 卌

    a. What fraction of the rolls are 2's? What percent is this?

    b. What fraction of the rolls are odd numbers? What percent is this?

    c. What percent of the rolls is greater than 3?

    d. Suppose Colby rolls the number cube 100 times. About how many times can she expect to roll a 2? Explain.

    e. If Colby rolls the number cube 1,000 times, about how many times can she expect to roll an odd number? Explain.

20. For each pair of fractions, find a fraction between the two fractions.

    a. $\frac{1}{10}$ and $\frac{8}{25}$ **b.** $\frac{3}{8}$ and $\frac{11}{40}$

For Exercises 21–23, use the bar graph below.

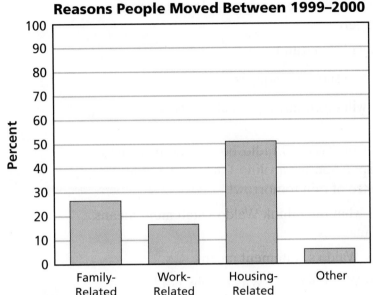

Reasons People Moved Between 1999–2000

SOURCE: U.S. Census Bureau

21. **Multiple Choice** Suppose 41,642 people moved. About how many of these people moved for family-related reasons?

   A. 28   **B.** 11,000   **C.** 21,000   **D.** 31,000

22. **Multiple Choice** About what fraction of the people represented in the chart moved for reasons other than work-related, housing-related, or family-related?

   F. $\frac{6}{10}$ **G.** $\frac{6}{100}$ **H.** $\frac{52}{100}$ **J.** $\frac{94}{100}$

23. **Multiple Choice** Suppose 41,642 people moved. About how many of these people moved for housing-related reasons?

   A. 52   **B.** 11,000   **C.** 21,000   **D.** 31,000

24. Suppose you write each factor of 42 on pieces of paper and put them in a bag. You shake the bag and then choose one piece of paper from the bag. Find the probability of choosing a factor that is

   a. an even number.

   b. a prime number.

25. Weather forecasters often use percents to give probabilities in their forecasts. For example, a forecaster might say that there is a 50% chance of rain tomorrow. For the forecasts below, change the fractional probabilities to percents.

   a. The probability that it will rain tomorrow is $\frac{2}{5}$.

   b. The probability that it will snow Monday is $\frac{3}{10}$.

   c. The probability that it will be cloudy this weekend is $\frac{3}{5}$.

26. Waldo, the meteorologist from WARM radio, boasts that he is the best weather predictor in Sunspot, South Carolina. On Monday, Waldo says, "There is only a 10% chance of rain tomorrow!"

   a. Ask at least two adults what they think Waldo's statement means. Write down their explanations.

   b. Explain what you think Waldo's statement means.

   c. If it rains on Tuesday, is Waldo wrong? Why or why not?

For Exercises 27–30, use this graph, which shows the average number of tornadoes per year in several states.

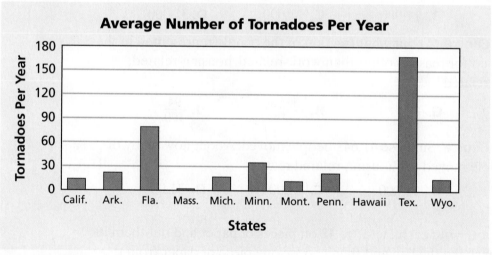

Source: National Oceanic and Atmospheric Administration

27. In an average year, is a tornado equally likely to occur in California as in Florida? Explain your reasoning.

28. In an average year, is a tornado equally likely to occur in Arkansas as in Pennsylvania?

29. In an average year, is a tornado equally likely to occur in Massachusetts as in Texas?

30. Based on these data, is a person living in Montana more likely to experience a tornado than a person living in Massachusetts? Explain.

Extensions

31. Monday is the first day Kalvin tosses a coin to determine his cereal. During the first five days, he has Cocoa Blast only twice. One possible pattern of Kalvin's coin tosses is shown.

Coin Toss Results

Monday	Tuesday	Wednesday	Thursday	Friday
H	H	T	T	T

Find every way Kalvin can toss the coin during the week and have Cocoa Blast cereal twice. Explain how you know that you found every possible way.

32. Yolanda watches a carnival game in which a paper cup is tossed. It costs $1 to play the game. If the cup lands upright, the player wins $5. The cup is tossed 50 times. It lands on its side 32 times, upside down 13 times, and upright 5 times.

   a. If Yolanda plays the game ten times, about how many times can she expect to win? How many times can she expect to lose?

   b. Do you expect her to have more or less money at the end of ten games? Why?

Mathematical Reflections 1

In this investigation, you conducted experiments with coins and paper cups. You used fractions and percents to express the chances, or probabilities, that certain results would occur. You also considered several actions and determined whether the possible results were equally likely. These questions will help you summarize what you have learned.

Think about your answers to these questions. Discuss your ideas with other students and your teacher. Then write a summary of your findings in your notebook.

1. How do you find the experimental probability that a particular result will occur? Why is it called the experimental probability?

2. In an experiment, are 30 trials as good as 500 trials to predict the chances of a result? Explain.

3. What does it mean for results to be equally likely?

Investigation 2

Experimental and Theoretical Probability

In the last investigation, you collected the results of many coin tosses. You found that the experimental probability of a coin landing on heads is $\frac{1}{2}$ (or very close to $\frac{1}{2}$).

The results of the coin-tossing experiment probably didn't surprise you. You already knew that the two possible results, heads and tails, are equally likely. In fact, you can find the probability of tossing heads by examining the possible results rather than by experimenting. There are two equally likely results. Because one of the results is heads, the probability of tossing heads is 1 of 2, or $\frac{1}{2}$.

The individual results of an action or event are called **outcomes.** The coin-tossing experiment had two outcomes, heads and tails. A probability calculated by examining outcomes, rather than by experimenting, is a **theoretical probability.**

When the outcomes of an action or event are equally likely, you can use the ratio below to find the theoretical probability.

$$\frac{\text{number of favorable outcomes}}{\text{number of possible outcomes}}$$

Favorable outcomes are the outcomes in which you are interested.

You can write the theoretical probability of tossing heads as $P(\text{heads})$. So,

$$P(\text{heads}) = \frac{\text{number of ways heads can occur}}{\text{number of outcomes}} = \frac{1}{2}.$$

In this investigation, you will explore some other situations in which probabilities are found both by experimenting and by analyzing the possible outcomes.

2.1 Predicting to Win

In the last 5 minutes of the *Gee Whiz Everyone Wins!* game show, all the members of the audience are called to the stage. They each choose a block at *random* from a bucket containing an unknown number of red, yellow, and blue blocks. Each block has the same size and shape. Before choosing, each contestant predicts the color of his or her block. If the prediction is correct, the contestant wins. After each selection, the block is put back into the bucket.

What do you think random *means? Suppose you are a member of the audience. Would you rather be called to the stage first or last? Why?*

Problem 2.1 Finding Theoretical Probabilities

A. 1. Play the block-guessing game with your class. Keep a record of the number of times a color is chosen. Play the game until you think you can predict the chances of each color being chosen.

2. Based on the data you collect during the game, find the experimental probabilities of choosing red, choosing yellow, and choosing blue.

B. 1. After you look in the bucket, find the fraction of the blocks that are red, the fraction that are yellow, and the fraction that are blue. These are the theoretical probabilities.

2. How do the theoretical probabilities compare to the experimental probabilities in Question A?

3. What is the sum of the theoretical probabilities in Question B, part (1)?

C. 1. Does each block have an equally likely chance of being chosen? Explain.

2. Does each color have an equally likely chance of being chosen? Explain.

D. Which person has the advantage—the first person to choose from the bucket or the last person? Explain.

ACE Homework starts on page 28.

Exploring Probabilities

In the next problem set, you will discover some interesting facts about probabilities.

Problem 2.2 Exploring Probabilities

A. A bag contains two yellow marbles, four blue marbles, and six red marbles. You choose a marble from the bag at random.

   1. What is the probability the marble is yellow? The probability it is blue? The probability it is red?

   2. What is the sum of the probabilities from part (1)?

   3. What color is the marble most likely to be?

   4. What is the probability the marble is *not* blue?

   5. What is the probability the marble is either red or yellow?

   6. What is the probability the marble is white?

   7. Mary says the probability the marble is blue is $\frac{12}{4}$. Anne says $\frac{12}{4}$ is impossible. Who is correct? Explain your reasoning.

B. Suppose the bag in Question A has twice as many marbles of each color. Do the probabilities change? Explain.

C. How many blue marbles do you add to the bag in Question A to have the probability of choosing a blue marble equal to $\frac{1}{2}$?

D. A bag contains several marbles. Each marble is either red, white, or blue. The probability of choosing a red marble is $\frac{1}{3}$, and the probability of choosing a white marble is $\frac{1}{6}$.

   1. What is the probability of choosing a blue marble? Explain.

   2. What is the least number of marbles that can be in the bag? Explain. Suppose the bag contains the least number of marbles. How many of each color does the bag contain?

   3. Can the bag contain 48 marbles? If so, how many of each color would it contain?

   4. Suppose the bag contains 8 red marbles and 4 white marbles. How many blue marbles does it contain?

ACE Homework starts on page 28.

2.3 Winning the Bonus Prize

To find the theoretical probability of a result, you need to count all the possible outcomes. In some situations, such as when you toss a coin or roll a number cube, it is easy to count the outcomes. In other situations, it can be difficult. One way to find (or count) all the possible outcomes is to make an organized list. Here is an organized list of all the possible outcomes of tossing two coins.

First Coin	Second Coin	Outcome
heads	heads	heads-heads
heads	tails	heads-tails
tails	heads	tails-heads
tails	tails	tails-tails

Another way to find all possible outcomes is to make a **tree diagram.** A tree diagram is a diagram that shows all the possible outcomes of an event. The steps for making a counting tree for tossing two coins are shown below.

Step 1   Label a starting point. Make a branch from the starting point for each possible result for the first coin.

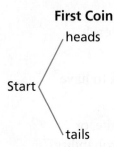

Step 2   Make a branch from each of the results for the first coin to show the possible results for the second coin.

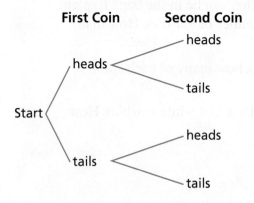

Step 3 When you follow the paths from left to right, you can find all the possible outcomes of tossing two coins. For example, the path shown in red represents the outcome heads-heads.

First Coin	Second Coin	Outcome
heads	heads	heads-heads
	tails	heads-tails
tails	heads	tails-heads
	tails	tails-tails

Both the organized list and the tree diagram show that there are four possible outcomes when you toss two coins. The outcomes are equally likely, so the probability of each outcome is $\frac{1}{4}$.

$$P(\text{heads, heads}) = \frac{1}{4}$$
$$P(\text{heads, tails}) = \frac{1}{4}$$
$$P(\text{tails, heads}) = \frac{1}{4}$$
$$P(\text{tails, tails}) = \frac{1}{4}$$

If you toss two coins, what is the probability that the coins will match?

What is the probability they won't match?

All the winners from the *Gee Whiz Everyone Wins!* game show have the opportunity to compete for a bonus prize. Each winner chooses one block from each of two bags. Both bags contain one red, one yellow, and one blue block. The contestant must predict which color she or he will choose from each of the two bags. If the prediction is correct, the contestant wins a $10,000 bonus prize!

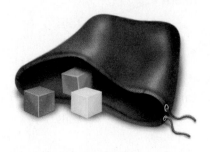

What are the contestant's chances of winning this game?

 **Using Strategies to Find Theoretical Problem 2.3 Probabilities**

A. 1. Conduct an experiment with 36 trials for the situation above. Record the pairs of colors that you choose.

2. Find the experimental probability of choosing each possible pair of colors.

3. If you combined your data with the data collected by your classmates, would your answer to part (1) change? Explain.

B. 1. List all the possible pairs that can be chosen. Are these outcomes equally likely? Explain your reasoning.

2. Find the theoretical probability of choosing each pair of blocks.

3. Does a contestant have a chance to win the bonus prize? Is it likely a contestant will win the bonus prize? Explain.

4. If you play this game 18 times, about how many times do you expect to win?

C. How do the theoretical probabilities compare with your experimental probabilities? Explain any differences.

ACE Homework starts on page 28.

2.4 Pondering Possible and Probable

Santo and Tevy are playing a coin-tossing game. To play the game, they take turns tossing three coins. If all three coins match, Santo wins. Otherwise, Tevy wins. Both players have won the game several times, but Tevy seems to be winning more often. Santo thinks the game is unfair.

Do you think this game is fair?

Problem 2.4 Pondering Possible and Probable

A. 1. How many possible outcomes are there when you toss three coins? Show all your work. Are the outcomes equally likely?

2. What is the theoretical probability that the three coins will match?

3. What is the theoretical probability that exactly two coins will match?

4. Is this a fair game? Explain your reasoning.

B. If you tossed three coins 24 times, how many times would you expect two coins to match?

C. Santo said, "It is *possible* to toss three matching coins." Tevy replied, "Yes, but is it *probable*?" What do you think each boy meant?

ACE Homework starts on page 28.

Applications

1. A bucket contains one green block, one red block, and two yellow blocks. You choose one block from the bucket.

   a. Find the theoretical probability that you will choose each color.

   $P(\text{green}) = \blacksquare$ $\qquad$ $P(\text{yellow}) = \blacksquare$ $\qquad$ $P(\text{red}) = \blacksquare$

   b. Find the sum of the probabilities in part (a).

   c. What is the probability that you will *not* choose a red block? Explain how you found your answer.

   d. What is the sum of the probability of choosing a red block and the probability of *not* choosing a red block?

2. A bubble-gum machine contains 25 gumballs. There are 12 green, 6 purple, 2 orange, and 5 yellow gumballs.

   a. Find each theoretical probability.

   $P(\text{green}) = \blacksquare$ $\qquad$ $P(\text{purple}) = \blacksquare$

   $P(\text{orange}) = \blacksquare$ $\qquad$ $P(\text{yellow}) = \blacksquare$

   b. Find the sum.

   $P(\text{green}) + P(\text{purple}) + P(\text{orange}) + P(\text{yellow}) = \blacksquare$

   c. Write each of the probabilities in part (a) as a percent.

   $P(\text{green}) = \blacksquare$ $\qquad$ $P(\text{purple}) = \blacksquare$

   $P(\text{orange}) = \blacksquare$ $\qquad$ $P(\text{yellow}) = \blacksquare$

   d. What is the sum of all the probabilities as a percent?

   e. What do you think the sum of the probabilities for all the possible outcomes must be for any situation? Explain.

3. A bag contains two white blocks, one red block, and three purple blocks. You choose one block from the bag.

   a. Find each probability.

   $P(\text{white}) = $ 　　　$P(\text{red}) = $ ■　　　$P(\text{purple}) = $ ■

   b. What is the probability of *not* choosing a white block? Explain how you found your answer.

   c. Suppose the number of blocks of each color is doubled. What happens to the probability of choosing each color?

   d. Suppose you add two more blocks of each color. What happens to the probability of choosing each color?

   e. How many blocks of which colors should you add to the original bag to make the probability of choosing a red block equal to $\frac{1}{2}$?

4. A bag contains exactly three blue blocks. You choose a block at random. Find each probability.

   a. $P(\text{blue})$　　　**b.** $P(not \text{ blue})$　　　**c.** $P(\text{yellow})$

For: Multiple-Choice Skills Practice
Web Code: ama-7254

5. A bag contains several marbles. Some are red, some are white, and some are blue. You count the marbles and find the theoretical probability of choosing a red marble is $\frac{1}{5}$. You also find the theoretical probability of choosing a white marble is $\frac{3}{10}$.

   a. What is the least number of marbles that can be in the bag?

   b. Can the bag contain 60 marbles? If so, how many of each color does it contain?

   c. If the bag contains 4 red marbles and 6 white marbles, how many blue marbles does it contain?

   d. How can you find the probability of choosing a blue marble?

6. Decide whether each statement is true or false. Justify your answers.

   a. The probability of an outcome can be 0.

   b. The probability of an outcome can be 1.

   c. The probability of an outcome can be greater than 1.

7. Melissa is designing a birthday card for her sister. She has a blue, a yellow, a pink, and a green sheet of paper. She also has a black, a red, and a purple marker. Suppose Melissa chooses one sheet of paper and one marker at random.

   a. Make a tree diagram to find all the possible color combinations.

   b. What is the probability that Melissa chooses pink paper and a red marker?

   c. What is the probability that Melissa chooses blue paper? What is the probability she does *not* choose blue paper?

   d. What is the probability that she chooses a purple marker?

8. Lunch at Casimer Middle School consists of a sandwich, a vegetable, and a fruit. Today there is an equal number of each type of sandwich, vegetable, and fruit. The students don't know what lunch they will get. Sol's favorite lunch is a chicken sandwich, carrots, and a banana.

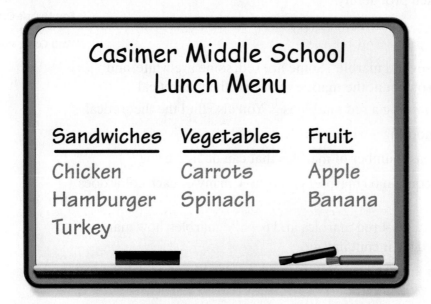

   a. Make a tree diagram to determine how many different lunches are possible. List all the possible outcomes.

   b. What is the probability that Sol gets his favorite lunch? Explain your reasoning.

   c. What is the probability that Sol gets at least one of his favorite lunch items? Explain.

9. Suppose you spin the pointer of the spinner at the right once and roll the number cube. (The numbers on the cube are 1, 2, 3, 4, 5, and 6.)

  a. Make a tree diagram of the possible outcomes of a spin of the pointer and a roll of the number cube.

  b. What is the probability that you get a 2 on both the spinner and the number cube? Explain your reasoning.

  c. What is the probability that you get a factor of 2 on both the spinner and the number cube?

  d. What is the probability that you get a multiple of 2 on both the number cube and the spinner?

10. Patricia and Jean design a coin-tossing game. Patricia suggests tossing three coins. Jean says they can toss one coin three times. Are the outcomes different for the two situations? Explain.

11. Pietro and Eva are playing a game in which they toss a coin three times. Eva gets a point if *no* two consecutive toss results match (as in H-T-H). Pietro gets a point if exactly two consecutive toss results match (as in H-H-T). The first player to get 10 points wins. Is this a fair game? Explain. If it is not a fair game, change the rules to make it fair.

12. Silvia and Juanita are designing a game. In the game, you toss two number cubes and consider whether the sum of the two numbers is odd or even. They make a tree diagram of possible outcomes.

For: Help with Exercise 12
Web Code: ame-7212

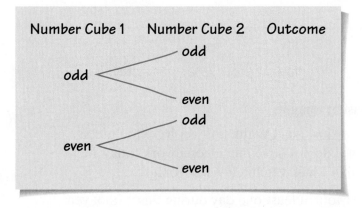

  a. List all the outcomes.

  b. Design rules for a two-player game that is fair.

  c. Design rules for a two-player game that is not fair.

  d. How is this situation similar to tossing two coins and seeing if the coins match or don't match?

Connections

13. Find numbers that make each sentence true.

   a. $\frac{1}{8} = \frac{\blacksquare}{32} = \frac{5}{\blacksquare}$ **b.** $\frac{3}{7} = \frac{\blacksquare}{21} = \frac{6}{\blacksquare}$ **c.** $\frac{6}{20} = \frac{\blacksquare}{5} = \frac{12}{\blacksquare}$

14. Which of the following sums is equal to 1?

   a. $\frac{1}{6} + \frac{3}{6} + \frac{2}{6}$ **b.** $\frac{4}{18} + \frac{1}{9} + \frac{2}{3}$ **c.** $\frac{1}{5} + \frac{1}{3} + \frac{1}{5}$

15. From Question 14, choose a sum equal to 1. Describe a situation whose events have a theoretical probability that can be represented by the sum.

16. Kara and Bly both perform the same experiment in math class. Kara gets a probability of $\frac{125}{300}$ and Bly gets a probability of $\frac{108}{320}$.

   a. Whose experimental probability is closer to the theoretical probability of $\frac{1}{3}$? Explain your reasoning.

   b. Give two possible experiments that Kara and Bly can do that have a theoretical probability of $\frac{1}{3}$.

For Exercises 17–24, estimate the probability that the given event occurs. Any probability must be between 0 and 1 (or 0% and 100%). If an event is impossible, the probability it will occur is 0, or 0%. If an event is certain to happen, the probability it will occur is 1, or 100%.

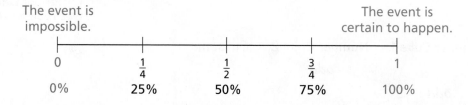

Sample   You watch television tonight.

   I watch some television every night, unless I have too much homework. So far, I do not have much homework today. I am about 95% sure that I will watch television tonight.

17. You are absent from school at least one day during this school year.

18. You have pizza for lunch one day this week.

19. It snows on July 4 this year in Mexico.

20. You get all the problems on your next math test correct.

21. The next baby born in your local hospital is a girl.

22. The sun sets tonight.

23. You win a game by tossing four coins. The result is all heads.

24. You toss a coin and get 100 tails in a row.

Multiple Choice For Exercises 25–28, choose the fraction closest to the given decimal.

25. 0.39

    A. $\frac{1}{2}$ **B.** $\frac{1}{4}$ **C.** $\frac{1}{8}$ **D.** $\frac{1}{10}$

26. 0.125

    F. $\frac{1}{2}$ **G.** $\frac{1}{4}$ **H.** $\frac{1}{8}$ **J.** $\frac{1}{10}$

27. 0.195

    A. $\frac{1}{2}$ **B.** $\frac{1}{4}$ **C.** $\frac{1}{8}$ **D.** $\frac{1}{10}$

28. 0.24

    F. $\frac{1}{2}$ **G.** $\frac{1}{4}$ **H.** $\frac{1}{8}$ **J.** $\frac{1}{10}$

29. Koto's class makes the line plot shown below. Each mark represents the first letter of the name of a student in her class.

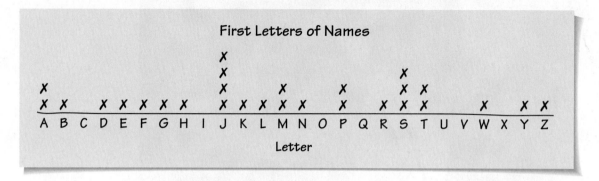

First Letters of Names

Letter

Suppose you choose a student at random from Koto's Class.

a. What is the probability that the student's name begins with J?

b. What is the probability that the student's name begins with a letter after F and before T in the alphabet?

c. What is the probability that you choose Koto?

d. Suppose two new students, Melvin and Tara, join the class. You now choose a student at random from the class. What is the probability that the student's name begins with J?

30. A bag contains red, white, blue, and green marbles. The probability of choosing a red marble is $\frac{1}{7}$. The probability of choosing a green marble is $\frac{1}{2}$. The probability of choosing a white marble is half the probability of choosing a red one. You want to find the number of marbles in the bag.

a. Why do you need to know how to multiply and add fractions to proceed?

b. Why do you need to know about multiples of whole numbers to proceed?

c. Can there be seven marbles in the bag? Explain.

31. Write the following as one fraction.

a. $\frac{1}{2}$ of $\frac{1}{7}$

b. $\frac{1}{7} + \frac{1}{14} + \frac{1}{2}$

32. Karen and Mia play games with coins and number cubes. No matter which game they play, Karen loses more often than Mia. Karen is not sure if she just has bad luck or if the games are unfair. The games are described in this table. Review the game rules and complete the table.

Games	Is It Possible for Karen to Win?	Is It Likely Karen Will Win?	Is the Game Fair or Unfair?
Game 1 Roll a number cube. • Karen scores a point if the roll is even. • Mia scores a point if the roll is odd.			
Game 2 Roll a number cube. • Karen scores a point if the roll is a multiple of 4. • Mia scores a point if the roll is a multiple of 3.			
Game 3 Toss two coins. • Karen scores a point if the coins match. • Mia scores a point if the coins do not match.			
Game 4 Roll two number cubes. • Karen scores a point if the number cubes match. • Mia scores a point if the number cubes do not match.			
Game 5 Roll two number cubes. • Karen scores a point if the product of the two numbers is 7. • Mia scores a point if the sum of the two numbers is 7.			

33. Karen and Mia invent another game. They roll a number cube twice and read the two digits shown as a two-digit number. So if Karen gets a 6 and then a 2, she has 62.

   a. What is the least number possible?

   b. What is the greatest number possible?

   c. Are all numbers equally likely?

   d. Suppose Karen wins on any prime number and Mia wins on any multiple of 4. Explain how to decide who is more likely to win.

Extensions

34. Place 12 objects of the same size and shape in a bag such as blocks or marbles. Use three or four different solid colors.

   a. Describe the contents of your bag.

   b. Determine the theoretical probability of choosing each color by examining the bag's contents.

   c. Conduct an experiment to determine the experimental probability of choosing each color. Describe your experiment and record your results.

   d. How do the two types of probability compare?

35. Suppose you are a contestant on the *Gee Whiz Everyone Wins!* game show in Problem 2.3. You win a mountain bike, a CD player, a vacation to Hawaii, and a one-year membership to an amusement park. You play the bonus round and lose. Then the host makes this offer:

> You can choose from the two bags again. If the two colors match, you win $5,000. If the two colors do not match, you do not get the $5,000 and you return all the prizes.

Would you accept this offer? Explain.

36. Suppose you compete for the bonus prize on the *Gee Whiz Everyone Wins!* game in Problem 2.3. You choose one block from each of two bags. Each bag contains one red, one yellow, and one blue block.

  a. Make a tree diagram to show all the possible outcomes.

  b. What is the probability that you choose two blocks that are *not* blue?

  c. Jason made the tree diagram shown below to find the probability of choosing two blocks that are *not* blue. Using his tree, what probability do you think Jason got?

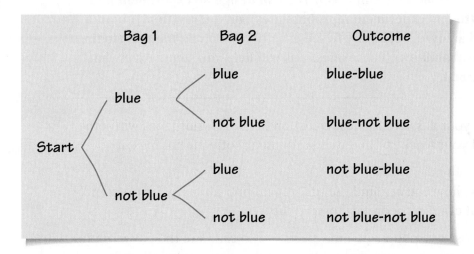

  d. Does your answer in part (b) match Jason's? If not, why do you think Jason gets a different answer?

37. Suppose you toss four coins.

  a. List all the possible outcomes.

  b. What is the probability of each outcome?

  c. Design a game for two players that involves tossing four coins. What is the probability that each player wins? Is one player more likely to win than the other player?

Mathematical Reflections 2

In this investigation, you explored two ways to get information about the probability that something will occur. You can design an experiment and collect data (to find experimental probabilities), or you can think about a situation and analyze it carefully to see exactly what might happen (to find theoretical probabilities). These questions will help you summarize what you have learned.

Think about your answers to these questions. Discuss your ideas with other students and your teacher. Then write a summary of your findings in your notebook.

1. Describe how you can find the theoretical probability of an outcome. Why is it called a theoretical probability?

2. **a.** Suppose two people do an experiment to estimate the probability that an outcome occurs. Will they get the same probabilities? Explain.

   b. Suppose two people analyze a situation to find the theoretical probability that an outcome occurs. Will they get the same probabilities? Explain.

   c. One person uses an experiment to estimate the probability that an outcome occurs. Another person analyzes the situation to find the theoretical probability that the outcome can occur. Will they get the same probabilities? Explain.

Investigation **3**

Making Decisions With Probability

Spring vacation has arrived! Kalvin thinks he can stay up until 11:00 P.M. every night. His father thinks Kalvin will have more energy for his activities (such as roller blading, cleaning out the garage, or washing dishes) during his vacation if he goes to bed at 9:00 P.M.

3.1 Designing a Spinner

Getting Ready for Problem 3.1

Kalvin makes the three spinners shown below. Kalvin hopes that his father lets him use one of the spinners to determine his bedtime.

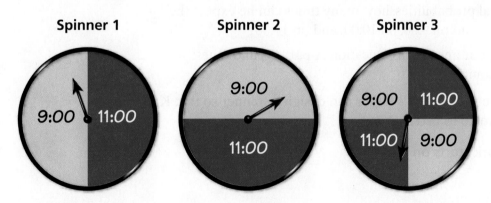

- Which spinner gives Kalvin the best chance of going to bed at 11:00? Explain.

Kalvin decides to design a spinner that lands on 11:00 the most. To convince his father to use this spinner, Kalvin puts three 9:00 spaces, two 10:00 spaces, and one 11:00 space on the spinner. However, he uses the biggest space for 11:00. Kalvin hopes the pointer lands on that space the most.

Which time do you think is most likely to occur?

Problem 3.1 Finding Probabilities With a Spinner

A. 1. Find the experimental probability that the pointer lands on 9:00, on 10:00, and on 11:00.

   2. After how many spins did you decide to stop spinning? Why?

   3. Suppose Kalvin spins the pointer 64 times. Based on your experiment, how many times can he expect the pointer to land on 9:00, on 10:00, and on 11:00?

B. 1. What is the theoretical probability that the pointer lands on 9:00, on 10:00, and on 11:00? Explain.

   2. Suppose Kalvin spins the pointer 64 times. Based on your theoretical probabilities, how many times can he expect the pointer to land on 9:00, on 10:00, and on 11:00?

   3. How do your answers to Question A part (3) and Question B part (2) compare?

C. Describe one way Kalvin's father can design a spinner so that Kalvin is most likely to go to bed at 9:00.

ACE Homework starts on page 44.

Kalvin begins to think that probability is a good way to make decisions. One day at school, Kalvin's teacher, Ms. Miller, has to decide which student to send to the office to get an important message. Billie, Evo, and Carla volunteer. Kalvin suggests they design a quick experiment to choose the student fairly.

Getting Ready for Problem

Which of these items can Kalvin's class use to choose a messenger? How can they make the decision fair?

- a coin
- a six-sided number cube
- colored cubes
- playing cards
- a spinner

Two suggestions for making a decision are shown in each question. Decide whether the suggestions are fair ways to make the decision. Explain your reasoning.

A. At lunch, Kalvin and his friends discuss whether to play kickball, soccer, baseball, or dodgeball. Ethan and Ava each have a suggestion.

Ethan: We can make a spinner that looks like this:

Ava: We can roll a number cube. If it lands on 1, we play kickball. A roll of 2 means soccer, 3 means baseball, 4 means dodgeball, and we can roll again if it's 5 or 6.

B. The group decides to play baseball. Tony and Meda are the team captains. Now they must decide who bats first.

Tony: We can roll a number cube. If the number is a multiple of three, my team bats first. Otherwise, Meda's team bats first.

Meda: Yes, let's roll a number cube, but my team bats first if the number is even and Tony's team bats first if it's odd.

C. There are 60 sixth-grade students at Kalvin's school. The students need to choose someone to wear the mascot costume on field day.

Huey: We can give everyone a number from 1 to 60. Then, we can roll 10 number cubes and add the results. The person whose number is equal to the sum wears the costume.

Sal: That doesn't seem fair. Everyone should have a number from 0 to 59. In one bag, we can have blocks numbered 0 to 5. In another bag, we can have blocks numbered 0 to 9. We can select one block from the first bag to represent the tens digit and one block from the second bag to represent the ones digit.

ACE Homework starts on page 44.

3.3 Scratching Spots

Have you ever tried to win a contest? Probability can often help you figure out your chances of winning.

Tawanda's Toys is having a contest. Any customer who spends at least $10 receives a scratch-off prize card.

TAWANDA'S TOYS
Prize Card

Sky Knight | | Sky Knight | |
A B C D E

Scratch off only two spots

- Each card has five gold spots that reveal the names of video games when you scratch them.
- Exactly two spots match on each card.
- A customer may scratch off only two spots on a card.
- If the spots match, the customer wins that video game.

It can be difficult to get enough prize cards to conduct an experiment. So, you can design a related experiment to help you find the probability of each outcome. A model used to find experimental probabilities is a **simulation.**

One way you can simulate the scratch-off card is by using five playing cards. First, make sure that exactly two out of the five cards match. Place the cards facedown on a table. While your eyes are closed, have a friend mix up the cards. Then open your eyes and choose two cards. If the cards match, you win. Otherwise, you lose.

Can you think of another way to simulate the scratch-off cards?

Problem 3.3 Using a Simulation

A. Use the card simulation above to find the probability of winning.

B. Examine the different ways you can scratch off two spots. Find the theoretical probability of winning with one prize card.

C. Suppose you have 100 prize cards from Tawanda.

    1. How many video games can you expect to win?

    2. How much money do you need to get 100 cards?

D. Tawanda thinks she may lose money with this promotion. The video games she gives away cost her $15 each. Will Tawanda lose money? Why or why not?

ACE Homework starts on page 44.

Applications

1. For parts (a)–(g), use a spinner similar to the one below.

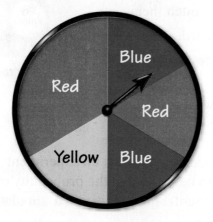

a. Use a paper clip or bobby pin as a pointer. Spin the pointer 30 times. What fraction of your spins land on red? What fraction land on blue? On yellow?

b. Use an angle ruler or another method to examine the spinner. What fraction of the spinner is red? What fraction is blue? What fraction is yellow? Explain.

c. Compare your answers to parts (a) and (b). Do you expect these answers to be the same? Why or why not?

d. Suppose you spin 300 times instead of 30 times. Do you expect your answers to become closer to or further from the fractions you found in part (b)? Explain your reasoning.

e. When you spin, is it equally likely that the pointer will land on red, on blue, or on yellow? Explain.

f. Suppose you use the spinner to play a game with a friend. Your friend scores a point every time the pointer lands on red. To make the game fair, for what outcomes should you score a point? Explain.

g. Suppose you use this spinner to play a three-person game. Player A scores if the pointer lands on yellow. Player B scores if the pointer lands on red. Player C scores if the pointer lands on blue. How can you assign points so that the game is fair?

2. The cooks at Kyla's school make the spinners below to help them choose the lunch menu. They let the students take turns spinning. For parts (a)–(c), decide which spinner you would choose. Explain your reasoning.

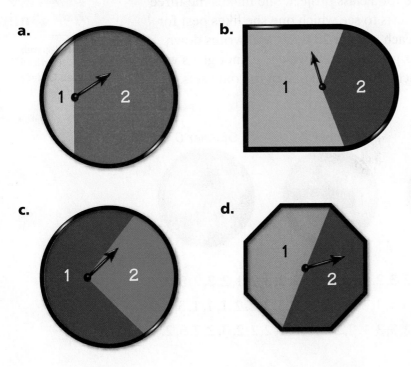

Spinner A   **Spinner B**

a. Your favorite lunch is pizza.

b. Your favorite lunch is lasagna.

c. Your favorite lunch is hot dogs.

3. When you use each of the spinners below, the two possible outcomes are landing on 1 and landing on 2. Are the outcomes equally likely? If not, which outcome has a greater theoretical probability? Explain.

a.

b.

c.

d.

4. A science club hosts a carnival to raise money. A game called Making Purple at the carnival involves using both of the spinners shown. If the player gets red on spinner A and blue on spinner B, the player wins because mixing red and blue makes purple.

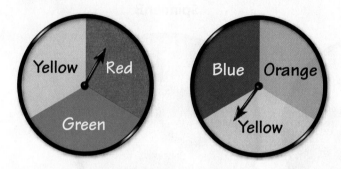

a. List the outcomes that are possible when you spin both pointers. Are these outcomes equally likely? Explain your reasoning.

b. What is the theoretical probability that a player "makes purple"? Explain.

c. If 100 people play the Making Purple game, how many people do you expect to win?

d. The club charges $1 per turn. A player who makes purple wins $5. Suppose 100 people play. How much money do you expect the club to make?

5. Molly designs a game for a class project. She makes the three spinners shown. She tests to see which one she likes best for her game. She spins each pointer 20 times and writes down her results, but she forgets to record which spinner gives which set of data. Match each spinner with one of the data sets. Explain your answer.

Homework Help Online
PHSchool.com

For: Help with Exercise 5
Web Code: ame-7305

First data set: 1, 2, 3, 2, 1, 1, 2, 1, 2, 2, 2, 3, 2, 1, 2, 2, 2, 3, 2, 2

Second data set: 2, 3, 1, 1, 3, 3, 3, 1, 1, 2, 3, 2, 2, 2, 1, 1, 1, 3, 3, 3

Third data set: 1, 2, 3, 3, 1, 2, 2, 2, 3, 2, 1, 2, 2, 2, 3, 2, 2, 3, 2, 1

6. Three people play a game on each spinner in Exercise 5. Player 1 scores a point if the pointer lands on 1. Player 2 scores a point if the pointer lands on 2. Player 3 scores a point if the pointer lands on 3.

   a. On which spinner(s) is the game a fair game? Why?

   b. Choose a spinner that you think doesn't make a fair game. Then, change the scoring rules to make the game fair by assigning different points for landing on the different numbers. Explain why your point system works.

7. a. Make a spinner and a set of rules for a fair two-person game. Explain why your game is fair.

   b. Make a spinner and a set of rules for a two-person game that is *not* fair. Explain why your game is not fair.

8. Multiple Choice Jake, Carl, and John try to decide what to do after school. Jake thinks they should play video games. Carl wants to see a movie. John thinks they should ride their bikes. Which choice is a fair way to decide?

   A. Let's toss three coins. If they all match, we play video games. If there are exactly two heads, we see a movie. If there are exactly two tails, we ride our bikes.

   B. Let's roll a number cube. If we roll a 1 or 2, we play video games. If we roll a 3 or 4, we go to the movies. Otherwise, we ride bikes.

   C. Let's use this spinner.

   D. None of these is fair.

9. Multiple Choice The Millers can't decide whether to eat pizza or burritos for dinner.

   F. Let's roll a number cube and toss a coin. If the number cube is even and the coin is heads, then we eat pizza. If the number cube is odd and the coin is tails, then we eat burritos. If neither happens, we try again.

   G. Let's toss a coin. If it is heads, we eat pizza. If it is tails, we do *not* eat burritos.

   H. Each of these is fair.

   J. Neither of these is fair.

10. Tawanda wants fewer winners for her scratch-off cards. She orders new cards with six spots. Two of the spots on each card match. What is the probability that a person who plays once will win on the card?

Connections

For Exercises 11–16, complete the following table. Write each probability as a fraction, decimal, or percent.

Probabilities

	Fraction	Decimal	Percent
11.	$\frac{1}{4}$	■	25%
12.	$\frac{1}{8}$	■	■
13.	■	■	$33\frac{1}{3}$%
14.	■	■	10%
15.	■	0.1666…	■
16.	■	0.05	■

Go Online
PHSchool.com

For: Multiple-Choice Skills Practice
Web Code: ama-7354

17. The cooks at Kyla's school let students make spinners to determine the lunch menu.

a. Make a spinner for which the chance of lasagna is 25%, the chance of a hamburger is $16\frac{2}{3}$% and the chance of a tuna sandwich is $33\frac{1}{3}$%. The last choice is hot dogs.

b. What is the chance of hot dogs?

18. Three of the following situations have the same probability of getting "spinach." What is the probability for these three situations?

a. Spin the pointer on this spinner once.

b. Roll a number cube once. You get "spinach" when you roll a multiple of 3.

c. Toss two coins. You get "spinach" with one head and one tail.

d. Roll a number cube once. You get "spinach" when you roll a 5 or 6.

For Exercises 19–21, rewrite each pair of numbers. Insert <, >, or = to make a true statement.

19. $\dfrac{1}{3\frac{1}{2}}$ ■ $\dfrac{1}{4}$

20. $\dfrac{3.5}{7}$ ■ $\dfrac{1}{2}$

21. 0.30 ■ $\dfrac{1}{3}$

22. Use the table of historic baseball statistics to answer parts (a)–(d).

Batting Averages

Player	At Bats	Hits
Nomar Garciaparra	4,089	1,317
Derek Jeter	5,457	1,715
Jackie Robinson	4,877	1,518

a. What percent of Nomar Garciaparra's at bats resulted in a hit?

b. What percent of Derek Jeter's at bats resulted in a hit?

c. What percent of Jackie Robinson's at bats resulted in a hit?

d. Suppose each player comes to bat today with the same skill his record shows. Who has the greatest chance of getting a hit? Explain.

For Exercises 23–25, rewrite each fraction as an equivalent fraction using a denominator of 10 or 100. Then, write a decimal number for each fraction.

23. $\dfrac{3}{20}$

24. $\dfrac{2}{5}$

25. $\dfrac{11}{25}$

26. A-1 Trucks used this graph to show that their trucks last longer than other trucks.

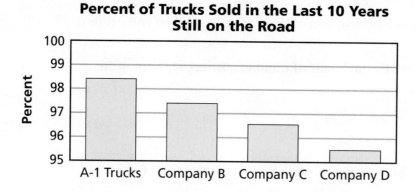

Percent of Trucks Sold in the Last 10 Years Still on the Road

a. The bar for A-1 Trucks is about six times the height of Company D's bar. Does this mean that the chance of one of A-1's trucks lasting ten years is about six times as great as the chance of one of Company D's trucks lasting ten years? Explain.

b. If you wanted to buy a truck, would this graph convince you to buy a truck from A-1 Trucks? Why or why not?

27. The Federal Trade Commission (FTC) makes rules for businesses that buy and sell things. One rule states that an advertisement may be found unlawful if it can deceive a person.

To decide whether an ad is deceptive, the FTC considers the "general impression" it makes on a "reasonable person." Even if every statement is true, the ad is deceptive if it gives an overall false impression. For example, cows can't appear in margarine ads because it gives the false impression that margarine is a dairy product.

a. Tawanda places this ad in a newspaper. Qualifying customers receive a prize card like the ones described in the introduction to Problem 3.3. According to the FTC, is it legal for Tawanda to say, "Every card is a winner"? Explain.

TAWANDA'S TOYS is having a HUGE CONTEST!

Every customer who spends at least $10 receives a prize card! EVERY CARD IS A WINNER!

b. Design a better ad that excites people but does not lead some to think they will win every time.

c. Find an ad that might be deceptive. Why do you think it is deceptive? What proof could the company provide to change your mind?

28. A sugarless gum company used to have an advertisement that stated:

Four out of five dentists surveyed recommend sugarless gum for their patients who chew gum.

Do you think this statement means that 80% of dentists believe their patients should chew sugarless gum? Explain your reasoning.

29. Portland Middle School students make a flag as shown. After it hangs outside for a month, it looks dirty so they examine it. They find more bugs stuck on the yellow part than on the green part. Cheng says bugs are more attracted to yellow than to green.

a. Students in a science class test Cheng's conjecture with a design the same as the flag design. Suppose Cheng's conjecture is true. What is the chance that a bug landing at random on the flag hits the yellow part?

b. Suppose 13 bugs land on the yellow part and 12 bugs land on the green part. Is this evidence that supports Cheng's conjecture?

Did You Know?

Pi can be estimated using probability. Take a square that is 2 units on each side and inscribe a circle inside which has a radius of 1 unit.

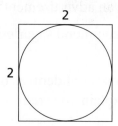

The area of the square is 4 square units and the area of the circle is $\pi \cdot r^2$ or $\pi \cdot 1^2 = \pi$ square units.

The ratio of the area of the circle to the area of the square is $\frac{\pi}{4}$. Ratios can be written as fractions.

Computer simulations can be done where the computer randomly places a dot inside the square. A computer can place 10,000 dots inside the square in less than 30 seconds.

This ratio $\dfrac{\text{number of dots inside the circle}}{\text{total number of dots inside the square}}$ should approximate $\frac{\pi}{4}$.

So, π should equal four times the ratio $\dfrac{\text{number of dots inside the circle}}{\text{total number of dots inside the square}}$.

---

30. Charlie runs three computer simulations such as the one described in the Did You Know? He records data for the three trials.

a. Complete the table below of Charlie's data.

Pi Estimations

Trial	Dots Inside the Circle	Dots Inside the Square	Ratio: $\dfrac{\text{Dots in Circle}}{\text{Dots in Square}}$
1	388	500	▦
2	352	450	▦
3	373	475	▦

b. Decide which trial is closest to an approximation for $\frac{\pi}{4}$. Explain your reasoning.

Extensions

31. Design a spinner with five regions so that the chances of landing in each region are equally likely. Give the number of degrees in the central angle of each region.

32. Design a spinner with five regions so that the chances of landing in one region are twice the chances of landing in each of the other four regions. Give the number of degrees in the central angle of each region.

For Exercises 33–35, design a contest for each company. Each contest should help the company attract customers, but not make the company lose money. Explain the rules, including any requirements for entering the contest.

33. The manager of a small clothing store wants to design a contest in which 1 of every 30 players wins a prize.

34. The director of operations for a chain of supermarkets wants to design a contest with a $100,000 grand prize!

35. An auto store sells new and used cars. The owner wants to have a contest with lots of winners and big prizes. She wants about one of every ten players to win a $500 prize.

Connections

Extensions

Mathematical Reflections 3

In this investigation, you used spinners and cubes in probability situations. You used both experimental and theoretical probabilities to help you make decisions. These questions will help you summarize what you learned.

Think about your answers to these questions. Discuss your ideas with other students and your teacher. Then write a summary of your findings in your notebook.

1. Describe a situation in which you and a friend can use probability to make a decision. Can the probabilities of the outcomes be determined both experimentally and theoretically? Why or why not?

2. Describe a situation in which it is difficult or impossible to find the theoretical probabilities of the outcomes.

3. Explain what it means for a probability situation to be fair.

Probability, Genetics, and Games

Have you ever heard of genes? (We don't mean the kind you wear!) What color are your eyes? Can you curl your tongue? Your birth parents gave you a unique set of genes that determine such things.

Scientists who study traits such as eye and hair color are called geneticists (juh NET uh sists). Geneticists use probability to predict certain traits in children based on traits in their parents or relatives.

4.1 Genetic Traits

Look at the earlobe of a classmate. Is it attached or does it dangle freely? The type of earlobe you have is a trait determined by your genes. Here is a description of four genetic traits:

- *Attached earlobe*: An earlobe is attached if its lowest point is attached directly to the head, as shown below.
- *Dimple*: A dimple is a small indentation, usually near the mouth.
- *Straight hair*: Straight hair has no waves or curls. (Note: Consider only how a person's hair is naturally.)
- *Widow's peak*: A widow's peak is a V-shaped hairline, as shown below.

Attached earlobe

Unattached earlobe

Widow's peak

No widow's peak

Problem 4.1 Applying Experimental Probability

The table lists four genetic traits.

Classroom Genetics Survey

Trait	Yes	No	Total
Attached Earlobes	■	■	■
Dimples	■	■	■
Straight Hair	■	■	■
Widow's Peak	■	■	■

A. Copy the table. Find the number of people in your class who have each trait and record the results in your table.

B. Use your table to complete parts (1)–(4).

  1. For each trait, find the probability that a person chosen at random has the trait.

  2. What is the probability that a person chosen at random does *not* have straight hair?

  3. How many students in your school do you expect to have attached earlobes?

  4. How many students in your school do you expect to have a widow's peak?

C. Below are the results of a study of students from around the country.

U.S. Genetics Survey

Trait	Yes	No
Attached Earlobes	443	1,080
Dimples	445	1,066
Straight Hair	623	666
Widow's Peak	734	777

  1. Find the probability that a person chosen at random has each trait.

  2. How do the probabilities in Question B compare to the probabilities from the national data?

ACE Homework starts on page 62.

4.2 Tracing Traits

In the last problem, you looked at experimental probabilities for certain traits. In some cases, you can determine the probability that a child will have a trait based on his or her parents' genes.

Geneticists use the word *allele* (uh LEEL) for one of a pair of genes that determines a trait. For example, you have two alleles that determine whether your earlobes are attached. You receive one of these alleles from your birth mother and one from your birth father. Of course, each parent has two earlobe alleles.

Let's use *e* to represent the allele for attached earlobes. Let *E* represent the allele for nonattached earlobes. If you receive an *e* allele from each parent, your earlobe alleles will be *ee*, and you will have attached earlobes. If you receive an *E* allele from each parent, your earlobe alleles will be *EE*. Then you will have nonattached earlobes.

What if you receive one *E* and one *e* allele? In nature, the *E* allele is *dominant* and the *e* allele is *recessive*. This means that you have an *Ee* combination, the *E* dominates, and you will have nonattached earlobes.

Earlobe Alleles

Letters	Earlobe Trait
EE	Nonattached
Ee or *eE*	Nonattached
ee	Attached

An Example: Bonnie and Evan's Baby

Bonnie and Evan are going to have a baby. Bonnie's earlobe alleles are *Ee*, and Evan's earlobe alleles are *ee*. You can determine the probability that their baby will have attached earlobes by making a tree diagram.

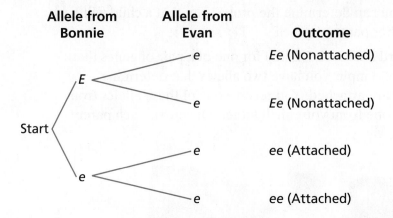

There are four possible allele pairs (outcomes). Two of these pairs, *ee* and *ee*, result in attached earlobes. The probability that Bonnie and Evan's baby will have attached earlobes is $\frac{2}{4}$, or $\frac{1}{2}$.

You can also find the probabilities by making a table such as the one at the right. List Evan's alleles along the side and Bonnie's alleles on top. The four white squares show the possible combinations.

Bonnie

	E	*e*
e	*Ee*	*ee*
e	*Ee*	*ee*

Evan

Bonnie and Evan's chart is sometimes called a *Punnett square* by geneticists. A Punnett square is a chart which predicts all possible gene combinations. Punnett squares are named for an English geneticist, Reginald Punnett. He discovered some basic principles of genetics. He studied the feather color traits of chickens in order to quickly determine whether chickens were male or female when they were born.

Go Online
PHSchool.com
For: Information about Punnett squares
Web Code: ame-9031

Problem 4.2 Applying Theoretical Probability

In Questions A–C, examine each family situation and answer the questions.

A. Dasan's mother is expecting her third child. His mother and father both have the earlobe alleles *Ee*.

  1. What is the probability that Dasan's new sibling will have attached earlobes?

  2. What is the probability that his new sibling will have nonattached earlobes?

B. Geoff's earlobe alleles are *EE* and Mali's earlobe alleles are *Ee*. What is the probability that their child will have nonattached earlobes?

C. Both of Eileen's parents have attached earlobes. What is the probability that Eileen has attached earlobes?

ACE Homework starts on page 62.

There are many other traits you can study in the way you studied earlobes. For example, having certain characteristics (dimples, curly or wavy hair, and widow's peak) is dominant over not having the characteristics.

Did You Know?

There are dominant traits that do not show up very often in the population. For example, the trait for six fingers on one hand is a dominant trait, and five fingers is a recessive trait. Because only a few people carry the allele for six fingers, very few people are born with this trait.

Greg Harris, a major-league baseball player from 1981 to 1995, has six fingers on one hand. He had a specially designed, reversible six-fingered glove. In 1995, he became the only pitcher since 1900 to pitch with both hands in a major-league game.

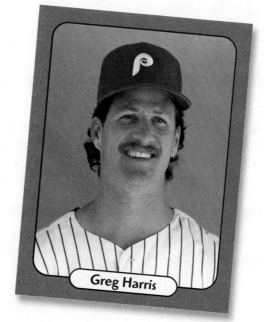

Greg Harris

Go Online
PHSchool.com
For: Information about genetic traits
Web Code: ame-9031

Have you ever figured out a strategy for winning a game?

Now that you know about making tables and diagrams to find probabilities, you can use these tools to find winning strategies for games. In this problem, you play a two-team game called Roller Derby.

Each team needs a game board with columns numbered 1–12, a pair of number cubes, and 12 markers (such as coins, buttons, or small blocks).

Roller Derby Rules

1. Each team places its 12 markers into their columns in any way it chooses.

2. Each team rolls a number cube. The team with the highest roll goes first.

3. Teams take turns rolling the two number cubes. They remove a marker from the column on their board with the same number as the total sum of the numbers on the number cubes. If the column is empty, the team does not get to remove a marker.

4. The first team to remove all the markers from its board wins.

As you play, think about strategies for winning and how probability relates to your strategies.

Problem 4.3 Analyzing a Game

A. Play the game at least twice. For each game, record the strategies you use to place your markers on the board. Also, record how many times each sum is rolled. What is a good strategy for placing your markers on the game board?

B. 1. Which sums seem to occur most often?

    2. Which sums do not come up very often?

C. Find all the possible outcomes (number pairs) of rolling two number cubes. Find the sums for each of these outcomes.

    1. Are all the sums equally likely? Explain.

    2. How many ways can you get a sum of 2?

    3. What is the probability of getting a sum of 4?

    4. What is the probability of getting a sum of 6?

    5. Which sums occur most often?

D. Now that you have looked at the possible outcomes of the Roller Derby game, do you have any new strategies for winning? Explain.

ACE Homework starts on page 62.

Did You Know?

Galileo was an Italian physicist, astronomer, and mathematician. He is famous for helping develop a model in which the sun was the center of the universe. He also studied problems in probability similar to the ones you have seen.

A famous problem he worked on involved rolling three number cubes. He looked at the possibilities for getting a sum of 9 or a sum of 10. A sum of 9 is made using six groups of numbers:

$$(1, 2, 6), (1, 3, 5), (1, 4, 4), (2, 2, 5), (2, 3, 4), \text{ and } (3, 3, 3).$$

A sum of 10 is made using six other groups of numbers:

$$(1, 3, 6), (1, 4, 5), (2, 2, 6), (2, 3, 5), (2, 4, 4), \text{ and } (3, 3, 4).$$

What puzzled people is that, when they did experiments, the sum of 10 occurred more often. By making a diagram similar to a counting tree, Galileo showed the theoretical probability matched the experimental results. There are actually 25 combinations that have a sum of 9 and 27 combinations that have a sum of 10.

For: Information about Galileo
Web Code: ame-9031

Applications

1. A foot arch is a genetic trait. A foot arch is a space between the middle of a person's foot and the floor when the person stands. In a national study, 982 people said they had a foot arch, while 445 people said they did not have a foot arch.

   a. Based on these data, what is the experimental probability that a person chosen at random has a foot arch?

   b. In a recent year, about 16,600 people participated in the Boston Marathon. Use the data above to estimate the number of participants who did *not* have a foot arch. Explain.

   c. If you know people who are runners, find out if they have foot arches. Does your data seem to match the national study data?

2. Some genetic traits are gender-linked. These traits are more prevalent in people of one gender than the other. For example, color blindness is far more common in men than in women. About 7% of the U.S. male population either cannot distinguish red from green, or sees red and green differently from most people. Red-green color blindness only affects about 0.4% of U.S. females.

   About 550 males and 600 females attend a middle school. How many males and females do you predict have red-green color blindness?

For Exercises 3–7, use the following information about the genetics of tongue curling to answer the question.

Let *T* stand for the allele for tongue curling and let *t* stand for the allele for non-curling. *T* is dominant, so people with *TT* or *Tt* can curl their tongues, while people with *tt* cannot.

3. Neither Greg nor Megan can curl their tongues. What is the probability that their daughter can curl her tongue? Explain.

4. Suppose a woman with tongue-curling alleles *TT* and her husband with tongue-curling alleles *tt* are expecting a baby. What is the probability that the baby will be able to curl his tongue? Explain.

5. If Laura can curl her tongue, is it possible that neither of her parents can curl their tongues? Why or why not?

6. Suppose Ryan can't curl his tongue. Is it possible that both of his parents can curl their tongues? Why or why not?

7. Suppose both Niran and Gen can curl their tongues. They are wondering how many of their children will have this ability.

   a. Gen's mother can curl her tongue, but her father can't. What are Gen's tongue-curling alleles? Explain.

   b. Niran's mother can't curl her tongue, but his father can. What are Niran's tongue-curling alleles? Explain.

   c. What is the probability that Niran and Gen's first child will have the tongue-curling ability?

   d. Suppose their first child has the tongue-curling ability. What is the probability that their second child will also have this ability?

   e. Suppose Niran and Gen have ten children. How many of their children would you expect to have the tongue-curling ability? Why?

Multiple Choice For Exercises 8 and 9, use your list of possible outcomes when you roll two number cubes from Problem 4.3.

8. What is the probability of getting a sum of 5 when you roll two number cubes?

   A. $\frac{1}{9}$ **B.** $\frac{1}{6}$ **C.** $\frac{1}{4}$ **D.** $\frac{1}{3}$

9. What is the probability of getting a sum greater than 9 when you roll two number cubes?

   F. $\frac{1}{9}$ **G.** $\frac{1}{6}$ **H.** $\frac{1}{4}$ **J.** $\frac{1}{3}$

Multiple Choice For Exercises 10 and 11, Ella is playing Roller Derby with Carlos. Ella places all her markers in column 1 and Carlos places all of his markers in column 12.

10. What is the probability that Ella will win?

   A. 0   **B.** $\frac{1}{3}$ **C.** $\frac{1}{2}$ **D.** 1

11. What is the probability that Carlos will win?

   F. 0   **G.** $\frac{1}{3}$ **H.** $\frac{1}{2}$ **J.** 1

12. In some board games, you can end up in "jail." One way to get out of jail is to roll doubles (two number cubes that match). What is the probability of getting out of jail on your turn by rolling doubles? Use your list of possible outcomes of rolling two number cubes. Explain your reasoning.

Homework Help Online
PHSchool.com
For: Help with Exercise 12
Web Code: ame-7412

Connections

For Exercises 13–17, use the data below to answer the question. If there is not enough information to answer the question, explain what additional information you need.

Careers and Goals for Young People

Career/Goal	Ages 8–12	Ages 13–21
Be a millionaire	65%	65%
Star in movie/TV	34%	47%
Make movies	32%	43%
Be a famous athlete	32%	24%
Be a musician/singer	28%	46%
Cure a disease	27%	43%
Start a big company	22%	37%
Be President of the United States	22%	18%
Be a famous writer	22%	33%
Win a Nobel Prize	20%	28%

SOURCE: *Harris Interactive Youthpulse*

13. Which group is more likely to want to be a musician/singer?

14. In a group of 1,500 young people (ages 13–21), about how many would choose to cure a disease?

15. Order the five lowest career/goal choices from least to greatest for ages 13–21.

16. About how many people in your school would select famous athlete as a career?

17. In order to find the percent of all young people (ages 8–12) who want to star in a movie/TV or make a movie, can you add the percents for the two careers/goals together? Why or why not?

18. Suppose you try to determine Fia's and Tomas's earlobe alleles. Here is the information you have:

- Fia has attached earlobes.

- Tomas has nonattached earlobes.

- Their two daughters have nonattached earlobes.

- Their son has attached earlobes.

a. What are Fia's earlobe alleles?

b. What are Tomas's earlobe alleles?

c. If they have another child, what is the probability that the child will have attached earlobes?

19. In *Shapes and Designs*, you built triangles and parallelograms with a given set of criteria. You know that sometimes two people can construct different geometric shapes, given the same set of directions.

a. Suppose your teacher tells you the lengths of all three sides of a given triangle. What is the probability that you construct a triangle congruent to the one that your teacher has in mind? Explain.

b. Suppose your teacher tells you the lengths of all four sides of a given parallelogram. What is the probability that you construct a parallelogram congruent to the parallelogram that your teacher has in mind? Explain.

c. Suppose your teacher tells you the lengths of all four sides of a given rectangle. What is the probability that you construct a rectangle congruent to the one that your teacher has in mind? Explain.

d. Suppose your teacher tells you the perimeter of a given rectangle. What is the probability that you construct a rectangle congruent to the one that your teacher has in mind?

e. Suppose your teacher tells you the lengths of all four sides and the area of a given parallelogram. What is the probability that you construct a parallelogram congruent to the one that your teacher has in mind?

Go Online
PHSchool.com

For: Multiple-Choice Skills
Practice
Web Code: ama-7454

20. What is the probability that the sum is a multiple of 4?

21. What is the probability that the sum is a common multiple of 2 and 3?

22. What is the probability that the sum is a prime number? Explain.

23. Which has a greater probability of being rolled on a pair of number cubes, a sum that is a factor of 6 or a sum that is a multiple of 6? Explain.

24. Suppose Jose and Nina play the game Evens and Odds. To play the game, they roll two number cubes and find the product of the numbers. If the product is odd, Nina scores a point. If the product is even, Jose scores a point.

    a. Make a table of the possible products of two number cubes.

    b. What is the probability that Nina wins? What is the probability that Jose wins? Explain your reasoning.

    c. Is this a fair game? If not, how could you change the points scored by each player so that it would be fair?

    d. What is the probability that the product is a prime number?

    e. What is the probability that the product is a factor of 4?

25. Aran knows that if you roll a number cube once, there is a 50% chance of getting an even number. He says that if you roll a number cube twice, the chance of getting at least one even number is doubled. Is he correct?

26. a. Suppose you fold this shape along the dashed lines to make a three-dimensional shape. How many faces will it have?

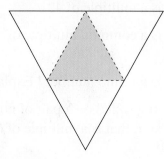

b. Suppose you roll the shape in part (a). What is the probability that the shaded face lands on the bottom?

c. Suppose you fold the shape below. Can you use it in a game? Will the game be fair? Explain.

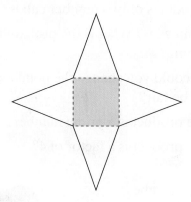

Extensions

27. Pick one of the following two options:

a. Investigate the earlobes in your family. Make a family tree that shows the earlobe alleles that you can find for each person. Trace back as many generations as you can.

b. Survey a large number of people to estimate the percentage of people in the population who have attached earlobes. Represent the data in a graph.

Mathematical Reflections 4

In this investigation, you explored probability related to genetics and games. You collected data to determine the probability that a person selected at random would have a genetic trait. You also found the probability that a child would have a trait based on information about his or her parents' genes. You examined a game to determine winning strategies for playing the game. These questions will help you summarize what you have learned.

Think about your answers to these questions. Discuss your ideas with other students and your teacher. Then write a summary of your findings in your notebook.

1. How can you collect the data to find the experimental probability that a person chosen at random from your school has a particular trait?

2. Describe a way you can find the theoretical probability that a baby will have a trait, such as attached earlobes or tongue-curling ability. Base your answer on the alleles of the parents.

3. Describe some of the strategies for determining the theoretical probabilities for situations in this unit. Give an example of a situation for each of the strategies.

Looking Back and Looking Ahead

The problems in this unit explored some of the big ideas in probability. You learned

- how to think about chance in activities for which individual trials have uncertain outcomes, but patterns of outcomes emerge after many trials
- how to use experimental and theoretical probabilities to predict outcomes with number cubes or coins
- that some outcomes are equally likely while others are not
- how to analyze games of chance to determine whether they are fair games

Go Online
PHSchool.com

For: Vocabulary Review Puzzle
Web Code: amj-7051

Use Your Understanding: Probability

Test your understanding of probability by solving the following problems.

1. Joanna designs a game for the school carnival. She prepares two bags of marbles.

   To play the game, a contestant selects one marble from each bag. If the colors of the marbles match, the contestant wins a prize.

   a. These are the win/loss results for the first 30 games.

   W L L W W L L W W L L W
   W L L L W L L L L W L W
   L L L L W W

   What do these data tell you about the experimental probability of winning the game?

   b. What is the theoretical probability of winning the game?

   c. What explains the difference between your answers to parts (a) and (b)?

Bag A

Bag B

2. Kiana designs a number-cube game for a carnival. To play the game, a contestant rolls two number cubes. If the greatest common factor of the two numbers rolled is even, the contestant wins a prize.

   a. Describe how to conduct an experiment to find the experimental probability of winning the game. Include how you would record results and use them to find experimental probabilities.

   b. What is the theoretical probability of winning the game?

   c. Is this a fair game? Explain your reasoning.

Explain Your Reasoning

3. Consider activities with uncertain outcomes like games of chance or genetic inheritance.

   a. How do you find experimental probabilities for the possible outcomes?

   b. How do you find theoretical probabilities for the possible outcomes?

   c. What relationship do you expect between experimental and theoretical probabilities for any event if the experimental probability is based on each of the following number of trials?

   i. 5   ii. 50   iii. 500

4. Explain the relationship between equally likely and fair when playing a game of chance.

5. What does it mean when a set of outcomes is *not* equally likely? Give an example.

6. For Question 1, suppose Joanna charges $5 to play her game and you can win $10 if you select a marble from each bag and they match. How can you use probability to decide if you want to play the game or not?

Look Ahead

The ideas of probability will be used and developed further in several other units of *Connected Mathematics*, especially *What Do You Expect?* You will also find that you can apply probability reasoning in areas of science, personal health care, safety, and games of chance.

C

certain outcome A result of an action or event that is certain to happen. For example, the sun will rise tomorrow (even if it stays behind clouds all day). The probability of a certain outcome is 1.

suceso seguro Resultado de una acción o suceso que ocurrirá. Por ejemplo, el sol saldrá mañana (incluso si hay nubes). La probabilidad de ese resultado es 1.

chance The likelihood that something will happen. Chance is often expressed as a percent. For example, a weather forecaster might say that there is a 30% chance that it will rain tomorrow.

posibilidad Probabilidad de que algo ocurra. La posibilidad se expresa como un porcentaje. Por ejemplo, un metereólogo puede decir que hay un 30% de probabilidad de que llueva mañana.

E

equally likely events Two or more events that have the same chance of happening. For example, when you toss a fair coin, heads and tails are equally likely. Each has a 50% chance of happening. When you toss a tack, it is not equally likely to land on its side and on its head. It is more likely to land on its side.

sucesos igualmente probables Dos o más sucesos que tienen las mismas posibilidades de suceder. Por ejemplo, cuando lanzas una moneda "justa," la probabilidad de que salga cara o cruz es igualmente probable. Cada resultado tiene una probabilidad del 50% de que suceda. Cuando tiras una tachuela, no existe la misma probabilidad de que caiga sobre un lado que de cabeza. Es más probable que caiga de lado.

event A set of outcomes. For example, when you toss two coins, getting two matching coins is an event consisting of the outcomes heads-heads (HH) and tails-tails (TT).

suceso Un conjunto de resultados. Por ejemplo, cuando se lanzan dos monedas, lograr que las dos monedas coincidan es un suceso que consiste en los resultados cara-cara (CC) y cruz-cruz (XX).

experimental probability A probability found as a result of an experiment. Experimental probabilities are used to predict behavior over the long run. For example, you could find the experimental probability of getting heads when you toss a coin by tossing the coin several times and keeping track of the outcomes. The experimental probability would be the relative frequency of heads, that is the ratio of the number of heads to the total number of trials.

probabilidad experimental Una probabilidad hallada mediante la experimentación. Las probabilidades experimentales se usan para predecir lo que podría suceder con el tiempo. Por ejemplo, podrías hallar la probabilidad experimental de que salgan caras cuando lanzas una moneda varias veces, si llevas la cuenta de los resultados. La probabilidad experimental sería la frecuencia relativa de que salgan caras, que es la razón del número de caras sobre el total del número de pruebas.

fair game A game is fair when each player has the same chance of winning. A game that is not fair can be made fair by adjusting the pay-offs (or scoring system). For example, suppose you play a game in which two coins are tossed. You score when the coins both land heads up. Otherwise, your opponent scores. The probability that you will score is $\frac{1}{4}$ and the probability that your opponent will score is $\frac{3}{4}$. To make the game fair, you must get three points each time you score, and your opponent must get only one point when he scores. A coin is fair when the probability of tossing a head equals the probability of tossing a tail.

juego justo Un juego en el que cada jugador tiene las mismas posibilidades de ganar. Un juego que no es justo se puede hacer justo mediante una adaptación del sistema de resultados. Por ejemplo, supón que juegas a tirar dos monedas. Obtienes un punto cuando las dos monedas caen cara arriba. Si no, tu oponente recibe un punto. La probabilidad de que consigas el punto es $\frac{1}{4}$ y la probabilidad de que tu oponente consiga un punto es $\frac{3}{4}$. Para hacer que el juego sea justo, deberás obtener tres puntos cada vez que las dos monedas caigan cara arriba y tu oponente deberá obtener un punto cuando las monedas caigan de otro modo. El juego de la moneda es justo cuando la probabilidad de que caiga en cara es igual a la probabilidad de que caiga en cruz.

favorable outcome An outcome that gives a desired result. A favorable outcome is sometimes called a *success*. For example, when you toss two coins to find the probability of the coins matching, HH and TT are favorable outcomes.

resultado favorable Un resultado en el que estás interesado. A veces, un resultado favorable se llama un *éxito*. Por ejemplo, cuando lanzas dos monedas para hallar la probabilidad de que las dos coincidan, los resultados CC y XX son resultados favorables.

impossible outcome An outcome that cannot happen. For example, the probability of getting a 7 by tossing a number cube is zero. We write $P(7) = 0$.

suceso imposible Un suceso que no puede ocurrir. Por ejemplo, la probabilidad de obtener un 7 al lanzar un cubo numérico es cero. Se escribe $P(7) = 0$.

outcome A possible result of an action. For example, when one number cube is rolled, the possible outcomes are 1, 2, 3, 4, 5, and 6.

resultado Lo que sucede como consecuencia o efecto de una acción. Por ejemplo, cuando se lanza un cubo numerado, los resultados posibles son 1, 2, 3, 4, 5 y 6.

possible A word used to describe an outcome or result that can happen. *Possible* does not imply anything about how likely the outcome is. For example, it is *possible* to toss a coin 200 times and get heads every time, but it is not at all likely.

posible Una palabra usada para describir un suceso que puede ocurrir. *Posible* no implica nada sobre la probabilidad de que suceda. Por ejemplo, es *posible* lanzar una moneda 200 veces y que salgan caras todas las veces pero no es nada probable.

probability A number with a value from 0 to 1 that describes the likelihood that an event will occur. For example, if a bag contains a red marble, a white marble, and a blue marble, then the probability of selecting a red marble is $\frac{1}{3}$.

probabilidad Un número entre 0 y 1 que describe la posibilidad de que un suceso ocurra. Por ejemplo, si una bolsa contiene una canica roja, una blanca y una azul, entonces la probabilidad de sacar una canica roja es $\frac{1}{3}$.

probable Another way to say *likely*. An outcome that is probable is likely to happen.

probable Otra manera de decir *posible*. Un resultado posible que seguramente ocurrirá.

random events Events for which the outcome is uncertain when they are viewed as individual events. Random events often exhibit a regular pattern when observed over many trials. For example, when you roll a number cube, the number that will result is uncertain on any one particular roll, but over a great many rolls each number will occur about the same number of times.

sucesos aleatorios Sucesos que no son seguros individualmente, pero que podrían exhibir un patrón regular cuando son observados a lo largo de muchas pruebas. Por ejemplo, cuando lanzas un cubo numerado, no hay ninguna manera de saber el resultado del próximo tiro, pero sabes que con el tiempo cada número saldrá aproximadamente la misma cantidad de veces.

simulation A model of an experiment used to find the likelihood of an event. For example, suppose you want to find the likelihood you will win a contest with ten contestants. Since it is difficult to gather information about the contestants, you can simulate the contest. Write the numbers 1–10 on cards and select a card at random. The number 1 represents a win and the numbers 2–10 represent a loss.

simulación Modelo de un experimento que se usa para hallar la probabilidad de un suceso. Por ejemplo, supón que quieres saber la probabilidad que tendrás de ganar un concurso con diez participantes. Como es difícil reunir información sobre los participantes, puedes simular el concurso. Escribe los números 1–10 en tarjetas y selecciona una tarjeta al azar. El número 1 representa una ganancia y los números 2–10 representa una pérdida.

theoretical probability A probability found by analyzing a situation. If all the outcomes are equally likely, you can find a theoretical probability of an event by first listing all the possible outcomes, and then finding the ratio of the number of outcomes you are interested in to the total number of outcomes. For example, there are 36 possible equally likely outcomes (number pairs) when two number cubes are rolled. Of these outcomes, 6 have a sum of 7, so the probability of rolling a sum of 7 is $\frac{6}{36}$, or $\frac{1}{6}$.

probabilidad teórica Una probabilidad hallada mediante el análisis de una situación. Si todos los resultados son igualmente probables, puedes hallar una probabilidad teórica de un suceso haciendo primero una lista de todos los resultados posibles y luego hallando la razón entre el número de resultados en los que estás interesado y el número total de resultados. Por ejemplo, hay 36 resultados (pares de números) posibles e igualmente probables cuando se lanzan dos cubos numerados. De estos resultados, 6 tienen una suma de 7, así que la probabilidad de lanzar una suma de 7 es $\frac{6}{36}$ ó $\frac{1}{6}$.

tree diagram A systematic way to find all the possible outcomes in a probability situation.

diagrama de árbol Manera sistemática de hallar todos los resultados posibles en una probabilidad.

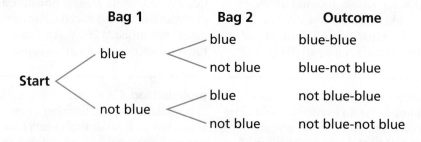

trial One round of an experiment. For example, if you are interested in the behavior of a coin, you might experiment by tossing a coin 50 times and recording the results. Each toss is a trial, so this experiment consists of 50 trials.

prueba Una parte en un experimento. Por ejemplo, si te interesan los resultados de tirar una moneda, puedes lanzarla al aire 50 veces y anotar los resultados. Cada lanzamiento es una prueba, por lo que este experimento consistiría en 50 pruebas.

Academic Vocabulary

The following terms are important to your understanding of the mathematics in this unit. Knowing and using these words will help you in thinking, reasoning, representing, communicating your ideas, and making connections across ideas. When these words make sense to you, the investigations and problems will make more sense as well.

D

design To make using specific criteria
related terms: draw, plan, outline, model

Sample: **Carlos noticed that he gets home from school first about $\frac{1}{3}$ of the time, his brother gets home first about $\frac{1}{2}$ of the time, and his sister is first about $\frac{1}{6}$ of the time. Design a spinner to predict who will get home first tomorrow.**

I designed a spinner with six equal sections. Three sixths or $\frac{1}{2}$ of these sections are labeled brother, two sixths or $\frac{1}{3}$ of them are labeled Carlos, and $\frac{1}{6}$ is labeled sister.

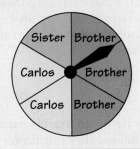

diseñar Hacer algo usando criterios específicos.
términos relacionados: dibujar, hacer un plan, hacer un esquema, hacer modelos

Ejemplo: **Carlos observó que llega a casa de la escuela primero alrededor de $\frac{1}{3}$ del tiempo, su hermano llega a casa primero alrededor de $\frac{1}{2}$ del tiempo y su hermana llega primero alrededor de $\frac{1}{6}$ del tiempo. Diseña una flecha giratoria para predecir quién llegará primero a casa mañana.**

Diseñé una flecha giratoria con seis secciones iguales. Tres sextos ó $\frac{1}{2}$ de estas secciones se rotularon hermano, dos sextos ó $\frac{1}{3}$ se rotularon Carlos y $\frac{1}{6}$ se rotuló hermana.

E

expect Using theoretical or experimental data to anticipate a certain outcome.
related terms: anticipate, predict

Sample: **Lizzie and her sister flip a coin every afternoon to see who will walk the dog. How often should Lizzie expect to walk the dog?**

There are two possible outcomes: heads or tails. The probability of heads or tails is $\frac{1}{2}$. Lizzie should expect to walk the dog half of the time.

esperar Usar datos teóricos o experimentales para anticipar un determinado resultado.
términos relacionados: anticipar, predecir

Ejemplo: **Lizzie y su hermana lanzan una moneda cada tarde para ver quién sacará a pasear al perro. ¿Con cuánta frecuencia debería esperar Lizzie sacar a pasear al perro?**

Hay dos resultados posibles: cara o cruz. La probabilidad de que caiga cara o cruz es la misma, $\frac{1}{2}$. Lizzie debería esperar sacar a pasear al perro la mitad del tiempo.

explain To give facts and details that make an idea easier to understand. Explaining can involve a written summary supported by a diagram, chart, table, or a combination of these.

related terms: clarify, describe, justify

Sample: Ellen made a spinner to choose an exercise activity. Which do you think will occur most often? Explain your reasoning.

Exercise Spinner

- ☐ Run
- ☐ Swim
- ☐ Bike

Ellen is most likely to go for a run since the run portion of the spinner is the largest. It takes up $\frac{1}{2}$ of the spinner, while swim takes up only $\frac{1}{3}$ of the spinner and bike takes up $\frac{1}{6}$ of the spinner.

explicar Dar hechos y detalles que hacen que una idea sea más fácil de comprender. Explicar puede implicar un resumen escrito apoyado por hechos, un diagrama, una gráfica, una tabla o una combinación de éstos.

términos relacionados: aclarar, describir, justificar

Ejemplo: Ellen hizo una flecha giratoria para elegir una actividad de ejercicio. ¿Cuál piensas que ocurrirá con mayor frecuencia? Explica tu razonamiento.

Flecha Giratoria de Ejercicio

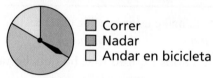

- ☐ Correr
- ☐ Nadar
- ☐ Andar en bicicleta

Es más probable que Ellen salga a correr puesto que la porción de correr de la flecha es la más grande. Ocupa la $\frac{1}{2}$ de la flecha, mientras nadar ocupa sólo $\frac{1}{3}$ de la flecha y andar en bicicleta ocupa $\frac{1}{6}$ de la flecha.

P

predict To make an educated guess.

related terms: anticipate, expect, estimate

Sample: Eli and Jake put colored crayons in a bag. Then they conducted an experiment to find the probability of pulling a green crayon out of the bag.

Eli: $P(\text{green}) = \frac{10}{45}$

Jake: $P(\text{green}) = \frac{5}{12}$

Whose results would you use to best predict the likelihood of pulling a green crayon out of the bag?

I would use Eli's results since he conducted the experiment more times than Jake did. The more often an experiment is repeated, the better the results are as a predictor of a future similar event.

predecir Hacer una estimación informada.

términos relacionados: anticipar, esperar, estimar

Ejemplo: Eli y Jake pusieron creyones de colores en una bolsa. Luego realizaron un experimento para hallar la probabilidad de sacar un creyón verde de la bolsa.

Eli: $P(\text{verde}) = \frac{10}{45}$

Jake: $P(\text{verde}) = \frac{5}{12}$

¿Los resultados de quién usarías para predecir mejor la probabilidad de sacar un creyón verde de la bolsa?

Usaría los resultados de Eli puesto que realizó el experimento más veces que Jake. Entre más se repite un experimento, son mejores los resultados como pronosticador de un evento futuro similar.

Index

Acting it out, 6–7, 9–10, 22, 26, 36, 40–44, 60–61

Algebra
area, 52
pi, 52
probability, 8, 109

Allele, 57–59, 63, 69
ACE, 66, 68
dominant, 57, 59
recessive, 57, 59

Analyzing games of chance, 60–61

Angle measurement, 44

Bar graph, 17–18, 50
deceptive, 50
prediction from, 17–18

Block guessing (see also Drawing from a bag), 22, 26, 36–37
experiment, 22, 26

Certain event, 32

Certain outcome, 72

Chance, *see* **Probability**

Coin toss, 6–7, 9–11, 21, 24–25, 27, 41, 70
ACE, 13–14, 19, 31, 33, 35, 37, 47
experiment, 6–7, 9–10

Computer simulation, 52

Cup toss, 7–9, 13–14, 19
experiment, 7–8

Deceptive advertising, 50–51

Deceptive graphs, 50

Designing a game, 31, 40, 47, 48, 53

Designing an experiment, 36, 38, 71

Drawing from a bag, 22–23, 26, 41–42, 70
ACE, 14–15, 17, 28–29, 34, 36–37
experiment, 22, 26, 36

Equally likely events, 11–12, 20, 21–22, 26–27, 61, 71, 72
ACE, 15, 18, 36, 44–46, 53

Evens and Odds game, 67

Event (see also Outcome and Trial), 72
certain, 32
equally likely, 11–12, 15, 18, 20, 21–22, 26–27, 36, 44–46, 53, 61, 71, 72
impossible, 32

Experiment
block guessing, 22, 26
coin toss, 6–7, 9–10
cup toss, 7–8
drawing from a bag, 22, 26, 36
designing, 36, 38, 71
number cubes, 60
Gee Whiz Everyone Wins!, *see* Block guessing
scratch-off cards, 43
spinner, 40, 44

Experimental probability, 8–12, 22, 26, 38, 39–40, 43, 54, 56–57, 69, 70–71, 72
ACE, 13–19, 32, 34, 36, 44, 49, 51–52, 62–68
computing, 8–10
genetics and, 56–57, 69, 71
prediction with, 22, 34, 38, 39–40, 43, 44, 51–52, 54, 56, 62–68, 70–71
theoretical probability and, 4, 22, 26, 32, 36, 38, 40, 44, 49, 54, 70–71

Fair, 4, 11, 27, 41–42, 54, 71, 73
ACE, 31, 35–36, 44, 47
coin toss game, 11, 27, 31, 35
number cube, 31, 35–36, 67, 68, 71
spinner, 42, 44, 47

Family tree, making, 68

Favorable outcome, 21, 73

Games of chance
analyzing, 60–61
block guessing, 22, 26, 36–37
coin toss, 6–7, 9–11, 13–14, 19, 21, 24–25, 27, 31, 33, 35, 37, 41, 47, 70
cup toss, 7–9, 13–14, 19
designing, 31, 40, 47, 48, 53
drawing from a bag, 14–15, 17, 22–23, 26, 28–29, 34, 36–37, 41–42, 70
Evens and Odds, 67
Gee Whiz Everyone Wins!, *see* Block guessing
number cubes, 5, 12, 16, 31, 35–36, 41–42, 47, 49, 54, 60–61, 64, 67, 70–71
Roller Derby, 60–61, 64
scratch-off cards, 43, 48
spinner, 13, 31, 39–42, 44–49, 53, 54

Genetics
ACE, 62–63, 66, 68
allele, 57–59, 63, 66, 68, 69
probability and, 55–59, 69, 71

Graph, making, 68

Impossible event, 32

Impossible outcome, 73

Interpreting data
bar graph, 17–18, 50
line plot, 34
number line, 32
organized list, 12, 15, 24–26, 30, 31, 37
picture, 7, 43, 51–52, 55, 60–61, 68, 70
Punnett square, 58
spinner, 13, 31, 39–42, 44–49, 53, 54
table, 6, 14, 16, 19, 35, 48, 49, 52, 56, 57, 65
tree diagram, 24–25, 30, 31, 37, 58

Acknowledgments

Team Credits

The people who made up the **Connected Mathematics2** team—representing editorial, editorial services, design services, and production services—are listed below. Bold type denotes core team members.

Leora Adler, Judith Buice, Kerry Cashman, Patrick Culleton, Sheila DeFazio, Richard Heater, **Barbara Hollingdale, Jayne Holman,** Karen Holtzman, **Etta Jacobs,** Christine Lee, Carolyn Lock, Catherine Maglio, **Dotti Marshall,** Rich McMahon, Eve Melnechuk, Kristin Mingrone, Terri Mitchell, **Marsha Novak,** Irene Rubin, Donna Russo, Robin Samper, Siri Schwartzman, **Nancy Smith,** Emily Soltanoff, **Mark Tricca,** Paula Vergith, Roberta Warshaw, Helen Young

Additional Credits

Diana Bonfilio, Mairead Reddin, Michael Torocsik, nSight, Inc.

Illustration

Michelle Barbera: 6

Technical Illustration

WestWords, Inc.

Cover Design

tom white.images

Photos

2 t, Russ Lappa; **2 b,** Michael Newman/PhotoEdit; **3,** Thinkstock/Getty Images, Inc.; **5,** Comstock Images/Getty Images, Inc.; **9 all,** Russ Lappa; **10,** ©1999 Scott Adams/Distributed by United Features Syndicate, Inc.; **12,** Camille Tokerud/Getty Images, Inc.; **14,** Richard Haynes; **19,** Gail Mooney/Masterfile; **21,** Jim Cummins/Getty Images, Inc.; **22,** Russ Lappa; **25,** Richard Haynes; **27,** Russ Lappa; **28,** Brian Hagiwara/Brand X Pictures/Getty Images, Inc.; **33,** Bob Daemmrich/PhotoEdit; **36,** Mark Scott/Getty Images, Inc.; **39,** David Young-Wolff/PhotoEdit; **41,** Gabe Palmer/Corbis; **42,** Michael Prince/Corbis; **55 l,** Corbis; **55 ml,** Alain Dex/Photo Researchers, Inc.; **55 mr,** David Young-Wolf/PhotoEdit; **55 r,** Michael Newman/PhotoEdit; **57,** Sarma Ozols/Getty Images, Inc.; **59,** AP/Wide World Photos; **62,** John Coletti/Index Stock Imagery, Inc.; **63,** Michael Newman/PhotoEdit; **64,** David Young-Wolff/PhotoEdit; **67,** Richard Haynes

Data Sources

The table of batting averages on page 49 is adapted from Major League Baseball Historical Player Statistics. Copyright © Major League Baseball.

The table "US Genetic Survey" on page 56 is from "The Genetics Project: Are We Alike?" Used with permission Dr. Jacalyn Willis, Director of PRISM, Montclair State University, Montclair, New Jersey.

Careers data on page 65 from The Harris Poll ® "Careers in the Arts (Coupled with Fame) Are High in Young People's Aspirations" Harris Interactive, Inc. All Rights Reserved.

Note: Every effort has been made to locate the copyright owner of the material reprinted in this book. Omissions brought to our attention will be corrected in subsequent editions.

Connected Mathematics 2

Data About Us

Statistics

Glenda Lappan

James T. Fey

William M. Fitzgerald

Susan N. Friel

Elizabeth Difanis Phillips

PEARSON

Boston, Massachusetts · Glenview, Illinois · Shoreview, Minnesota · Upper Saddle River, New Jersey

Data About Us

Statistics

What is the greatest number of pets owned by students in your class? How can you find out?

Suppose two classes competed in a jump-rope contest. They recorded the number of jumps for each student. How would you determine which class did better?

A group of students collected data on the number of movies they watched last month. How would you find out the "typical" number of movies watched?

Every 10 years the United States government conducts a *census*, or survey, of every household in the country. The census gathers information about many things including education, employment, and income. Because people are naturally curious about themselves and others, many people are interested in information from the census. Of course, collecting data from every household in the United States is a huge task.

You often hear people making statements about the results of surveys. For example, what does it mean when reports say the average middle-school student has four people in his or her family, or watches three hours of television on a weekday?

In *Data About Us,* you will learn to collect and analyze data for situations similar to those on the previous page. You will also learn to use your results to describe people and their characteristics.

Mathematical Highlights

Statistics

In *Data About Us*, you will explore ways of collecting, organizing, displaying, and analyzing data.

You will learn how to

- Conduct data investigations by posing questions, collecting and analyzing data, and making interpretations to answer questions
- Represent distributions of data using line plots, bar graphs, stem-and-leaf plots, and coordinate graphs
- Compute the mean, median, mode, or range of the data
- Distinguish between categorical data and numerical data and identify which graphs and statistics may be used to represent each kind of data
- Choose the most appropriate statistical measures (mean, median, mode, range, etc.) to describe a distribution of data
- Develop strategies for comparing distributions of data

As you work on problems in this unit, ask yourself questions about situations that involve data analysis:

What is the question being asked?

What organization of the data can help me analyze the data?

What statistical measures will provide useful information about the distribution of data?

What will statistical measures tell me about the distribution of the data?

How can I use graphs and statistics to describe a data distribution or to compare two data distributions in order to answer my original question?

Unit Project

Is Anyone Typical?

What are the characteristics of a typical middle-school student? Who is interested in knowing these characteristics? Does a typical middle-school student really exist? As you proceed through this unit, you will identify some "typical" facts about your classmates, such as these:

- The typical number of letters in a student's full name
- The typical number of people in a student's household
- The typical height of a student

When you have completed the investigations in *Data About Us,* you will carry out a statistical investigation to answer this question:

What are some of the characteristics of a typical middle-school student?

These characteristics may include

- Physical characteristics (for example, age, height, or eye color)
- Family and home characteristics (for example, number of brothers and sisters or number of MP3 players)
- Behaviors (for example, hobbies or number of hours spent watching television)
- Preferences, opinions, or attitudes (for example, favorite musical group, or choice for class president)

As you study this unit, make and improve your plans for your project. Keep in mind that a statistical investigation involves posing questions, collecting data, analyzing data, and interpreting the results of the analysis. As you work through each investigation, think about how you might use what you are learning to help you with your project.

Looking at Data

The problems in this investigation involve people's names. Family traditions are often involved when a child is named. A person's name may reveal information about his or her ancestors.

Many people have interesting stories about how they were named. Here is one student's story: "I'm a twin, and my mom and dad didn't know they were going to have twins. My sister was born first. She was named Sukey. I was a surprise. My mom named me after the woman in the next hospital bed. Her name was Takara."

- Do you know anything interesting about how you were named or about the history behind your family's name?

Rhoshandiatellyneshiaunneveshenk Koyaanisquatsiuth Williams is the longest name on a birth certificate.

Shortly after Rhoshandiatellyneshiaunneveshenk was born, her father lengthened her first name to 1,019 letters and her middle name to 36 letters. What is a good nickname for her?

Organizing and Interpreting Data

Most parents do not worry about the number of letters in their children's names. Sometimes though, name length does matter. For example, only a limited number of letters may fit on a bracelet or a library card.

Getting Ready for Problem

What do you think is the typical number of letters in the full names (first and last names) of your classmates?

- What data do you need to collect and how would you collect it?
- How would you organize and represent your data?
- If a new student joined your class today, how might you use your results to predict the length of that student's name?

The students in Ms. Jee's class made a **line plot** to display the distribution of their class's data.

Name Lengths of Ms. Jee's Students

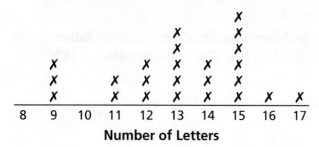

Another group displayed the same data using a **bar graph.**

Name Lengths of Ms. Jee's Students

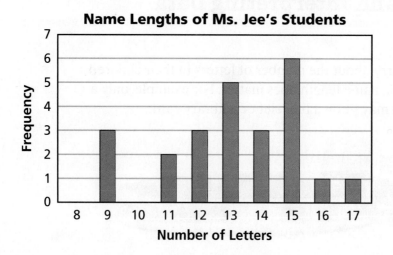

To describe how the data are distributed, you might look at where the data values cluster, how much they vary, and the high and low values.

Problem 1.1 Organizing and Interpreting Data

Examine the line plot and the bar graph.

  A. Describe the distribution of the data. Do you see any patterns?

  B. How are the two graphs alike? How are they different?

  C. How can you use each graph to determine the total number of letters in all the names?

  D. Fahimeh Ghomizadeh said, "My name has the most letters, but the bar that shows my name length is one of the shortest on the graph. Why?" How would you answer this question?

E. Collect the data for your class's name lengths. Represent the data distribution using a line plot or a bar graph.

F. What are some similarities and differences between the data distribution from Ms. Jee's class and the data distribution from your class?

ACE Homework starts on page 21.

Did You Know?

In Africa, a child's name is often very meaningful. Names such as Sekelaga, which means "rejoice," and Tusajigwe, which means "we are blessed," reflect the happiness the family felt at the child's birth. Names such as Mvula, meaning "rain," reflect events that happened at the time the child was born.

Go Online
PHSchool.com   **For:** Information about African names
Web Code: ame-9031

1.2 Useful Statistics

In the data for Ms. Jee's class, the name length of 15 letters occurs most often. Notice that 15 has the highest stack of X's in the line plot and the tallest bar in the bar graph. We call the most frequent value the **mode** of the data set.

The least value and the greatest value are important values in a data set. They give a sense of the variability in the data. In Ms. Jee's class, the data vary from 9 letters to 17 letters. The difference between the least value and the greatest value is called the **range** of the data. The range of Ms. Jee's class data is 17–9, or 8 letters.

Still another important statistic is the **median,** or the midpoint, of the data set.

The table and line plot below show the distribution of the name-length data for Mr. Gray's class. Notice that these data have two modes, 11 letters and 12 letters. We say the distribution is *bimodal*. The data vary from 7 letters to 19 letters. The range of the data is 19 – 7, or 12 letters.

Name Lengths of Mr. Gray's Students	
Name	Number of Letters
Jeffrey Piersonjones	19
Thomas Petes	11
Clarence Jenkins	15
Michelle Hughes	14
Shoshana White	13
Deborah Black	12
Terry Van Bourgondien	19
Maxi Swanson	11
Tonya Stewart	12
Jorge Bastante	13
Richard Mudd	11
Joachim Caruso	13
Robert Northcott	15
Tony Tung	8
Joshua Klein	11
Jan Wong	7
Bob King	7
Veronica Rodriguez	17
Charlene Greene	14
Peter Juliano	12
Linora Haynes	12

Name Lengths of Mr. Gray's Students

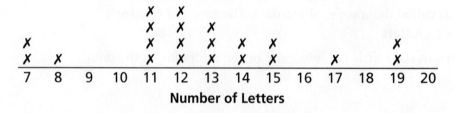

Problem 1.2 Useful Statistics

Here is a way to help you think about how to identify the median. Cut a strip of 21 squares from a sheet of grid paper. Each square is for the length of a student's name in Mr. Gray's class. Write the name lengths of Mr. Gray's students in order from least to greatest on the grid paper as shown.

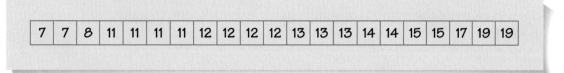

| 7 | 7 | 8 | 11 | 11 | 11 | 11 | 12 | 12 | 12 | 12 | 13 | 13 | 13 | 14 | 14 | 15 | 15 | 17 | 19 | 19 |

A. Fold the strip in half.

  1. On what number is the crease caused by the fold?

  2. How many numbers occur to the left of this number?

  3. How many numbers occur to the right of this number?

  4. The median is the value of the midpoint marker in a set of data. The same number of data values occur before and after this value. What is the median for these data?

B. Suppose a new student, Suzanne Mannerstrale, joins Mr. Gray's class. The class now has 22 students. On a strip of 22 squares, list the name lengths, including Suzanne's, in order from least to greatest. Fold the strip in half.

  1. On what number is the crease caused by the fold?

  2. How many numbers occur to the left of the crease?

  3. How many numbers occur to the right of the crease?

  4. What is the median for these data?

C. Suzanne has six pets. She made the line plot shown of her pets' name lengths. Find the median length of her pets' names. Find the mode for the data set.

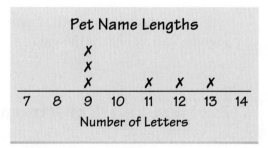

D. There are 15 students in a class. Use the information about the class's name lengths below.

  ● Mode: 12 letters

  ● Median: 12 letters

  ● The data vary from 8 letters to 16 letters

  1. Find a possible set of name lengths for the class.

  2. Make a line plot to display your data distribution.

  3. Compare your graph with the graphs of your classmates. How are the graphs alike? How are they different?

ACE Homework starts on page 21.

You can use the median and the mode of a set of data to describe what is typical about the distribution. They are sometimes called *measures of center*.

Use the following ten names. Write each name on an index card. On the back of each card, write the number of letters in the name. A sample index card is shown below.

Student Name Lengths

Name	Number of Letters
Thomas Petes	11
Michelle Hughes	14
Shoshana White	13
Deborah Black	12
Tonya Stewart	12
Richard Mudd	11
Tony Tung	8
Janice Wong	10
Bobby King	9
Charlene Greene	14

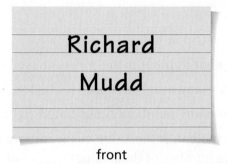

front

back

Order the cards from shortest name length to longest name length, and identify the median of the data.

Problem 1.3 Experimenting With the Median

Use your cards to complete each task below. Keep a record of your work.

A. Remove two names from the original data set so that

   1. the median stays the same.

   2. the median increases.

   3. the median decreases.

B. Add two new names to the original data set so that

    1. the median stays the same.

    2. the median increases.

    3. the median decreases.

C. How does the median of the original data set change if you add a name

    1. with 16 letters?

    2. with 1,019 letters?

ACE Homework starts on page 21.

Did You Know?

Names from many parts of the world have special origins. European family names (last names) often came from the father's first name. For example, Ian Robertson was the son of Robert, Janos Ivanovich was the son (vich) of Ivan, and John Peters was the son of Peter.

Family names also came from words that described a person's hometown or job. This resulted in such names as William Hill and Gilbert Baker.

Family names in China and Vietnam are almost always one-syllable words that are related to names of ruling families. Chang is one such example.

You can read more about names in books such as *Names from Africa* by Ogonna Chuks-Orji and *Do People Grow on Family Trees?* by Ira Wolfman.

 **For:** Information about names
PHSchool.com **Web Code:** ame-9031

Using Different Data Types

When you are interested in learning more about something, you ask questions about it. Some questions have answers that are words or categories. For example, what is your favorite sport? Other questions have answers that are numbers. For example, how many inches tall are you?

Categorical data are data that have been grouped into categories, such as "favorite sport." They are usually not numbers. Suppose you ask people in which month they were born or what kinds of pets they have. Their answers would be categorical data.

Numerical data are data that are counts or measures. Suppose you ask people how tall they are or how many pets they have. Their responses would be numerical data.

Getting Ready for Problem

Read each of the questions below. Which questions have words or categories as answers? Which questions have numbers as answers?

- In which month were you born?
- What is your favorite kind of pet?
- How many pets do you have?
- Who is your favorite author?
- How much time do you spend watching television in a day?
- What's your highest score in the game?
- How many movies have you watched in the past week?

The kinds of pets people have often depend on where they live. People who live in cities often have small pets. People who live on farms often have large pets. People who live in apartments sometimes cannot have pets at all.

One middle-school class gathered data about their pets by tallying students' responses to these questions:

- What is your favorite kind of pet?
- How many pets do you have?

The students made tables to show the tallies or frequencies. Then they made bar graphs to display the data distributions.

Do you think the students surveyed live in a city, the suburbs, or the country? Explain.

Number of Pets

Number	Frequency
0	2
1	2
2	5
3	4
4	1
5	2
6	3
7	0
8	1
9	1
10	0
11	0
12	1
13	0
14	1
15	0
16	0
17	1
18	0
19	1
20	0
21	1

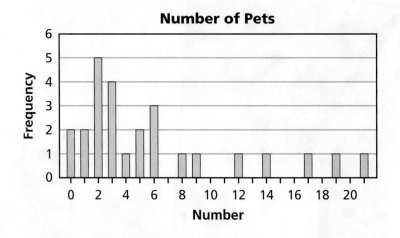

Favorite Kinds of Pets

Pet	Frequency
cat	4
dog	7
fish	2
bird	2
horse	3
goat	1
cow	2
rabbit	3
duck	1
pig	1

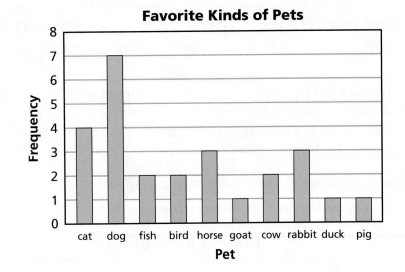

Favorite Kinds of Pets

Problem 1.4 Using Different Data Types

Decide whether each question can be answered by using data from the graphs and tables the students created. If so, give the answer and explain how you got it. If not, explain why not and tell what additional information you would need to answer the question.

A. Which graph shows categorical data?

B. Which graph shows numerical data?

C. What is the total number of pets the students have?

D. What is the greatest number of pets a student has?

E. How many students are in the class?

F. How many students chose cats as their favorite kind of pet?

G. How many cats do students have as pets?

H. What is the mode for the favorite kind of pet?

I. What is the median number of pets students have?

J. What is the range of the numbers of pets students have?

K. Tomas is a student in this class. How many pets does he have?

L. Do the girls have more pets than the boys?

ACE Homework starts on page 21.

You have used bar graphs to display distributions of data. *Vertical bar graphs* display data on the horizontal axis with vertical bars. On vertical bar graphs, the heights can be compared to the vertical frequency axis.

Look at the vertical bar graph below.

- What information does the horizontal axis show?
- What information does the vertical axis show?

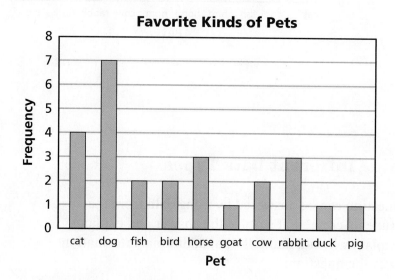

Favorite Kinds of Pets

- How do you find out how many people chose "dog" as their favorite kind of pet using the vertical bar graph?

Suppose five more students are surveyed. Three identify birds as their favorite kind of pet. Two identify cats as their favorite kind of pet.

- What changes would you make in the vertical bar graph to show the new distribution?

Below is the distribution of the original pet data shown on a *horizontal bar graph*.

- Compare the vertical bar graph to the horizontal bar graph. How are they alike? How are they different?

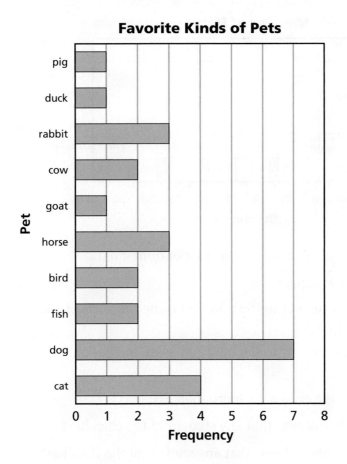

Favorite Kinds of Pets

- How do you find out how many people chose "dog" as their favorite kind of pet using the horizontal bar graph?

Suppose five more students were surveyed. Three identify birds as their favorite kind of pet. Two identify cats as their favorite kind of pet.

- What changes would you make in the horizontal bar graph to show the new distribution?

Below is a vertical bar graph showing the distribution of the number of pets students have.

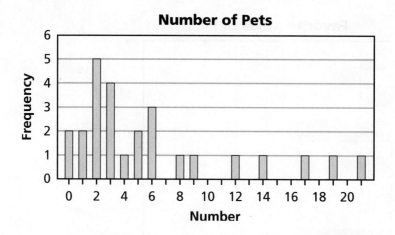

Number of Pets

A. Make a horizontal bar graph to show this distribution of data.

For each question below, explain:

- how you can find the answer to the question using the vertical bar graph
- how you can find the answer to the question using the horizontal bar graph

B. How many students in the class have more than five pets?

C. What is the least number of pets that any student in the class has?

D. What is the greatest number of pets that any student in the class has?

E. What is the median number of pets?

F. Three students were absent when these data were collected. Malcolm has 7 pets, Makana has 1 pet, and Jake has 3 pets. Add their data to each graph. What is the median number of pets now?

ACE Homework starts on page 21.

Applications

For Exercises 1 and 2, use the names of Mr. Young's students listed below.

Ben Foster	Rosita Ramirez
Ava Baker	Kimberly Pace
Lucas Fuentes	Paula Wheeler
Juan Norinda	Darnell Fay
Ron Weaver	Jeremy Yosho
Bryan Wong	Cora Harris
Toby Vanhook	Corey Brooks
Katrina Roberson	Tijuana Degraffenreid

1. Make a table showing the length of each name. Then make both a line plot and a bar graph of the name lengths.

2. What is the typical name length for Mr. Young's students? Use the mode, median, and range to help you answer this question.

For Exercises 3–6, make a line plot or bar graph of a data distribution that fits each description.

3. 24 names, with a range of 12 letters

4. 7 names, with a median length of 14 letters

5. 13 names, with a median length of 13 letters, and with data that vary from 8 letters to 17 letters

6. 16 names, with a median length of $14\frac{1}{2}$ letters, and with data that vary from 11 letters to 20 letters

For Exercises 7–12, use the bar graph below.

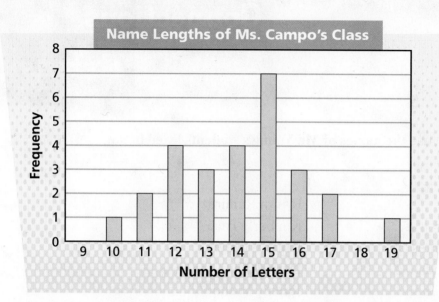

Name Lengths of Ms. Campo's Class

7. How does the data distribution from Ms. Campo's class compare with the data distribution from Mr. Young's class in Exercise 1?

8. **Multiple Choice** For Ms. Campo's students, which value (name length) occurs most frequently?

   A. 12 letters   **B.** 14 letters   **C.** 15 letters   **D.** 16 letters

9. **Multiple Choice** What is the name of the value found in Exercise 8?

   F. range   **G.** median   **H.** mode   **J.** none of these

10. How many students are in Ms. Campo's class? Explain how you got your answer.

11. What is the range of name lengths for this class?

12. What is the median name length? Explain how you got your answer.

13. Look at the table and graph for Number of Pets from the introduction to Problem 1.4. Four new students join the class. One student has 3 pets, two students each have 7 pets, and the last student has 16 pets.

    a. Copy the graph and show these data included.

    b. With these new data included, does the median change or stay the same? Explain your reasoning.

Go Online
PHSchool.com

For: Multiple-Choice Skills Practice
Web Code: ama-8154

For Exercises 14–20, tell whether the answers to the questions are numerical or categorical data.

14. What is your height in centimeters?

15. What is your favorite musical group?

16. What would you like to do after you graduate from high school?

17. Are students in Mr. Perez's class older than students in Ms. Sato's class?

18. What kind(s) of transportation do you use to get to school?

19. How much time do you spend doing homework?

20. On a scale of 1 to 7, with 7 being outstanding and 1 being poor, how would you rate the cafeteria food?

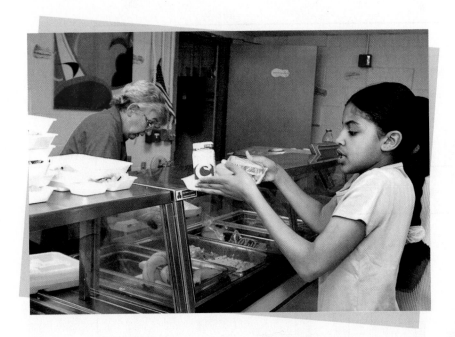

21. Use the graph for Name Lengths from Exercises 7–12. Make a horizontal bar graph of Ms. Campo's students' name length data.

a. What is the median name length? How does it compare with the answer you found in Exercise 12? Why do you think this is so?

b. A new student joins Ms. Campo's class. The student has a name length of 16 letters. Add this data value to your graph. Does the median change? Explain.

Connections

For Exercises 22–25, use the bar graphs below. The graphs show information about a class of middle-school students.

Graph A

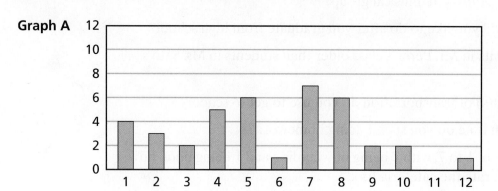

Graph B

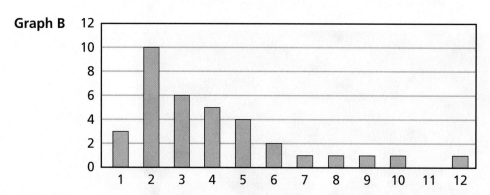

Graph C

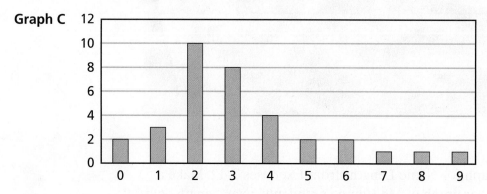

22. Which graph might show the number of children in the students' families? Explain.

23. Which graph might show the birth months of the students? Explain.
Hint: Months are often written using numbers instead of names. For example, 1 means January, 2 means February, etc.

24. Which graph might show the number of toppings students like on their pizzas? Explain.

25. Give a possible title, a label for the vertical axis, and a label for the horizontal axis for each graph based on your answers to Exercises 22–24.

For Exercises 26–31, use the graph below. The graph shows the number of juice drinks 100 middle-school students consume in one day.

Juice Drinks Consumed by Students in One Day

26. A student used this graph to estimate that the median number of juice drinks students consume in a day is five. How can you tell that this estimate is not correct without finding the median?

27. Another student estimates that the median number of juice drinks is 1. Explain why the student is not correct.

28. **Multiple Choice** What is the range of these data?

   A. 9 drinks   **B.** 10 drinks   **C.** 11 drinks   **D.** 12 drinks

29. **a.** What fraction of the students consumed two juice drinks?

   b. What percent of the students consumed three juice drinks?

30. What is the total number of juice drinks these 100 students consume in one day? How did you determine your answer?

31. Are these data numerical or categorical? Explain.

Homework Help Online
PHSchool.com
For: Help with Exercise 29
Web Code: ame-8129

32. Alex has a rat that is three years old. He wonders if his rat is old compared to other rats. At the pet store, he finds out that the median age for a rat is $2\frac{1}{2}$ years.

   a. What does the median tell Alex about the life span for a rat?

   b. How would knowing how the data vary from the least value to the greatest value help Alex predict the life span of his rat?

Extensions

For Exercises 33–39, use the bar graphs below.

A greeting card store sells stickers and street signs with first names on them. The store ordered 12 stickers and 12 street signs for each name. The table and the four bar graphs show the numbers of stickers and street signs that remain for the names that begin with the letter A.

Sales of Stickers and Street Signs

Name	Stickers Remaining	Street Signs Remaining
Aaron	1	9
Adam	2	7
Alicia	7	4
Allison	2	3
Amanda	0	11
Amber	2	3
Amy	3	3
Andrea	2	4
Andrew	8	6
Andy	3	5
Angela	8	4
Ana	10	7

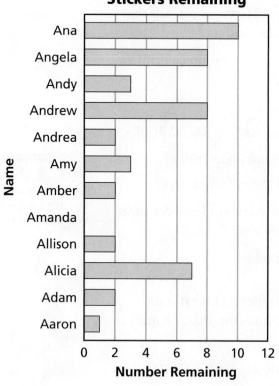

Graph A: Stickers Remaining

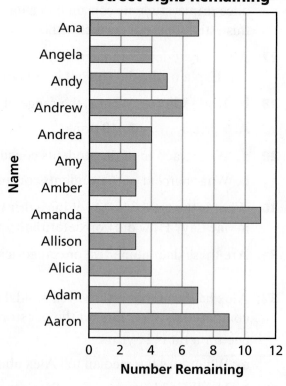

Graph B: Street Signs Remaining

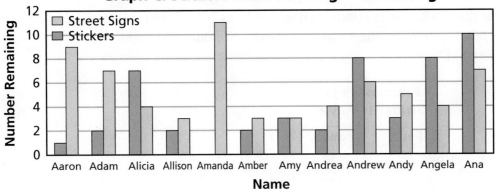

Graph C: Stickers and Street Signs Remaining

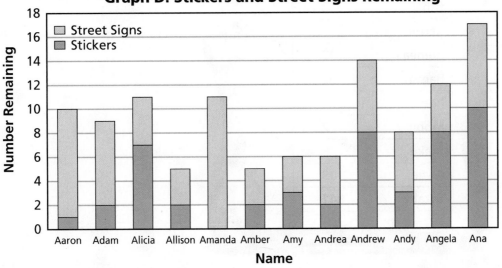

Graph D: Stickers and Street Signs Remaining

33. Use Graph A. How many Alicia stickers are left? How many Alicia stickers have been sold? Explain.

34. Use Graph B. How many Alicia street signs are left? How many Alicia street signs have been sold? Explain.

35. Are the stickers more popular than the street signs? Explain.

36. If each sticker costs $1.50, how much money has the store collected from selling name stickers for names beginning with the letter A?

37. For which name has the store sold the most stickers? For which name has the store sold the least stickers?

38. Graph C is a *double bar graph*. Use this graph to determine the name(s) for which the number of street signs sold and the number of stickers sold are the same.

39. Graph D is a *stacked bar graph*. Use this graph to determine whether some names are more popular than others. Justify your answer.

For Exercises 40–43, use the data below.

These data show the kinds of pets middle-school students have. From these data we cannot tell how many students were surveyed. We only know that 841 pets were counted.

**Kinds of Pets
Students Have**

Pet	Frequency
bird	61
cat	184
dog	180
fish	303
gerbil	17
guinea pig	12
hamster	32
horse	28
rabbit	2
snake	9
turtle	13
Total	**841**

40. Make a bar graph to display the distribution of these data. Think about how you will design and label the horizontal and vertical axes.

41. Use the information displayed in your graph to write a paragraph about the pets these students have. Compare these data with the data in Problem 1.4.

42. Jane said that close to 50% of the animals owned were birds, cats, or dogs. Do you agree or disagree? Explain.

43. What might be a good estimate of how many students were surveyed? (Use the data about number of pets each student had from Problem 1.4 to help you.) Explain.

Mathematical Reflections 1

In this investigation, you learned some ways to describe what is typical about a set of data. The following questions will help you summarize what you have learned.

Think about your answers to these questions. Discuss your ideas with other students and your teacher. Then write a summary of your findings in your notebook.

1. How are a table of data, a line plot, and a bar graph alike? How are they different?

2. What does the mode tell you about the distribution of a set of data? Can the mode be used to describe both categorical data and numerical data?

3. What does the median tell you about the distribution of a set of data? Can the median be used to describe both categorical data and numerical data?

4. Can the mode and the median of a set of data be the same values? Can they be different? Explain.

5. Why is it helpful to give the range when you describe the distribution of a set of data? Can the range be used to describe both categorical and numerical data?

6. How is the range of a set of data related to how the data vary from the least value to the greatest value?

7. How can you describe what is typical about the distribution of a set of data?

Unit Project   What's Next?

To carry out a research project about characteristics of the typical middle-school student, you will need to pose questions. What questions might you ask that would have categorical data as answers? What questions might you ask that have numerical data as answers? How would you display the information you gather about each of these questions? Write your thoughts in your notebook.

Investigation 2

Using Graphs to Explore Data

Sometimes data may be spread out. When these data are displayed on a line plot or a bar graph, it is not easy to see patterns. In this investigation, you will learn how to highlight data using displays called stem-and-leaf plots and back-to-back stem-and-leaf plots to help you see patterns.

In Investigation 1, you analyzed single sets of data. Sometimes you may want to analyze whether there is a relationship between two different data sets. In this investigation, you will learn how to display data pairs from two different data sets using a coordinate graph.

2.1 Traveling to School

While investigating the times they got up in the morning, a middle-school class was surprised to find that two students got up almost an hour earlier than their classmates. These students said they got up early because it took them a long time to get to school. The class then wondered how much time it took each student to travel to school. The data they collected are on the next page.

Getting Ready for Problem 2.1

Use the table on the next page to answer these questions:

- What three questions did the students ask?
- How might the students have collected the travel-time data?
- Would a line plot be a good way to show the data? Why or why not?

Times and Distances to School

Student's Initials	Time (minutes)	Distance (miles)	Mode of Travel
DB	60	4.50	Bus
DD	15	2.00	Bus
CC	30	2.00	Bus
FH	35	2.50	Bus
SE	15	0.75	Car
AE	15	1.00	Bus
CL	15	1.00	Bus
LM	22	2.00	Bus
QN	25	1.50	Bus
MP	20	1.50	Bus
AP	25	1.25	Bus
AP	19	2.25	Bus
HCP	15	1.50	Bus
KR	8	0.25	Walking
NS	8	1.25	Car
LS	5	0.50	Bus
AT	20	2.75	Bus
JW	15	1.50	Bus
DW	17	2.50	Bus
SW	15	2.00	Car
NW	10	0.50	Walking
JW	20	0.50	Walking
CW	15	2.25	Bus
BA	30	3.00	Bus
JB	20	2.50	Bus
AB	50	4.00	Bus
BB	30	4.75	Bus
MB	20	2.00	Bus
RC	10	1.25	Bus
CD	5	0.25	Walking
ME	5	0.50	Bus
CF	20	1.75	Bus
KG	15	1.75	Bus
TH	11	1.50	Bus
EL	6	1.00	Car
KLD	35	0.75	Bus
MN	17	4.50	Bus
JO	10	3.00	Car
RP	21	1.50	Bus
ER	10	1.00	Bus

The students decide to make a stem-and-leaf plot of the travel times.

A **stem-and-leaf plot** looks like a vertical stem with leaves to the right of it. It is sometimes simply called a *stem plot*.

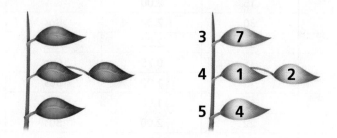

To make a stem plot to represent travel times, separate each data value into a left "stem" and a right "leaf."

For these data, the "stem" will be the tens digits. Because the travel times include values from 5 minutes to 60 minutes, the stem will be the digits 0, 1, 2, 3, 4, 5, and 6.

- Make a vertical list of the tens digits in order from least to greatest.
- Draw a line to the right of the digits to separate the stem from the "leaves."

```
0 |
1 |
2 |
3 |
4 |
5 |
6 |
```

The "leaves" will be the ones digits. For each data value, add a leaf next to the appropriate tens digit on the stem.

- The first data value is 60 minutes. Write a 0 next to the stem of 6.
- The next value is 15 minutes. Write a 5 next to the stem of 1.
- The travel times of 30 and 35 minutes are shown by a 0 and 5 next to the stem of 3.

```
0 |
1 | 5
2 |
3 | 0 5
4 |
5 |
6 | 0
```

A. Use the Travel to School data to make the stem plot. The plot is started for you.

```
0 |
1 | 5 5 5 5
2 | 2 5 0
3 | 0 5
4 |
5 |
6 | 0
```

B. Now redraw the stem plot, putting the data in each leaf in order from least to greatest. Include a title for your plot. Also include a key like the following that tells how to read the plot.

Key
2 | 5 means 25 minutes

C. Which students probably get to sleep the latest in the morning? Why do you think this?

D. Which students probably get up the earliest? Why do you think this?

E. What is the median of the travel-time data? Explain how you found this.

F. What is the range of the travel-time data? Explain.

ACE **Homework starts on page 40.**

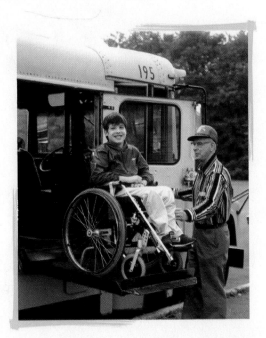

Mrs. Reid's class competed against Mr. Costo's class in a jump-rope contest. Each student jumped as many times as possible. Another student counted the jumps and recorded the total. The classes made the *back-to-back stem plot* shown to display their data. Look at this plot carefully. Try to figure out how to read it.

When the two classes compare their results, they disagree about which class did better.

- Mr. Costo's class says that the range of their data is much greater.

- Mrs. Reid's class says this is only because they had one person who jumped many more times than anybody else.

- Mrs. Reid's class claims that most of them jumped more times than most of the students in Mr. Costo's class.

- Mr. Costo's class argues that even if they do not count the person with 300 jumps, they still did better.

Number of Jumps

Mrs. Reid's class		Mr. Costo's class
8 7 7 7 5 1 1	0	1 1 2 3 4 5 8 8
6 1 1	1	0 7
9 7 6 3 0 0	2	3 7 8
7 6 5 3	3	0 3 5
5 0	4	2 7 8
	5	0 2 3
2	6	0 8
	7	
9 8 0	8	
6 3 1	9	
	10	2 4
3	11	
	12	
	13	
	14	
	15	1
	16	0 0
	17	
	18	
	19	
	20	
	21	
	22	
	23	
	24	
	25	
	26	
	27	
	28	
	29	
	30	0

Key: 7 | 3 | 0 means 37 jumps for Mrs. Reid's class and 30 jumps for Mr. Costo's class

A. Which class did better overall in the jump-rope contest? Use what you know about statistics to help you justify your answer.

B. In Mr. Costo's class, there are some very large numbers of jumps. For example, one student jumped 151 times, and another student jumped 300 times. We call these data outliers. **Outliers** are data values that are located far from the rest of the other values in a set of data. Find two other outliers in the data for Mr. Costo's class.

C. An outlier may be a value that was recorded incorrectly, or it may be a signal that something special is happening. All the values recorded for Mr. Costo's class are correct. What might account for the few students who jumped many more times than their classmates?

ACE Homework starts on page 40.

In earlier problems, you worked with one measure at a time. For example, you looked at the number of letters in students' names and travel times to school. In this problem, you will look at the relationship between two different counts or measures.

If you look around at your classmates, you might guess that taller people have wider arm spans. But is there *really* any relationship between a person's height and his or her arm span? The best way to find out more about this question is to collect some data.

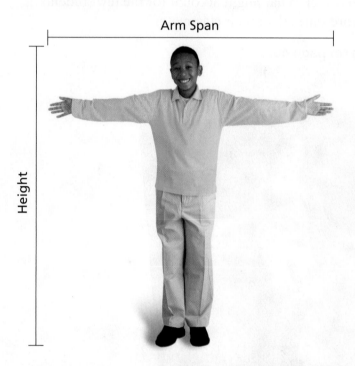

Arm Span

Height

Here are data on height and arm span (measured from fingertip to fingertip) that one class collected.

Height and Arm Span Measurements

Initials	Height (inches)	Arm Span (inches)
NY	63	60
JJ	69	67
CM	73	75
PL	77	77
BP	64	65
AS	67	64
KR	58	58

You can show two different data values at the same time on a **coordinate graph.** Each point on a coordinate graph represents two data values. The horizontal axis, or *x*-axis, represents one data value. The vertical axis, or *y*-axis, represents a second data value. The graph below shows data for height along the *x*-axis and data for arm span along the *y*-axis. Each point on the graph represents the height and the arm span for one student.

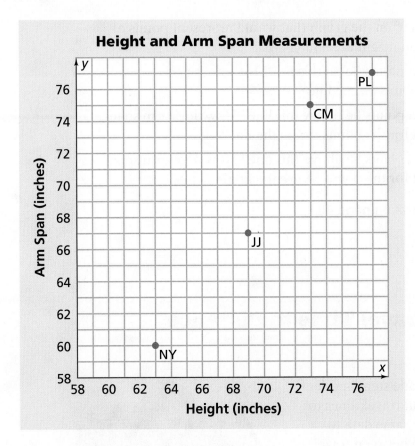

Study the table of data on the previous page and the coordinate graph. Four points have already been plotted and labeled with the students' initials. The location of each point is shown in the table at the right.

Initials	Point
NY	(63, 60)
JJ	(69, 67)
CM	(73, 75)
PL	(77, 77)

Getting Ready for Problem

- Where would you place the points and initials for the remaining three people?
- Why do the axes of the graph start at (58, 58)?
- What would the graph look like if the axes started at (0, 0)?

Problem 2.3 Making and Reading Coordinate Graphs

Collect the height and arm span data of each person in your class. Make a coordinate graph of your data. Use the graph to answer the questions.

A. If you know the measure of a person's arm span, do you know his or her height? Explain.

B. Draw a diagonal line on the graph that would represent points at which arm span and height are equal.

    1. How many data points lie on this line? How does arm span relate to height for the points *on* the line?

    2. How many data points lie below this line? How does arm span relate to height for the points *below* the line?

    3. How many data points lie above this line? How does arm span relate to height for the points *above* the line?

ACE | Homework starts on page 40.

2.4 Relating Travel Time to Distance

In Problem 2.1, you made stem-and-leaf plots to show data about travel times to school. You can use the same data to look at the relationship between travel time and distance from home to school on a coordinate graph.

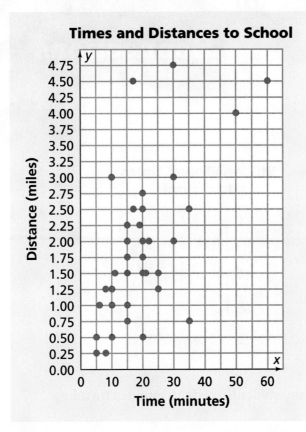

Times and Distances to School

Distance (miles) vs *Time (minutes)*

Problem 2.4 Using Coordinate Graphs to Find Relationships

Study the graph above and the data from Problem 2.1.

A. Copy the coordinate graph. Mark and label a point with the student's initial for the first five students in the table.

B. If you know a student's travel time, what do you know about that student's distance from school? Use the graph to justify your answer.

C. Locate each set of points on the coordinate graph. What can you tell about travel time and distance from school for the students these points represent?

1. (17, 4.50) and (60, 4.50)

2. (30, 2.00), (30, 3.00), and (30, 4.75)

3. (17, 4.50) and (30, 4.75)

D. 1. Why do the axes have different scales?

2. What would the graph look like if both axes used the same scales?

ACE Homework starts on page 40.

active math online

For: Statistical Tool
Visit: PHSchool.com
Web Code: amd-8204

Applications

For Exercises 1–4, use the stem-and-leaf plot at the right.

Student Travel Times to School

```
0 | 3 3 5 7 8 9
1 | 0 2 3 5 6 6 8 9
2 | 0 1 3 3 3 5 5 8 8
3 | 0 5
4 | 5
```
Key: 2 | 5 means 25 min

1. **Multiple Choice** How many students spent 10 minutes traveling to school?

   A. 1   **B.** 9   **C.** 10   **D.** 19

2. **Multiple Choice** How many students spent 15 minutes or more traveling to school?

   F. 10   **G.** 16   **H.** 17   **J.** 25

3. How many students are in the class? Explain.

4. What is the typical time it took these students to travel to school? Explain.

For Exercises 5–8, use the table on the next page.

5. Make a stem-and-leaf plot of the students' ages. The plot has been started for you at the right. Notice that the first value in the stem is 6, because there are no values less than 60 months.

6. What ages, in years, does the interval of 80–89 months represent?

7. What is the median age of these students?

8. **a.** On a piece of grid paper, make a coordinate graph. Show age (in months) on the horizontal axis and height (in centimeters) on the vertical axis. To help you choose a scale for each axis, look at the least and greatest values for each measure.

   b. Explain how you can use your graph to find out whether the youngest student is also the shortest student.

```
 6
 7
 8
 9
10
11
12
13
14
15
```

c. Use your graph to describe what happens to students' heights as the students get older.

d. What would happen to the graph if you extended it to include people in their late teens or early twenties? Explain.

Student Ages, Heights, and Foot Lengths

Age (mo)	Height (cm)	Foot Length (cm)	Age (mo)	Height (cm)	Foot Length (cm)
76	126	24	148	164	26
73	117	24	140	152	22
68	112	17	114	135	20
78	123	22	108	135	22
81	117	20	105	147	22
82	122	23	113	138	22
80	130	22	120	141	20
90	127	21	120	146	24
101	127	21	132	147	23
99	124	21	132	155	21
103	130	20	129	141	22
101	134	21	138	161	28
145	172	32	152	156	30
146	163	27	149	157	27
144	158	25	132	150	25

9. The coordinate graph below shows the height and foot length data from the table on the previous page. Notice that the scale on the *x*-axis uses intervals of 5 centimeters and the scale on the *y*-axis uses intervals of 1 centimeter.

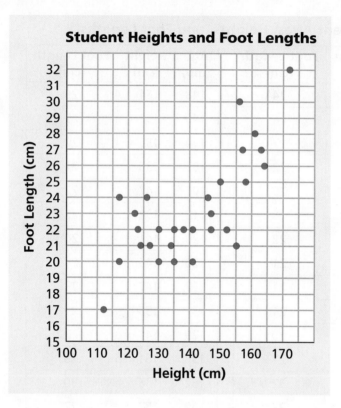

Student Heights and Foot Lengths

a. If you know a person's foot length, can you tell that person's height? Explain.

b. Find the median height and the median foot length. The median height is about how many times the median foot length?

c. Measure the length of your foot in centimeters. Your height is about how many times your foot length?

d. Look at your responses to parts (b) and (c). How can you use this information to answer part (a)? Explain.

e. What would the graph look like if you started each axis at 0?

Connections

10. a. Use the data in the Student Ages, Heights, and Foot Lengths table from Exercises 5–8. Make a stem-and-leaf plot of the students' heights.

b. Describe how to make a line plot of the students' heights. What are the least and greatest data values? How does this help you make the line plot?

c. Describe how to make a bar graph of the students' heights. What are the least and greatest data values? How does this help you make the graph?

d. Why might you display these data using a stem-and-leaf plot instead of a line plot or a bar graph?

11. The table below shows some of the Student Ages, Heights, and Foot Lengths data in centimeters. The table includes two new columns. Copy and complete the table to show heights and foot lengths in meters.

For: Help with Exercise 11
Web Code: ame-8211

a. Round the height for each student to the nearest tenth of a meter.

b. Make a line plot showing these rounded height data.

c. What is the typical height for these students in meters? Explain.

Student Ages, Heights, and Foot Lengths

Age (mo)	Height (cm)	Height (m)	Foot Length (cm)	Foot Length (m)
76	126	■	24	■
73	117	■	24	■
68	112	■	17	■
78	123	■	22	■
81	117	■	20	■
82	122	■	23	■
80	130	■	22	■
90	127	■	21	■
138	161	■	28	■
152	156	■	30	■
149	157	■	27	■
132	150	■	25	■

12. The pie chart shows the portion of time Harold spent on homework in each subject last week.

Time Spent on Homework

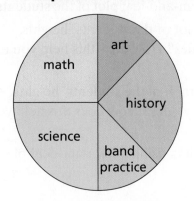

a. If Harold spent two hours on math homework, about how many hours did he spend on homework altogether?

b. About what percent of his time did Harold spend on math, science, and history homework? Explain.

Extensions

For Exercises 13 and 14, use the jump-rope data on the next page.

13. Make a back-to-back stem-and-leaf plot that compares either the girls in Mrs. Reid's class with the girls in Mr. Costo's class or the boys in Mrs. Reid's class with the boys in Mr. Costo's class. Did the girls (or boys) in one class do better than the girls (or boys) in the other class? Explain your reasoning.

14. Make a back-to-back stem-and-leaf plot that compares the girls in both classes with the boys in both classes. Did the girls do better than the boys? Explain.

Number of Jumps

Mrs. Reid's Class Data		Mr. Costo's Class Data	
Boy	5	Boy	1
Boy	35	Boy	30
Girl	91	Boy	28
Boy	62	Boy	10
Girl	96	Girl	27
Girl	23	Girl	102
Boy	16	Boy	47
Boy	1	Boy	8
Boy	8	Girl	160
Boy	11	Girl	23
Girl	93	Boy	17
Girl	27	Boy	2
Girl	88	Girl	68
Boy	26	Boy	50
Boy	7	Girl	151
Boy	7	Boy	60
Boy	1	Boy	5
Boy	40	Girl	52
Boy	7	Girl	4
Boy	20	Girl	35
Girl	20	Boy	160
Girl	89	Boy	1
Boy	29	Boy	3
Boy	11	Boy	8
Boy	113	Girl	48
Boy	33	Boy	42
Girl	45	Boy	33
Girl	80	Girl	300
Boy	36	Girl	104
Girl	37	Girl	53

15. A group of students challenged each other to see who could come the closest to guessing the number of seeds in his or her pumpkin. The data they collected are shown in the table and the graph.

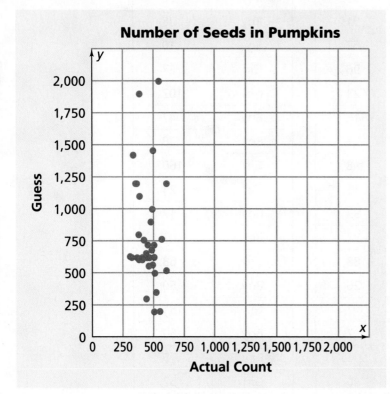

Number of Seeds in Pumpkins

Guess	Actual
630	309
621	446
801	381
720	505
1,900	387
1,423	336
621	325
1,200	365
622	410
1,000	492
1,200	607
1,458	498
350	523
621	467
759	423
900	479
500	512
521	606
564	494
655	441
722	455
202	553
621	367
300	442
200	507
556	462
604	384
2,000	545
1,200	354
766	568
624	506
680	486
605	408
1,100	387

a. What do you notice about how the actual counts vary? What are the median and the least and greatest values of the actual counts?

b. What do you notice about how the guesses vary? What are the median and the least and greatest values of the guesses?

c. Make your own coordinate graph of the data. Draw a diagonal line on the graph to connect the points $(0, 0)$, $(250, 250)$, $(500, 500)$, all the way to $(2,250, 2,250)$.

d. What is true about the guesses compared to the actual counts for points near the line you drew?

e. What is true about the guesses compared to the actual counts for points above the line?

f. What is true about the guesses compared to the actual counts for points below the line?

g. In general, did the students make good guesses? Use what you know about median and range to explain your reasoning.

h. The scales on the axes are the same, but the data are bunched together. How would you change the scale to show the data points better?

Mathematical Reflections 2

In this investigation, you learned how to make stem-and-leaf plots as a way to group a set of data so you can study its shape. You have also learned how to make and read coordinate graphs. Coordinate graphs let you examine two things at once so you can look for relationships between them. The following questions will help you summarize what you have learned.

Think about your answers to these questions. Discuss your ideas with other students and your teacher. Then write a summary of your findings in your notebook.

1. Describe how to locate the median and range using a stem plot.

2. When you make a coordinate graph of data pairs, how do you determine where to place each point?

3. What do you consider when choosing a scale for each axis of a coordinate graph?

4. Numerical data can be displayed using more than one kind of graph. How do you decide when to use a line plot, a bar graph, a stem-and-leaf plot, or a coordinate graph?

Unit Project What's Next?

Think about the survey you will be conducting about middle-school students. What kinds of questions can you ask that might involve using a stem-and-leaf plot to display the data? Can you sort your data into two groups and use a back-to-back stem plot to help you compare the data?

Investigation 3

What Do We Mean by *Mean*?

The main use of the United States Census is to find out how many people live in the United States. The census provides useful information about household size. In the census, the term *household* means all the people who live in a "housing unit" (such as a house, an apartment, or a room of a boarding house).

In earlier investigations, you used median and mode to describe a set of data. Another measure of center is the *mean*. It is the most commonly used measure of center for numerical data. Another word often used to indicate the mean of a set of data is *average*.

3.1 Finding the Mean

Six students in a middle-school class use the United States Census guidelines to find the number of people in their household. Each student then makes a stack of cubes to show the number of people in his or her household.

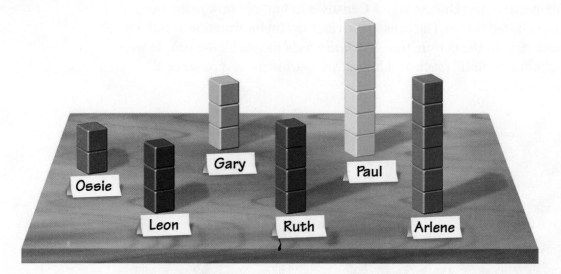

You can see from the stacks that the six households vary in size.

Getting Ready for Problem 3.1

Use cubes and make stacks like the ones shown above. Use the stacks to answer these questions:

- What is the median of these data?
- What is the mode of these data?

Make the stacks all the same height by moving cubes.

- How many cubes are in each stack?
- The average stack height you found represents the mean number of people in a household. What is the mean number of people in a household?

Another group of students made the table below.

Household Size

Name	Number of People
Reggie	6
Tara	4
Brendan	3
Felix	4
Hector	3
Tonisha	4

A. Make stacks of cubes to show the size of each household.

    1. How many people are in the six households altogether? Explain.

    2. What is the mean number of people per household? Explain.

    3. How does the mean for these data compare to the mean for the data in the Getting Ready?

B. What are some ways to determine the mean number of a set of data other than using cubes?

ACE Homework starts on page 56.

The line plots below show two different distributions with the same mean.

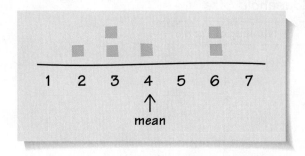

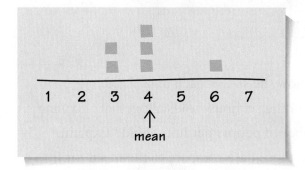

Getting Ready for Problem 3.2

- How many households are there in each situation?
- What is the total number of people in each situation?
- How do these facts relate to the mean in each case?

A. Find two new data sets for six households that each has a mean of 4 people per household. Use cubes to show each data set. Then make line plots from the cubes.

B. Find two different data sets for seven households that each has a mean of 4 people per household. Use cubes to show each set. Then make line plots from the cubes.

C. A group of seven students find they have a mean of 3 people per household. Find a data set that fits this description. Then make a line plot for this data.

D. 1. A group of six students has a mean of $3\frac{1}{2}$ people per household. Find a data set that fits this description. Then make a line plot for this data.

    2. How can the mean be $3\frac{1}{2}$ people when "half" a person does not exist?

    3. How can you predict when the mean number of people per household will not be a whole number?

ACE Homework starts on page 56.

A group of middle-school students answered the question: How many movies did you watch last month? The table and stem plot show their data.

Movies Watched

Student	Number
Joel	15
Tonya	16
Rachel	5
Swanson	18
Jerome	3
Leah	6
Beth	7
Mickey	6
Bhavana	3
Josh	11

Movies Watched

```
0 | 3 3 5 6 6 7
1 | 1 5 6 8
2 |
```
Key: 1 | 5 means 15 movies

You have found the mean using cubes to represent the data. You may know the following procedure to find the mean: The **mean** of a set of data is the sum of the values divided by the number of values in the set.

Problem 3.3 Using the Mean

A. Use the movie data to find each number.

1. the total number of students

2. the total number of movies watched

3. the mean number of movies watched

B. A new value is added for Carlos, who was home last month with a broken leg. He watched 31 movies.

1. How does the new value change the distribution on the stem plot?

2. Is this new value an outlier? Explain.

3. What is the mean of the data now?

4. Compare the mean from Question A to the new mean. What do you notice? Explain.

C. Data for eight more students are added:

Tommy	5	Robbie	4
Alexandra	5	Ana	4
Trevor	5	Alicia	2
Kirsten	4	Brian	2

1. How do these values change the distribution on the stem plot?

2. Are any of these new data values outliers? Explain.

3. What is the mean of the data now?

4. Compare the means you found in Questions A and B with this new mean. What do you notice? Explain.

D. 1. What happens to the mean of a data set when you add one or more data values that are outliers? Explain.

2. What happens to the mean of a data set when you add data values that cluster near one end of the original data set? Explain.

3. Explain why you think these changes might occur.

ACE **Homework starts on page 56.**

Applications

For Exercises 1 and 2, use the line plot.

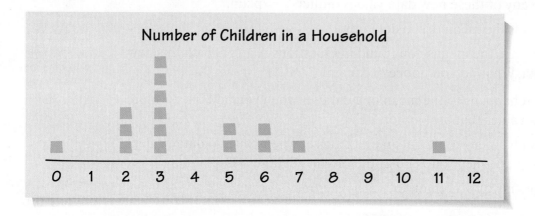

Number of Children in a Household

1. a. What is the median number of children for the 16 households? Explain how to find the median. What does the median tell you?

  b. Do any of the 16 households have the median number of children? Explain.

2. a. What is the mean number of children per household for the 16 households? Explain how to find the mean. What does the mean tell you?

  b. Do any of the 16 households have the mean number of children? Explain.

For Exercises 3 and 4, the mean number of people per household for eight households is 6 people.

3. Multiple Choice What is the total number of people in the eight households?

  A. 11   **B.** 16   **C.** 48   **D.** 64

4. a. Make a line plot showing one possible arrangement for the numbers of people in the eight households.

  b. Make a line plot showing a different possible arrangement for the numbers of people in the eight households.

  c. Are the medians the same for the two arrangements you made?

5. A group of nine students has a mean of $3\frac{1}{3}$ people per household. Make a line plot showing a data set that fits this description.

6. A group of nine students has a mean of 5 people per household. The largest household in the group has 10 people. Make a line plot showing a data set that fits this description.

Connections

7. The students in Mr. Wilson's study hall spent the following amounts of time on their homework.

$\frac{3}{4}$ hour $\frac{1}{2}$ hour $1\frac{1}{4}$ hours $\frac{3}{4}$ hour $\frac{1}{2}$ hour

What is the mean time his students spent on homework?

8. Multiple Choice Use the data from Exercise 7. What is the median time Mr. Wilson's students spent on homework?

F. $\frac{1}{2}$ hour   **G.** $\frac{3}{4}$ hour   **H.** 1 hour   **J.** $1\frac{1}{4}$ hour

9. A soccer league wants to find the average amount of water the players drink per game. There are 18 players on a team and 10 teams in the league. The players drank a total of 5,760 ounces of water during one day in which each team played exactly one game.

a. How much water did each player drink per game if they each drank the same amount of water?

b. Does this value represent the mean or the median? Explain.

10. A grocery store carries nine different brands of granola bars. What are possible prices for the nine brands if the mean price is $2.66? Explain. You may use pictures to help you.

11. Ralph has a pet rabbit that is 5 years old. He wonders if his rabbit is old compared to other rabbits. He finds out that the mean life span for a rabbit is 7 years.

    a. What does the mean tell Ralph about the life span for a rabbit?

    b. What additional information would help Ralph to predict the life span of his rabbit?

12. Sabrina, Diego, and Marcus entered a dance contest that ran from 9 a.m. to 7 p.m. Below are the times that each student danced.

Homework Help Online
PHSchool.com
For: Help with Exercise 12
Web Code: ame-8312

Dance Contest Schedule

Student	Time
Sabrina	9:15 a.m. to 1:00 p.m.
Diego	1:00 p.m. to 4:45 p.m.
Marcus	4:45 p.m. to 7:00 p.m.

    a. Write the time each student spent dancing as a mixed number.

    b. Look at the data from part (a). Without doing any computations, do you think the mean time spent dancing is the same as, less than, or greater than the median? Explain your reasoning.

For Exercises 13–16, a recent time study of 3,000 children ages 2–18 years old was conducted. The data are in the table below.

How Children Spend Their Time

Activity	Time (minutes per day)
Watching videos	39
Reading for fun	44
Using the computer for fun	21

13. Did each child watch videos for 39 minutes per day? Explain.

14. Thelma decides to round 39 minutes to 40 minutes. Then she estimates that children spend about $\frac{2}{3}$ of an hour watching videos. What percent of an hour is $\frac{2}{3}$?

15. Estimate what part of an hour children spend reading for fun. Write your answer as a fraction and as a decimal.

16. Children use a computer for fun for about 20 minutes per day. How many hours do they spend using a computer for fun in 1 week (7 days)? Write your answer as a fraction and as a decimal.

17. Three candidates are running for mayor of Slugville. Each has determined the typical income for the people in Slugville, using this information to help in their campaigns.

Mayor Phillips is running for re-election. He says, "Slugville is doing great! The average income for each person is $2,000 per week!"

Candidate Lily Jackson says, "Slugville is nice, but it needs my help! The average income is only $100 per week."

Candidate Ronnie Ruis says, "Slugville is in a lot of trouble! The average income is $0 per week."

Some of the candidates are confused about "average." Slugville has only 16 residents, and their weekly incomes are $0, $0, $0, $0, $0, $0, $0, $0, $200, $200, $200, $200, $200, $200, $200, and $30,600.

a. Explain which measure of center each of the candidates used as an "average" income for the town. Check their computations.

b. Does any person in Slugville have the mean income? Explain.

c. Does any person in Slugville have an income that equals the median? Explain.

d. Does any person in Slugville have an income that equals the mode? Explain.

e. What do you consider to be the typical income for a resident of Slugville? Explain.

f. Suppose four more people move to Slugville. Each has a weekly income of $200. How would the mean, median, and mode change?

18. A recent survey asked 25 middle-school students how many movies they watch in one month. The data are shown below. Notice that the data varies from 1 to 30 movies.

Movies Watched

Student	Number
Wes	2
Tomi	15
Ling	13
Su Chin	1
Michael	9
Mara	30
Alan	20
Jo	1
Tanisha	25
Susan	4
Gil	3
Enrique	2
Lonnie	3
Ken	10
Kristina	15
Mario	12
Henry	5
Julian	2
Alana	4
Tyrone	1
Rebecca	4
Anton	11
Jun	8
Raymond	8
Angelica	17

a. Make a stem-and-leaf plot to show these data. Describe the shape of the data.

b. Find the mean number of movies watched by the students. Explain.

c. What do the mean and how the data vary tell you about the typical number of movies watched for this group of students?

d. Find the median number of movies watched. Are the mean and the median the same? Why do you think this is so?

19. Six students each had a different number of pens. They put them all together and then distributed them so that each student had the same number of pens.

    a. Choose any of the following that could be the number of pens they had altogether. Explain your reasoning.

        A. 12   **B.** 18   **C.** 46   **D.** 48

    b. Use your response from part (a). How many pens did each person have after the pens were distributed evenly?

    c. Your classmate says that finding the mean number of pens per person is the same as finding the number of pens each person had after the pens were distributed evenly. Do you agree or disagree? Explain.

Extensions

For Exercises 20 and 21, use the newspaper headline.

Daily News

Volume 1

How much TV is too much?
Third Graders Spend an Average of 900 Hours a Year in School and 1,170 Hours Watching TV

In a study done this year in over 500 cities in the US, reports of very high

20. Do you think that this headline is referring to a mean, a median, or something else? Explain.

21. About how many hours per day does the average third grader watch television if he or she watches 1,170 hours in a year?

22. Review the jump-rope data from Problem 2.2.

    a. What are the median and the mean for each class's data? How do the median and the mean compare for each class?

    b. Should Mr. Costo's class use the median or the mode to compare their performance with Mrs. Reid's class? Why?

    c. What happens to the median of Mr. Costo's class data if you leave out the data for the student who jumped rope 300 times? Why does this happen?

    d. What happens to the mean of Mr. Costo's class data if you leave out the data for the student who jumped rope 300 times? Why does this happen?

    e. Can Mrs. Reid's class claim they did better if Mr. Costo's class leaves out the data of 300 jumps? Explain.

23. A group of middle-school students answered the question: How many TV shows did you watch last week? The table at the right shows their data.

    a. Use the data to find the mean number of TV shows watched.

    b. A new value is added for Albert. He watched only 1 TV show last week.

        i. Is this new value an outlier?

        ii. What is the mean of the data now?

        iii. Compare this mean to the mean you found in part (a). What do you notice? Explain.

Student	Number of TV Shows Watched
Caleb	17
Malek	13
Jenna	20
Mario	8
Melania	11
Bennett	13
Anna	16

Mathematical Reflections 3

In this investigation, you have explored a type of measure of center called the mean. It is important to understand this mean, or average, and to relate it to the mode and the median. The following questions will help you summarize what you have learned.

Think about your answers to these questions. Discuss your ideas with other students and your teacher. Then write a summary of your findings in your notebook.

1. Describe a method for calculating mean. Explain why this method works.

2. You have used three measures of center: mode, median, and mean.

   a. Why do you suppose they are called "measures of center"?

   b. What does each tell you about a set of data?

   c. Why might you use the median instead of the mean?

3. You have also used range and how data vary from least to greatest values to describe data. Why might you use these with a measure of center to describe a data set?

4. Once you collect data to answer questions, you must decide what statistics you can use to describe your data.

   a. One student says you can only use the mode to describe categorical data, but you can use the mode, median, and mean to describe numerical data. Is the student correct? Explain.

   b. Can you find range for categorical data? Explain.

Unit Project What's Next?

For your project for the unit, you are developing your own survey to gather information about middle-school students. What statistics can you use to describe the data you might collect for each question in your survey?

Unit Project

Is Anyone Typical?

You can use what you have learned in *Data About Us* to conduct a statistical investigation. Answer the question, "What are some characteristics of a typical middle-school student?" Complete your data collection, analysis, and interpretation. Then make a poster, write a report, or find some other way to display your results.

Your statistical investigation should consist of four parts:

- Asking Questions

    Decide what information you want to gather. You will want to gather both numerical data and categorical data. Your data may include physical characteristics, family characteristics, behaviors (such as hobbies), and preferences or opinions.

    Once you have decided what you want to know, write clear and appropriate questions. Everyone who takes your survey should interpret your questions the same way. For some questions, you may want to give answer choices. For example, instead of asking, "What is your favorite movie?" you could ask, "Which of the following movies do you like best?" and list several choices.

- Collecting the Data

    You can collect data from just your class or from a larger group of students. Decide how to distribute and collect the survey.

- Analyzing the Data

    Once you have collected your data, organize, display, and analyze them. Think about what types of displays and which measures of center are most appropriate for each set of data values you collect.

- Interpreting the Results

    Use the results of your analysis to describe some characteristics of the typical middle-school student. Is there a student that fits all the "typical" characteristics you found? If not, explain why.

Looking Back and Looking Ahead

Working on the problems in this unit, you explored some of the big ideas involved in conducting statistical investigations. You learned how to

- use a process of statistical investigation to pose questions, collect and analyze data, and interpret results
- represent data using bar graphs, line plots, stem-and-leaf plots, and coordinate graphs
- explore ways of using statistics such as mean, median, mode, and range to describe what is "typical" about data
- develop a variety of ways to compare data sets

Go Online
PHSchool.com

For: Vocabulary Review
Puzzle
Web Code: amj-8051

Use Your Understanding: Statistical Reasoning

Naturalists in their studies of wild animal populations often use statistical reasoning. The data in the table on the next page show the lengths (in inches) and weights (in pounds) of 25 alligators captured in central Florida.

Lengths and Weights of Captured Alligators

Gator Number	Length (inches)	Weight (pounds)	Gator Number	Length (inches)	Weight (pounds)
1	74	54	14	88	70
2	94	110	15	58	28
3	85	84	16	90	102
4	61	44	17	94	130
5	128	366	18	68	39
6	72	61	19	78	57
7	89	84	20	86	80
8	90	106	21	72	38
9	63	33	22	74	51
10	82	80	23	147	640
11	114	197	24	76	42
12	69	36	25	86	90
13	86	83			

1. Consider the lengths of the alligators in the sample.

   a. Make a graph of the lengths of the 25 alligators. Describe the distribution of lengths in the graph.

   b. What are the mean and median lengths? Which might you use to describe the typical length of an alligator?

   c. What are the range and the least and greatest values of the lengths?

2. Consider the weights of alligators in the sample.

   a. Make a graph of the weights of the 25 alligators. Describe the distribution of weights in the graph.

   b. What are the mean and median weights? Which might you use to describe the typical weight of an alligator?

   c. What are the range and the least and greatest values of the weights?

3. **a.** Make a coordinate graph of the (*length*, *weight*) data.

   b. What do you notice about the relationship between length and weight of alligators in the sample that are

      i. 61 and 63 inches long?   **ii.** 82, 85, and 86 inches long?

      iii. 90, 94, and 114 inches long?

   c. What weight would you predict for an alligator that is

      i. 70 inches long?   **ii.** 100 inches long?

      iii. 130 inches long?

   d. Do you believe it is possible to make a good estimate for the weight of an alligator if you know its length?

Explain Your Reasoning

When you describe a collection of data, you look for the shape of the distribution of the data. You can often visualize data patterns using graphs.

4. How do the mean and the median help in describing the distribution of data in a data set?

5. How do the range and how data vary from least to greatest values help in describing the distribution of data in a data set?

6. How do you know when to use each graph to display numerical data?

   a. line plots   **b.** stem-and-leaf plots   **c.** coordinate graphs

7. What does it mean to say that a person's arm span *is related to* his or her height, or that the weight of an alligator *is related to* its length?

Look Ahead

The ideas about statistics and data analysis that you have learned in this unit will be used and extended in a variety of future *Connected Mathematics* units. In *Data Distributions*, you will explore how data vary and ways to compare data sets. In *Samples and Populations*, you will explore sampling, comparing samples, and comparing different variables in a sample. You'll also find that various statistical plots and data summaries appear in everyday news reports and in the technical work of science, business, and government.

B

bar graph (bar chart) A graphical representation of a table of data in which the height or length of each bar indicates its frequency. The bars are separated from each other to highlight that the data are discrete or "counted" data. In a vertical bar graph, the horizontal axis shows the values or categories, and the vertical axis shows the frequency or tally for each of the values or categories on the horizontal axis. In a horizontal bar graph, the vertical axis shows the values or categories, and the horizontal axis shows the frequencies.

gráfica de barras (tabla de barras) Representación gráfica de una tabla de datos en la que la altura o longitud de cada barra indica su frecuencia. Las barras están separadas entre sí para subrayar que los datos son discretos o "contados". En una gráfica de barras vertical, el eje horizontal representa los valores o categorías, y el eje vertical representa la frecuencia o el cómputo de cada uno de los valores o categorías en el eje horizontal. En una gráfica de barras horizontal, el eje vertical representa los valores o categorías, y el eje horizontal representa las frecuencias.

Vertical Bar Graph

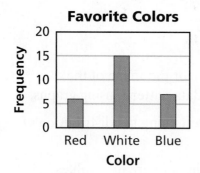

Horizontal Bar Graph

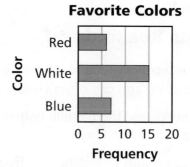

C

categorical data Data that are "words" that represent possible responses within a given category. Frequency counts can be made of the values for a given category. The table below shows examples of categories and their possible values.

datos categóricos Valores que son "palabras" que representan respuestas posibles en una categoría dada. Se pueden contar las frecuencias de los valores para una categoría dada. La siguiente tabla muestra ejemplos de categorías y sus posibles valores.

Category	Possible Values
Month people are born	January, February, March
Favorite color to wear	magenta, blue, yellow
Kinds of pets people have	cats, dogs, fish, horses

coordinate graph A graphical representation in which points are used to denote pairs of related numerical values. For each point, the two coordinates of the point give the associated numerical values in the appropriate order. Using the table below, the *x*-coordinate could represent height, and the *y*-coordinate could represent arm span. The coordinate graph would look like the one below the table.

gráfica de coordenadas Representación gráfica en la que se usan puntos para denotar los pares de valores numéricos relacionados. Para cada punto, las dos coordenadas del punto dan los valores numéricos asociados en el orden apropiado. En la tabla de abajo, la coordenada *x* podría representar la altura y la coordenada *y* podría representar la longitud del brazo. La gráfica de coordenada sería como la que está debajo de la tabla.

Height and Arm Span Measurements

Initials	Height (inches)	Arm Span (inches)
JJ	69	67
NY	63	60
CM	73	75
PL	77	77

Height and Arm Span Measurements

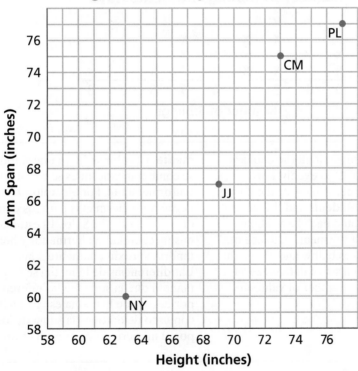

D

data Values such as counts, ratings, measurements, or opinions that are gathered to answer questions. The data in this table show mean temperatures in three cities.

datos Valores como cómputos, calificaciones, medidas u opiniones que se recogen para responder a preguntas. Los datos en esta tabla representan las temperaturas medias en tres ciudades.

Daily Mean Temperatures

City	Mean Temperature (°F)
Mobile, Ala.	67.5
Boston, Mass.	51.3
Spokane, Wash.	47.3

L

line plot A quick, simple way to organize data along a number line where the Xs (or other symbols) above a number represent how often each value is mentioned.

diagrama de puntos Una manera rápida y sencilla de organizar datos en una recta numérica donde las X (u otros símbolos) colocadas encima de un número representan la frecuencia con que se menciona cada valor.

Number of Siblings Students Have

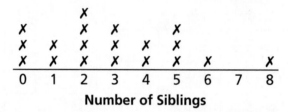

Number of Siblings

M

mean The value you would get if all the data are combined and then redistributed evenly. For example, the total number of siblings for the above data is 56 siblings. If all 19 students had the same number of siblings, they would each have about 3 siblings. Differences from the mean "balance out" so that the sum of differences below and above the mean equal 0. The mean of a set of data is the sum of the values divided by the number of values in the set.

media El valor se logra que si todos los datos se combinan y después se redistribuyen uniformemente. Por ejemplo, el número total de hermanos y hermanas para los datos en el diagrama de arriba es de 56. Si los 19 estudiantes tuvieran la misma cantidad de hermanos y hermanas, cada uno tendría aproximadamente 3 hermanos o hermanas. Las diferencias de la media se "equilibran" de tal manera que la suma de las diferencias por encima y por debajo de la media es igual a 0. La media de un conjunto de datos es la suma de los valores dividido por el número de valores en el conjunto.

median The number that marks the middle of an ordered set of data. At least half of the values lie at or above the median, and at least half lie at or below the median. The median of the distribution of siblings is 3 because the tenth (middle) value in the ordered set of 19 values (0, 0, 0, 1, 1, 2, 2, 2, 2, 3, 3, 3, 4, 4, 5, 5, 5, 6, 8) is 3 siblings.

mediana El número que señala la mitad en un conjunto ordenado de datos. Por lo menos mitad de los datos ocurre en o encima de la mediana, y por lo menos mitad de los datos ocurre en o debajo de la mediana. La mediana de la distribución de hermanos y hermanas es 3 porque el décimo valor (el del medio) en el conjunto ordenado de 19 valores (0, 0, 0, 1, 1, 2, 2, 2, 2, 3, 3, 3, 4, 4, 5, 5, 5, 6, 8) es 3 hermanos o hermanas.

mode The category or numerical value that occurs most often. The mode of the distribution of siblings is 2. It is possible for a set of data to have more than one mode.

moda En una distribución, es la categoría o el valor numérico que ocurre con mayor frecuencia. La moda de la distribución de hermanos o hermanas es 2. Es posible que un conjunto de datos tenga más de una moda.

N

numerical data Values that are numbers such as counts, measurements, and ratings. Here are some examples.
- Number of children in families
- Pulse rates (number of heart beats per minute)
- Height
- Amount of time people spend reading in one day
- Amount of value placed on something, such as: on a scale of 1 to 5 with 1 as "low interest," how would you rate your interest in participating in the school's field day?

datos numéricos Valores que son números como, por ejemplo, cómputos, medidas y calificaciones. Aquí hay algunos ejemplos.
- Número de hijos e hijas en las familias
- Pulsaciones por minuto (número de latidos del corazón por minuto)
- Altura
- Cantidad de tiempo que las personas pasan leyendo en un día
- El valor que las personas le dan a algo, como por ejemplo: en una escala de 1 a 5, en la que 1 representa "poco interés", ¿cómo calificarías tu interés por participar en el día de campo de tu escuela?

O

outlier A value that lies far from the "center" of a distribution. Outlier is a relative term, but it indicates a data point that is much higher or much lower than the values that could be normally expected for the distribution.

valor extremo Valor que se sitúa lejos del "centro" de una distribución. El valor extremo es un término relativo, pero indica un dato que es mucho más alto o mucho más bajo que los valores que se podrían esperar normalmente de la distribución.

R

range The difference between the least value and the greatest value in a distribution. For example, in the distribution below, the range of the number of siblings is 8 people.

gama Diferencia entre el valor mínimo y máximo en una distribución. Por ejemplo, en la siguiente distribución, la gama del número de hermanos o hermanas es 8 personas.

Number of Siblings Students Have

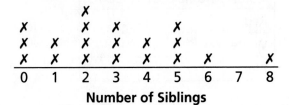

Number of Siblings

S

scale The size of the units on an axis of a graph or number line. For instance, each mark on the vertical axis might represent 10 units.

escala El tamaño de las unidades en un eje de una gráfica o recta numérica. Por ejemplo, cada marca en el eje vertical puede representar 10 unidades.

stem-and-leaf plot (stem plot) A quick way to picture the shape of a distribution while including the actual numerical values in the graph. For a number like 25, the stem 2 is written at the left of the vertical line, and the leaf, 5 is at the right.

diagrama de tallo y hojas Una manera rápida de representar la forma de una distribución y al mismo tiempo incluir los valores numéricos reales en la gráfica. Para un número como 25, el tallo 2 se escribe a la izquierda de la recta vertical, y la hoja 5, a la derecha de la recta.

Travel Time

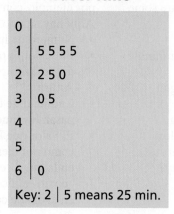

```
0 |
1 | 5 5 5 5
2 | 2 5 0
3 | 0 5
4 |
5 |
6 | 0
```
Key: 2 | 5 means 25 min.

survey A method for collecting data that uses interviews. Surveys ask questions to find out information such as facts, opinions, or beliefs.

encuesta Un método para reunir datos que utiliza entrevistas. En las encuestas se hacen preguntas para averiguar información tal como hechos, opiniones o creencias.

T

table A tool for organizing information in rows and columns. Tables let you list categories or values and then tally the occurrences.

tabla Una herramienta para organizar información en filas y columnas. Las tablas permiten que se hagan listas de categorías o de valores y luego se computan los sucesos.

Favorite Colors

Color	Number of Students
Red	6
White	15
Blue	9

X

x-axis The horizontal number line used to make a graph.

eje x Recta numérica horizontal que se usa para hacer una gráfica.

Y

y-axis The vertical number line used to make a graph.

eje y Recta numérica vertical que se usa para hacer una gráfica.

Academic Vocabulary

The following terms are important to your understanding of the mathematics in this unit. Knowing and using these words will help you in thinking, reasoning, representing, communicating your ideas, and making connections across ideas. When these words make sense to you, the investigations and problems will make more sense as well.

A

analyze To study using a logical or mathematical system.

related terms: examine, evaluate, determine, observe, investigate

Sample: Analyze the following data to find the mean and the mode.

Getting to School

Student	Krista	Mike	Lupe	Kareem
Time (min)	10	15	20	10

The mean is $\frac{10 + 15 + 20 + 10}{4} = 13.75$. The mode of this data is 10 because 10 is the value that occurs most often.

analizar Estudiar usando un sistema lógico o matemático.

términos relacionados: examinar, evaluar, determinar, observar, investigar

Ejemplo: Analiza los siguientes datos para hallar la media y la moda.

Tiempos a la escuela

Estudiante	Krista	Mike	Lupe	Kareem
Tiempo (minutos)	10	15	20	10

La media es $\frac{10 + 15 + 20 + 10}{4} = 13.75$. La moda de estos datos es 10 porque 10 es el valor que ocurre con mayor frecuencia.

E

explain To give facts and details that make an idea easier to understand. Explaining can involve a written summary supported by a diagram, chart, table, or a combination of these.

related terms: analyze, clarify, describe, justify, tell

Sample: Explain why the mean may not be the best statistical measure of how many sit-ups students can do.

How many sit-ups?

```
0 | 9 9
1 | 0 1 2 2 5 5 6
2 |
3 |
4 | 1
Key 1 | 2 = 12
```

The mean is affected by the outlier 41, which is much greater than the rest of the data. The median or mode would be better measures of the data.

explicar Dar hechos y detalles que hacen que una idea sea más fácil de comprender. Explicar puede implicar un resumen escrito apoyado por hechos, un diagrama, una gráfica, una tabla o una combinación de éstos.

términos relacionados: analizar, aclarar, describir, justificar, decir

Ejemplo: Explica por qué la media puede no ser la mejor medida estadística de cuántas sentadillas pueden hacer los estudiantes.

¿Cuántas sentadillas?

```
0 | 9 9
1 | 0 1 2 2 5 5 6
2 |
3 |
4 | 1
Clave 1 | 2 = 12
```

La media se ve afectada por el valor extremo 41, que es mucho más grandes que el resto de los datos. La mediana o la moda serían mejores medidas de los datos.

predict To make an educated guess based on the analysis of real data.

related terms: estimate, guess, expect

Sample: Dan knows that the mean life span of his type of tropical fish is 2 years. What other information could help Dan predict how long his fish will live?

> If Dan also knew the median life span he would have more information to predict how long his fish will live. The mean could be skewed because of one or more outliers.

predecir Hacer una conjetura informada basada en el análisis de datos reales.

términos relacionados: estimar, conjeturar, esperar

Ejemplo: Dan sabe que la duración de la vida media de su tipo de pez tropical es de 2 años. ¿Qué otra información podría ayudar a Dan a predecir cuánto vivirá su pez?

> Si Dan también supiera la duración de la vida media, tendría más información para predecir cuánto vivirá su pez. La media podría estar sesgada debido a uno o más valores extremos.

represent To stand for or take the place of something else. Symbols, equations, charts, and tables are often used to represent particular situations.

related terms: symbolize, stand for

Sample: Jerry surveyed his classmates about the number of pets they have. He recorded his data in a table. Represent the results of Jerry's survey in a bar graph.

representar Significar o tomar el lugar de algo más. Con frecuencia se usan símbolos, ecuaciones, gráficas y tablas para representar situaciones particulares.

términos relacionados: simbolizar, significar

Ejemplo: Jerry hizo una encuesta entre sus compañeros de clases sobre el número de mascotas que tienen. Anotó sus datos en una tabla. Representa los resultados de la encuesta de Jerry en una gráfica de barras.

How Many Pets?

Number of Pets	Number of Students
0 pets	10
1 pet	11
2 or more pets	8

¿Cuántas mascotas?

Número de mascotas	Número de estudiantes
0 mascotas	10
1 mascota	11
2 ó más mascotas	8

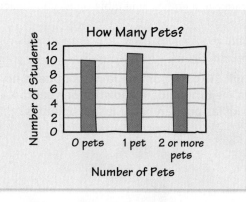

Index

Index

Acknowledgments

Team Credits

The people who made up the **Connected Mathematics 2** team—representing editorial, editorial services, design services, and production services— are listed below. Bold type denotes core team members.

Leora Adler, Judith Buice, Kerry Cashman, Patrick Culleton, Sheila DeFazio, Richard Heater, **Barbara Hollingdale, Jayne Holman,** Karen Holtzman, **Etta Jacobs,** Christine Lee, Carolyn Lock, Catherine Maglio, **Dotti Marshall,** Rich McMahon, Eve Melnechuk, Kristin Mingrone, Terri Mitchell, **Marsha Novak,** Irene Rubin, Donna Russo, Robin Samper, Siri Schwartzman, **Nancy Smith,** Emily Soltanoff, **Mark Tricca,** Paula Vergith, Roberta Warshaw, Helen Young

Additional Credits

Diana Bonfilio, Mairead Reddin, Michael Torocsik, nSight, Inc.

Illustration

Michelle Barbera: 7, 20, 30, 59, 60

Technical Illustration

WestWords, Inc.

Cover Design

tom white.images

Photos

2 t, Chris Pinchbeck/IPN; **2 m,** Kwame Zikomo/ SuperStock; **2 b,** Michael Newman/PhotoEdit; **3,** Jeff Greenberg/Peter Arnold, Inc.; **6,** Kwame Zikomo/SuperStock; **9,** Ariadne Van Zandbergen/ Lonely Planet Images; **13,** Steve Vidler/ SuperStock; **15 l,** Rick Gomez/Corbis; **15 r,** Myrleen Ferguson Cate/PhotoEdit; **18,** Ron Kimball/Ron Kimball Stock; **20,** Chris Pinchbeck/IPN; **23,** Ellen Senisi/The Image Works; **33,** Ray Stott/The Image Works; **35,** Kwame Zikomo/SuperStock; **36,** Richard Haynes; **38,** David Young-Wolff/PhotoEdit; **41,** Ellen Senisi/The Image Works; 43, Richard Haynes; **44,** Journal-Courier/Steve Warmowski/ The Image Works; **47,** Jim Cummins/Getty Images, Inc.; **49,** Ron Stroud/Masterfile; **53,** Creatas/PictureQuest; **55,** Michael Newman/ PhotoEdit; **57,** Bob Daemmrich Photography; **62,** Syracuse Newspapers/The Image Works; **65,** Joe McDonald/Corbis